Bipolar Disorder
FOR DUMMIES®
A Wiley Brand

3rd Edition

by Candida Fink, MD,
and Joe Kraynak MA

FOR DUMMIES®
A Wiley Brand

Bipolar Disorder For Dummies®, **3rd Edition**

Published by: **John Wiley & Sons, Inc.,** 111 River Street, Hoboken, NJ 07030-5774, www.wiley.com

Copyright © 2016 by John Wiley & Sons, Inc., Hoboken, New Jersey

Published simultaneously in Canada

No part of this publication may be reproduced, stored in a retrieval system, or transmitted in any form or by any means, electronic, mechanical, photocopying, recording, scanning or otherwise, except as permitted under Sections 107 or 108 of the 1976 United States Copyright Act, without the prior written permission of the Publisher. Requests to the Publisher for permission should be addressed to the Permissions Department, John Wiley & Sons, Inc., 111 River Street, Hoboken, NJ 07030, (201) 748-6011, fax (201) 748-6008, or online at http://www.wiley.com/go/permissions.

Trademarks: Wiley, For Dummies, the Dummies Man logo, Dummies.com, Making Everything Easier, and related trade dress are trademarks or registered trademarks of John Wiley & Sons, Inc., and may not be used without written permission. All other trademarks are the property of their respective owners. John Wiley & Sons, Inc., is not associated with any product or vendor mentioned in this book.

LIMIT OF LIABILITY/DISCLAIMER OF WARRANTY: THE CONTENTS OF THIS WORK ARE INTENDED TO FURTHER GENERAL SCIENTIFIC RESEARCH, UNDERSTANDING, AND DISCUSSION ONLY AND ARE NOT INTENDED AND SHOULD NOT BE RELIED UPON AS RECOMMENDING OR PROMOTING A SPECIFIC METHOD, DIAGNOSIS, OR TREATMENT BY PHYSICIANS FOR ANY PARTICULAR PATIENT. THE PUBLISHER AND THE AUTHORS MAKE NO REPRESENTATIONS OR WARRANTIES WITH RESPECT TO THE ACCURACY OR COMPLETENESS OF THE CONTENTS OF THIS WORK AND SPECIFICALLY DISCLAIM ALL WARRANTIES, INCLUDING WITHOUT LIMITATION ANY IMPLIED WARRANTIES OF FITNESS FOR A PARTICULAR PURPOSE. IN VIEW OF ONGOING RESEARCH, EQUIPMENT MODIFICATIONS, CHANGES IN GOVERNMENTAL REGULATIONS, AND THE CONSTANT FLOW OF INFORMATION, THE READER IS URGED TO REVIEW AND EVALUATE THE INFORMATION PROVIDED IN THE PACKAGE INSERT OR INSTRUCTIONS FOR EACH MEDICINE, EQUIPMENT, OR DEVICE FOR, AMONG OTHER THINGS, ANY CHANGES IN THE INSTRUCTIONS OR INDICATION OF USAGE AND FOR ADDED WARNINGS AND PRECAUTIONS. READERS SHOULD CONSULT WITH A SPECIALIST WHERE APPROPRIATE. NEITHER THE PUBLISHER NOR THE AUTHOR SHALL BE LIABLE FOR ANY DAMAGES ARISING HEREFROM.

For general information on our other products and services, please contact our Customer Care Department within the U.S. at 877-762-2974, outside the U.S. at 317-572-3993, or fax 317-572-4002. For technical support, please visit www.wiley.com/techsupport.

Wiley publishes in a variety of print and electronic formats and by print-on-demand. Some material included with standard print versions of this book may not be included in e-books or in print-on-demand. If this book refers to media such as a CD or DVD that is not included in the version you purchased, you may download this material at http://booksupport.wiley.com. For more information about Wiley products, visit www.wiley.com.

Library of Congress Control Number: 2015951120

ISBN: 978-1-119-12186-2

ISBN 978-1-119-12186-2 (pbk); ISBN 978-1-119-12187-9 (ebk); ISBN 978-1-119-12188-6 (ebk)

10 9 8 7 6 5 4 3 2 1

MIX
Paper from
responsible sources
FSC® C013604

Contents at a Glance

Introduction 1

Part I: Getting Started on Your Bipolar Journey.............. 5
Chapter 1: Grasping Bipolar Disorder: Symptoms and Diagnosis.............................7
Chapter 2: Finding the Cause: The Brain and Body Science
of Bipolar Disorder...29
Chapter 3: Reining in Bipolar Disorder: Prognosis and Treatments.....................47

Part II: Obtaining a Diagnosis and Building
a Treatment Plan and Team 61
Chapter 4: Diagnosis Step 1: Ruling Out Other Health Issues.....................63
Chapter 5: Diagnosis Step 2: Obtaining a Psychiatric
Evaluation and Treatment Plan..75
Chapter 6: Building a Winning Mood-Management Team 93

Part III: Managing the Biology of Bipolar Disorder..... 107
Chapter 7: Leveling Moods with Medication.....................................109
Chapter 8: Coming to Terms with Medications
and Their Side Effects 141
Chapter 9: Expanding Your Biological Treatment Options.....................159
Chapter 10: Treating Bipolar Disorder in Women
and Other Specific Populations..171

Part IV: Developing Essential Survival Skills.............. 185
Chapter 11: Exploring Self-Help Strategies, Therapies, and Other Supports.........187
Chapter 12: Making Lifestyle Adjustments 201
Chapter 13: Communicating Effectively..221
Chapter 14: Solving Problems and Resolving Conflict 233
Chapter 15: Planning Ahead for a Mood Episode 243

Part V: Dealing with the Fallout 253
Chapter 16: From Hospitalization to Recovery....................................255
Chapter 17: Returning to Work . . . or Not..269
Chapter 18: Overcoming Financial Setbacks.....................................281

Part VI: Assisting a Friend or Relative with Bipolar Disorder 295

Chapter 19: Supporting Your Loved One 297
Chapter 20: Dealing with Crisis Situations 311
Chapter 21: Backing Your Bipolar Child or Teen 327

Part VII: The Part of Tens 353

Chapter 22: Ten Tips for Managing Bipolar 355
Chapter 23: Ten Ways to Help a Loved One with Bipolar Disorder 361

Index 367

Table of Contents

Introduction *1*

    About This Book 1

    Foolish Assumptions 2

    Icons Used in This Book 3

    Beyond the Book 3

    Where to Go from Here 4

Part I: Getting Started on Your Bipolar Journey *5*

Chapter 1: Grasping Bipolar Disorder: Symptoms and Diagnosis. 7

    Cracking Open the Diagnostic Manual: DSM-5 8

    Exploring the Poles of Bipolar Disorder: Mania and Depression 9

        Manic episode 9

        Hypomanic episode 10

        Major depressive episode 11

        Not your average moodiness 12

        Not attributable to other psychotic disorders 13

    Distinguishing Types of Bipolar Disorder 13

        Bipolar I 14

        Bipolar II 14

        Cyclothymic disorder 14

        Substance/medication-induced bipolar disorder 15

        Bipolar and related disorder due to another
medical condition 15

        Other specified bipolar and related disorder 15

        Unspecified bipolar disorder 16

    Digging Deeper with Bipolar Specifiers 17

        Current or most recent episode 17

        Severity of illness 17

        Presence or absence of psychosis 18

        Course of illness 19

        Additional features that often accompany bipolar disorder 19

    Distinguishing Bipolar from Conditions with Similar Symptoms 20

    Considering Comorbidity: When Bipolar Coexists
with Other Conditions 22

        Anxiety disorders 23

        Substance use disorder 23

        Attention deficit hyperactivity disorder 24

Personality disorders 24
Memory and thinking problems 25
Confronting the Challenges of Diagnosing Children and Teens 25

Chapter 2: Finding the Cause: The Brain and Body Science of Bipolar Disorder 29

Digging Up Bipolar's Genetic Roots 30
Shaking the family tree... 31
Realizing that genetic susceptibility is only one risk factor ... 32
Grasping the genetic complexities 32
Flipping the bipolar switch: Epigenetics................................. 33
Investigating Nongenetic Factors 34
Examining the Circuitry of Bipolar 37
Brushing up on brain structure and function 37
Connecting the brain to bipolar disorder............................... 41
Recognizing How Medications Do Their Thing............................... 45

Chapter 3: Reining in Bipolar Disorder: Prognosis and Treatments 47

So, Doc, What's the Prognosis? 47
Responding Reactively and Proactively to Bipolar Disorder 48
Reacting: Extinguishing the flames.. 49
Preventing future flare-ups 50
Recognizing the Components of an Effective Treatment Plan......... 51
Exploring medication and other biological remedies 51
Making lifestyle adjustments: The big five 54
Sampling self-help treatments.. 55
Comparing psychotherapies and other
professional counseling 56
Rounding up the troops: Relationship and family support 58
Ensuring continuity of care 59

Part II: Obtaining a Diagnosis and Building a Treatment Plan and Team 61

Chapter 4: Diagnosis Step 1: Ruling Out Other Health Issues 63

Could It Be Something Else?... 64
Singing the body blues 64
Considering other culprits: Medication, alcohol,
and other substances 66
Seeking Your Doctor's Advice... 67
Identifying your symptoms.. 68
Knowing when your problem started 69
Recognizing what makes your symptoms better or worse 70
Figuring out what else to tell your doctor 70
Getting a physical exam 71

Digging Deeper with Additional Tests and Procedures............................71
  Medical tests that your doctor may order 71
  Thyroid tests 72
  Other hormone tests 73
Receiving a Clean Bill of Health — Now What?..................................73

Chapter 5: Diagnosis Step 2: Obtaining a Psychiatric Evaluation and Treatment Plan 75
Finding Professional Help...76
  Ask your family doctor...76
  Call your insurance company...76
  Pick your therapist's brain 77
  Go online...77
  Consult your support group...78
  When having a psychiatrist isn't an option........................78
Knowing What to Look for in a Psychiatrist 79
What to Bring to Your First Meeting..81
  Why you (or others) think you need help 81
  More symptom information, please! 82
  Medical history 83
  Family history...84
  List of legal and . . . yes . . . illegal drugs.........................85
  Sleep log...86
Arriving at a Diagnosis..86
  Evaluating your symptoms...86
  Considering other causes 87
  Receiving the diagnosis 88
  Gauging the severity of your illness 89
Responding to Your Diagnosis...90
Receiving Your Treatment Plan...91

Chapter 6: Building a Winning Mood-Management Team. 93
A Psychiatrist for Diagnosis and Medication Management 94
  Diagnostician...94
  Master planner 94
  Medicine man (or woman)..95
A Lifestyle Director: Highlighting the Therapist's Roles 95
  Coach, trainer, and referee..96
  Mood thermometer 96
  Resident soundboard 97
  Wellness manager 97
  Referral service 97
  When having a therapist isn't an option............................98
Assembling Your Personal Support Staff: Family and Friends 98
  Building a network based on trust 99
  Understanding their fears, anxieties, anger,
    and other emotions...99

Educating your supporters...100
Establishing your team's level of involvement 101
Encouraging open communication.....................................102
Working as a Team 104
Expanding Your Network through Local Support Groups 104

Part III: Managing the Biology of Bipolar Disorder 107

Chapter 7: Leveling Moods with Medication 109

Unlocking the Bipolar Medicine Cabinet 110
Lithium 110
Anticonvulsants 112
Antipsychotics 114
Mood-boosting antidepressants 118
Calming anxiolytics and sleep agents 123
Exploring Bipolar Psychopharmacology.................................127
Selecting the best medications for you.............................128
Knowing what to expect...129
Testing for med levels and health issues.........................130
Mixing your pharmaceutical cocktail..............................130
Juggling meds for comorbid conditions 133
Treating Mood Episodes and Preventing Future Episodes 134
Muffling mania 134
Lifting bipolar depression..134
Keeping mania and depression at bay:
    Maintenance treatment 135
Treatment-resistant bipolar disorder 136
Peering into the Promising Future of Bipolar Medications...................137
Meds that target the glutamergic pathways.......................137
Protein kinase C inhibitors 138
Other meds worth mentioning.....................................139

Chapter 8: Coming to Terms with Medications and Their Side Effects 141

Facing Your Emotional Reactions 142
Examining objections to taking meds 142
Accepting that your reluctance is normal.........................148
Performing a Cost-Benefit Analysis 149
Alleviating Undesirable Side Effects...................................150
Tweaking your doses and times 151
Trying different meds in the same class...........................151
Exploring other options 152
Dealing with specific side effects................................152
Switching, Reducing, and Stopping Meds............................156

Chapter 9: Expanding Your Biological Treatment Options.........159

Treating Your Moods to Supplements...............................159
    Fishing for a cure: Omega-3 fatty acids............................160
    Pumping up your brain with vitamins and minerals...................161
    Investigating herbs and other supplements........................163
    Assessing the safety of all-natural ingredients 165
Treating Depression with Light Therapy 166
Stimulating Your Brain with Electricity and Magnetism 167
    Zapping your moods with electroconvulsive therapy (ECT).......167
    Moderating moods with repetitive transcranial magnetic
        stimulation (rTMS)...169
    Soothing depression with neurostimulation......................169

**Chapter 10: Treating Bipolar Disorder in Women
and Other Specific Populations............................171**

Bipolar Disorder in Women.......................................171
    Considering the nature of the illness 172
    Tracing hormonal changes......................................172
    Bipolar disorder and pregnancy.................................174
    Dealing with bipolar during menopause..........................180
Older Adults and Bipolar Disorder................................180
    What's so different about older adults?..........................180
    Addressing dementia and bipolar 181
    Medication issues for older adults 181
Accommodating Cultural Differences.............................183
Bipolar in the LGBT Community..................................184

Part IV: Developing Essential Survival Skills............... 185

**Chapter 11: Exploring Self-Help Strategies,
Therapies, and Other Supports 187**

Monitoring Your Moods 187
Charting Sleep and Energy Levels................................188
Identifying Stressors and Triggers 189
Seeking Out Therapy and Support 191
    Psychoeducation 191
    Cognitive behavioral therapy (CBT) 192
    Dialectical behavioral therapy (DBT) 194
    Interpersonal and social rhythm therapy (IPSRT) 195
    Mindfulness and other centering activities......................198
    Relationship and family therapies..............................200
    Support groups 200

Chapter 12: Making Lifestyle Adjustments 201

Cultivating a Healthy Home Environment 201
Educating all household members 201
Establishing a structured schedule 202
Cranking down the volume 202
Reducing conflict and criticism 203
Establishing expectations 204
Considering the kids 206
Establishing Healthy Routines 207
Regulating your sleep 207
Scheduling social activities 209
Leaving room for spontaneity 210
Serving Healthy Foods 210
Cutting back on simple carbohydrates 211
Getting your fill of vegetables and fruits 212
Powering up with protein 213
Feeding your brain healthy fats 214
Building Healthy Relationships 215
Checking relationship vitals 215
Having some fun 216
Taking breaks from one another 217
Relieving Stress through Exercise 217
Avoiding the Bad Stuff 218

Chapter 13: Communicating Effectively 221

Setting the Stage 221
Choosing the right time and place 222
Establishing ground rules 222
Watching what you say 223
Expressing yourself in a positive tone 224
Being sensitive to posture, position, and body language 224
Adding mood symptoms to the mix 225
Avoiding the Four Big Tiff-Makers 226
Criticism 226
Judgment 227
Demand 227
Blame 227
Becoming Less Confrontational with "I" Statements 228
Validating Other People's Feelings 229
Disengaging from Unproductive Conflicts 230

Chapter 14: Solving Problems and Resolving Conflict 233

Setting the Stage for Effective Problem Solving 234
Identifying the Problem 235
Redefining the Problem/Conflict: From Right
Versus Wrong to Unmet Needs 237

Brainstorming Possible Solutions 238
Planning and Implementing Agreed-Upon Solutions............................. 239
Avoiding Unproductive Approaches.. 240
Letting Go of Problems You Can't Solve on Your Own........................... 241

Chapter 15: Planning Ahead for a Mood Episode.................243

Teaming Up with Your Care Providers.. 243
Thwarting a Mood Episode 245
Choosing a Psychiatric Facility.. 245
Documenting Essential Information 247
Signing Releases . . . Or Not... 249
    Release of information authorization... 249
    Power of attorney 250
    Advanced directive.. 251

Part V: Dealing with the Fallout 253

Chapter 16: From Hospitalization to Recovery 255

Coming to Terms with Hospitalization 255
Knowing What to Expect 256
    Seeing the doctor.. 256
    Adjusting your medications 256
    Engaging in therapy... 257
    Looking into seclusion and restraint policies 257
    Exploring variations in visiting hours 258
    Knowing about how long you'll stay 259
    Getting released 259
Knowing Your Patient Rights... 259
Making Your Stay More Comfortable... 260
Keeping Your Team in the Loop... 261
Making Recovery Your Top Priority 262
    Anticipating the aftershock... 262
    Mastering the art of selfishness.. 263
    Retreating to a safe, quiet place.. 264
    Following your doctor's orders 265
Reclaiming Your Life 266
    Knowing when you're ready... 266
    Returning to friends and family 267

Chapter 17: Returning to Work . . . or Not......................269

Reality Check: Are You Ready to Return to Work? 269
Getting Back into the Swing of Things 271
Disclosing Your Diagnosis . . . or Not.. 272
    Weighing the pros and cons of disclosure 272
    Talking to supervisors and coworkers... 273

Requesting Workplace Accommodations 274
Finding More Suitable Work 276
Dreaming up your ideal work situation 277
Taking a skills and interests inventory 277
Pursuing your dream job 278
Is Not Returning to Work Right for You? 279

Chapter 18: Overcoming Financial Setbacks 281

The Public Mental Health System 281
Surveying available resources 282
Accessing local financial support 283
Public systems in Canada and the U.K. 283
Filing for Disability Benefits 284
Meeting the guidelines 285
Improving your chances of approval 286
Exploring Health Insurance Options 287
Low- or No-Cost Healthcare Resources 288
Tracking down a university program 289
Finding peer support 289
Contacting religious organizations 290
Prescription assistance programs 290
Haggling with a psychiatrist or therapist 291
Other Ways to Survive the Hard Times 291
Asking family and friends for help 291
Finding temporary financial relief 292
Government safety net programs 293

Part VI: Assisting a Friend or Relative with Bipolar Disorder 295

Chapter 19: Supporting Your Loved One 297

Establishing the Right Mindset 297
Forming realistic expectations 298
Disassociating the disorder from the one you love 298
Figuring out how not to take it personally 299
Nurturing a Sense of Empathy 300
Recognizing Your Limitations 301
Doing what you can 301
Recognizing what you can't do 302
Remaining Vigilant for Warning Signs 302
Knowing when to step in 303
Knowing when to step back 303
Making a deal: Drawing up a contract 304

Helping Someone Who Refuses Help 304
    Taking action in an emergency 305
    Expressing your concerns 305
    Calling the doctor or therapist 306
    Contacting a local support group 306
    Contacting a local mental health center 306
    Seeking a court order 306
Taking Care of Yourself 307

Chapter 20: Dealing with Crisis Situations 311
Consulting Your Loved One's Doctor or Therapist 311
Discussing the Emergency Plan 313
    Figuring out how involved to be 313
    Determining when to intervene 315
    Knowing whom to call for help 316
    Deciding where to go 316
Responding in a Crisis 317
    Suicidal threats or attempts 318
    Agitated behavior 318
    Reckless driving 319
    Overspending 320
    Hypersexual behavior 321
    Substance abuse 322
    Runaways and disappearances 322
    Arrests 323

Chapter 21: Backing Your Bipolar Child or Teen 327
Recognizing the Diagnostic Difficulties 328
Diagnosing Bipolar Disorder in Children 329
    Attention deficit hyperactivity disorder (ADHD) 330
    Oppositional defiant disorder (ODD) 332
    Unipolar depression 332
    Disruptive mood dysregulation disorder 335
    Anxiety disorders 336
    Trauma 337
    Autism spectrum disorders 338
    Toxic exposures 339
Requesting a Professional Evaluation 339
    Finding the right doctor 340
    Knowing what to do when seeking help 341
Breaking Out the Treatment Toolbox 342
    Considering medication issues 343
    Understanding the diagnosis and treatment plan 344
Parenting a Child with Bipolar Disorder 347
    Fine-tuning your parenting skills 347
    Tending to school matters 348
    Practicing lifestyle management 350
    Recognizing suicidal red flags 351

Part VII: The Part of Tens *353*

Chapter 22: Ten Tips for Managing Bipolar .... .355
  Team Up with Your Doctor and Therapist 355
  Take Medications as Prescribed 356
  Regulate Your Sleep 356
  Develop Daily Routines 357
  Build Mindfulness and Other Self-Centering Skills 357
  Clearly Communicate Your Needs 358
  Avoid Alcohol and Stimulants 358
  Monitor Your Moods 359
  Identify Your Early Warning Signs 359
  Get Help at the First Sign of Trouble 360

Chapter 23: Ten Ways to Help a Loved One
with Bipolar Disorder .... .361
  Find Out More about Bipolar Disorder 361
  Treat Your Loved One with Respect 362
  Hone Your Communication Skills 362
  Become a Problem Solver 363
  Disengage When Tensions Rise 363
  Keep Detailed Records 364
  Partner with Your Loved One 364
  Brush Up on Medications 364
  Flex Your Expectations 365
  Enjoy Your Life 366

Index *367*

Introduction

Imagine yourself cruising down the highway at a comfortable speed of 65 miles per hour when your cruise control goes berserk. The speedometer climbs to 75 and then 85 . . . you hit the button to cancel . . . tap the brakes . . . 90 . . . nothing slows you down . . . 95 . . . your car is shaking and weaving . . . 100 . . . people are honking . . . 105 . . . police cars are chasing you . . . 110 . . . your spouse is yelling at you to SLOW DOWN . . . 115 . . . 120 . . . .

Or imagine the opposite: You're driving through town in a 30-mile-per-hour speed limit zone. Nobody's in front of you — you're practically pushing the accelerator through the floor — but your car can only creep along at 3 miles per hour. Your neighbors are honking, passing you on the right — on bicycles — and giving you dirty looks and other gestures of discontent.

When you have bipolar disorder, your brain's accelerator is stuck. At full speed, it launches you into a manic episode. In low gear, it grinds you down into a deep depression. If this were a situation with your heart, somebody would call an ambulance; doctors and nurses would flock to your bedside; loved ones would fly in from other states; and you'd get flowers and fruit baskets. But when your brain is stuck in park or overdrive, people tend to think you're lazy, you've snapped, or you're too weak to deal with life. Instead of flowers and fruit baskets, you get a pink slip and divorce papers.

The good news is that the mind mechanics — psychiatrists, psychologists, and therapists — have toolboxes packed with medications and therapies that can repair your brain's accelerator. In this book, we reveal those tools along with strategies and techniques you can use to achieve and maintain mood stability and to help yourself feel a whole lot better.

About This Book

Although psychiatrists, psychologists, and therapists are better equipped than ever to treat bipolar disorder, studies increasingly show that the more involved patients and their loved ones are in the treatment plan, the better the outcome. Our goal in writing this book is to make you a well-informed patient or support person and to empower you to become a key player on the treatment team.

Organized in an easy-to-access format and presented in plain English, the newest edition of *Bipolar Disorder For Dummies* brings you up to speed on bipolar disorder, explaining what it is, what causes it, and how it's diagnosed and treated. We present the most effective treatments, explain why preventive treatment plays such a critical role in keeping symptoms at bay, and point out the positive prognosis that you can expect with the right combination of medication, therapy, lifestyle adjustments, and support.

In addition to comprehensive coverage of bipolar disorder, this book contains numerous first-person accounts from people living with bipolar disorder and their loved ones. These stories give you a glimpse inside the minds of people living with bipolar disorder along with additional insight into how people deal with the challenges in their own lives.

When we refer to medications or drugs, we use this format on first reference: generic name (Brand name), as in fluoxetine (Prozac), and in an attempt to be fair to both sexes, we alternate the use of "he" and "she" as we change from one section to the next instead of using the bulky "he or she" approach or the really weird "s/he" solution.

Foolish Assumptions

When you (or your loved ones) are diagnosed with bipolar, you automatically become a rank beginner. You never needed information about this illness before and probably had little interest in the topic. Now you have to get up to speed in a hurry. With that in mind, we assume that you know very little about bipolar disorder. If you've been to a doctor or therapist and received a diagnosis, however, you know at least a little. And if you got burned by a misdiagnosis or the wrong approach, you know you don't want that to happen again. But no matter how experienced you are, this book can help.

We also assume that you or someone you know has bipolar or that you're at least somewhat curious about the condition. The more the disorder affects you, your family, or someone else you know, the more this book can help.

Finally, we assume that you have a sense of humor. Yes, bipolar disorder can be brutal, but laughter is one tool that enables you to rise above the absurdity and frustration of dealing with it.

Icons Used in This Book

Throughout this book, we sprinkle the following icons in the margins to cue you in to different types of information that you may or may not care to see:

If you happen to forget the rest of the stuff in this book, at least remember what we mark with these icons.

Tips provide insider insight from behind the scenes. When you're looking for a better, faster way to do something, check out information flagged with this icon.

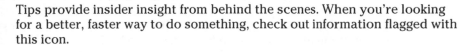

"Danger, Will Robinson, danger!" This icon appears when you need to be extra vigilant or seek professional help.

Throughout the book, we feature cameos of people living with bipolar disorder. This icon shows you where to meet them.

This icon points out supplemental (and free) information at `www.dummies.com/extras/bipolardisorder`.

Beyond the Book

Every *For Dummies* book has a Cheat Sheet chock-full of helpful information that you can refer to on a regular basis. You can find this book's Cheat Sheet at `www.dummies.com/cheatsheet/bipolardisorder`.

We also offer some bonus goodies at `www.dummies.com/extras/bipolardisorder`. You can read a bonus Part of Tens chapter on ten questions to ask a psychiatrist, a bipolar disorder glossary, and additional articles related to bipolar disorder.

Where to Go from Here

Think of this book as an all-you-can-eat buffet. You can grab a plate, start at the beginning, and read one chapter right after another, or you can dip into any chapter and pile your plate high with the information it contains.

If you want a quick overview of bipolar disorder, check out the chapters in Part I. Before you visit a psychiatrist for a diagnosis, see Chapters 4 and 5 to find out what to expect during the diagnostic process. For information and insight into the medications used to treat bipolar disorder, head to Chapter 7. Turn to the chapters in Part IV for self-help strategies. If you have a friend or family member with bipolar, skip to Part VI. Use the index to look up any bipolar term you're unfamiliar with and find out where we cover it in the book. Wherever you choose to go, you'll find plenty of useful information.

Part I
Getting Started on Your Bipolar Journey

In this part . . .

✔ Understand what bipolar disorder is and what it isn't according to the diagnostic categories spelled out in the *Diagnostic and Statistical Manual of Mental Disorders, 5th Edition* (*DSM-5*) — the book psychiatrists look to when developing their diagnosis.

✔ Explore genetic and nongenetic factors, such as physical and emotional stress, that likely team up to trigger the manic and depressive episodes characteristic of bipolar disorder.

✔ Take a look inside the different parts of the brain to understand the biology of bipolar disorder.

✔ Get a bird's-eye view of the diagnosis and treatment of bipolar disorder, so you know what's involved and the sort of outcome you can expect when treatment proceeds according to plan.

Chapter 1

Grasping Bipolar Disorder: Symptoms and Diagnosis

In This Chapter

▶ Meeting the manual used to diagnose bipolar disorder

▶ Recognizing the two poles of bipolar: mania and depression

▶ Telling the difference between bipolar I, bipolar II, and other types

▶ Augmenting the diagnosis with specifiers and distinguishing it from other conditions

▶ Diagnosing bipolar in children . . . or not

*W*hen you initially encounter bipolar disorder, one of the first questions you're likely to ask is, "What is it?" The short answer is this: *Bipolar disorder* is a medical illness characterized by alternating periods of abnormally elevated and depressed mood. The second question that most people ask is, "Can I get tested for it?" And the short answer is no. Doctors arrive at a diagnosis by conducting a physical and mental status examination; taking a close look at a person's symptoms, medical history, and family history; and ruling out other possible causes. For guidance, doctors use a book called the *Diagnostic and Statistical Manual of Mental Disorders (DSM),* which presents the diagnostic criteria for determining whether a person is likely to have bipolar disorder.

This chapter digs deep into the *DSM* to reveal what bipolar disorder is and isn't. It describes what elevated and depressed moods look like and provides you with the details you need to tell the difference between the various bipolar diagnoses, including bipolar I, bipolar II, and a form of bipolar called rapid-cycling. We discuss diagnostic *specifiers* that enable doctors to more precisely describe a person's symptoms and inform his treatment decisions. We distinguish bipolar disorder from conditions that may have similar symptoms and discuss other conditions that commonly accompany bipolar disorder, such as alcoholism and substance use disorder. We wrap up with a discussion of the challenges of diagnosing bipolar in children and young adults.

Cracking Open the Diagnostic Manual: DSM-5

When a doctor in the United States diagnoses a mental illness, such as bipolar disorder, she turns to the American Psychiatric Association's (APA) *Diagnostic and Statistical Manual of Mental Disorders (DSM)* for guidance. This manual defines numerous patterns of symptoms and illnesses that are supported by scientific research and a consensus among a wide variety of experts. During the writing of this book, the APA recommends using *DSM-5*, the fifth edition, which was published in May 2013. Don't be surprised if you see references to earlier editions, particularly *DSM-IV*, the fourth edition.

Throughout this chapter, we describe the symptoms of bipolar disorder according to the diagnostic criteria presented in *DSM-5*. Although the fundamental criteria haven't changed all that much from *DSM-IV* to *DSM-5*, some of the language has been modified and criteria have been added to help doctors arrive at and describe a person's condition more fully.

Diagnosis isn't a simple matter of matching a list of symptoms to a label. Doctors are expected to use the *DSM* along with their training, clinical experience, and professional judgment to arrive at the correct diagnosis.

The International Classification of Diseases (ICD)

Doctors in countries throughout the world (not the United States) rely on the World Health Organization's (WHO) *International Classification of Diseases,* a classification system for all health issues. Chapter V of the *ICD* specifically addresses mental and behavioral disorders.

The major difference between *DSM-5* and *ICD-10* is that the WHO manual doesn't use the labels bipolar I and bipolar II as primary distinctions. Instead, *ICD-10* refers to the disorder as *bipolar affective disorder* and then further classifies it by the nature of the current episode: currently hypomanic, currently manic, currently depressed, mixed disorder, or in remission. In addition, the *ICD-10* requires two or more mood episodes, with at least one being manic or hypomanic, to qualify for a bipolar diagnosis, while the *DSM* requires only a single manic or hypomanic episode.

The APA and WHO work together closely to coordinate their efforts. So in clinical practice, a doctor using one manual should arrive at a similar diagnosis as a doctor using the other.

Exploring the Poles of Bipolar Disorder: Mania and Depression

Bipolar diagnoses rely heavily on the type of mood episode(s) a person is experiencing or has experienced in the past, so to understand the different diagnoses, you need to know what constitutes a mood episode — specifically a manic, hypomanic, and major depressive episode. In the following sections, we present the *DSM-5* diagnostic criteria for each mood episode type.

Manic episode

A *manic episode* is a period of abnormally elevated energy and mood that interferes with a person's ability to function as he normally does. Merely having some manic symptoms isn't the same as experiencing a manic episode. The symptoms must meet the following four criteria.

Distinct period

The episode must last for at least one week *or* require hospitalization, and it must be characterized by "abnormally and persistently elevated, expansive, or irritable mood and abnormally and persistently increased goal-directed activity or energy" that's "present most of the day, nearly every day."

Three or more manic symptoms

Three of the following symptoms must also be present during the week of mania (four, if the mood is irritable rather than elevated or expansive). The symptoms must be present to a significant degree and represent a change from usual behavior.

- Markedly inflated self-esteem or *grandiosity*

- Decreased need for sleep (for example, feeling well rested after three hours or less of sleep)

- Excessive talking or the need to talk continuously *(pressured speech)*

- *Flight of ideas* — when thoughts flow rapidly and shift topics rapidly and indiscriminately — and/or the feeling that one's thoughts are racing

- Inability to concentrate and being easily distracted by insignificant external stimuli

✔ Significant increase in goal-directed activity (socially, at work or school, or sexually) or significant physical movement or agitation (aimless activity)

✔ Excessive involvement in risky, potentially self-destructive activities, including sexual indiscretions, unrestrained shopping sprees, and optimistic investments in pyramid schemes

Functional impairment

The mood episode must be severe enough to

✔ Impair the person's ability to socialize or work, or

✔ Require hospitalization to prevent the person from harming herself or others, or

✔ Cause psychotic features (paranoia, hallucinations, or delusions) indicating that the person is out of touch with reality

For more details, see the later section, "Presence or absence of psychosis."

Not caused by something else

For a manic episode to count toward bipolar diagnosis, the mania must satisfy the following conditions:

✔ **The mania can't be exclusively drug-induced or attributed to medical treatments.** For example, if you're taking an antidepressant, steroid, or cocaine at the time you experience manic symptoms, then the episode doesn't count toward a diagnosis of bipolar disorder, unless symptoms persist after the effects of the substance have worn off.

✔ **The mania isn't attributable to another medical condition.** Mania that is caused by a medical condition is identified as a separate form of bipolar disorder, as described in the later section, "Distinguishing Types of Bipolar Disorder."

Hypomanic episode

A *hypomanic episode* requires the same number and types of symptoms as a manic episode that we discuss in the preceding section. For instance, the symptoms must represent a distinct change from a person's usual behavior patterns, and the changes must be observable by others. However, a hypomanic episode differs from a manic episode in the following ways:

✔ May be shorter in duration (just four consecutive days is enough to qualify as a hypomanic episode)

✔ Doesn't cause severe functional impairment

> ✔ Doesn't require hospitalization
>
> ✔ Doesn't include psychosis

Hypomania doesn't typically result in serious relationship problems or extremely risky behavior, but your hypomanic behavior may make people around you uncomfortable. On the other hand, hypomania can make you more engaging, so you may become the center of attention, at least until the mania intensifies, which may bring much unwanted attention.

Major depressive episode

During a *major depressive episode* you may feel like you're swimming in a sea of molasses. Everything is slow, dark, and heavy. To qualify as a major depressive episode, five or more of the following symptoms must be present for at least two weeks straight. These symptoms must be changes from usual behavior, and the episode must include at least one symptom of depressed mood or loss of interest or pleasure.

✔ Depressed mood most of the day nearly every day

✔ Markedly diminished interest nearly every day in activities previously considered pleasurable, which may include sex

✔ Notable increase or decrease in appetite nearly every day or a marked change in weight, up or down (5 percent or more) in a span of one month or less that isn't due to planned dietary changes

✔ Sleeping too much or too little nearly every day

✔ Moving uncharacteristically slowly or having physical agitation observable by others, not just internal sensations

✔ Daily fatigue

✔ Feelings of worthlessness, excessive guilt, or inappropriate guilt nearly every day

✔ Uncharacteristic indecisiveness or diminished ability to think clearly or concentrate on a given task nearly every day, experienced internally and/or observed by others

✔ Recurrent thoughts of death or suicide *(suicide ideation),* a suicide attempt, or a plan to commit suicide

These symptoms must cause significant problems in your day-to-day life and function to qualify as indicators of a major depressive episode. If they occur solely in response to use of a medication or substance, or another medical condition, then the episode has its own category, such as *substance/ medication-induced depressive disorder* or *depressive disorder due to another medical condition,* and, therefore, doesn't count toward a diagnosis of either unipolar or bipolar depression.

Of course, people who experience a significant loss or crisis in their lives may have many of these same symptoms. Doctors must rely on their clinical experience, observations, and what their patient tells them in order to determine whether the person is experiencing a major depressive episode or intense sadness that's a normal part of the grieving process. In addition, cultural factors may play a role in how deeply a person feels and expresses emotion in response to a loss.

Not your average moodiness

Most people experience mood fluctuations to some acceptable degree, but bipolar mood episodes are amplified and extend far beyond the levels of discomfort — to the point of impairing a person's ability to function and enjoy life. Episodes associated with bipolar disorder make a person think, feel, speak, and behave in ways that are extremely uncharacteristic of the individual. And they may drag on for weeks or even months. They strain relationships, disrupt lives, and often land people in the hospital or in legal trouble. And they're not something a person can just snap out of. Figure 1-1 illustrates the difference between normal mood fluctuations and those related to bipolar disorder.

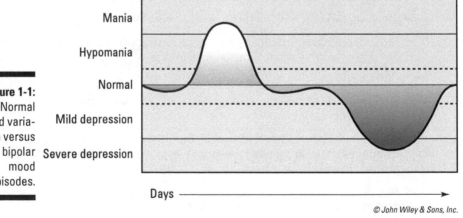

Figure 1-1: Normal mood variation versus bipolar mood episodes.

© John Wiley & Sons, Inc.

Not attributable to other psychotic disorders

For any mood episode to count toward a diagnosis of bipolar disorder, the mood episode can't be better explained by schizoaffective disorder, schizo- phrenia, schizophreniform disorder, delusional disorder, other specific or unspecified schizophrenia spectrum disorders, or other psychotic disorders. All these conditions have at least some period of psychosis that's not part of a mood episode. The point is to clarify that a bipolar diagnosis can't be decided if symptoms include disordered thinking and reality testing that aren't part of a mood episode. (For more about psychosis, see "Presence or absence of psychosis," later in this chapter.)

Distinguishing Types of Bipolar Disorder

Bipolar disorder wears many masks. It can be happy, sad, fearful, confident, sexy, or furious. It can seduce strangers, intimidate bank tellers, throw extravagant parties, and steal your joy late into the night. However, based on research, psychiatrists have managed to bring order to the disorder by grouping the many manifestations of bipolar into categories that include bipolar I, bipolar II, and cyclothymic disorder. In the following sections, we offer guidance for distinguishing among the many different types of bipolar disorder.

You're in good company

Bipolar disorder is often considered the Cadillac of brain disorders because so many famous and creative individuals — Vincent van Gogh, Abraham Lincoln, Winston Churchill, and Virginia Woolf — are thought to have struggled with it and perhaps even benefited from it. This may be small comfort when your symptoms are severe and painful, but it can give you a sense of kinship with people who made a positive impact despite this disorder. Maybe it can motivate you to find and focus on the talents that make you stand out in this world.

More good news: With advances in treatment, people with bipolar no longer have to swap creativity for good health. In fact, most people with bipolar find that they're more consistently creative and productive with the right combination of medication, self-help, and therapy.

Bipolar I

To earn the *bipolar I* label, you must experience at least one manic episode sometime during your life (see "Manic episode," earlier in this chapter). A major depressive episode isn't required for the bipolar I diagnosis, although many people with bipolar I have experienced one or more major depressive episodes at some point in their lives. In fact, depression is actually the phase of bipolar that causes the most problems for people with bipolar.

Bipolar I requires a manic episode. If you've never had a manic episode, you don't have bipolar I. If you've only ever had a hypomanic episode, you don't have bipolar I.

Bipolar II

Bipolar II is characterized by one or more major depressive episodes with at least one hypomanic episode sometime during the person's life. The major depressive episode must last at least two weeks, and the hypomania must last at least four days. (For more about what qualifies as hypomania, check out the earlier section "Hypomanic episode.")

Bipolar II requires at least one major depressive episode and one hypomanic episode. If you've ever had a manic episode that can't be attributed to some other cause, then you have bipolar I, not bipolar II.

Cyclothymic disorder

Cyclothymic disorder involves multiple episodes of hypomania and depressive symptoms that don't meet the criteria for a manic episode or a major depressive episode in intensity or duration. Your symptoms must last for at least two years (or one year in children or adolescents) without more than two months of a stable, or *euthymic,* mood during that time to qualify for a cyclothymic disorder diagnosis.

Some people with cyclothymic disorder eventually experience a full-blown manic or depressive episode, leading to an additional diagnosis of bipolar I or II. Medical supervision is important so that treatment planning can change if symptoms change.

Substance/medication-induced bipolar disorder

The *substance/medication-induced bipolar disorder* diagnosis applies when someone presents with all the symptoms of bipolar disorder (elevated, expansive, or irritable mood with or without depression), but only in the context of acute substance intoxication or withdrawal or medication effects. When this diagnostic category is used correctly, the mood disorder doesn't predate the introduction of the substance or persist long after the substance effects or withdrawal is over.

Bipolar and related disorder due to another medical condition

When a person's mania or hypomania can be traced to another medical condition, such as *hyperthyroidism* (overactive thyroid), based on medical history, physical examination, or lab results, the person may receive a diagnosis of bipolar and related disorder due to another medical condition, and the doctor will identify that other medical condition.

Other specified bipolar and related disorder

Introduced in *DSM-5,* this diagnosis enables doctors to diagnose bipolar disorder when symptoms characteristic of bipolar disorder significantly impair normal function or cause considerable distress, but don't quite meet the full diagnostic criteria for the other bipolar diagnostic classes. Here are some examples:

✔ **Major depression with short-duration hypomanic episodes:** An individual has experienced one or more major depressive episodes and two or more hypomanic episodes, but the hypomanic episodes have lasted for only a couple days (not the full four consecutive days required). In addition, the hypomanic episodes don't overlap with the major depressive episodes, which would call for a diagnosis of major depression with mixed features.

✔ **Major depression with hypomania that fails to meet the criteria for a hypomanic episode:** An individual has experienced one or more major depressive episodes along with periods of hypomania that fall short of the symptoms required for a hypomanic episode. For example, the person may have an elevated or expansive mood for four consecutive days, but she has only two of the three other symptoms required to qualify as having had a hypomanic episode.

- **Hypomanic episode without a major depressive or manic episode:** This designation enables doctors to diagnose bipolar disorder in the absence of a full-blown major depressive episode (which would result in a diagnosis of bipolar II) or a manic episode (which would result in a diagnosis of bipolar I).

- **Short-duration cyclothymia:** An individual has experienced multiple periods of depression and hypomania that don't meet the criteria for major depressive episode or hypomanic episode in the course of fewer than 24 months (or fewer than 12 months in children or adolescents).

All bipolar diagnoses require that the symptoms cause significant clinical distress or functional impairment. Although doctors certainly want to diagnose and treat people with bipolar disorder and other conditions covered in the *DSM,* they don't want to overdiagnose and overmedicate. Treatment is provided only when it begins to disrupt a person's ability to function normally and enjoy life's pleasures.

Unspecified bipolar disorder

The *unspecified bipolar disorder* designation is used to diagnose individuals who present with symptoms characteristic of bipolar disorder that cause clinically significant distress or functional impairment but don't fully meet the diagnostic criteria for the other bipolar disorder diagnostic categories. This diagnosis is used instead of *other specified bipolar and related disorder* when a doctor, for whatever reason, doesn't want to go into detail about why the criteria for a specific bipolar diagnosis hasn't been met; for example, in emergency room settings by doctors who need to diagnose and treat the symptoms immediately and may not have the time or sufficient details to make a more specific diagnosis.

Clarifying the purpose of the bipolar label

Your doctor doesn't use *bipolar disorder* to label *you* or minimize your worth as a human being. The label provides a convenient way to refer to your condition among insurance and healthcare providers. It helps all the people involved in your treatment to quickly recognize the illness that afflicts you and to provide the appropriate medications and therapy. You aren't bipolar disorder. Bipolar disorder is an illness you have, and you can manage it with the right treatments.

Digging Deeper with Bipolar Specifiers

The *DSM* provides *specifiers* to help doctors more fully describe a person's condition. Think of specifiers as adjectives used to describe nouns, the noun being the primary diagnosis.

Specifiers indicate the nature of the person's current or most recent episode, the severity of symptoms, the presence or absence of psychosis, the course of the illness, and other features of the illness, such as anxiety or a seasonal pattern. Specifiers serve two useful purposes:

- ✔ They allow for the subgrouping of individuals with bipolar disorder who share certain features, such as people who have bipolar disorder with anxious distress.

- ✔ They convey information that's helpful and relevant to the treatment and management of a person's condition. For example, someone who has bipolar with anxious distress likely needs treatment for both bipolar and anxiety.

In the following sections, we describe the bipolar specifiers in greater detail.

Current or most recent episode

This specifier identifies the most active or recent phase of illness, with a primary goal of identifying the most appropriate treatment. These specifiers are coded in the patient's medical record, where they're also important for insurance reimbursement purposes:

- ✔ **Manic:** The current or most recent episode is primarily mania.

- ✔ **Hypomanic:** The most recent or current episode is primarily hypomania.

- ✔ **Depressed:** The most recent or current episode is primarily depression.

Severity of illness

These specifiers have been part of the diagnostic system for a long time, and they continue to be part of the *DSM-5*. They assist in treatment planning and in following the course of illness; for example, a patient moving from severe to mild symptoms suggests that the acute episode is resolving. Historically the doctor making the diagnosis would use his clinical judgment and experience to estimate severity. *DSM-5* strongly encourages the use of more objective data, particularly by using scales that patients or doctors fill out, to provide more consistent ratings across patients and across treatment providers.

Severity typically relates to the intensity and frequency of symptoms as well as the degree to which symptoms impair function:

- ✔ **Mild:** Symptoms are less frequent, milder in intensity (causing some distress), and sometimes affect function seriously.

- ✔ **Moderate:** Symptoms are more persistent and intense (causing more distress) and often affect function seriously.

- ✔ **Severe:** Symptoms are very persistent to continuous, very intense (causing high levels of distress), and often affect function seriously.

Presence or absence of psychosis

Perhaps the most frightening accompaniment to depression or mania is *psychosis,* which may include delusional thinking, paranoia, and hallucinations (typically auditory as opposed to visual). Although psychosis isn't a necessary part of the bipolar diagnosis, it can accompany a mood episode. The extremes of depression and mania are sometimes associated with profound changes in the reality-testing system of the brain, which lead to severe distortions in perception and thinking. During a psychotic episode, you may experience any of the following symptoms:

- ✔ Feel as though you have special powers

- ✔ Hear voices that other people can't hear and that make you believe they're talking about you or instructing you to perform certain acts

- ✔ Believe that people can read your mind or put thoughts into your head

- ✔ Think that the television or radio is sending you special messages

- ✔ Think that people are following or trying to harm you when they're not

- ✔ Believe that you can accomplish goals that are well beyond your abilities and means

Psychotic symptoms usually reflect the pole of the mood disorder. So if you're in a major depressive episode, the psychotic thoughts are typically dark and negative; in a manic state, the symptoms tend to be more about super strengths, abilities, and insights. However, this doesn't always hold true; psychotic content can be all over the map.

Course of illness

This specifier overlaps with the presence or absence of psychosis when a diagnosis is coded. If the illness is active, the specifier notes whether or not psychosis is present.

If the illness is moving out of active phase, then one of the following specifiers is used:

- ✔ **In partial remission:** If symptoms have started to decline in severity and/or frequency, function has improved to some degree, and these improvements have been sustained over at least several weeks, this label is appropriate.

- ✔ **In full remission:** If function has returned to levels that existed before the illness, symptoms are much less active, and this state has sustained for several weeks to months, this label would be appropriate.

Additional features that often accompany bipolar disorder

Bipolar is often accompanied by other conditions, such as anxiety, and may have some features that vary among those who have the diagnosis. The following specifiers are used to label these extras:

- ✔ **With anxious distress:** Anxiety commonly co-occurs with bipolar disorder even in the absence of a full-blown anxiety disorder and the presence of this anxiety may influence treatment decisions.

- ✔ **With mixed features:** Mood episodes in bipolar disorder often aren't completely clear-cut. People with mostly manic symptoms may still express symptoms of depression, such as guilt and hopelessness or suicidal thoughts. Or someone who is primarily depressed may have a lot of physical agitation and racing thoughts characteristic of mania. This specifier accounts for these types of presentations, which may affect treatment planning.

- ✔ **With rapid cycling:** *Rapid cycling* is a specifier that identifies bipolar disorder that presents with four or more mood episodes in a 12-month period. This subtype is thought to be more severe and often doesn't respond as well to medications.

- ✔ **With melancholic features:** This subtype of depression is quite severe. It includes features such as very low mood that shows little or no response to improved external circumstance, very low energy, almost no interest in or response to pleasurable stimuli, agitation or slowing of movements, *diurnal variation* (mood and energy worse in the morning), sleep interruptions including early morning awakening, impaired thinking and concentration, and loss of appetite. It's really the most extreme presentation of most or all of the symptoms of a major depressive episode.

✔ **With atypical features:** This specifier describes a pattern of depression symptoms that used to be considered less typical of depression, but are now recognized as a frequent feature of depression. The name has stuck though. Symptoms include responsiveness to changes in external stimuli — feeling better if things improve or worse if something bad is going on, increased appetite or weight gain, excessive sleep and severe fatigue, feelings of *leaden paralysis* (heaviness in the limbs), and longstanding patterns of sensitivity to interpersonal rejection.

✔ **With mood-congruent psychotic features:** This label is used when psychosis is present and the hallucinations and delusions are similar to the mood episode — delusions of grandiosity and power in mania or delusions of guilt and hurting other people in depressed periods.

✔ **With mood-incongruent psychotic features:** This label is used when the hallucinations or delusions don't match the mood episode.

✔ **With catatonia:** *Catatonia* is a state of minimal responsiveness to the environment and abnormal movement. Symptoms can include stupor, immobility, rigid muscles or movements, very slowed or very fast movements, repetitive movements or speech, *mutism* (not speaking at all), odd mannerisms or postures, staring, unusual muscle responses when someone moves her limbs, *negativism* (oppositional or no response to external stimuli), and *echolalia and echopraxia* (repeating other people's language or movements). Catatonia can be present in many psychiatric conditions, and it can occur with either depressive or manic poles of bipolar disorder.

✔ **With peripartum onset:** This specifier is used when the onset of the bipolar mood episode is any time during pregnancy or in the four weeks after delivery, which is important because pregnancy and childbirth influence treatment decisions. (See Chapter 10 for details.)

✔ **With seasonal pattern:** This label indicates a well-established pattern of mood episodes that start and end at specific times of the year.

Distinguishing Bipolar from Conditions with Similar Symptoms

Before arriving at any medical diagnosis, doctors review a *differential diagnosis* to consider all the possible causes of the presenting symptoms. In bipolar disorder, the differential diagnosis often includes the following conditions that may involve symptoms similar to those of bipolar disorder:

✔ **Unipolar depression:** A major depressive episode without a history of mania or hypomania doesn't qualify as bipolar disorder. However, if you experience depression and you have a history of bipolar disorder in any first-degree relatives (parent, sibling, or child), your doctor may want to monitor you closely if she starts treatment with an antidepressant, because of the increased risk that you may have bipolar disorder that hasn't shown its manic pole yet. Additionally, the differentiation between unipolar and bipolar depression can be quite difficult. If a symptom such as agitation is present, it can be part of a mixed-mood episode of bipolar disorder, but it can also just be part of unipolar depression. Another difficult diagnostic situation is when during recovery from depression a person has periods of feeling particularly well. Are these periods symptomatic of hypomania or simply a strong recovery from a depressive episode?

✔ **Anxiety:** Anxiety may make you feel wired or tired with racing thoughts, poor sleep, and irritability, all of which overlap with symptoms characteristic of depression and mania. Many people with bipolar disorder also have an anxiety disorder, so they can happen together, but determining whether anxiety is the primary disorder rather than bipolar is important.

✔ **Attention deficit hyperactivity disorder (ADHD):** ADHD and mania are both characterized by impaired concentration and attention, impulsivity, high energy levels, and problems with organization and planning. However, for those with bipolar disorder, these symptoms are present only during a manic episode, not all the time. In addition, diagnostic criteria for hypomania or mania include an increase in goal-directed behavior, a decreased need for sleep, and grandiose thinking; ADHD doesn't include any of these. The pattern of symptoms, especially the episodic nature of mood episodes, is a key way to distinguish bipolar disorder from ADHD.

✔ **Schizophrenia and schizoaffective disorders:** Schizophrenia and schizoaffective disorders are thought disorders characterized by psychosis — delusional thinking, paranoia, and auditory or visual hallucinations. Although psychosis may accompany mania and depression, the bipolar psychosis is present only during an acute mood episode and goes away during times of normal mood. In schizoaffective disorders, psychosis occurs for at least some period of time separate from the mood episodes. Schizophrenia and related disorders are persistent and severe disruptions of thinking and reality testing unrelated to mood episodes.

✔ **Borderline personality disorder (BPD):** BPD shares a few characteristics with bipolar. For instance, someone with BPD may be impulsive, irritable, and argumentative much like someone who's experiencing a manic episode. However, BPD mood shifts are typically abrupt, short-lived, and in response to an external trigger, such as a conflict with another person; bipolar mood shifts are slower to develop, last longer, and may not appear to be in response to anything external. The rages that often characterize BPD aren't equivalent to mania. BPD symptoms are chronic, representing the person's baseline behaviors, whereas bipolar symptoms are episodic and different from the person's usual behavior patterns.

✔ **Other medical conditions:** Many medical conditions — including brain tumors, meningitis, encephalitis, seizure disorders, brain injury, hormone imbalances, anxiety disorders, autism, and pervasive developmental disorder (PDD) — can produce symptoms similar to those of bipolar mania or depression.

✔ **Mood instability caused by medications, alcohol, or drugs:** A variety of prescription medications, alcohol, marijuana, and street drugs can affect moods. You and your doctor must rule out these possible causes before arriving at a diagnosis of bipolar disorder.

Be sure to tell your doctor if anyone in your immediate or close extended family has been diagnosed with bipolar disorder, schizophrenia, or substance use disorder (formerly known as substance abuse), especially if you're seeking treatment only for depression. A close family history of these conditions increases the risk that you may eventually experience a manic or hypomanic episode resulting in a bipolar diagnosis. Medication treatment of unipolar and bipolar depressions is different — treatment with antidepressant alone in someone with bipolar disorder can trigger a shift to mania. Knowing about a family history of bipolar, you and your doctor can make a plan for close monitoring of your response to treatment for depression.

Considering Comorbidity: When Bipolar Coexists with Other Conditions

Bipolar disorder carries the distinction of having some of the highest rates of *comorbidity* with other psychiatric illnesses, which means that someone diagnosed with bipolar disorder is likely to have at least one other psychiatric diagnosis. Some researchers suspect that because bipolar disorder may actually be closely related to some of these illnesses, in terms of underlying brain changes — they may not really be separate disorders at all. Given how psychiatric illness is diagnosed at this point in time, we describe the disorders as separate entities and call them *comorbidities,* which we discuss in these sections.

Anxiety disorders

Anxiety disorders occur very frequently with bipolar disorder. One study of a large community sample found that more than 90 percent of people with bipolar I disorder had a co-occurring anxiety disorder diagnosis. When all bipolar groups were considered, it was about 70 percent. Most studies have found rates of anxiety disorders to occur in somewhere between a third and slightly more than a half of people diagnosed with all types of bipolar disorder. Here are a few of the anxiety disorders commonly associated with bipolar:

- ✔ **Panic disorder** occurs in about 21 percent of people with a bipolar diagnosis. That's more than 20 times the rate seen in the general population. Researchers suspect an underlying genetic relationship between the two disorders in some people and families.

- ✔ **Generalized anxiety disorder** seems to occur in nearly a third of all individuals with bipolar.

- ✔ **Social anxiety** seems to occur in about 50 percent of people with bipolar, in some studies.

- ✔ **Obsessive compulsive disorder (OCD)** has been found in about 21 percent of people with all types of bipolar disorder — about ten times the rate seen in the general population.

- ✔ **Post-traumatic stress disorder (PTSD)** has a high rate of occurrence in the general population, but an even higher rate in bipolar disorder. Women have higher rates than men with PTSD, both with and without bipolar disorder.

Treatment of anxiety disorders may complicate or complement the treatments of bipolar disorder, but reducing anxiety symptoms is an important part of managing bipolar disorder effectively.

Substance use disorder

Although the studies vary in exact numbers, studies overall suggest that about 60 percent of people with a bipolar diagnosis have had a substance abuse problem at least sometime in their lives, with more than 40 percent having current or past problems with alcohol abuse and similar but slightly lower numbers having had problems with drug abuse. Psychiatric hospitalization rates are generally higher for people with both bipolar and substance use disorder. The course of the illnesses seems to be more severe when both are present. Males with bipolar disorder have more substance abuse than females, but the rates are high in both groups. The rates decline as people get older but are still higher than rates of substance abuse in older people without bipolar disorder.

Treatment of both substance abuse and bipolar disorder is challenging, and having both adds many layers of challenges to the treatment. Resolution of bipolar symptoms may be quite difficult to achieve in the context of active substance abuse, and substance abuse is particularly difficult to address during active mood episodes. Successfully managing both disorders is necessary for long-term recovery from both.

Attention deficit hyperactivity disorder

Research in this area has suggested that about 20 percent of adults with all types of bipolar disorder have ADHD. Researchers have suggested that bipolar disorder that overlaps with ADHD might be a particular subtype of bipolar. In children with bipolar disorder, the distinction between bipolar and ADHD and the levels of overlap remain difficult issues to resolve. Some researchers have suggested significantly high levels of comorbidity in children, but others have found the levels to be much lower. Stay tuned for more information as the research unfolds.

The general consensus is that those with ADHD and bipolar disorder have worse outcomes for their bipolar disorder. Treatment is complicated because use of stimulants such as Ritalin to treat ADHD can significantly exacerbate bipolar symptoms. And with the high rates of substance use disorder in bipolar disorder, potential misuse of these medications must also be considered.

Personality disorders

Personality disorders are conditions in which the development of emotional, social, and behavioral systems is disrupted, causing significant, lifelong problems with function. Personality disorders are divided into *clusters* and then further into specific types; for example Cluster B personality disorders include borderline, antisocial, histrionic, and narcissistic personality disorders. Studies suggest that about 30 to 40 percent of people with bipolar disorder also meet criteria for a personality disorder.

Personality disorders are difficult to treat and often don't respond to medications. Psychotherapies are becoming more and more effective; people with personality disorders often have difficulty gaining insight into how their problems affect their lives, because they've never known a more adaptive level of functioning. Without insight, trying to address the problems is quite difficult. Layering these challenges onto a bipolar disorder adds tremendously to the difficulties of achieving sustained recovery.

Childhood trauma may be closely related to the development of some personality disorders, including borderline personality disorder. Early trauma can have damaging effects on the development of emotional and interpersonal skills. Identifying and addressing trauma is an important part of managing these conditions.

Memory and thinking problems

Problems with cognitive skills such as memory and attention and the ability to think clearly are common in bipolar disorder, both during and between mood episodes. Compounding the cognitive issues inherent in bipolar is that fact that some medications used to treat bipolar can cloud thinking as a side effect. Addressing problems with thinking and memory is important in recovery from bipolar disorder to help people get back on their feet in terms of work, life management, and interpersonal and leisure time skills.

Certain medications used to treat bipolar disorder may have *neuroprotective properties;* that is, they may prevent damage and perhaps help the recovery or regeneration of brain cells. Some recent studies have suggested that lithium, while sometimes causing short-term mental cloudiness, may actually protect brain cells over time and may prevent or reduce cognitive decline.

Confronting the Challenges of Diagnosing Children and Teens

The diagnosis of bipolar disorder in children (up to the age of 12) and adolescents (teenagers) has been an area of debate and controversy for close to 20 years. Even professionals in the field fundamentally disagree about some features of diagnosing this disorder in young age groups. The consensus that's evolving, however, is straightforward: To be diagnosed with bipolar disorder, children need to exhibit the same patterns of energy and mood changes that adults do — at least one period of mania or hypomania, often associated with episodes of depression.

Adolescents are more likely than younger children to show classic symptoms of bipolar — mania in particular. True mania does occur in children before puberty, but it's infrequent. And recent research suggests that children who exhibit a lot of problems with mood dysregulation, particularly anger and irritability, aren't more likely to exhibit bipolar disorder later in life. Instead, they more often experience anxiety and/or depression when they get older.

The high energy and impulsivity that are prominent in manic episodes are core symptoms of one of the most common psychiatric conditions in children — ADHD. The evolving diagnostic criteria for bipolar disorder in children don't count high energy and impulsivity toward a manic episode diagnosis unless these symptoms become significantly worse during a sustained period of time (not just a few hours).

Irritable mood — one possible symptom in mania — is also a common symptom in childhood, and many medical, developmental, or psychiatric issues can cause it. Unless the irritability occurs in cycles — sustained periods of time in which it's much more severe than the child's usual temperament — it doesn't count toward a diagnosis of bipolar disorder. *DSM-5* contains a new diagnosis called *disruptive mood dysregulation disorder*. The purpose of introducing this diagnosis is to have a way to describe and research chronically irritable and explosive children without inappropriately labeling them as having bipolar disorder. The criteria for DMDD include

- ✔ Severe recurrent temper outbursts that are grossly out of proportion in intensity or duration to the situation or provocation.

- ✔ The temper outbursts are inconsistent with developmental level.

- ✔ The outbursts occur on average three or more times per week.

- ✔ The mood between outbursts is persistently irritable or angry most of the day, nearly every day, and is observable by others.

- ✔ The symptoms have been present for 12 or more months and there hasn't been a period lasting three or more consecutive months without the patterns of irritability and outbursts.

- ✔ The symptoms aren't part of a manic episode or better explained by major depression or other psychiatric or neurodevelopmental disorders, including anxiety disorders and autism.

This research is ongoing, and many researchers are still exploring whether bipolar disorder can look significantly different in children and teens. But, whatever the studies reveal, doctors know that they must be cautious and diligent when evaluating young patients with mood symptoms. The medications used to treat mania are powerful and have many side effects, and a diagnosis of bipolar may prevent the use of medications to treat ADHD or anxiety and depression. Therefore, a misdiagnosis in a child can have significant long-term consequences.

Obtaining an early, accurate diagnosis of a child's difficulties and identifying whether the cause is bipolar disorder or something else is the most critical step in helping the child or adolescent manage a mood problem. See Chapter 21 for more about diagnosis and treatment options for children and teenagers who may be dealing with a mood disorder.

BIPOLAR BIO

Battling the stigma of a bipolar diagnosis

During my battle with bipolar disorder, I was unaware of the consequences of my risky behavior — abusing substances, having promiscuous sex, staying up all night, and counterfeiting art — but I was high-functioning.

My diagnosis put me in a category of the population called *bipolar*. In my mind, I was a lunatic, freak, psycho, crack-up, and mental case. I had officially stigmatized myself, long before anyone else had the chance.

I invited my parents to dinner to tell them the news, and they had a ton of questions. "Are you sure your doctor is right? Where did it come from? What's going to happen to you? Is it genetic?" They struggled with the stigma of having a son with bipolar, and, even worse, they worried that it might run in the family — we might have more like me!

Family and friends didn't come rushing to my side to support me in my battle. In 1993, the mere mention of bipolar disorder frightened people; someone with bipolar was "crazy." And because my insidious illness wasn't tangible, like diabetes or MS, it was easier for people to blame it on me. At a time when I was most in need of support from my friends and family, stigma pushed them away.

Most people thought I had the skills and strength to "kick" my bipolar disorder and get better on my own because the symptoms didn't show up on my body as a wound. Many people thought it was a figment of my imagination, that I was lazy or just seeking attention, and I started believing these ideas. But when symptoms surfaced, I was reminded that I really was suffering from bipolar disorder.

When medication didn't quell the mania, I opted for the last resort — electroshock therapy. That decision in itself pretty much confirmed that I was officially mentally ill. It was too much for some of my friends to handle, and they simply disappeared. Nobody seemed to want a friend who was now a psychiatric patient and, after electroshock, a "certifiable zombie."

Stigma prevents many us from seeking help and isolates us when we're most in need of supportive friends and family. Even in my recovery today, when I speak openly about my diagnosis, I'm keenly aware that many people are uncomfortable and afraid. Stigma is a form of discrimination, and debunking the myths about bipolar disorder and disseminating the truths are critical to educating the public and creating a social environment that's more conducive to mental health and recovery.

— Andy Behrman
(http://electroboy.com),
author of *Electroboy: A Memoir of Mania*

Chapter 2

Finding the Cause: The Brain and Body Science of Bipolar Disorder

. . . .

In This Chapter

▶ Examining genetic vulnerabilities

▶ Investigating other possible contributing factors

▶ Understanding the brain and the way it functions and dysfunctions

▶ Looking at how medications can help

. . . .

As with all mental illnesses, at this point in time, doctors diagnose bipolar disorder by observation only — identifying patterns of change in how a person is feeling and behaving. Medical science has no brain scans or blood tests that can conclusively make the diagnosis, and research now shows that the chances of eventually developing one simple screening test are next to nothing. In fact, it seems likely that what's referred to as *bipolar disorder* isn't just one disorder but rather many different disorders of brain and body function that share similar emotional and behavioral patterns.

These underlying disorders develop from complex combinations of genetic and nongenetic factors that the scientific community is only just beginning to understand. Importantly, the growing science of bipolar disorder can help eliminate the commonly held myth that it's some type of weakness or defect in moral character. Make no mistake — bipolar disorder is a real *physical* illness or illnesses.

Another fact that's also becoming clear is that although the brain is the site of many of the problems found in bipolar disorder, bipolar also affects the rest of the body in important ways. And the environment's interactions with brain and body play critical roles in the development and evolution of bipolar disorder.

In this chapter, we explore the biological basis of bipolar disorder, looking at factors inside and outside the human body that may contribute to its onset and progression with the goal of understanding what is currently known about what causes bipolar disorder and what is yet to be uncovered by science.

Digging Up Bipolar's Genetic Roots

Now that scientists are able to map human genes fairly easily and inexpensively, genetic research is exploding. Understanding the genetics of an illness doesn't just shed light on causes but also seeks to identify specific biological processes that contribute to the illness, which in turn helps to develop more effective treatments. But before even jumping into a search for genes, scientists need to know if they have any reason to suspect that genetics are partly to blame. Studies of families, particularly studies of twin siblings, have been the gold standard of this research. These genetic studies reveal the following:

✔ The identical twin of a person with bipolar I disorder has about a 50 percent risk of developing the disorder. Because identical twins share all their genes, this finding means genetics accounts for some, but not all, of the chance of developing bipolar disorder. (If the genetics were fully responsible and one identical twin had bipolar I, then the other twin would have a 100 percent chance of developing the disorder.)

✔ If someone has an immediate family member with bipolar I disorder, the person has about a 10 percent chance of developing the disorder, which is much higher than the 1 to 2 percent chance of having the disorder if for an individual with no family history of bipolar.

✔ The familial risks of bipolar II and cyclothymia — so called bipolar spectrum disorders — are less clear in the research. *First-degree family members* (parents, siblings, or offspring) of people with bipolar disorder are more likely to have other disorders as well, such as unipolar depression, schizophrenia, autism disorder, anxiety disorders, substance abuse, attention deficit hyperactivity disorder (ADHD), and personality disorders.

Putting together all the family and twin studies, researchers say that *heritability* — how much of bipolar disorder is due to genetics — accounts for between 60 and 70 percent of the risk of getting the illness.

Shaking the family tree

A history of bipolar disorder in an immediate family member is important to know, because it increases your risk of getting the disorder. However, families of people with bipolar disorder have higher rates of many other psychiatric conditions, as well. When considering your risk for bipolar disorder, a look at all major psychiatric disorders in close family members can help identify some genetic susceptibility to bipolar disorder. If you ask relatives whether anyone in your family has had bipolar disorder, they may not know the answer. Older relatives may have been misdiagnosed as having schizophrenia or may have never been diagnosed but had a history of self-treating with alcohol or drugs. Or a relative may have been considered eccentric, but for whatever reason was never diagnosed.

To obtain better answers, try rephrasing the question:

- **Has anyone in the family had alcohol or substance abuse problems?** Many people with bipolar disorder self-medicate with alcohol and drugs, which does significantly more harm than good but may provide temporary relief from the psychological pain. Some research also suggests that bipolar disorder and substance abuse may share some genetic risk factors.

- **Have any family members been diagnosed with schizophrenia?** In the not-so-distant past, doctors commonly misdiagnosed bipolar disorder as schizophrenia. Schizophrenia is more common in the relatives of people with bipolar disorder, likely because of some shared genetic risks.

- **Has any family member been treated for any other mental illness?** If a family member has received treatment for depression, psychosis, or other mental illnesses, he may not have received the correct diagnosis. Also, relatives of people with bipolar disorder are more likely to have many other types of mental illness, which may be partly genetic and may be due to other mechanisms.

- **Has anyone in the family had to go away for a while to an institution, sanatorium, or rehab center?** Families sometimes cover up memories of relatives who had to be hospitalized for mental illnesses by saying that they had to go away for a while.

- **Have any family members been known to be particularly energetic or eccentric?** In the past, people politely described relatives with various degrees of mental illness as eccentric.

- **Has anyone in the family suffered from physical symptoms such as chronic exhaustion, pain, or digestive problems?** These symptoms may be physical manifestations of mood and anxiety disorders.

Families can be particularly secretive, especially when protecting the reputation of the dead. People can become even more defensive if you confront them while you're in the throes of mania. Choose a time when you're level-headed to explain how important an accurate and detailed family history is for your diagnosis.

Realizing that genetic susceptibility is only one risk factor

Having a genetic susceptibility to bipolar disorder doesn't guarantee that you'll experience symptoms. The most recent research, described in the next two sections, suggests that a variety of genetic changes can create a *susceptibility* to developing the disorder. But susceptibility isn't destiny — bipolar disorder seems to occur due to a combination of genetic and nongenetic factors. Although you can't control all the possible triggers, managing the ones you can control may reduce your risk of developing the disorder, and doing so certainly may help lessen the severity of your illness and improve your prognosis if it occurs.

Highly charged life events, both positive and negative, seem to relate to the development of symptoms, but other biological events — including the number of episodes that you experience — are likely to be involved, as the next section explains. The severity of your underlying susceptibility is also important. Some subtypes of bipolar found in some families that are more extreme and more likely to evolve into illness without major or well-defined triggers, whereas other forms may require higher doses of stress responses to fully develop.

Grasping the genetic complexities

Even though indisputable evidence proves that bipolar disorder has strong genetic components, science has more recently been able to show clearly that that there is no single bipolar gene. What's called bipolar disorder, based on emotional and behavioral symptoms, actually seems to be a group of disorders that have different underlying biological stories. Because genetics play a big role in these stories, scientists are likely to find many different types of genetic changes that contribute to the various causes of bipolar disorder. Current research has started to put some pieces of these stories together and suggests the following main points:

✔ Bipolar disorder seems to be the result of small changes in a high number of genes rather than big changes in just a few genes; high-volume studies that look at thousands of genomes are needed to pin down the specific genes involved in bipolar. (A *genome* is an organism's complete set of DNA, its genetic makeup.) The small changes that have been found aren't usually unique to bipolar disorder, but have a higher rate of occurrence in people with bipolar disorder compared to those without bipolar.

✔ Studies show a number of genetic changes that overlap between bipolar disorder and other conditions, especially schizophrenia and unipolar depression. Recently, a large and much publicized study published by the Cross-Disorder Group of the Psychiatric Genomics Consortium entitled "Genetic relationship between five psychiatric disorders estimated from genome-wide SNPs, published in the journal *Nature Genetics,* uncovered a shared genetic risk with autism spectrum and ADHD, in addition to depression and schizophrenia. However, researchers have also identified a number of genetic changes that seem to be specific to bipolar disorder.

✔ The numerous genetic factors uncovered so far affect a wide variety of structures and functions throughout the body. Many other studies are looking at how the brains and bodies of people with bipolar disorder differ from those without (see the later section, "Examining the Circuitry of Bipolar"). The integration of the genetic studies and this other research is where the big picture of bipolar disorder is unfolding.

✔ Because bipolar isn't 100 percent genetic, another important goal is to understand how nongenetic factors interact with the genetic risk factors to cause someone to actually develop bipolar disorder, as we explain in the next two sections.

Flipping the bipolar switch: Epigenetics

Epigenetics is the study of changes that affect how genes are expressed without affecting the genes themselves. These changes occur through a variety of chemical interactions with the DNA. Sometimes these changes in expression occur as part of typical development and function, but some changes can disrupt normal processes and healthy cell function.

The science of epigenetics helps to explain the interplay between nature and nurture — how an organism's *genotype* (genetic makeup) interacts with the environment to produce the organism's *phenotype* (observable characteristics). External events such as parental neglect or other trauma or stress may trigger chemical changes to DNA, which affect how a person's genes are expressed. And these changes can pass to the next generation. So, for example, if an expectant mom has been exposed to chronic stress that has affected her mood-related genes, then the stress effect on the gene (not just the gene itself) can be passed on to her child. As a result, the child's own genes as well as the effects of long-term stress on her mother's genes affect the child's likelihood of eventually exhibiting depression or other mood disorders.

Investigating Nongenetic Factors

Genetic studies indicate that about 60 to 70 percent of bipolar disorder is related to inherited factors, but a variety of nongenetic factors affect how these genes are expressed. Many of these stressors are present in the very early phase of brain development — before birth and in the first months and years of life. However, scientists also believe that ongoing nongenetic factors contribute to the development of bipolar disorder and its course over time. Some of these factors include the following:

- **Stressful life events:** Studies of people with bipolar disorder have found a number of abnormalities in the biological systems that regulate the body's response to various types of stress. Interactions between these vulnerable systems and environmental stress more than likely play an important role in both the development and progression of bipolar disorder. Acute life events have been found to occur more frequently before mood episodes in people with bipolar disorder.

- **Early life stress:** That same interaction between impaired stress response systems and stress may occur many years before the development of bipolar disorder. Studies suggest that early childhood trauma is associated with a higher risk of bipolar disorder in adulthood.

- **Substances:** Alcohol and/or drug abuse often accompanies bipolar disorder. Some of this may be self-medication — using substances to dull pain and discomfort in the short run. However, substance abuse and bipolar disorder may have overlapping genetic risk factors, so that rather than being a behavioral response to the illness, these conditions may develop alongside one another. Some evidence even suggests that the use of alcohol and drugs may increase the risk of developing bipolar disorder, which raises the question of whether early intervention with drug and alcohol use can help reduce the likelihood of ever having that first mood episode. Tobacco use is also being looked at as possibly interacting negatively with genetic vulnerabilities to bipolar disorder.

- **Nutrition:** Although no research points to specific nutritional triggers for bipolar disorder, people with bipolar disorder have higher rates of illnesses such as cardiovascular disease and type 2 diabetes. These conditions create their own stress and physical damage. Healthful nutrition is an important part of limiting the development and progression of these conditions, which can reduce their negative effects.

- **Infection:** Studies have suggested that maternal infections, particularly with the flu virus, during pregnancy are associated with higher rates of bipolar disorder I in adulthood. The overlap of the infection with genetic risk factors may be a contributing factor to some people's bipolar disorder. Some research shows a higher rate of infection with *toxoplasmosis* (a parasite found in cat feces) in people with bipolar disorder, and the current thinking is that the infection interacts in some way with the genetic risk factors to cause psychiatric symptoms.

- **Sleep/circadian rhythms:** Researchers have identified a strong relationship between bipolar disorder and sleep problems. A number of different genetic variations may contribute to these difficulties. Some data suggests that sleep deprivation can be a trigger for mania, and because people with bipolar disorder are already poor sleepers, they're at much higher risk of sleep deprivation. Sleeplessness creates a vicious negative spiral with bipolar, causing sleeplessness and sleeplessness contributing to bipolar. Sleep management is important in trying to hinder the progression of bipolar disorder.

- **Hormones:** Hormones are mood modulators and may contribute to mood symptoms and patterns. Research suggests that they interact with the genetically vulnerable brain and body systems in people with bipolar disorder to influence the onset and progression of their illness. Women are particularly vulnerable to this effect because of their frequent hormone shifts throughout their lives. Hormonal transition times such as the onset of puberty, pregnancy, and menopause are vulnerable periods for mood episodes (refer to Chapter 10 for more discussion).

Some of the genetic differences in people with bipolar disorder interfere with their body's ability to regulate or turn off their stress responses — even between mood episodes. These factors stress the body, adding to the already hyped-up response from genetic factors. Finding ways to limit or reduce distress, avoid or treat substance use, and manage sleep and nutrition are some strategies that may help you reduce the severity of the illness. Throughout this book, we describe various techniques for reducing the risks of experiencing mood episodes and managing them when they do occur.

BIPOLAR BIO

All of the above

Was it the drugs, the genetic predisposition, or the trauma? Likely, all of the above.

My parents, Marcia and Martino, were impoverished, had two kids, and were using illicit drugs. I was born premature and addicted. Each had manic depression, now called bipolar disorder.

They coped with their mental battles by using drugs and alcohol. They would leave my brother Jordache and me unattended, lying in our own filth, screaming, barely clothed, to score. They left us just one too many times. On that day, at a seedy motel, the clerk heard our cries and called the police, and we were then taken into child protective services. It was a gift, our first.

Clearly Jordache and I were predisposed to bipolar disorder. The question remains, did we have a chance? How much did neglect, malnutrition, and abandonment have to do with my condition? How much did the drugs in my system, in utero, contribute to the eventual onset of bipolar disorder?

After Jordache and I were placed into foster care, he developed bronchitis and died. Feeling even more abandoned, I developed a detachment disorder, which would follow me into adulthood. Even today, I battle with anxiety, detachment disorder, and abandonment issues on top of bipolar disorder.

I bounced around from foster home to foster home. Day after day was spent vomiting and having ongoing diarrhea. I was every foster parent's nightmare. Finally, at nine months of age, I was placed into the loving arms of Patrick and Debi Hines. They were my second gift, my greatest blessing next to getting taken in by child protective services.

Soon after I was placed in their care, Patrick and Debi decided to try and adopt me. They fought a two-year court battle to keep me.

Patrick hired the best lawyers he could find to retain custody and won. He and Debi proceeded to adopt me. They cared for me throughout this time and were there throughout the progression of my bipolar disorder I with psychotic features. Even though our lives were rough when I struggled most, we got through it and have come out on the other side.

I will never know to what extent my traumatic infancy, the drugs that entered my system before birth, my predisposition to a mental health condition, or any other factors may have contributed to my getting bipolar disorder. There is no way to measure those things that changed my brain forever. There is no way to tell which played a bigger role or when they overlapped.

For now, I remain confident that no matter my suffering, I will prevail. The chronic suicidal thoughts will not kill me. I won't let them. I have far too much to live for. After my suicide attempt and survival, I know I deserve to be here. I have made a promise to myself and to my family. I will never attempt to take my life again. I will live until the ripe old age of 110, fighting for my mental wellbeing, and I will die in my sleep, holding my wife's hand, just as in the film *The Notebook* (which I'll never admit to having seen, or cried during, twice).

— Kevin Hines
(www.kevinhinesstory.com),
mental health advocate, speaker, and
author of *Cracked, Not Broken: Surviving and Thriving after a Suicide Attempt*

Examining the Circuitry of Bipolar

Many people refer to bipolar disorder as a chemical imbalance, but this phrase oversimplifies what's actually going on and creates the false impression that your brain has too much of this or too little of that. The biological anomalies being discovered in people with bipolar disorder are complex and affect numerous biological structures and systems — throughout the body and brain — as well as how these systems interact with each other. Keep in mind that the current knowledge about bipolar disorder is still only beginning, and things are likely to change quickly and substantially as more research is done. In the following sections, we explore the facets of bipolar at work in the body that science has discovered so far.

The discussion of brain structure and function that follows is heavy and dense, but you need to know some basic terminology before you can begin to understand any discussion of how brain dysfunction plays a role in producing bipolar symptoms. We start by discussing the *anatomy* (structure) and *physiology* (function) of the brain and the cells that comprise it in order to bring you up to speed on the basics. Then, you get to the good stuff — where we explain how structural and functional anomalies in the brain may be linked to bipolar.

Brushing up on brain structure and function

Pinpointing the location of bipolar disorder in your brain is almost as difficult as finding affordable health insurance. Brain imaging studies have found few consistent changes when looking at large brain structures. They've had much more success looking at changes at the cellular level and, in particular, at functional changes in cells and groups of cells in particular brain areas. Here is some basic brain anatomy and physiology that helps explain the research.

Dissecting the brain

Looking at a whole human brain from the outside, as shown in Figure 2-1, you see the *cerebral hemispheres* (the large sections, not labeled in the figure, that comprise most of the brain), the *cerebellum* (the small ball toward the back of the hemispheres), and the *brain stem* (a long, thin structure leaving the brain and connecting it to the spinal cord). The cerebral hemispheres are divided into four sections that serve broadly different functions — the frontal lobe, the parietal lobe, the temporal lobe, and the occipital lobe.

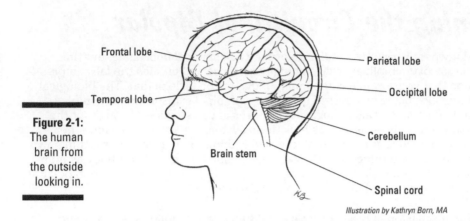

Figure 2-1:
The human
brain from
the outside
looking in.

Illustration by Kathryn Born, MA

When you open the brain up, pulling the two hemispheres apart into two
equal parts, and look inside, you see a number of brain structures within
the hemispheres (see Figure 2-2). Within the outer layer, researchers have
identified a number of cell areas related to different functions. Several of
these areas appear frequently in studies of bipolar, including the *prefrontal
cortex* and the *anterior cingulate cortex.* Below the large outer layer are
a number of structures, some of which are quite important in bipolar
disorder research, including the thalamus, hypothalamus, hippocampus,
and amygdala.

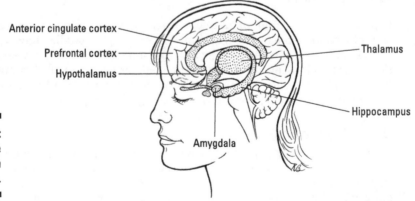

Figure 2-2:
Inside the
human
brain.

Illustration by Kathryn Born, MA

Exploring the functions of different areas of the brain

Now that you have a bird's-eye view of the brain, consider the functions of some of these areas:

✔ **Cerebral hemispheres:** The cerebral hemispheres include most of the thinking and planning parts of the brain as well as areas important to sensory input and learning and memory. The areas are as follows:

- The *frontal lobe* is the executive of the brain, serving to coordinate and manage the many functions within the body and brain.

- The *parietal lobe* is involved in managing sensory experiences, in addition to playing a role in many other functions.

- The *temporal lobe* is involved in smell and auditory sensory input, speech and language, and memory and learning.

- The *occipital lobe* is the center for processing visual stimuli.

All these areas perform many other functions, as well, and functions may overlap between areas.

✔ **Cerebellum:** The *cerebellum* appears to manage the fine-tuning of complex movements and also seems to be involved in regulating thought, language, and mood responses.

✔ **Brain stem:** The *brain stem* manages basic survival mechanisms, such as breathing and the heartbeat, and is involved in the management of consciousness, alertness, and sleep/wake cycles.

✔ **Cerebral cortex:** The *cerebral cortex* is the outer layer of brain cells in the hemispheres. It's considered to be the site of higher level thinking, coordinating incoming information and generating movement, actions, and thoughts. It's broken down into a number of smaller areas associated with specific types of function.

✔ **Prefrontal cortex:** The *prefrontal cortex* is a section of the cerebral cortex that is highly developed and is involved in regulating complex thinking and behavior; it's considered a center of judgment and planning.

✔ **Hippocampus:** The *hippocampus* is located in the cortex *(subcortical)* and is especially important in learning and memory.

✔ **Thalamus:** The *thalamus* is a structure that sits below the cortex *(subcortical)* that serves as a relay station for sensorimotor input, conveying it to areas of the cortex. It also regulates sleep, consciousness, and levels of alertness.

✔ **Hypothalamus:** The *hypothalamus* is also subcortical and regulates many survival mechanisms such as hunger/thirst and sleep/wake and energy cycles, all components of *circadian rhythms* — physical, mental, and behavioral patterns that occur in approximately 24-hour cycles.

✔ **Amygdala:** The *amygdala,* another subcortical area, is a major player in the brain's reaction to emotions.

✔ **Limbic system:** The term *limbic system* is used to describe a number of brain areas important to emotional function. The list of areas can be different in different textbooks but the hippocampus, thalamus, hypothalamus, and amygdala are considered main components of this system.

✔ **Anterior cingulate cortex:** The *anterior cingulate cortex* is a part of the cortex that has strong associations between the prefrontal cortex and the limbic system and is thought to play an important role in regulation of strong emotions.

Viewing the brain under a microscope

The brain has several layers. The outer layer of the brain is referred to as the *cortex,* often referred to as the gray matter. The layer beneath the cortex is a network of fibers that connect different areas of the brain that's often referred to as the white matter. The fibers are protected and insulated by a layer called the *myelin sheath.* Within the brain is a system of cavities, including spaces called the ventricles, that make, circulate, and then re-absorb *cerebrospinal fluid.* This fluid serves as a mechanical shock absorber to the brain but also brings nutrients from and filters waste back into the blood stream.

Another important component of brain anatomy is comprised of cells that make up all these structures. Brain cells include neurons and glia.

✔ *Neurons* form the telecommunications system in the brain and body, dictating body functions by generating, sending, and reacting to electrochemical signals.

✔ *Glial cells,* once thought to be just a support network for neurons, play a major role in brain function and in the brain's communications and reaction systems.

The gray matter of the cortex includes the *cell bodies* (central section) and *dendrites* (one of the connecting ends) of neurons, as well as glial cells. The white matter is made up of the *axons* (another type of connecting end) of neurons.

Understanding how brain cells communicate

Neurons communicate with one another in many different ways, but communication occurs primarily across the *synapse* — the space between neurons or between neurons and other cells such as a gland or muscle cell. The most common type of communication occurs when one end of the neuron (often the axon but not always) releases a chemical messenger into the synapse (as in Figure 2-3). The next cell (often the dendrite of another neuron) receives the chemical messenger.

Receptors on the outside of the second cell latch onto the chemical messenger. Cells have many different types of receptors for all of the chemical messengers; the type of receptor influences how the message is received and processed and how the instructions are transmitted to the second cell. After a chemical messenger occupies the receptor, it can generate many different responses in the receiving cell, depending on the chemical messenger and the receptor type. After the messenger has done its job, it's released from the receptor and then taken back into the first cell, a process called *reuptake.* In the brain, the chemical messengers are often referred to as *neurotransmitters.*

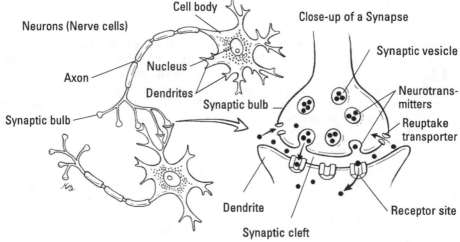

Figure 2-3:
Cell-to-cell communication via neurotransmitters.

Illustration by Kathryn Born, MA

Nervous system cells communicate in ways beyond the synapse; for example, chemicals called *neuropeptides* communicate between cells but not across synapses. Of great importance in the current research on bipolar disorder is the communication between glial cells and neurons.

Disruptions in these communication systems may be at least as important as problems in neuron-to-neuron transmissions. *Intracellular* (within-cell) communication may also play a role, as we explain in the later section, "Intracellular signaling."

Connecting the brain to bipolar disorder

Given the complexity of the brain's structures and functions, the many interactions throughout the body, and the heterogeneous nature of bipolar disorder, research has been difficult, and findings are often inconsistent from study to study. Major ways of studying the brain, which overlap with the genetic research, include imaging studies that can look at structure or function of brain areas, microscopic examination of brain tissue *postmortem* (after someone with bipolar has died), blood tests, *neuropsychological tests* (having a patient answer questions and do specific mental tasks), and a variety of other ways of examining the brain and body.

Scientists are still working toward developing a clear picture of bipolar disorder at work in the brain, but some findings are beginning to shed light on what goes on in the brain of someone with bipolar, and others are just beginning to be explored. In these sections, you get a glimpse of the emerging picture.

These findings only touch the surface of the tremendous work being done to better understand bipolar disorder. All these factors, along with many others not discussed here, interact with one another in numerous complex ways. Uncovering the various components and their relationships is actually starting to put together the puzzle that is bipolar disorder, but much work remains to be done.

Structure

Despite many studies, finding consistent changes in any one large brain structure has been difficult. Some research reveals changes in the cerebellum, but findings are inconsistent. Some research shows that the ventricles increase in size, a sign of damage to the brain, with every manic episode that occurs. Changes in the hippocampus have also been reported but, again, the findings are inconsistent between studies. Changes in the size of amygdala have also been observed, but may be different depending on the age of the person or how long he's had the illness.

Circuitry/wiring

This is one of the most productive areas of research. Circuits (or networks) are communication loops between brain areas that affect particular types of function. The studies examine patterns of communication within and between these circuits to see whether they're significantly and consistently different between people with and without bipolar disorder. One of the many challenges is that researchers have to look at these networks in different states — depressed, manic, or between episodes.

Although researchers are studying a number of circuits, the *cortico-limbic theory* seems most promising. This theory describes abnormalities in the balance between the cortex, which is more about regulation and control, and the limbic system, which is about emotional reaction. Too much limbic activation and inadequate or inconsistent activation of the control mechanisms in the cortex seem to play a role in the development of bipolar disorder.

Neurotransmitters

The body uses a wide range of *neurotransmitters* (chemical messengers) to communicate between cells. Bipolar research has found that abnormalities in these transmitters are associated with bipolar disorder:

- ✓ **Glutamate** is an *activating* neurotransmitter, often having to do with turning things on rather than off. Many studies consistently have found problems in the networks that use glutamate.

- ✓ **Dopamine** is a neurotransmitter related to reward- and pleasure-seeking behaviors, attention and focus, and muscle movement. Some research has identified dopamine as possibly being poorly regulated during manic episodes.

- ✓ **Serotonin** is a chemical messenger highly involved in networks related to mood, anxiety, and general survival mechanisms such as eating, sleeping, and reproduction, with well-established relationships to depression. Extensive research shows a clear and consistent connection between serotonin and depression.

- ✓ **Gamma-aminobutyric acid (GABA)** is a transmitter that plays a role in *inhibitory systems* (systems that turn things off) and may be abnormally regulated in bipolar disorder.

- ✓ **Norepinephrine** is important in the brain stem and may also exhibit some abnormalities in bipolar.

Intracellular signaling

Intracellular signaling refers to the changes that happen inside a nerve cell after the receptor on the outside of the cell latches on to the transmitter. Genetic studies point toward a number of these signaling systems being disturbed in bipolar disorder, and interestingly many of the medications that treat bipolar disorder affect and re-regulate some of these same pathways. This implies that although research often focuses attention on the neurotransmitter at the synapse, the underlying abnormalities and the treatment effects may also be in other parts of the neuronal communication system. Perhaps this is why some medications take days or weeks to become fully effective.

Stress circuits

The body systems that control chemical responses to stress show abnormalities in people with bipolar disorder. *Cortisol* is a chemical that is part of normal body function, but is raised during periods of stress. In bipolar disorder, the body's ability to turn off or tone down the cortisol response appears to be impaired. These stress responses are risk factors for worsening bipolar disorder. In addition, having too much cortisol is harmful to the body in many ways and is associated with problems in blood sugar and insulin management as well as heart disease, among other significant medical problems found more often in people with bipolar disorder.

Circadian rhythms

The brain and body have their own daily rhythms, which are significantly disrupted in bipolar disorder. Some researchers see these circadian rhythms as possibly central to the underlying abnormalities in bipolar disorder.

Inflammation

Research looking at the role of inflammation in psychiatric disorders, including bipolar disorder, is growing. *Inflammation* is one of the ways the body reacts to injury/damage, generating a number of chemicals and cellular processes to repair the damage.

When you have the flu, your symptoms of achy muscles and fatigue aren't actually from the virus, but rather from your body's inflammatory response, which is trying to help manage the virus attack. More and more evidence shows that people with bipolar disorder have higher levels of these inflammatory chemicals in their brains and throughout the bodies. These inflammatory responses seem to both contribute to developing bipolar disorder and be the result of the illness. Stress on the brain and body, of all kinds, not just physical illness, triggers inflammatory responses, which may be one of the ways that emotional stress contributes to the onset and progression of bipolar.

Neuroplasticity

For a long time the medical community thought that after the brain was finished developing in childhood, it stayed the same throughout adulthood. More recent research shows clearly that *plasticity* — the ability of the brain to reorganize and rebuild itself in response to events within the body and changes in the environment — extends into adulthood. Plasticity can apply to synapses, such as building new synapses, pruning unnecessary ones, and keeping existing ones healthy, or more broadly to nerve cells and the connections between them.

Normal brain development requires plasticity as do learning and memory; the brain changes at some level whenever you learn something. Evidence that neuroplasticity is impaired in bipolar disorder is growing, suggesting that genetic risks and environmental interactions interfere with the ability of brain cells to respond adaptively to change and stress and that these abnormalities contribute to the symptoms of bipolar disorder.

Recognizing How Medications Do Their Thing

Medications that work for bipolar disorder continue to puzzle researchers, who don't yet fully understand how they do their thing — their *mechanism of action*. For example, although antidepressants and antianxiety medications are known to target certain neurotransmitters, this may not be their major effect in treating bipolar. Lithium and valproate (Depakote) — the primary antimanic medications — seem to operate on processes within the cell itself rather than on the transmitters between synapses.

The mechanism of action of mood medications may include any of the following activities or others still being discovered, depending on the type of medication:

✔ Increase the levels of a particular neurotransmitter within the synapse by preventing its breakdown by enzymes or by preventing it from being sucked back into the first neuron

✔ Change how a neuron receives a neurotransmitter — by blocking, opening, or otherwise changing the receiving cell's receptor proteins

✔ Strengthen neuroprotective factors that help cells recover from injury and maintain healthy cell development, growth, and function

✔ Inhibit or increase the activities of enzymes that are important to the signaling systems in neurons

✔ Change patterns of electrochemical pulses in the neurons

✔ Alter pathways that trigger changes in gene expression and possibly even alleviate negative environmental effects on the chemical packaging of DNA (epigenetics)

Flip to Chapter 7 for more about medications used to treat bipolar disorder.

Chapter 3

Reining in Bipolar Disorder: Prognosis and Treatments

In This Chapter

▶ Gaining hope through a positive prognosis

▶ Relieving current symptoms and reducing the likelihood of future episodes

▶ Taking a sneak peek at what treatment looks like

You can't fight an affliction you can't identify, so an accurate diagnosis is the first step on the path to wellness. If you know your enemy, you can draw up a proactive battle plan to defeat it . . . or at least keep it from ruining your life.

In this chapter, we reveal the positive *prognosis* (outlook for recovery) that accompanies the bipolar diagnosis. We show you not only how to conquer bouts of depression and mania when they afflict you, but also how to quiet them before they begin to roar. And we provide a list of treatment options, therapies, and self-help skills so you can begin assembling your own customized treatment plan.

So, Doc, What's the Prognosis?

The difference between a negative and positive prognosis for bipolar disorder largely depends on the choices that you, your doctor, and your family and friends make. If you accept the bipolar diagnosis, if you and your doctor can discover an effective medicine or combination of medicines, and if your family and friends pitch in to support you, the prognosis is very positive indeed. But if you try to ignore the problem, avoid working on an effective treatment plan, or don't follow your plan, the illness and consequences of it will likely worsen.

A few lucky souls have only one major mood episode throughout their lives. They experience deep depression or full-blown mania that eventually passes, with or without treatment, and then they proceed to live out the rest of their lives symptom-free. In an overwhelming majority of cases, however, when left untreated, when self-treated, or when treated with the wrong interventions, people with bipolar can expect the following problems:

- ✔ Increased frequency and severity of mood episodes
- ✔ Increased stress from the fallout of mood episodes
- ✔ Damaged relationships
- ✔ Loss of job or career status
- ✔ Increased financial problems
- ✔ Problems with thinking and memory

That's the bad news.

The good news is that effective medicines, self-help strategies, and therapies are available, and researchers are constantly developing newer and better treatments to add to the arsenal. Through medication, therapy, support, and your own efforts, you can look forward to achieving the following goals:

- ✔ Reduce or eliminate symptoms of mania and depression.
- ✔ Reduce the chances of experiencing major mood episodes in the future.
- ✔ Reduce or eliminate stressors that trigger mania or depression.
- ✔ Find and retain fulfilling and rewarding work.
- ✔ Repair damaged relationships and build new, healthy relationships.
- ✔ Restore your social and financial security.
- ✔ Keep your thinking and memory sharp.

Recovery isn't necessarily a return to the way things used to be, although it very well can be. For some people, finding out they have bipolar disorder is the first step toward a different life that's better and more fulfilling.

Responding Reactively and Proactively to Bipolar Disorder

Major mood episodes can sneak up on you with the silence of a brooding sadness or the furtive stirrings of enthusiasm. Maybe you feel a little less tired one day, a little more energetic. That's normal. You figure it's nothing to worry about. After all, you have every right to enjoy your life, and you're looking forward to the weekend — TGIF! After work, you head to Wilma's Watering Hole for an evening of rowdiness with your old college pals.

You get home a little late — actually, early Saturday morning — and you're not even tired. You lie in bed for two hours, replaying the excitement of the evening on the insides of your eyelids. You finally manage to doze off, expecting to sleep until noon, but you wake up bright and early, raring to go. Why sleep when life's smorgasbord summons you to its feast?

Requiring less sleep and more stimulation, you race through each day of the week. By week's end, pedal to the metal, you're highballing down the hypomanic highway, and you don't even know how you got there. Now what?

Reacting: Extinguishing the flames

Enveloped by full-blown mania or depression, you face limited choices. If you pose no threat to yourself or others, you can choose to wait out the storm and hope the raging currents subside. But if your behavior becomes unbearable or dangerous — if you have suicidal or delusional — thoughts or become increasingly belligerent, for example — you or someone on your behalf may want to seek medical intervention in one or more of the following forms:

- **Hospitalization:** The safety and retreat that hospitalization provides is a good choice when you pose a threat to yourself or others, even though you may not think so at the time.

- **Intensive outpatient therapy:** A structured outpatient program allows you to focus on getting well by day and return home in the evening.

- **Medication:** You may require medicine to lift the depression or quell the mania.

During a major mood episode, you may need to make some immediate changes, such as taking time off work and delegating responsibilities at home, especially if you're hospitalized. But even if you decide to use outpatient resources, allow yourself time away from immediate responsibilities at least until the medication takes effect and you regain solid footing. Keep in mind that non-medication treatment options such as self-help and psychotherapy can be tough to get going and don't work as quickly as medication during active episodes. Those types of intervention are often better suited to long-term recovery, as we explain later in this chapter.

Preventing future flare-ups

How you respond to your diagnosis and how ambitiously you pursue treatment have a huge effect on your outcome. If you deny that you have a problem, lose hope, or try to self-medicate with alcohol and other substances, the disorder wins. If you discover the right medication, acquire some coping skills, confront your hidden demons through therapy, and remain vigilant, you prevail.

One of the best ways to derail a major mood episode is to remain attentive for signs of impending depression or mania and to consult your doctor or therapist if you observe any warning signs. A medication adjustment or some help dealing effectively with a situation that's currently stressing you out may be all you need to avoid a major meltdown. To find out more about monitoring your moods, turn to Chapter 11.

Does it take less stress to trigger later episodes?

Some researchers exploring the connections between life stress and mood episodes suggest that early mood episodes require a larger stress load whereas later episodes can be triggered with less severe stress. This is the *kindling hypothesis,* which is rooted in studies of seizures and epilepsy — the more seizures a person has, the lower threshold that person's brain seems to have for seizures.

Seizures and mood episodes are both associated with abnormal electrochemical patterns in the brain, and some antiseizure medicines help to reduce bipolar disorder symptoms. Therefore, some researchers suggest a similar kindling model in bipolar mood episodes, but the evidence is inconsistent. A number of studies have tried to connect mood and behavioral symptoms of bipolar disorder to stressful life events based on the underlying neurobiological theories of the disorder. But given the complexity of these theories, their related models are tentative. Evidence does seem clear that the more episodes a person has, the more damage occurs to his brain. But evidence isn't clear that these brain changes make it easier for someone to have a mood episode without a stress trigger.

However, studies have shown clearly that stressful life events, including good stress (very happy events or goal attainment) and bad stress (loss, in particular), are associated with the onset of some mood episodes in many people with bipolar disorder. How the events actually trigger the biological responses of mood episodes is still being worked out.

Recognizing the Components of an Effective Treatment Plan

Bipolar disorder is a physical illness related to the neurobiology of the brain and the body (see Chapter 2), so standard protocol for treating it involves medication — typically a mood stabilizer and/or antipsychotic with or without an antidepressant added.

In rare circumstances, medication works so well that it's the only treatment needed. In most situations, however, medication isn't sufficient to offset the stressors and triggers in a person's life and to manage the new challenges that arise due to the illness. Additional interventions in the form of self-help, lifestyle changes, certain types of psychotherapies, and relationship and family education and counseling are usually needed. The following sections describe the treatment options and interventions that many people with bipolar have found most useful.

What works for one person may not work for another. In addition, some people prefer certain treatments to others. Our approach is to present various treatment options as a menu from which to choose, typically in consultation with your treatment team. Although medication is usually the main course, many people find that adding self-help skills, making lifestyle changes, and pursuing therapy improve the fullness, speed, and duration of recovery.

Exploring medication and other biological remedies

The first order of business in treating bipolar disorder is to treat the brain. Such treatment usually requires medication and may also include other biological methods that specifically target brain function, such as light therapy. In the following sections, we touch on some common biological treatment options for bipolar. Chapters 7 through 9 describe these options in greater detail.

Getting the right meds for your condition

The first, fastest, and generally most effective treatment for mania or depression is medication, which treats *acute* (severe, short-term) symptoms and is used as a *prophylaxis* (preventive) to avoid further cycles. Chapter 7 introduces you to the medications most often used to treat bipolar depression and mania. The medication choices are based on where someone is in the cycle of the disorder:

- ✔ **Acute mania:** Lithium and valproate (Depakote) have historically been the mainstays of treatment for an acute manic episode. However, antipsychotics, such as olanzapine (Zyprexa), risperidone (Risperdal), or asenapine (Saphris) are increasingly used as first choices when someone is suffering with acute mania. Doctors usually try to use just one medication, but sometimes a combination of lithium or valproate with an antipsychotic is needed.

- ✔ **Acute bipolar depression:** For a long time the medical community thought that depression in bipolar disorder was the same thing as unipolar depression, but research has increasingly shown that they're not so similar. Treatment with antidepressant *monotherapy* (using a medication by itself without any other medications), such as fluoxetine (Prozac) or paroxetine (Paxil), appears to be less effective in bipolar depression and also carries a risk of switching someone from depression to mania. The research suggests that antidepressants, if used in bipolar disorder, should be prescribed with one of the antimanic agents, such as lithium or valproate, or an antipsychotic. Depression causes some of the most chronic and devastating effects in bipolar disorder, but it's still one of the hardest parts to treat. Currently, three medications are specifically approved to treat bipolar depression: Symbyax (a combination of the antipsychotic olanzapine and the antidepressant fluoxetine) and two additional antipsychotics — quetiapine (Seroquel) and lurasidone (Latuda). Lithium is well established as a *booster agent* in unipolar depression (to increase the effectiveness of an antidepressant), but not enough studies have been done to clearly show whether it's useful in bipolar depression. Importantly, though, it remains the only medication to clearly reduce the risk of suicide in bipolar disorder.

- ✔ **Maintenance treatment:** After an acute episode is resolved, medication is often part of the plan to help reduce the likelihood of having another mood episode of either the depressive or manic type. Lithium is the gold standard for maintenance care in bipolar disorder. The benefits of valproate for this purpose aren't as clear-cut, but it has been used in this way for a long time. Lamotrigine (Lamictal) is a medication that's approved for the maintenance treatment of bipolar disorder, but it's not helpful in acute mania. Lamotrigine may have some benefits in acute depressive episodes, but the data so far has been inconsistent.

These general treatment guidelines apply primarily to bipolar I. The treatment guidelines for bipolar II are much less clear. Although antidepressants may play a larger role in bipolar II than in bipolar I, the risk of switching to a manic or hypomanic episode while taking antidepressants still seems to be present.

Other categories of medications may be used to treat associated problems of bipolar disorder, including sedatives, such as lorazepam (Ativan) for agitation or anxiety, and sleep medications, such as zolpidem (Ambien) for severe insomnia.

The goal of medication treatment is to get maximum benefit while taking the fewest medications. Unfortunately, because bipolar disorder presents with completely opposite symptoms (manic and depressive) in the same person at different times, most people require more than one medication.

Prescription medication isn't designed to cure bipolar or to solve all your problems. It's prescribed to treat the biological side of the disorder in your brain so the rest of your being can function without the interference of mania or depression. When your brain is functioning more normally, you may be able to make adjustments to your lifestyle and attitudes that accelerate your recovery, improve your life, and offer added protection against new episodes.

Few people *like* taking medicine, especially to treat a chronic or long-term condition such as diabetes or bipolar disorder. Taking medication regularly is a hassle, some medications have undesirable side effects, and people don't want to think of themselves as needing a pill to function normally. Even people without bipolar have a tough time sticking with their treatment plans; just think of how many times people stop taking their antibiotics as soon as they start feeling better, even though the doctor and pharmacist made a point of telling them to take it until the bottle's empty. Coming to terms with medication is a big first step toward recovery. We address this issue in Chapter 8.

Exploring other biological treatment options

Although medication is typically the most effective approach for treating bipolar disorder, other treatments demonstrate varying degrees of effectiveness in alleviating mood symptoms. These treatments fall into two categories:

- ✓ **Vitamins and supplements:** Omega-3 fatty acids (fish oil), folic acid, and N-acetyl cysteine (NAC)

- ✓ **Brain stimulation:** Light therapy, electroconvulsive therapy (ECT), repetitive transcranial magnetic stimulation (rTMS), and deep brain stimulation (DBS)

See Chapter 9 for more about these and other alternative treatments, along with some cautionary words about the potential drawbacks and dangers of using alternative treatments.

Making lifestyle adjustments: The big five

Overall health and stress levels impact the brain. Recent research even suggests that these factors can flip certain genes on or off to protect against or trigger illness. To give your body, including your brain, what it needs to function well, focus on five major areas: sleep, nutrition, exercise, stress management, and relationships.

Sleep

A decreased need for sleep is not only an early warning sign of an impending mood episode, but it's also a possible trigger for mania or depression. Sleep deprivation traumatizes the brain and the body and increases your risk of illness and injury, both of which make managing bipolar disorder more difficult.

Your doctor may prescribe medication to help you sleep, but you can take additional steps to improve sleep quantity and quality. Many people find that establishing a regular routine of going to bed at the same time every night and waking at the same time every morning does wonders. Avoiding caffeine and other stimulants close to bedtime also helps. For more suggestions, check out Chapter 12.

Nutrition

Although no particular diet can stop the symptoms of bipolar disorder, making healthy nutritional choices can help to reduce the risk of other major health problems, such as cardiovascular disease and diabetes, and improve your overall sense of wellbeing. Choosing healthy nutrition is more important than an overemphasis on losing weight; weight can be fickle and difficult to change, whereas your food choices are more manageable. Chapter 12 spells out how to incorporate nutrition into you daily life.

Exercise

Exercise is particularly helpful for relieving depression, but overdoing it can be a sign of a looming manic episode. Think about adding moderate exercise to your daily routine; walking is a good start. Consider a super short period of vigorous movement; strongly increasing your heart rate even for just one minute a day may be enough to improve your overall health. Start with as light a workout as you need and find an exercise or activity you enjoy, so you'll be more likely to do it and stick with it. Check out Chapter 12 for more details about exercise.

Stress

Stress is anything that stimulates or places a demand on the mind, body, or emotions. It can come from inside or outside and be negative or positive. A ringing phone is a stress, but the actual content and intensity of the stress varies widely depending on several factors, including who's calling and about what. In response to a stress or demand, the body kicks off a variety of internal changes to help respond appropriately to the situation.

Bipolar disorder affects the stress response system, making it harder for the body to turn off the internal chemical responses when they're no longer needed. High doses of stress such as big life events, both good and bad, can destabilize mood and trigger episodes, so look for ways to dial down the pressure in your life. You can't eliminate all stress, but identifying sources of high intensity stress or distress that's chronic and never lets up is a good first step. You can then troubleshoot or problem-solve to begin to reduce the dose of stress from each source, therefore reducing the total stress load in your life. Avoiding especially demanding or painful situations is one way to cope, but there are others, including changing the way you respond to the stressors and teaming up with others in your life to reduce everyone's overall stress level. (See Chapter 14 for additional suggestions.)

Relationships

When you have bipolar disorder, you quickly find out who your true friends are. They're the ones who don't judge you, who try to learn about the disorder, and who offer to lend an ear and a hand without treating you like a child. Having at least one good friend in your corner is essential. Surrounding yourself with a network of supportive friends, family members, and others is even better. However, you may need to make some tough relationship choices along the way and work on the relationships you decide to invest in. (See Chapters 13 and 14 for communication and problem-solving tips that can help.)

Sampling self-help treatments

Assuming that you're *not* in the throes of a major mood episode, you can do a great deal on your own to maintain mood stability and avoid future manic and depressive episodes, especially if the people closest to you are on board. Here are some of the most effective ways to help (see Part IV for details):

- ✔ **Take your meds.** The best way to improve the course of the illness is to prevent mood episodes, and the most effective means for doing so is medication. The urge to stop taking bipolar meds is common and understandable, as we explain in Chapter 8, but it significantly increases the chances of a future mood episode, and every mood episode you have is likely to worsen the course of the illness.

✔ **Monitor your moods.** Keeping track of your ups and downs can help you identify what works to help you stay within a comfortable range and what doesn't. It can also reduce the chances that you'll experience a major mood episode. If you know you're starting to cycle into mania or depression, your doctor may be able to adjust your medications to help you avoid hospitalization.

✔ **Identify your triggers.** Certain situations, seasons, people, or activities may trigger mood instability. Try to identify patterns in your life that match up with your shifting moods. These patterns may help you pin down triggers and open your eyes to creative solutions for dealing with them. For example, some people who tend to have mood episodes around the holidays scale back their traditional holiday activities.

✔ **Establish healthy routines.** Many people with bipolar disorder discover that a well-regulated life helps to regulate their mood. Routines may cover sleep/wake times, meal times, a regular work schedule, and even social engagements.

You're already engaged in one of the most important self-help activities — *psychoeducation.* Finding out more about bipolar disorder and how to successfully live with it empowers you to make well-informed decisions about the various treatment options available. Psychoeducation also helps your friends and family develop the empathy they need to accept your illness and support you.

Comparing psychotherapies and other professional counseling

Certain therapies and types of professional counseling, if available and affordable, are often valuable additions to a bipolar treatment plan. Here are some therapies and other professional offerings to consider:

✔ **Cognitive behavioral therapy (CBT):** The premise of CBT is that thoughts, feelings, and behaviors are closely interconnected. Through CBT, you identify negative thought and behavior patterns and retrain your mind and body to develop more adaptive behaviors and thought patterns, thereby training your body to react differently to stress triggers. As we explain in Chapter 11, CBT is especially effective in treating depression and anxiety. Its effectiveness in reducing manic symptoms is less studied.

✔ **Dialectical behavioral therapy (DBT):** A type of cognitive behavioral therapy, DBT is focused on helping individuals dial down their emotional responses to stress triggers. It involves training in a specific set of emotional skills that help to improve mood regulation and interpersonal interactions. It was originally developed to help in the treatment of borderline personality disorder, but it's now being used for a wide range of psychiatric conditions, including depression, anxiety, and substance use disorders.

✔ **Interpersonal and social rhythm therapy (IPSRT):** Living a structured lifestyle and establishing healthy routines can give your life a rhythm that's conducive to mood stability. Studies show that mood episodes commonly erupt when you experience life changes (both positive and negative) that break down your daily rhythms, including the rhythms of interactions with other people. Changes in these rhythms seem to disrupt the body's systems of mood regulation. IPSRT strives to restore a healthy rhythm to your life and improve interpersonal and social function. It targets resolution of acute episodes as well as reduction of recurrent episodes.

✔ **Mindfulness:** Mindfulness (refer to Chapter 11 for more information) involves bringing your attention to the present moment and not getting drawn into negative or extraneous thoughts that take you out of the moment and make it hard to concentrate or that trigger negative mood responses. *Mindfulness meditation* is a type of meditation that, when practiced regularly, has been shown to improve mood, attention, and general sense of wellbeing. Studies show positive changes in brain function in people who are taught this technique and who then practice it routinely. Although mindfulness meditation is a specific discipline of its own that has been supported by medical research, other practices (including yoga and tai chi) may have similar positive effects on calming the mind and increasing awareness in the moment.

✔ **Vocational therapy or career counseling:** Jobs, bosses, and coworkers can be major stressors, especially if you're dealing with bipolar as well. A vocational therapist may be able to help you work with your employer to establish reasonable work accommodations that enable you to continue performing your current duties. Or a career counselor may be able to help you find work that's more conducive to your situation.

✔ **Financial-resource guidance:** People with bipolar often have serious financial problems that don't reflect their financial prowess; bipolar depletes resources, especially for those who can't afford or qualify for health insurance. A financial advisor may be able to help you better manage the resources you have, but guidance on where and how to access free and affordable assistance may be vital. See Chapter 18 for tips on overcoming financial setbacks related to this illness.

Hiring a professional therapist or advisor may be the ideal option, but this help may not be accessible because of where you live or what you can afford. You can still benefit from some of these therapies by reading about them, watching videos, and/or participating in support groups.

Rounding up the troops: Relationship and family support

Studies show that bipolar recovery is faster and more durable when it occurs in a community that understands and supports the person who has the disorder. Ideally, when someone experiences a major mood episode, the person's entire family becomes involved and the treatment team keeps them informed about what's going on and how to help. However, what often happens is that the person who has bipolar is treated and released to return to a family or community that doesn't understand the condition and lacks the knowledge and skills needed to cope with it. If you're a family member or friend of someone with bipolar disorder, we encourage you to explore the following:

- **Psychoeducation:** Understanding and accepting the fact that bipolar disorder is a physical illness are two big steps toward being able to empathize with a family member or friend who has the disorder.

- **Communication skills:** Even if you have no problem communicating with people in general, bipolar disorder can make it feel that typical communication is useless. You can develop and practice certain techniques to help you express yourself more effectively with your loved one. You can also develop strategies to allow for everyone to listen more fully and to reduce knee-jerk emotional responses on all sides. Flip to Chapter 13 to find out more.

- **Problem-solving skills:** Bipolar may seem to be one big problem, but it's actually a number of smaller problems, and if you approach it that way, you're more likely to improve your success. Sometimes, what you may think is a relationship issue is just a problem that needs to be solved, not a battle that needs to be won. In Chapter 14, we explore some problem-solving strategies.

- **Boundaries:** You can't control what someone else says or does, but you can decide how you respond. By establishing reasonable boundaries, you give yourself some protection from factors outside of your control.

- **Self-help:** Taking care of yourself physically, emotionally, spiritually, and socially is essential to maintaining the health and strength required to support a loved one with bipolar.

Families often require intensive, rescue-type support and intervention during an acute mood episode, but it's often best to wait until the depression or mania has lifted before attempting intensive relationship or family therapy. Trying to resolve issues with someone who's in the throes of depression or mania is likely to be counterproductive and lead to more conflict, not less.

Ensuring continuity of care

Continuity of care is an extremely important factor in the success of long-term management of bipolar disorder. If you shuffle from one doctor or therapist to the next and the changes result in medication and therapy adjustments, your moods are likely to fluctuate. Unfortunately, changes in health insurance and other factors outside of your control often lead to changes in doctors and treatments. A therapist, caseworker, family member, or friend can often help you advocate for services and maintain an effective and consistent treatment plan.

If you have an insurance provider, call and ask whether it has case managers. Many insurance companies have case managers to help control costs, but these folks can also serve as treatment advocates if you're having trouble obtaining certain medications or getting in to see your doctor or therapist. After all, hospitalizations are expensive, and insurance companies have a strong financial incentive to keep you out of the hospital. They can also help you maintain the continuity of care you need to stay healthy.

Part II

Obtaining a Diagnosis and Building a Treatment Plan and Team

Bipolar Disorder Symptoms

Mania*	Depression**
Inflated self-esteem or grandiosity	Depressed mood most of the day nearly every day
Decreased need for sleep	Diminished interest in activities previously considered pleasurable
Excessive talking (pressured speech)	Increase or decrease in appetite or weight
Flight of ideas or racing thoughts	Sleeping too much or too little
Inability to concentrate	Moving slowly or having physical agitation
Significant increase in goal-directed activity	Feelings of worthlessness or excessive guilt
Significant increase in mental or physical activity	Indecisiveness or diminished ability to think clearly or concentrate on a given task
Hypersexuality, gambling, unrestrained spending, and other risky behaviors	Recurrent thoughts of death or suicide

*Three or more mania symptoms must be present and last for at least one week or require hospitalization.

**Five or more depression symptoms must be present, and they must represent significant changes from usual behavior and last for at least two weeks straight.

Visit www.dummies.com/cheatsheet/bipolardisorder for a handy Cheat Sheet that you can refer to on a regular basis to help you with the ins and outs of bipolar.

In this part . . .

✔ Visit your primary care physician to rule out other health conditions that may cause symptoms of mania or depression (such as thyroid disorders).

✔ Understand what's involved in a psychiatric evaluation and prepare for a visit with a psychiatrist for evaluation and treatment planning.

✔ Get suggestions on how to team up with your doctors and therapists for optimal results.

✔ Build an effective and efficient mood management team with a doctor/psychiatrist to prescribe medication, one or more counselors to provide therapy, and one or more carefully selected family members or friends to help with everything else.

Chapter 4

Diagnosis Step 1: Ruling Out Other Health Issues

· ·

In This Chapter

▶ Considering health issues that mimic bipolar symptoms

▶ Talking to your doctor and examining your symptoms for clues

▶ Undergoing additional medical tests

▶ Moving beyond the medical evaluation

· ·

*I*f you show up at your doctor's office in the throes of mania or major depression and you have a strong family history of bipolar disorder, your doctor probably won't waste time considering other medical conditions. If your doctor has any doubt at all, however, she performs a physical exam and orders some medical tests to rule out other conditions that could possibly produce similar symptoms. Hey, you're not the only one wondering, "Could it be something else?" Your doctor has the same question in her mind.

This chapter reveals what that diagnostic process looks like, so you know what to expect and can start formulating questions you may want to ask your doctor during the process. We introduce you to some of the medical tests your doctor may order and to certain ailments that can trigger or mimic mood imbalances, and we help you through the process of exploring possible causes.

We also show you what to do after you and your physician rule out other medical issues. This is only Step 1 in the process. Step 2 involves a psychiatrist, as explained in Chapter 5.

Could It Be Something Else?

From the time of Aristotle to now, Western thought has endeavored to divide and conquer, to label and dissect. Western medicine is no different, holding firm to the distinction between "physical ailments" and "brain disorders," as if people push their brains around in grocery carts.

The fact is that your brain is an integral part of your body, not only acting as the puppet master but also being subjected to imbalances and illnesses in other organs and physiological systems. Your brain affects and is affected by your body and various substances your body ingests.

In these sections, we investigate other medical conditions that may produce symptoms similar to those of bipolar disorder and certain substances that can destabilize mood.

Singing the body blues

Many physical ailments and conditions can cause changes in your brain function — changes that produce symptoms very similar to those of bipolar disorder. Here's a list of some conditions with symptoms that may mimic those of mood disorders or magnify symptoms of co-occurring mood disorders:

- **Thyroid malfunction:** Located at the base of your neck, your thyroid gland produces hormones that regulate metabolism, development, and reproductive function. A malfunction can cause the thyroid gland to overproduce hormones *(hyperthyroidism)* and cause symptoms similar to mania or underproduce hormones *(hypothyroidism)* and generate symptoms of depression. Mild thyroid problems may co-occur with some types of bipolar disorder.

- **Sex hormone changes and disruptions:** Hormones modulate many body and brain processes as well as neurotransmitters, which carry messages between cells in the body; when hormones fluctuate, moods may also change (refer to Chapter 2 for more on neurotransmitters). During puberty, during a woman's menstrual cycle, through pregnancy and postpartum periods, and over the course of a person's life, hormone production rises and falls. Some mood disorders, including depression, are related to hormone changes in men and women. For instance, men with low testosterone levels are more likely to be depressed than those with normal levels, and women with severe *premenstrual mood dysphoric disorder* (a severe form of PMS) can present with behavioral and emotional changes that can look a lot like bipolar. Even so, discovering the real cause of symptoms is critical in choosing the right treatment.

- ✔ **Infections:** Some viral infections, such as mononucleosis, can present with mood and energy changes, including fatigue, so a careful physical exam and lab studies are important to rule these out.

- ✔ **Fibromyalgia:** This chronic condition is associated with fatigue, sleep and cognitive changes, and widespread pain. People with fibromyalgia also often suffer from depression and anxiety, but these conditions require different (although sometimes overlapping) treatments. When evaluating depressive symptoms, doctors need to ask about pain and sleep to determine whether fibromyalgia is a possible cause.

- ✔ **Lupus and other autoimmune diseases:** Lupus, an autoimmune disorder, causes painful swelling of the connective tissue and can inflame numerous organs, including the brain. It's typically accompanied by extreme fatigue, irritability, and other physical symptoms. Your doctor can perform a blood test to rule out lupus if he suspects you may have it. Treatment may call for the use of corticosteroids, which can induce mood swings. Other autoimmune diseases such as rheumatoid arthritis are associated with depression but typically have more specific physical symptoms that reduce the likelihood of confusing them with bipolar disorder.

- ✔ **Cushing's syndrome:** Sometimes referred to as *hypercortisolism,* Cushing's syndrome results in a host of growth and development abnormalities and often mood instability. People with Cushing's syndrome commonly exhibit obesity in the torso, increased fat around the neck, a rounded face, and thinning arms and legs.

- ✔ **Hepatitis:** Hepatitis is an inflammation of the liver, typically caused by a virus or a buildup of toxins. In addition to the characteristic yellowing of the eyes, hepatitis can make you feel weak and nauseous and may produce symptoms similar to those of depression. If certain waste products accumulate to toxic levels, Hepatitis can cause hallucinations.

- ✔ **HIV/AIDS:** Human immunodeficiency virus (HIV) and acquired immune deficiency syndrome (AIDS) compromise the entire immune system, leaving you vulnerable to many kinds of infections that can affect mood. HIV can also directly attack brain cells, creating problems with thinking and mood changes. In addition, the daily stress of living with AIDS can burden you with tremendous anxiety.

- ✔ **Degenerative brain diseases, such as Alzheimer's and Parkinson's:** Early dementia may present with significant mood and behavior changes, so doctors must examine cognitive brain function, especially in older adults with symptoms related to bipolar (see Chapter 10). Parkinson's and other motor conditions are accompanied by high rates of depression, which may present as a primary symptom.

✔ **Chronic traumatic encephalopathy (CTE):** CTE is a pattern of brain changes related to recurrent traumatic head injuries; it's found in a variety of athletes, especially boxers and American football players. Depression and other mood or personality changes are common symptoms of CTE, so a doctor needs to take a careful history of head injuries when evaluating someone with mood symptoms.

✔ **Vitamin and iron deficiencies:** Vitamin B-12 deficiency can present with mood symptoms, such as depression. Vitamin B-12 deficiency can easily be missed and can cause significant neurologic problems if not treated correctly. Doctors may check for B-12 levels in an initial screening of a patient presenting with severe depression.

Studies about whether or not folic acid or vitamin D deficiencies can be related to depression conflict, but many doctors routinely screen for these levels as well. Anemia from low iron levels can present with fatigue, which sometimes has symptoms that overlap with depression; most people are screened for anemia during routine checkups.

Any physical ailment that makes you feel miserable or interferes with your ability to function properly can make you feel depressed. This is especially true of chronic illnesses. Realize that feeling chronically miserable isn't normal. Ask your doctor for help.

Identifying a medical condition that can cause mood instability doesn't rule out a mood disorder. You may have a medical condition *and* bipolar that both require treatment. The only way to find out is to talk to your doctor.

Considering other culprits: Medication, alcohol, and other substances

Because bipolar disorder has so much to do with brain chemistry and physiology (see Chapter 2), everything you consume, from cocaine to candy bars, can influence your moods. As soon as you start chewing, swallowing, inhaling, snorting, or injecting a substance into your system, your body begins breaking it down into chemical compounds and distributing the compounds to your heart, brain, muscles, organs, and appendages.

The list of medications and other substances that can affect your moods and thinking is too long to include in this book, but here are a few of the big names that can cause serious problems:

✔ Alcohol

✔ Cocaine

✔ Marijuana

- Amphetamines

- Ecstasy (NMDA), ketamine (Special K), and other "club drugs"

- LSD, mushrooms, and other hallucinogens

- Stimulants, including Vivarin and NoDoz

- Caffeine

- Sleeping aids, including those containing antihistamines, valerian, and melatonin

- Decongestants containing pseudoephedrine, ephedra, or ephedrine

- Corticosteroids

- Cough suppressants containing dextromethorphan

- Accutane

If you're taking any of these medications or substances, let your doctor know. Stopping cold turkey isn't always the best option. Your doctor can suggest safe ways to wean you off the substances if he thinks they may be causing the bipolar-like symptoms you're experiencing.

Keep in mind that just because something is "herbal" or "natural" doesn't mean it's mood and behavior neutral. Products sold as "dietary supplements" may include stimulating or sedating natural chemicals that can wreak havoc on your body and brain just as much as synthetic medications or drugs.

Seeking Your Doctor's Advice

Self-diagnosis can be addictive. You notice something about yourself that seems out of the ordinary, so you fire up your web browser, plug a few descriptive words into a search engine, and proceed to convince yourself that you have any variety of ailments known to humanity.

For most people, the mind latches onto any idea or quack diagnosis that seems remotely possible. To set your mind at ease and avoid making any mistakes that could possibly worsen your condition, visit your doctor instead of letting your imagination run wild. Your doctor should ask you a series of questions and gather information to form a *history* — the story of your condition — that will guide her during the physical examination and help her decide which tests and further studies to order.

Identifying your symptoms

The search for the cause of most illnesses begins with a careful examination of symptoms (how the illness *presents* itself) and the onset of the symptoms (where, when, and with whom the disease presents itself). During a medical examination, you basically enlist the aid of your doctor to solve a mystery.

To ensure that your collaboration can successfully unravel the mystery, provide your doctor with a detailed list of your symptoms. You should be able to supply your doctor with answers to the following questions:

- ✔ Do you feel depressed? Sad? Blue? Down? Empty? Numb? Do you feel different than how you usually feel?

- ✔ Have your energy levels changed? Do you feel more energetic? More fatigued?

- ✔ Do you feel angry or irritable more often than usual?

- ✔ Do you feel more anxious or worried than usual?

- ✔ Do you have difficulty enjoying things that used to be fun or pleasurable?

- ✔ Have you had more problems than usual getting to sleep or staying asleep?

- ✔ Have you been sleeping more than usual?

- ✔ Have you been eating significantly more or less than usual?

- ✔ Have you noticed behavior changes — doing significantly more or less than usual?

- ✔ Have you had any serious conflicts at home or work?

- ✔ Have you been drinking/drugging or wanting to drink and party more than usual?

Of course, the questions your doctor asks may not be as pointed as the ones we list here. When dealing with mood disorders, doctors often ask more open-end questions to find out how your life is going in general and to observe how you react to various questions and issues that arise during your meeting.

Your doctor may also ask about your other medical symptoms, focusing on particular areas, such as the nervous system. Through these questions, she looks for clues that point to other possible conditions that could cause your presenting symptoms. This inquiry is called a *review of systems*. Here are a few possible questions you may hear:

✔ Have you experienced headaches, muscle aches, or weakness?

✔ Do you limit your diet in any way for medical or other reasons? Are you allergic to anything? Are you vegan or vegetarian?

✔ Have you experienced nausea, vomiting, or changes in bowel habits?

✔ Do you have joint pain or swelling?

✔ Have you noticed rashes or skin changes?

✔ Have you noticed any changes in your appetite or weight?

✔ Are you thirsty all the time? Do you have to urinate frequently?

✔ Has your sex drive or ability to function sexually changed at all?

At this point, you may have a question of your own: "What do all these questions have to do with my moods?" Although these questions may seem unrelated to your chief complaint, your answers guide your doctor through a targeted physical examination and help her choose lab tests or other studies she may want to order.

Knowing when your problem started

Doctors are very cause-and-effect oriented, so your doctor is likely to ask whether you've experienced any recent events in your life that may be contributing to your symptoms. Do your homework and try to pinpoint events or times of change in your life that correspond with the onset of your symptoms. Here are some events or changes that may help jog your memory:

✔ Medication change

✔ Illness

✔ Auto accident or a fall

✔ Loss of a loved one

✔ Job loss or conflict

✔ Final exams

✔ Broken relationship

✔ Change in family structure, such as a child leaving or returning home

✔ Pregnancy, menopause, or change in menstrual cycle

Mood disorders can build up over many years, so you may not be able to point your finger at one particular incident or variation in your life that started the ball rolling. But it's worth a try.

The event or change that triggers an illness or begins to make it significantly worse is rarely the entire cause of the illness. Sometimes the original causes are buried so deeply in your brain development that you and your doctor will never find them. Or maybe you need to unravel a recent spiral — perhaps you took a medication that torpedoed your libido, which eventually wore away at your relationship, leaving you more depressed, which led to substance abuse and insomnia, which led to a manic episode. If you catch the initial cause early enough to stop the avalanche, great. If not, you may have to deal with (and treat) a long chain of causes and effects.

Recognizing what makes your symptoms better or worse

Your symptoms crept up on you, and you and your doctor can't pinpoint the cause. Frustrating? Yes. Hopeless? No. It's time to expand the search. Even if you've identified a trigger, focus on answering this next set of questions as you and your doctor try to arrive at a diagnosis and formulate a treatment plan. The next step is to examine the most troublesome and annoying symptoms to see whether anything changes them. To zero in on possible symptom amplifiers and reducers, answer the following questions:

- ✔ Do you feel better or worse at any specific time of day? In the morning? After lunch? After work? Before bed?

- ✔ Are you symptom-free during any seasons?

- ✔ Do your symptoms worsen near certain holidays or anniversaries, particularly anniversaries of losses or other traumatic events?

- ✔ Do any medications you currently take make you feel better or worse?

- ✔ Do any activities make you feel better or worse?

- ✔ Do any substances, such as caffeine, nicotine, or alcohol, alleviate symptoms or make them worse? (No, we're not recommending that you try these substances to see if they make you feel better.)

Figuring out what else to tell your doctor

In addition to a list of your symptoms, your recollections of when the symptoms first appeared, and your observations of what makes them better or worse, your doctor gathers the following information:

✓ **Your medical history:** To determine whether any past conditions may be causing your current symptoms

✓ **A list of medications you're taking:** To figure out if any of them may be related to your symptoms

✓ **Your family history:** To identify illnesses that may be genetic

Getting a physical exam

After piecing together a history of your condition, your doctor typically performs a brief physical examination to test your reflexes, check for enlarged glands, and observe your overall physical health and your temperament and behavior. As always, the nurse takes your temperature (to check for possible infection) and your blood pressure. Depending on the answers and information you provide as part of your history, the doctor may examine certain parts of you (for example, your joints if you report joint pain) more thoroughly than usual.

On the off chance that your physician immediately spots the condition that's causing your current mood misery, she diagnoses it, recommends one or more treatment options, bills you, and then heads out to lunch. However, if nothing shows up, you can look forward to additional medical tests, which we describe in the next section.

Digging Deeper with Additional Tests and Procedures

Depending on what your doctor digs up when taking your history and performing the physical exam, he may order additional tests or procedures to pin down or rule out certain medical conditions. The following sections describe some of the common lab tests that your doctor may order and point out what the results of these tests may reveal.

Medical tests that your doctor may order

No standard, routine medical tests are required in the work-up of bipolar disorder. However, if your doctor hasn't yet discovered a probable cause for your symptoms and he has specific concerns that he wants to confirm or rule out (making sure a certain diagnosis is or isn't present), he may order one or more of the following tests:

- ✔ **Blood tests:** Your doctor may order blood tests to check your blood counts (red blood cell count for anemia or white blood cell count for infections); iron levels and *ferritin* (a measure of iron stores in your body); glucose and lipid/cholesterol levels; blood chemistries to screen liver, kidney, and other organ function; and sometimes levels of vitamin B-12, folic acid, or other vitamins. Additional blood tests may be necessary if the initial ones indicate a problem.

- ✔ **MRI or CAT scan:** If the doctor finds specific neurologic symptoms (changes in muscle strength, movement, balance, or sensation, for example), he may order an MRI or CAT scan to check for structural abnormalities in the brain or other areas that could possibly cause the symptoms you're experiencing.

- ✔ **EEG:** If your doctor suspects that you may have a seizure disorder, he may order an EEG.

- ✔ **Spinal tap:** If you have an accompanying fever and your doctor suspects an infection of the brain, such as spinal meningitis or encephalitis, he may order a spinal tap.

Notice that we don't include any kind of blood test or scan for bipolar disorder in this list. A common misconception is that your doctor can test you for bipolar. It seems reasonable enough: If bipolar disorder is a "chemical imbalance," why can't you just measure the chemicals to see if they're abnormal? As we explain in other chapters, including Chapter 2, bipolar is more complicated than a simple chemical imbalance; it's a complex set of neurological abnormalities that are hard to pin down. Eventually, scientists will likely establish tests of some kind, but such a test doesn't yet exist.

Thyroid tests

The thyroid gland has a tremendous influence on moods and on the effectiveness of medications used to treat mood disorders, including mania and depression. It produces hormones that regulate your body's energy use. Low levels of thyroid hormones (hypothyroidism) lead to sluggishness, weight gain, and depression, while excessively high levels (hyperthyroidism) can have you bouncing off the walls.

Early in the diagnostic stage, your physician or psychiatrist should order thyroid tests to check your level of thyroid hormones to determine whether your thyroid gland is functioning properly. During the course of your treatment, your doctor may want to run the tests again, especially if you take medication that can affect thyroid function (such as lithium).

If your thyroid hormones are out of whack, your doctor may also order a *thyroid scan,* which is basically an X-ray of your thyroid gland that indicates how well it's functioning, and refer you to an *endocrinologist* (a doctor who specializes in the diagnosis and treatment of conditions related to the glands that secrete hormones) for a more in-depth evaluation of your thyroid.

Other hormone tests

Surges of reproductive hormones can make you feel pumped full of superhuman strength or rocket your libido to the stratosphere. Just imagine what they can do when they rock and roll to wild highs and lows during puberty and pregnancy.

Even so, doctors don't routinely run tests to check levels of estrogen, progesterone, testosterone, androgens, or other hormones that may be related to moods. These types of hormones modulate brain development and function throughout life, but their effects are indirect. Normal growth and a changing range of hormone levels tell the doctor little about mood disorders. Some tumors and medical conditions can cause huge changes in your hormone levels, but additional medical symptoms help identify these problems.

If your doctor suspects that wildly fluctuating reproductive hormones are contributing to your mood symptoms, he may recommend further testing or refer you to a specialist.

Although the word *hormones* usually makes people think *sex,* many hormone systems keep the entire body running smoothly. Thyroid hormones are the best known, but many others chip in to help. Insulin, which is related to diabetes, is a hormone. Cortisol, a hormone from the adrenal gland, modulates energy and wakefulness, fat metabolism, and many other body processes. A cortisol surplus causes Cushing's syndrome, which can be related to mood symptoms. Your doctor examines these and other hormonal systems more closely if blood test results or symptoms point in their direction.

Receiving a Clean Bill of Health — Now What?

Your doctor whacked you on the knee with her rubber mallet, extracted a few ounces of blood, and grilled you on your medical history and private indiscretions. She poked and prodded you, but you still don't have an explanation for what's wrong with you. Now what?

You have a few choices:

- ✔ **Get a second opinion from another physician.** Another physician or specialist, such as a neurologist or gynecologist, may be able to find other potential causes for the symptoms you're experiencing.

- ✔ **Let your physician treat your symptoms.** Primary-care physicians can prescribe antimanics, antidepressants, and other psychotropic medications that may help alleviate mood symptoms.

- ✔ **Consult a psychiatrist.** After your physician rules out medical issues, you can turn your focus to psychiatric illnesses, which a psychiatrist is usually more qualified to sort out and treat. As we note in Chapter 5, a psychiatrist can work through a differential diagnosis to identify or eliminate certain psychiatric illnesses in relation to your symptom profile.

Even if your physician finds and treats a medical condition that may be related to the depression or mania, you may still need psychiatric treatment or therapy. The medical condition may play only a partial role in your mood instability, or it may play no role at all. Turn to Chapter 5 for more on psychiatric diagnosis and treatment.

Chapter 5

Diagnosis Step 2: Obtaining a Psychiatric Evaluation and Treatment Plan

· ·

In This Chapter

▶ Tracking down a qualified psychiatrist

▶ Preparing for your first meeting

▶ Sailing through your psychiatric evaluation and dealing with your diagnosis

▶ Obtaining a treatment plan that works for you

· ·

*T*he bipolar tempest not only rocks your boat but also washes the captain overboard. Your rational mind flails in the waves, and nobody on deck has the wherewithal to throw it a lifesaver. You need someone on the outside to intervene. You need a psychiatrist.

A qualified psychiatrist can help you reset your rudder and steer your ship through the surrounding turbulence. She can explain what happened during your most recent mood episode, provide an objective evaluation of your psychiatric condition, offer one or more possible diagnoses, and develop a personalized treatment plan for you.

Because your psychiatrist plays such a significant role in your evaluation, recovery, and continued stability, this chapter offers advice on finding a qualified psychiatrist who makes you feel comfortable and confident. We point out what you can do to help your psychiatrist develop an accurate assessment of your condition and psychiatric needs. We also list items for you to take to your first appointment and offer ideas for keeping your relationship with your psychiatrist in good working order.

Finding Professional Help

Most people are happy to tell you all about their favorite doctors or healers; they eagerly share the names of their bone doctors, lung doctors, or gynecologists. But if you ask someone for the name of a good psychiatrist, you can feel the temperature of the room drop. Unlike plastic surgeons, psychiatrists don't advertise on billboards. You can flip through the phone book, but don't expect it to steer you in the direction of a bipolar specialist; all psychiatrists are pretty much lumped together.

Is finding a qualified psychiatrist a hit-or-miss proposition? Not exactly. You just need to do a little homework, remain persistent, and test-drive a few options until you find the one that's right for you. In this section, we offer suggestions on where to start your search.

Ask your family doctor

When you stump your doctor with an illness, he has a list of specialists to whom he can refer you. "Weird heart murmur? See Dr. Pulmonic, the cardiologist." "Skin discoloration? Here's a referral to Dr. Rasho, the dermatologist." The same is true of psychiatrists. Your family doctor, or *internist,* probably knows at least one psychiatrist whom he can recommend. So when you report mood-related symptoms that your doc can't trace to a medical cause and he recommends that you see a psychiatrist, ask for names.

If you're a woman and your gynecologist fills the role as your primary-care physician (a common arrangement in the U.S.), ask her for a psychiatric referral. The two fields often team up on diagnoses such as PMS and postpartum depression. She's likely to name psychiatrists with whom she likes to work. (For more women-specific advice, check out Chapter 10.)

Call your insurance company

Insurance companies have contracts with certain doctors, including psychiatrists, whom they refer to as *preferred providers.* These doctors agree to the insurance company's rates, which may make you responsible for only your co-pay (depending on your plan). If you go to a doctor who's not on this list, you may have to pay the full fee, so finding an in-network psychiatrist makes financial sense. Another perk of choosing in network is that the psychiatrist probably works with other doctors and hospitals in your network.

When looking at a preferred-provider list from your insurance company, ask for more information about the doctors. You can ask whether a doctor is board certified; request information about his level of experience; and check on any areas of subspecialty, such as mood disorders. If you can't find a doctor qualified to care for your type of illness, you can appeal to your insurance company to cover a doctor outside the plan so you get appropriate care without paying extra.

Pick your therapist's brain

Treatment need not begin with your family doctor or psychiatrist. If you're currently seeing a therapist (a psychologist or social worker) you like, ask him for a referral to a psychiatrist. He's probably familiar with psychiatrists in your area, possibly within the same office, whom he works with best.

Successful treatment almost always demands a consistent, coordinated combination of medicine and therapy, so you want a treatment duo that works well as a team. If your therapist and psychiatrist graduated from different schools of thought, they may be unwilling and unable to provide the integrated treatment you deserve. By obtaining a referral from your therapist, you increase your odds of building a treatment team with a unified vision.

If your therapist and psychiatrist work out of the same office, the proximity often enhances communication.

Go online

The Internet is an excellent tool for tracking down professional help of all kinds. When searching online for names of psychiatrists, use established, professional websites provided by a local medical society or a specialty society, such as the following:

- **WebMD:** WebMD has a physician directory at doctor.webmd.com.
- **American Psychiatric Association (APA):** Go to http://apps.psychiatry.org/dblisting to find the district branch nearest you, and then contact the branch by phone or email to obtain a list of members in your area.
- **American Academy of Child & Adolescent Psychiatry (AACAP):** Head to AACAP's home page at www.aacap.org and click Child and Adolescent Psychiatrist Finder.

> ✔ **Depression and Bipolar Support Alliance (DBSA):** Use DBSA's Find A Pro tool at `http://findapro.dbsapages.org` to find or recommend a treatment facility or professional. When we visited, the directory contained listings for major cities but few for the small towns we searched.

University, hospital, and medical school sites have physician search tools, and they usually list each doctor's subspecialty. By checking subspecialties, you may be able to find a provider who's researching bipolar disorder.

If you search more broadly and find other sites about mood disorders and doctors, be sure to get additional references about the doctor or clinic before you make an appointment. The Internet has its share of misinformation. If you're unsure whether a doctor who looks good to you is legitimate, double-check the doctor's licensing and complaint history with your local medical society, which you can do for any doctor you consider seeing.

Consult your support group

As your symptoms develop, you may seek help from a support group — a therapy or self-help group, a 12-step program, or an advocacy group. Maybe a loved one, a judge, or a therapist recommends or demands that you attend anger management or parenting groups. These settings are gold mines for information about local doctors. Seasoned veterans freely vent about doctors they adore and those they don't. Ask around and expect an earful!

Don't limit your search to official support groups. Consult your personal support group, too: The people who provide you daily guidance and care and who know you best may have connections with psychiatrists and can make recommendations with your temperament and needs in mind.

When having a psychiatrist isn't an option

Although psychiatrists are generally the most qualified to diagnose and treat bipolar and other brain disorders, a psychiatrist isn't always readily available, or you may want to consult a different type of doctor for diagnosis, treatment planning, and medication management. In some treatment settings, the psychiatrist is involved in the initial diagnosis and treatment plan development but falls back to serve as a consultant after your moods have stabilized. Following are some psychiatrist-alternative models that you may want to consider:

> ✔ **Primary-care physician:** If your primary-care physician (also called a PCP or family doctor) has known you for a long time and is familiar with your personal and medical history, she's a valuable team member even if

a psychiatrist is involved. Your PCP can help you rule out other medical conditions that may be causing symptoms and narrow down the possible diagnoses. She may also become the lead treatment provider when you're on a stable course of medication. In settings where psychiatrists are difficult to access, PCPs may provide a lot of psychiatric care, including diagnoses and treatment planning.

✔ **Obstetrician/gynecologist:** Many women regularly see an obstetrician/gynecologist (OB/GYN); therefore, this doctor functions essentially as a primary-care physician. If an OB/GYN sees symptoms that suggest bipolar and a referral to a psychiatrist isn't an option, she's likely to enlist the help of an internist or family doctor, because an OB/GYN's training in psychiatric care is often more limited than that of physicians with more training in general medicine.

✔ **Neurologist:** *Neurologists* (nervous system specialists) and psychiatrists share a lot of territory in terms of the symptoms and illnesses they treat. Both are certified by the same specialty board, so neurologists must have at least a baseline of psychiatric knowledge. (Likewise, psychiatrists must have a fundamental understanding of neurology.) Neurologists are specialists, which means they're harder to find than PCPs, but they're still more accessible than psychiatrists in some areas.

Neurologists aren't typically frontline providers for major psychiatric illnesses such as bipolar disorder, but they can certainly provide the care if necessary. Neurologists have strong skills in neurologic diagnoses, so they're able to recognize evidence of coexisting neurologic disorders that may be contributing to bipolar symptoms.

Knowing What to Look for in a Psychiatrist

When you're shopping for a psychiatrist, you may begin to wonder who's doing the shopping. Everyone is grilling *you* with questions. When do you get to ask questions and obtain the information you need to make an educated choice? The answer to that question is "the sooner, the better."

We provide a list of ten questions to ask a psychiatrist or therapist online at www.dummies.com/extras/bipolardisorder.

Before your first visit, review those questions and prepare yourself. If you're not the assertive type, ask a friend or relative who's a little pushier to join you. Bringing along a trusted ally, especially for the first visit, can make all the difference in getting the information you need and walking away with a good sense of how a psychiatrist may (or may not) work for you.

Your support person can also provide valuable information to the doctor — details you may forget to share or consider too insignificant to mention. Don't be afraid to bring a list of questions with you and to jot down notes during your meeting. This list and the notes you take help you remember the important questions you want to ask and highlight what the doctor has told you that you may not remember clearly after you leave.

When scouting for a psychiatrist, consider the following criteria:

- ✔ **Experience:** Experience in treating mood disorders usually ensures a more accurate diagnosis and use of more effective and current treatments. Be sure to ask the psychiatrist how much experience she has in treating bipolar disorder.

- ✔ **Sensitivity:** Your psychiatrist should be a team player who listens, answers your questions, and considers your input when prescribing medications and making adjustments.

- ✔ **Willingness to communicate:** Your psychiatrist should not only prescribe medications but also explain how she arrived at her diagnosis and treatment plan. She should carefully review the potential risks, benefits, and alternatives to any medications she prescribes.

- ✔ **Availability:** Your psychiatrist may need to adjust your diagnosis and medications frequently, especially in the early stages of treatment. Hence, you need her to be easy to reach and available to see you.

- ✔ **Affordability:** Is the doctor you've chosen included in your insurance plan? Do fees for office visits fit in your budget? Does the doctor offer a payment plan?

Your doctor should be *board certified* in psychiatry, meaning she has passed a rigorous set of exams that indicate her mastery of the specialty of psychiatry. In the United States, you can find out whether a psychiatrist is board certified by going to www.abpn.com, clicking the ABPN verifyCERT link, and searching for the doctor by name. The American Board of Psychiatry and Neurology (ABPN) is one of many specialty boards that certify doctors as competent within a specialty. Doctors can have licenses to practice medicine, but they may not be board certified in a specialty. Doctors without board certification may have the required skills to diagnose and treat your condition, but the designation makes it much easier for you to verify their credentials. Starting in the 1990s, all the medical specialty certification boards put into place a program called "Maintenance of Certifications." Under this program, psychiatrists must retest for their board certifications every ten years to ensure that they keep up with the rapid changes in the field. However, if a doctor was first certified before this program, she doesn't have to recertify.

What to Bring to Your First Meeting

During your first meeting, your psychiatrist tries to write your story in medical terms that accurately describe your symptoms. He needs a great deal of information about you, so he must ask a string of personal questions. He can't literally get inside your head to see what you think and feel, so he relies on the following information to guide his diagnosis:

- **Subjective information:** The insight and details you choose to provide about how you feel, what you're thinking, how you've been behaving recently, and what other people have been noticing about you

- **Objective information:** Your psychiatrist's observations of your appearance, behaviors, speech, mood state, and thoughts as well as your reactions to the interview

Your psychiatrist may also ask you to complete questionnaires or scales, such as the PHQ-9 depression scale, the Beck Depression Inventory, or the Young Mania Rating Scale. Your psychiatrist then uses all this information to perform a psychiatric evaluation, which he uses to determine a likely diagnosis. The evaluation, usually made after your first one or two meetings, is considered a *working diagnosis.* As in other fields of medicine, new information or developments during the course of treatment may lead to adjustments in the diagnosis.

Your best shot at receiving an accurate diagnosis is to be honest and open with your psychiatrist and to clearly describe your thoughts, behaviors, and feelings. If you withhold important information because you're embarrassed or for any other reason, you can't expect your psychiatrist to paint an accurate diagnostic portrait.

To prepare for your evaluation, gather the information we describe in this section in your head or on paper and get ready to share the intimate details.

Why you (or others) think you need help

The first thing your psychiatrist wants to know is your *chief complaint* — in other words, what's going on that prompted you to seek a psychiatric evaluation. This is a story that starts at the end and then goes back to fill in the details. Perhaps you've been bedridden for days, raging for weeks, watching your mood episodes chip away at your marriage, spending money extravagantly, feeling completely overwhelmed by everything on your to-do list, or getting into arguments with friends and relatives. If someone recommended that you see a psychiatrist or therapist, explain why that person thinks you need help — or even bring that person along for part of your initial meeting with the psychiatrist if you feel comfortable doing so.

Can't you just test me?

Unfortunately, at the time of this writing, the technology to test for bipolar disorder doesn't exist for several reasons. Among them are that bipolar disorder is probably a collection of different conditions; the related brain changes are at microscopic levels that are difficult for scans to detect; and blood chemistry doesn't accurately depict brain chemistry and function.

But don't throw in the towel just yet. The future holds out hope in the form of some new and improved detection tools. Some innovations include the following:

✔ A functional magnetic resonance imaging (MRI) scan measures tiny metabolic changes that determine activity patterns in different parts of your brain during mental tasks and mood states. This and other *functional imaging* technologies may someday be able to detect consistent differences between brains with bipolar disorder and those without.

✔ Genetic research is looking for genetic and epigenetic patterns associated with bipolar disorder in humans with the illness and in animal models of mania and depression. By identifying genetic patterns that are consistently associated with bipolar disorder, researchers can find out which proteins and patterns of proteins and enzymes play a role in the development of symptoms. This knowledge may allow for the development of blood tests for these *biomarkers* (substances whose presence indicate a condition).

✔ Neuropsychological tests (paper-and-pencil testing) may help map patterns of attention, memory, and information processing (executive function) that appear to be associated with bipolar disorder. These tests may eventually aid in the early identification of bipolar disorder in children with attention and behavioral problems.

More symptom information, please!

Your chief complaint simply states the problem. After you establish the problem, your psychiatrist can start collecting details about your physical and mental development, emotional life, and your behavior patterns over the years. He may refer to these details as the *history of present illness* and *review of systems*. Through this systematic, information-gathering approach, your psychiatrist attempts to understand your pattern of psychiatric symptoms. To gather a list of symptoms, your psychiatrist is likely to ask many of the following questions:

✔ **Depression-related questions:** How sad do you get and for how long? Do you feel hopeless or helpless? Do you think about death and dying? Do you think about killing yourself? Have you ever tried to kill yourself? Do you enjoy things anymore? Can you concentrate? Are you tired all the time?

✔ **Mania-related questions:** How happy or angry do you get and for how long? Do you have periods of high energy and productivity? Have you gotten into trouble during those times by spending money, having an affair, or "borrowing" money from your employer, for example? Do you ever feel like you're the best at everything?

✔ **General questions on thought content and processes:** How's your thinking? Do your thoughts feel slow or hyperactive? Do you feel as though you can't think clearly? Does your brain play tricks on you; do you hear voices, believe you have magical powers, or think people want to harm you?

✔ **Questions about anxieties and compulsive behaviors:** How much do you worry about things? Have you ever had a panic attack? Do you have unwanted thoughts that don't go away or illogical behaviors you can't stop doing? Do you freeze in social situations or avoid them altogether?

✔ **Mental health history questions:** What's your psychiatric history? Have you ever been hospitalized? Have you ever been on medications? Have you seen a therapist at some time in your life?

✔ **Questions about your life in the past:** What was your childhood like? How did you do in school? How did you relate to other kids? Did you have close friends? Did you experience any depression or manic symptoms as a teenager or child? Have you had a traumatic experience?

✔ **Questions about your life now:** What's your life like? Do you work? How's work going? How's your marriage/love life? How's sex for you? How are things with your kids, your parents, and/or your siblings? Do you have hobbies? Do you exercise? How much alcohol do you consume? Do you use any recreational drugs? Is anyone in your life hurting you physically or emotionally? Has this ever happened in your life? Do you feel safe in your current relationship?

Some of the questions are much easier to answer with the help of a significant other or a close family member who can offer some details that you may not remember or see in yourself. If your significant other or family member is willing and you're comfortable with him being in the office with you, the two of you can provide more valuable information more quickly and completely than if you go it alone.

Medical history

Have you seen your primary-care physician about your chief complaint? If you haven't, refer to Chapter 4 for a better understanding of why doing so is such an important first step. After you explore that avenue, provide your psychiatrist with test results and recommendations from your doctor.

Although your primary-care physician probably conducted a thorough physical exam and interview, you can expect your psychiatrist to ask several questions about your current physical condition as well. Any headaches, weakness, or dizziness? Any history of head injuries? Belly or bowel troubles? Joint pain or swelling? Skin problems? Diabetes or heart disease? History of stroke or cancer? Eye problems (such as glaucoma)? Have you had any surgeries? Allergic reactions to medications? Other allergies? How about your kidneys, liver, and lungs? Do you follow any type of particular diet — vegan, vegetarian, or gluten and/or dairy free? Have you had any noticeable weight loss or weight gain, especially if it wasn't something you were trying to do?

Your psychiatrist needs your medical history for two purposes: to help rule out other physical conditions that may be causing or aggravating your symptoms and to determine the safest, most effective medications to prescribe if you need medication.

Family history

When you start shaking the family tree of a person who exhibits classic bipolar symptoms, skeletons often rain down from the branches. Those skeletons, so to speak, can help your psychiatrist do the following:

- **Simplify the diagnosis.** If a first-degree relative (immediate family member) has a mood disorder, a schizophrenia diagnosis, or a history of suicidal thoughts or behaviors, your risk of having a mood disorder is significantly higher (see Chapter 2). Second-degree relatives (uncles, aunts, and cousins) count, too, but to a lesser degree.

- **Explore the risk of bipolar disorder if your only symptoms are depressive.** If you're experiencing depression and haven't experienced any manic or hypomanic symptoms but do have a family history of mania or schizophrenia, then you have a higher risk of eventually experiencing a manic or hypomanic episode.

  Prescribing an antidepressant alone to a person who has bipolar may be less effective for the depression and, in some cases, may actually increase the risk of a manic shift. So if bipolar is part of your immediate family history — even if you have no manic symptoms — your psychiatrist will likely be cautious in prescribing antidepressants and may need to monitor you closely, especially in the first weeks of treatment. And he may be quicker to add an antimanic or med to prevent mood cycles for you than for those without this family history.

✔ **Determine the most effective medications.** If a particular medication or therapy has effectively treated one of your first-degree relatives or caused a terrible side effect in someone in your family, your psychiatrist may use that information when choosing your initial medications. But just because a certain medication worked or didn't for a close relative doesn't mean it'll have the same effect on you.

Following are a few points to keep in mind regarding your family history:

✔ You may not have a formal diagnosis for people in your family — especially in previous generations. But if one or more people in the family showed serious behavioral quirks — never left the house, drank or used pills excessively, or kept tinfoil on the windows to keep out the aliens — they're worth mentioning.

✔ Don't limit your family history to diagnoses of bipolar disorder. Report all psychiatric problems: schizophrenia, depression, anxiety disorders, panic attacks, anger/aggression, substance abuse, and so on. Different disorders often share common genetic factors, and substance abuse in a relative can hint at underlying mood or anxiety disorders.

✔ Tell your psychiatrist about any suicides in your family. The risk of suicide seems to run genetically, apart from bipolar and depression.

List of legal and . . . yes . . . illegal drugs

Your psychiatrist needs to know about all the chemicals, dietary supplements, and herbs that you pop and pour into your body. You already know that you need to hand over a list of prescription medications, but don't overlook the other stuff you may take regularly, including over-the-counter medications, vitamins, herbs, alcohol, marijuana, caffeine, energy drinks, diet medications, amphetamines or other stimulants, or illicit drugs such as cocaine and ecstasy.

If you're using illicit drugs, tell your psychiatrist. These substances affect emotions and behavior drastically, and this information is critical to your psychiatric evaluation. Embarrassment and worry about being found out have no place here. Your psychiatrist won't report your drug use to anyone unless you pose a risk of serious harm to yourself or someone else. Full disclosure is the only workable policy.

Hiding drug or alcohol use from your psychiatrist can be fatal. Don't do it. Muster up all your courage, ditch your shame, and spill your guts. This will aid your recovery, and it may save your life.

Sleep log

Whether you're sleepless in Seattle or drowsy in Denver, your psychiatrist needs to know about it. Sleep changes and energy patterns are core biological markers in bipolar disorder; they provide important clues that tell you and your doctor when you need help. Report any of the following:

- Excessive need for sleep
- Inability to feel rested even after sleeping for a long time
- Persistent fatigue
- Little or no need for sleep
- Significant changes in sleep patterns

Note your sleep cycles *and* energy levels. Being awake all night and dragging around the next day are normal. Having a three-day wakeful jag and still feeling perky, however, may be symptomatic of mania. Yet remembering how well you sleep from one week to the next can be a challenge, so write it down. (Find a mood chart you can use to track your sleep in Chapter 11.) And ask your significant other for help; he may have an entirely different read on how well you sleep. You can also look into a variety of phone apps and devices that track sleep and activity patterns — high tech stuff that can give you important information to share with your psychiatrist.

Arriving at a Diagnosis

You spilled your guts, confessed your sins, and admitted to doing things that could have landed you in jail. All you want in return are clear answers to two simple questions: "What do I have?" and "How do I get rid of it?" You, your friends, and your significant other have slogged through months of unexplained, self-destructive, and unbearable symptoms, and you need an answer. Unfortunately, unraveling the mystery may take some time.

Evaluating your symptoms

To arrive at a diagnosis, your psychiatrist compares your symptoms to criteria specified in the *Diagnostic and Statistical Manual of Mental Disorders (DSM)* or the *International Classification of Diseases (ICD)*. These are the bibles of psychiatry that describe various syndromes and conditions and the symptoms that must be present to declare a particular diagnosis. (For more about these manuals and the diagnostic criteria for bipolar disorder, see Chapter 1.)

What symptoms are characteristic of bipolar disorder? Here are some highlights that doctors look for:

- ✔ **Evidence of mania:** You experience a week or more of high energy, excessively happy or angry moods, little need for sleep, excessive activity and pleasure seeking, impaired judgment or impulse control, grandiose thinking and behaviors, and racing thoughts . . . to the degree that they create problems in your life.

- ✔ **Evidence of major depression:** You experience two weeks or more of sad mood, low energy, decreased enjoyment of things, poor concentration, low activity and low productivity, thoughts of death and suicide, excessive feelings of guilt or bad feelings about yourself, and slowed thinking . . . to the degree that they create problems in your life.

- ✔ **Evidence of hypomania:** An elevated mood that lasts four days, *hypomania* is a "light" version of mania. Hypomania doesn't create as many problems in function as mania, but it can be difficult to live with.

- ✔ **Presence of psychosis:** Psychosis can go along with either depression or mania. It can include disorganized thinking, paranoia, delusional thinking (significant distortions of reality), or hearing voices.

The symptoms of a given mood episode must be noticeable changes from baseline, and they must be present most of the day, every day, for the minimum time period, as specified in the preceding list.

Considering other causes

After you and your psychiatrist develop the picture of your mood symptoms and lay out your family history on the table, your psychiatrist considers all of the possible diagnoses that could explain your pattern of symptoms. This *differential diagnosis* helps her carefully choose the most appropriate diagnosis or diagnoses and *rule out* the diagnoses she doesn't think apply to you at this particular time. Some diagnoses that are commonly considered in the differential diagnosis of bipolar disorder include but aren't limited to the following (see Chapter 1 for details about these conditions):

- ✔ Unipolar depression
- ✔ Anxiety disorders
- ✔ Attention deficit hyperactivity disorder (ADHD)
- ✔ Schizophrenia or schizoaffective disorder

✔ Borderline personality disorder (BPD)

✔ Other medical conditions

✔ Substance abuse

✔ Psychosis

Receiving the diagnosis

You've been poked and prodded, examined and cross-examined. Your psychiatrist has even climbed the branches of your family tree looking for clues. Now you want to know: What is it? What's causing all this discomfort and misery?

BIPOLAR BIO

Effective treatment starts with the correct diagnosis

I have borderline personality disorder (BPD), which was misdiagnosed as bipolar disorder for 15 years. The two conditions have many overlapping symptoms, so it's crucial that diagnosing clinicians really take the time to tease them out. When I was first given lithium in my early 20s to help treat bipolar, it was a disaster; but when I switched to valproic acid (Depakote), things got a little better. The hypomanic highs decreased a bit, but the underlying depression never went away. As a result, my psychiatrists proceeded to prescribe basically every new antidepressant to hit the market, plus a number of antipsychotics. I suffered the side effects of 22 different psych meds before finally getting the right ones, which wouldn't have happened if I'd been given the right diagnosis in the first place.

The mood stabilizer I now take, lamotrigine (Lamictal), was the first that ever touched my depression. When I first started taking lamotrigine back in 2005, I interpreted my rapid,

positive response to mean that I really was bipolar after all. Why else would I respond to mood stabilizers? But in 2011, when I started working for the Active Minds Speakers Bureau, I gave a talk to clinicians that helped me understand what was actually going on. A psychiatrist who treats adolescents with BPD at one of the top inpatient facilities in the U.S. told me that her patients tend to respond well to lamotrigine. We discussed the idea that people with BPD often suffer from the same deep depression as people with bipolar, but not the mania. While emotion dysregulation in BPD can manifest as short periods of hypomania, especially when lack of sleep is involved, I think it much more commonly manifests as suicidal depression. The antidepressant effect of lamotrigine, in combination with dialectical behavior therapy, made all the difference for me.

— Stacy Pershall,
author of *Loud in the House
of Myself: Memoir of a Strange Girl*

If you don't present textbook-like symptoms, your diagnosis may be murky and tentative. Perhaps you have an anxiety disorder with some depression, obsessive-compulsive disorder with some characteristics of attention deficit hyperactivity disorder, or a touch of mania with paranoia. In other words, your diagnostic portrait may look a lot like an abstract painting. Your psychiatrist may provide you with an initial diagnosis and then continue watching your progress over time to confirm, refute, or modify the diagnosis.

The diagnostic system in use right now is prone to a lot of murkiness and overlapping diagnoses, because it's based on observed symptoms rather than on underlying physical causes. Many different psychiatric illnesses share similar emotional and behavioral symptoms, so diagnosis can be a tricky process. In certain cases, time is an important diagnostic factor, because more clear-cut patterns of symptoms may take a while to emerge.

Gauging the severity of your illness

The severity of bipolar disorder varies from one person to the next. Some people go for years without a major mood episode, whereas others cycle four or more times a year. A depressive episode can drag on for months or end in a matter of weeks. Some individuals experience only mild episodes that have limited effects on their ability to function. Determining the severity or predicting the overall course of bipolar is difficult, but the following factors clue you in to what you can expect:

- ✔ The presence of psychosis commonly marks more severe mood episodes.

- ✔ Early onset of the disorder, in childhood or adolescence in particular, often indicates increased severity and predicts a worsening of the mood episodes over time.

- ✔ An increase in the frequency, duration, and intensity of mood episodes over time often indicates that the disorder is more severe.

- ✔ An early and full response to medication, such as lithium, often indicates a more classic form of the disorder with a more positive prognosis over the course of your life with treatment.

- ✔ Rapid cycling may indicate a more-difficult-to-treat type of bipolar.

You and your psychiatrist should discuss these factors. Although some factors may indicate a harsher outcome, no factor locks in your destiny. Stress management, lifestyle changes, and careful and comprehensive medical management over time can significantly diminish the severity of symptoms and improve the course of the disorder.

Responding to Your Diagnosis

A host of social reactions to mental illness may influence how you respond to receiving a diagnosis of bipolar disorder. How will people see you and judge you? Will your employer fire you? Will your landlord evict you? The questions swirl through your mind and spark panic. So what exactly is the point of the bipolar diagnosis? Why do you need it in your life, and what are its benefits and limitations? The following list provides some answers:

- ✔ **A diagnosis guides treatment decisions.** Just like a diagnosis of diabetes tells your doctor to initiate a certain treatment regimen, a bipolar diagnosis triggers a process for medication and therapy choices.

- ✔ **A diagnosis lets you know what to expect over time.** Your doctor can't see the future outcome of a complicated illness like bipolar disorder, but he can anticipate certain risks and patterns you're likely to encounter over the course of the illness and possibly help you avoid them.

- ✔ **A bipolar diagnosis doesn't define you.** You're not bipolar; you *have* bipolar disorder. This is a huge difference, because language can influence perception. Consider your condition something you manage, not as a label that identifies you.

- ✔ **You choose whether and with whom you want to share your diagnosis.** HIPAA privacy laws prevent your doctor and therapist from revealing your condition to anyone unless you give them permission to do so. In addition, disability rights provide some protection against discrimination based on a bipolar diagnosis. If your boss fires you or your landlord evicts you and you have proof that he did so just because of bipolar or its symptoms, you have grounds for a lawsuit.

- ✔ **Some people may judge you based on your diagnosis.** Judgment is a risk that comes with the diagnosis. Your task is to remember that people who make such judgments are uninformed and afraid. Sometimes you may choose to advocate, educate, and inform, but in other situations, you may choose to limit your interactions with certain people.

- ✔ **Your diagnosis places you in a community of support.** You have opportunities for support and networking that will be invaluable over the years. People who are going through the situation you're experiencing "get it," and they band together in many ways — formal and informal — to take care of one another and advocate for the group.

Receiving Your Treatment Plan

Your psychiatrist gives you more than a diagnosis; she also provides a well-defined treatment plan that covers your immediate needs and future directions. Your treatment plan should include the following:

- Medication names, dosing schedules, potential side effects, and time frames for them to begin working (in other words, some explanation of why your doctor chose particular medicines for you at this time)

- Written prescriptions, or electronic scripts sent directly to your pharmacy, for any medications you're supposed to take

- Forms necessary for any blood tests, other medical consultations, or examinations that your psychiatrist recommends

- Instructions for any changes in your current medications, including dose adjustments or changes in times for taking medications

- The date and time of your next appointment or information on how to set up your next appointment

Psychiatrist appointments, particularly at times of the day that are convenient for you, may be hard to come by. Before you leave (or right after your visit, if you must call the office to make appointments), schedule a series of appointments for four to six months out. This ensures that your appointments are planned at times that work for you.

- The cost of follow-up visits and the expected length of each visit

- Information on how to reach your psychiatrist in between visits if you have a question or if problems arise and guidance on what to do if you can't reach your doctor in an emergency

- If therapy is available, a plan that includes the recommended type of therapy, names and phone numbers of potential therapists, and/or consent forms that enable your psychiatrist to speak to your therapist

- Names of support groups in your area, books, or other helpful resources

Write down the treatment plan as your doctor describes it. (If you have someone with you, you can assign her this job.) Ask questions about anything in the plan that you don't understand. At all your visits, don't be afraid to bring a written list of questions to ask your doctor. With all that goes on during your first few appointments, you may easily and understandably forget to express your most pressing concerns and ask important questions.

Get several of your psychiatrist's business cards so you can give them to your other caregivers, including your therapist, family doctor, and cardiologist. And plug all her relevant contact information into your cellphone or other organizers so you have it with you at all times.

Make sure that you have signed any necessary consent forms for the psychiatrist to speak to your primary-care doctor, other physicians, and family members if that's appropriate and acceptable to you. Chapter 15 includes a sample release of information form to grant your psychiatrist permission to speak to a designated friend or family member.

Chapter 6

Building a Winning Mood-Management Team

In This Chapter

▶ Appreciating the roles your psychiatrist plays

▶ Teaming up with a competent and versatile therapist

▶ Recruiting supportive friends and family members

▶ Adding support groups to your team

*Y*ou can successfully treat many common ailments on your own. You can pop an antacid tablet to relieve indigestion, sip lemon tea at the first sign of a cold, or down a couple of aspirin to ease headache pain. But bipolar disorder is more sinister. You can be so blinded by the darkness of depression or so bewildered by the maelstrom of mania that you can't recognize your altered state of mind — let alone settle on an effective treatment.

If it takes a village to raise a child, it takes at least a small team to help you prevent your moods from swinging out of control. Your team ideally includes a psychiatrist and perhaps a therapist and one or more supportive family members or friends. Your psychiatrist typically makes the diagnosis and prescribes the medications that enable your brain to function properly; your therapist helps you solve problems, develop coping skills, and let go of issues beyond your control; and family members and friends provide feedback, support, and encouragement.

In this chapter, you find out how to begin to build your mood-management team. You discover the key role that each person on your team plays and the criteria required for each position. We also provide some suggestions for tracking down and selecting qualified professionals and supportive friends and family members to add to your team roster.

A Psychiatrist for Diagnosis and Medication Management

When your moods are out of sync with reality, your brain's physiology is disrupted. A psychiatrist, fondly referred to by many with bipolar disorder as a *p-doc,* prescribes medications to help adjust the neurobiological systems in your brain to enable it to respond appropriately. Medication doesn't cure your bipolar disorder, but it helps regulate your moods so you can function and begin to deal with real-life issues that may trigger mania or depression.

Your psychiatrist's primary functions are to accurately diagnose your illness, develop a comprehensive treatment plan that includes education and support as well as appropriate medications, and help you manage your medications, as we explain in the following sections.

 Although any medical doctor can diagnose and treat bipolar, a *psychiatrist* is a medical doctor who has specialized training in treating mental illnesses. Doctors who've completed this rigorous training run the gamut from relaxed and amiable to hurried and detached. When choosing a psychiatrist, remember that while knowledge and experience trump congeniality, listening skills are essential for the doctor to appropriately apply her expertise. (For more about choosing a psychiatrist, turn to Chapter 5.)

Diagnostician

Before you can begin any sensible treatment, you need a diagnosis, and your psychiatrist is usually the one who gives it to you. To find out how a psychiatrist performs a diagnosis and what you can do to improve the accuracy of that diagnosis, see Chapter 5. Turn to Chapter 1 for a description of the diagnostic criteria used to arrive at a bipolar diagnosis.

Master planner

Typically, your psychiatrist or your treatment team (usually a doctor and a therapist) draw up the initial game plan with you — a comprehensive treatment plan that typically includes a combination of medication, education, therapy, and self-help tailored specifically to your system profile. However, many people with bipolar disorder expand and personalize their plan as they become more aware of their own needs and the available treatments and supports. As your treatment plan evolves, having a master plan is an important component to address all facets of treatment.

Medicine man (or woman)

In the old days, psychiatrists handled all aspects of treatment. They diagnosed the illness, prescribed any necessary medications, and offered therapy and counseling. Although this is still the case for some psychiatrists, many people work with a treatment team that includes a psychiatrist, who primarily manages the medical end of things, and a therapist, often a psychologist or clinical social worker, who provides the psychotherapy. Unfortunately nowadays, some psychiatrists spend more time scribbling on prescription pads than they do listening to their patients or answering questions. The insurance reimbursement system encourages seeing as many patients as possible rather than spending extended time with each patient. The resulting time limits with patients are challenging, because the medical management of bipolar disorder is complex and requires adequate time to address many important topics at each appointment.

If the time you spend with your psychiatrist is insufficient for successfully communicating your needs, voice your concern. You and your doctor may be able to arrange for longer visits that can be appropriately reimbursed.

A Lifestyle Director: Highlighting the Therapist's Roles

After a psychiatrist effectively tweaks brain function with the right brew of medications, your problems may be mostly solved. For many people with bipolar disorder, however, medications provide only partial relief; some symptoms persist and you need additional interventions to reach a more complete recovery. Even if you experience full symptom relief, your system may react in ways that override the medication's mood-moderating effects if you live under constant stress, don't get enough sleep, or use ineffective strategies to resolve problems and deal with conflict in your life.

This is where a good therapist comes into play. Your therapist's primary roles are to help you develop strategies to relieve symptoms, make positive lifestyle changes that reduce stress, and establish healthy thinking and behavioral patterns so you can cope more effectively with life's ups and downs. For example, a therapist may teach you how to identify triggers and develop healthy responses instead of getting caught up in unhealthy thought patterns.

A therapist can play many additional roles on your mood-management team, acting as coach, career consultant, mood monitor, and wellness manager. We describe these roles in the following sections.

Your therapist and psychiatrist often function as co-leaders of your treatment team, and their roles may overlap to some degree. Psychiatrists tend to play some role in therapy, education, and support functions, whereas therapists, with their patients' permission, may contact psychiatrists to voice concerns when they think medication adjustments are necessary.

Coach, trainer, and referee

An effective therapist addresses not only the symptoms of your illness but all aspects of your life that may be suffering from bipolar symptoms or worsening the illness, including but certainly not limited to the following:

- **Your thought processes** can often darken your perceptions and create a vortex that spins you into a deeper depression.

- **Your daily patterns,** including a regular sleep schedule and consistent daily routines, can help to stabilize your mood.

- **Interpersonal conflict with partners, family members, and friends** often affects the illness and other aspects of your life.

- **Family issues** may include raising children or managing finances.

- **Career challenges** can span from problems on the job and conflicts with coworkers to time off needed to manage your symptoms. A therapist may provide valuable assistance in suggesting reasonable workplace accommodations, for example.

- **Social situations** that stress you out or that have suffered due to your illness may exacerbate mood episodes.

Look for a therapist who specializes in the form of therapy you need most. Chapter 11 describes therapies that are proven to improve mood stability and help people deal with the fallout from bipolar disorder.

Mood thermometer

You can and should monitor your moods, as we explain in Chapter 11, but when depression weighs on you like a lead blanket or mania thrusts your moods into the dizzying stratosphere, staying motivated and objective enough to create an accurate mood map may be nearly impossible. And friends and family members may be too busy with their own needs to be of much help.

Your therapist can function as a mood thermometer, providing you with objective observations concerning your moods and demeanor. He may be able to help you strategize ways to monitor your moods more regularly or effectively even when you aren't feeling well. Sometimes mood observations and advice are easier to accept from a third party than from a loved one.

Resident soundboard

Some forms of therapy don't offer any particular advice. The therapist sits and listens attentively as you, the client, describe a particular issue. Sure, he uses a little body language to indicate his interest, but he says very little overall. Often, airing out your issues allows you to calm down so the therapist can gently guide you toward your own solutions, which may have been there all along. Other therapy models are much more proactive and focused on problem solving, but active listening remains the starting point in developing solutions and strategies that will work for you.

If you can find a therapist who listens well and inspires you to solve your own problems, you've struck gold. But keep in mind that even if this is your therapist's primary way of working, it's likely to be less effective during more active periods of your illness. When a mood episode is brewing or active or even tapering off, a good therapist usually needs to play a role that's much more active than just listening.

Wellness manager

One of the most important factors in the success of long-term management of bipolar disorder is the *continuity of care* — carefully planned and executed treatment that's consistent over time. A therapist (or a caseworker, family member, or close friend) can improve your continuity of care by helping you keep detailed records of medications and therapies that have (and have not) worked for you in the past. Your wellness manager can also help smooth the transition if you change doctors or therapists so the new care provider doesn't engage in a process of trial and error that's already been done.

Referral service

Therapists are people who know people. If your therapist can't solve your problem, he probably has the contact information for someone who can. He'll dig through his desk and hand you a business card or flip through his smartphone and jot down the name and number of a specialist you need. "Buried in debt? Here's a financial consultant that other clients rave about!" "Need a job? Here's a career coach I know." "Need a break from the drudgery of daily life? Here's the travel agent I use." "Can't pay me? Check out this information on government-subsidized health insurance."

When having a therapist isn't an option

Not everyone has access to a therapist or the money to afford one. When a therapist isn't an option, you may need to rely more on self-help strategies and your personal support network and formal support groups. Books, and in some cases videos, can bring you up to speed on the basics of various do-it-yourself therapies, including cognitive behavioral therapy (CBT) and mindfulness training. Family members, friends, and fellow support group members can fill the role as soundboards and problem solvers, helping you track down solutions and resources to meet your needs.

Be skeptical of self-help titles in bookstores; many self-help books espouse ideas that haven't been researched at all. Seek out reputable resources for information. National organizations, including the Depression and Bipolar Support Alliance (DBSA), the National Alliance on Mental Illness (NAMI), and the National Institute of Mental Health (NIMH), offer reliable information and resources. These organizations and your psychiatrist or primary care physician can guide you toward reliable books and other resources for learning about well-researched treatments to try on your own.

Assembling Your Personal Support Staff: Family and Friends

A strong support network of family and friends can function as a valuable ally in the battle for mood stability. However, if your allies are lugging around their own agendas and emotional baggage, they can compound your problem and increase the likelihood of a mood episode. When you begin recruiting your support staff, you need to do three things:

- ✔ Decide whom you can trust.
- ✔ Talk about each candidate's fears and anxieties and establish a focus on open communication.
- ✔ Encourage your support staff to become educated about your illness and what they can do to help. (See Chapter 23 for a list of ten ways a loved one can help.)

Building a network based on trust

When scouting for family members or friends to add to your support network, look for stable and trustworthy people. Ask yourself the following questions:

- ✔ **Can I confide in this person?** Some people like to buddy up to others who have problems just so they can obtain some juicy gossip to pass along. Be sure the people on your support staff know how to keep information confidential.

- ✔ **Is this person stable enough to support me?** People with bipolar are commonly drawn to others who experience roller coaster moods and emotions. Only someone who's steady can help you steady yourself.

- ✔ **Do I interact with this person frequently enough?** An ideal support person sees or talks to you at least once a week so she can let you know if she notices significant shifts in mood. The more people you have in your support network, the more objective observers you have to monitor your moods. However, you need to choose these monitors carefully and train them accordingly, so they know when to step in and when to step back.

- ✔ **Does this person judge me for having a mental illness?** If a person thinks your illness is due to a character flaw, she can't provide the support you need. You don't need people around who make you feel guilty for having bipolar disorder.

- ✔ **Is this person reliable?** If you foresee a possible support person bailing out at the first sign of trouble, she may not be there when you need her most. Be sure that you trust the people on your team to stick with you and do what's best for *you*.

- ✔ **Does this person respect me?** You don't want an intrusive caretaker who constantly nags you about your moods and meds and treats you like a child. Choose individuals who demonstrate genuine respect for you and who respect mutually agreed-upon boundaries. You don't want to surround yourself with mood police who try to control your life.

Understanding their fears, anxieties, anger, and other emotions

Family and friends who genuinely care about you and appreciate your unique gifts can often get under your skin, especially when they want to help or when you're in the middle of a mood episode. These people in your life have their own set of fears, anxieties, anger, and other emotions. For example, as you battle a lengthy bout of depression, they may be anxious, not knowing how long it will last, or angry that you don't seem to be doing enough to help yourself. When you're in the throes of mania, your loved ones may be unable to understand you or they may tell you to calm down. Something you say or do may trigger strong negative emotions in them.

Although some people have thicker skin than others, nobody's skin is impervious. Remember that members of your support team are imperfect people and try to cut them some slack. Doing so isn't easy, especially when you're wrestling with your own demons, but if everyone on your team gives other team members the benefit of the doubt, you're all much more likely to work collectively toward the goal of maintaining a stable emotional environment.

Educating your supporters

Whenever you throw a party, you probably have guests who strategically avoid the after-party cleanup. If you're lucky, one or two close friends who know their way around your kitchen will start tidying up. You may see a couple others who linger around, waiting for instructions.

You can observe many of these same behaviors in your support team. When you're depressed or manic, most people — those who don't understand what's going on or what you expect of them — flee the scene. If they don't bolt, they stick around, become frustrated by not knowing what to do, and lose their tempers or pepper you with sarcasm. What you want is a close friend or relative who knows about mood disorders to intervene and provide a compassionate and gentle but firm guiding hand to help you stabilize.

You want as many knowledgeable people on your mood-management team as possible, and the only way to achieve that goal is to educate people in your life who want to learn about bipolar and are committed to helping you succeed. Knowledge gives people the confidence they need to jump in when you need them most. Whenever friends or family members ask what they can do to help, encourage them to discover more about the disorder, drawing from any of the following resources:

- **You:** You're the most qualified expert on *your* moods and what helps or hurts your mood stability. If you feel ready to discuss your situation with others, you can be a valuable source of information.

- **Depression and Bipolar Support Alliance (DBSA):** An organization that focuses on bipolar disorder and depression (run by and for people with the illness), DBSA offers free and confidential support groups for individuals with depression or bipolar as well as their families and friends. DBSA also offers free and easy-to-understand educational materials. Check out the DBSA website at www.dbsalliance.org.

✔ **NAMI Family to Family:** The National Alliance on Mental Illness (NAMI) offers a 12-week course called *Family-to-Family* that educates friends and family members of people with mental illness about major conditions and treatments. The course also functions as a support group. Visit the NAMI website at www.nami.org for more info and to find a local NAMI affiliate.

✔ **Books:** This book and many others on bipolar disorder can help friends and family members understand this illness and empathize with those who have it. Books can offer great tips on how to help someone with bipolar. We offer this information in Part VI and in Chapter 23.

✔ **TV shows and songs:** A variety of entertainment media, including TV shows and songs, address the topic of mental illness. In recent years more and more television dramas have included characters with bipolar disorder, and although they may not always portray the condition accurately, they do start conversations. The music industry has a long history of songs that speak to mental illness, and more and more artists are sharing their own struggles in their lyrics and videos. If any of these songs or TV shows are meaningful to you, sharing them with loved ones can be a powerful way to help them start to understand your experience.

✔ **Movies and theater:** Although Hollywood takes a little poetic license with "true" stories, some movies, including *Silver Linings Playbook* and *Canvas,* help remove the stigma of mental illness. Plays and musicals, including the Broadway show *Next to Normal,* are also excellent for fostering understanding, empathy, and discussion.

✔ **Websites and blogs:** Numerous websites and blogs offer valuable information about bipolar disorder and provide insight specifically for friends and family members of people who suffer from this illness. Check out our blog, Bipolar Beat, at blogs.psychcentral.com/bipolar.

When researching bipolar on the web, remain skeptical. The Internet has plenty of good information, but it also attracts its share of quacks and armchair quarterbacks. Consult your doctor before making any change to your treatment plan, including stopping medication or starting a home remedy.

Establishing your team's level of involvement

Everyone on your support team needs to have the sensitivity to know when to remain silent and when to voice concerns, along with the strength to step in and help when you need it most, especially when you can't or don't want to ask for or accept assistance. Such people are rare, and even the best of them can't always get it right. But you can help your loved ones become better supporters by educating them about bipolar, communicating your needs, and defining the parameters for assisting you.

You're probably aware that some people will gladly volunteer to live your life for you if you let them. They'd be happy to cook your meals, clean your house, raise your kids, and maybe even pay your bills (with your money, of course) — all in the name of charity. Such assistance may seem nice in the short term, when you really need help, but when charity becomes chronic and invasive, the lifesaver quickly becomes an anchor, keeping you from moving forward. Beware of the following personality types:

- **The Nagger:** "Did you take your meds today?" Every day, sometimes two or three times a day, you can expect this nagging question. If you want or need to be reminded to take your medications, the Nagger can be useful if she's willing to remind you within guidelines that you prearrange; otherwise, the nagging is just another stressor.

- **Clueless:** A Clueless helper watches you, but she never does or says anything that she thinks may offend you. You can be teetering on the edge of the cliff, and Clueless will patiently watch the events unfold. Giving this person permission to speak up may be necessary.

- **The Party Animal:** If you're prone to hypomanic or manic episodes that entail spending sprees, bar hopping, wild sex, and other frenetic activities, you can find plenty of Party Animals to join you for the fun, but they usually don't stick around when the hangover kicks in. Avoid people who encourage your most unhealthy behaviors.

- **The Heavy:** Unlike the Party Animal, who encourages you to have too much fun, the Heavy doesn't let you have any fun at all. And that's not . . . well, any fun. You should be able to enjoy a full life within the limits you set for yourself. Being happy and having fun aren't the same as being hypomanic, and you have to enjoy some pleasure in life.

Encouraging open communication

Announcing that you're bipolar is a foolproof way to silence an audience. Most people don't know what to say, so they instantly go mute. In some cases, that's the desired effect; but when you approach your support team, you want to encourage open communication to achieve two goals:

- Help your supporters understand you and your illness more intimately.

- Become more aware of how your moods and behaviors affect others.

Establishing a relationship is like learning to dance together. You and your partner must move in sync, and communication is pivotal. At first, you step on each other's toes quite frequently, but as you become more accustomed to each other's movements, you begin to instinctively move to the rhythms that surround you. Here are some techniques that can open the channels of communication so you can start working on your rhythm:

- ✓ Write down what you want to discuss in advance.

- ✓ Sit in a quiet, private place whenever you discuss confidential topics.

- ✓ Agree on a physical sign or secret word that you can use to end a discussion, no questions asked, if it becomes too heated.

- ✓ Encourage your friend or loved one to ask questions about bipolar disorder and the way it makes you feel.

- ✓ Ask your friend or loved one to describe her observations and emotions concerning your moods and behaviors. How is bipolar disorder affecting your loved one's life and her ability to satisfy personal needs?

You can help a person become more knowledgeable about bipolar disorder and your specific needs, but you can't force anyone to accept you or the illness. Some people, due to their own limitations, may not be ready to accept the illness and adapt to a new reality. For your own mental wellness, you may need some distance from these people for a while.

Reaping the benefits of honesty

I realized the importance of telling the truth to my family and providers when I was first hospitalized at the age of 19. It didn't take long to figure out that communicating honestly with the doctors and nurses caring for me allowed them to help me and respond to my needs. I also learned that signing a release form meant there was little I could hide from my family even if I wanted to.

After this initial hospitalization, I continued to communicate with my family about what I was going through, allowing them to be honest as well. We developed a deeper understanding of one another as we shared our fears, worries, and triumphs. I continued to be honest with my medical providers as well. I made it a goal to always tell the truth to my doctors; in turn, they helped me get the treatment I need, found

the medications that work best for me, and created a strong bond with me, allowing the trust to grow.

Sharing my truth with people is hard, but I'm rewarded for it over and over again. Whether it's closer bonds with my family, a truthful discussion about side effects with my psychiatrist, or an open talk with my therapist, I've seen positive results of honesty. What has inspired me the most, however, is that my honesty has allowed others to be honest as well. Honesty has made all the difference in my recovery, my stability, and my wellness.

— Linea Johnson,
coauthor of *Perfect Chaos: A Daughter's Journey to Survive Bipolar, a Mother's Struggle to Save Her*

Working as a Team

All the key players on your mood-management team should be able to communicate openly with you and one another to ensure that you receive comprehensive, integrated treatment. If your therapist notices that your moods are fluctuating or that you seem more anxious and irritable than usual, he should be able to contact your psychiatrist to talk about how to help you. You may need a medication adjustment or additional therapy sessions.

An effective strategy is to put one member of your support staff in charge of communications. Your communications manager should introduce the members of your mood-management team and ensure that critical information gets passed along. Such communication is especially important in situations that involve complications or transitions, such as the following:

- ✔ **Hospitalization:** Some hospitals have their own doctors in charge of treatment, so when you're hospitalized, the psychiatrist who usually sees you may no longer be in charge of your care. Communication between your psychiatrist and the new doctor at the hospital is essential.

- ✔ **Hospital release:** Before the hospital releases you, your regular psychiatrist, therapist, and the person acting as your primary caregiver need to be informed in advance so they can provide a smooth transition to the outside world and make any necessary arrangements.

- ✔ **Changing doctors:** When you change doctors or therapists, your complete records need to be transferred to the new care provider.

Because of privacy laws, you need to sign a release with each doctor and therapist you see to allow them to openly communicate with one another. You also need to sign a release if you want your doctor or therapist to be able to discuss your treatment with specific friends or family members. See Chapter 15 for a sample release of information authorization letter.

Expanding Your Network through Local Support Groups

Friends and family have much more invested in your well-being than any third party, including your psychiatrist or therapist, but other people who have bipolar may be able to offer much more in terms of empathy, insight, and connections. Bipolar support groups can offer the following perks:

✔ Camaraderie with people who share your experiences and emotions

✔ Understanding that a mood disorder doesn't define who you are

✔ Motivation to follow your treatment plan

✔ Opportunity to rediscover strengths and humor you thought you lost when you became ill

✔ Insider information on medications, treatments, and therapies

✔ First-hand perspectives of local doctors and therapists

✔ Information about your legal rights

✔ Tips about education and IEPs (Individualized Education Plans) for children with bipolar disorder

✔ Access to credible books and videos about bipolar

You can tap in to the resources a support group offers by joining one. Organizations such as the Depression and Bipolar Support Alliance (DBSA) and the National Alliance on Mental Illness (NAMI) sponsor support groups in most cities and many towns to help people with mental illnesses find peer support and encourage advocacy. To find out about support groups in your area, contact the following organizations:

✔ **Bipolar Scotland:** Visit www.bipolarscotland.org.uk.

✔ **Bipolar UK:** Call 020-7931-6480 or visit www.bipolaruk.org.uk.

✔ **Church:** Many churches provide meeting places for support groups, including those affiliated with DBSA and NAMI.

✔ **Depression and Bipolar Support Alliance:** Call 800-826-3632 or go to www.dbsalliance.org.

✔ **Local mental health centers:** Most states and large counties have mental health services that can refer you to support groups in your area.

✔ **Mental Health America:** Call 800-969-6642 or go to www.nmha.org.

✔ **MIND:** Enter your location or postcode at www.mind.org.uk to find a local support group.

✔ **National Alliance on Mental Illness:** Call 800-950-6264 or go to www.nami.org to find contact information for local NAMI affiliates.

✔ **Your psychiatrist or therapist:** Ask your psychiatrist or therapist for information about local support groups.

What can you expect when you walk into your first support group session? That depends on the composition of the group and its organization. Some groups are more structured than others. Some invite experts in the field to give presentations; others encourage members to talk about their emotions and engage in group problem solving. Generally, you can expect members to be very open, welcoming, and willing to lend an empathetic ear.

Every support group has its own chemistry and dynamic, so don't give up if you feel out of place at the first one you visit. Try a few groups until you find one that feels comfortable. And if you don't like support groups, that's okay, too; not everyone is comfortable in a support group setting.

Part III
Managing the Biology of Bipolar Disorder

Medications for Mania and Depression

For Mania	For Bipolar Depression
Aripiprazole (Abilify)	Bupropion (Wellbutrin)
Asenapine (Saphris)	Citalopram (Celexa)
Carbamazepine (Tegretol)	Desvenlafaxine (Pristiq)
Lamotrigine (Lamictal)	Duloxetine (Cymbalta)
Lithium (Eskalith, Lithobid)	Escitalopram (Lexapro)
Olanzapine (Zyprexa)	Fluoxetine (Prozac)
Quetiapene (Seroquel)	Lamotrigine (Lamictal)
Risperidone (Risperdal)	Lithium (Eskalith, Lithobid)
Valproic acid (Depakote)	Lurasidone (Latuda)
Ziprasidone (Geodon)	Olanzapine+fluoxetine (Symbyax)
	Paroxetine (Paxil)
	Quetiapine (Seroquel)
	Sertraline (Zoloft)
	Venlafaxine (Effexor)

Go to www.dummies.com/extras/bipolardisorder for a bonus article on differences between name brand medications and their generic counterparts.

In this part . . .

- ✔ Check out medications used to treat bipolar mania and depression and to treat other conditions that often accompany bipolar disorder, including anxiety and insomnia.

- ✔ Weigh medication benefits against their side effects to perform your own cost-benefit analysis.

- ✔ Recognize the reasons why many people stop taking their medications and find ways to address many of the most common issues and deal with emotional factors that often play a role.

- ✔ Discover other ways to treat the biology of bipolar disorder — include supplements, light therapy, and various methods of physically stimulating the brain — when medications are insufficient or produce unacceptable side effects.

- ✔ Recognize challenges in treating bipolar disorder in certain populations, such as pregnant women and older people, and find solutions for meeting these challenges.

Chapter 7

Leveling Moods with Medication

・・・

In This Chapter

▶ Recognizing the different classes of mood-regulating medications

▶ Choosing the right medications for you and sticking to your prescribed regimen

・・・

*M*ost people with bipolar disorder need to take medication to help manage their moods, but doctors have no magic pill. Because bipolar disorder cycles through periods of vastly different symptoms, medications have a lot of ground to cover. The treatments work differently for everyone; a godsend to some may be a disaster for others. Medications that are effective in regulating for some people may cause intolerable side effects for others. Medications that work today may stop working later.

Using medications off label

Throughout this chapter (and the book), we discuss many medications and how licensed physicians can prescribe them for bipolar disorder and related conditions. They've been researched in scientific studies that help to understand what effects and side effects the medicines have and how they work in the body. The Food and Drug Administration (FDA) also labels medications in the United States as *approved* for use in certain conditions. If a pharmaceutical company wants to be able to market one of its medications for a particular illness, it must show the FDA a certain number of well-designed studies that support its use in that illness. The FDA then decides whether or not to approve the medication for that condition. If the FDA gives approval, then when a doctor

prescribes the medication for that condition, she is using it *on label*.

Frequently, though, doctors also use medications *off label* — in ways that don't have specific FDA approval. In such situations, they're relying on other evidence, such as scientific research and clinical *standards of practice* patterns of prescribing that are common in a particular specialty.

Discussions about medication in this book include both on-label and off-label uses. Your doctor should let you know when she's using a medication off label, but because doing so is such a common practice, many prescribers may not spell this out in detail, so feel free to ask.

We can't tell you which medications are best for you, but in this chapter we introduce you to those that have proven useful in treating the most common bipolar symptoms and offer guidance on working with your prescriber in choosing and managing your meds.

Unlocking the Bipolar Medicine Cabinet

This section introduces you to many of the most routinely prescribed medications that treat bipolar and commonly associated conditions. The information you find here is based on the knowledge and prescribing practices in place at the time of this writing. We highlight the primary benefits and most common potential side effects of each medication and encourage you to use this information when talking with your doctor about the safest and most effective medication choices for you.

If you're pregnant or planning to become pregnant, see Chapter 10 for additional considerations regarding medications to use based on possible effects on the developing fetus.

Lithium

Since the 1960s, lithium has been the gold standard, treating the range of bipolar symptoms more fully than any other medication in use today. It treats mania. It may treat bipolar depression. It's also used in *maintenance therapy,* as long-term medication to prevent or reduce recurrent depressive or manic episodes. And perhaps most importantly, it's the only medication that's proven to reduce the risk of suicide associated with bipolar.

Lithium truly is in a league of its own. Interestingly, this wonder med wasn't cooked up in a multimillion-dollar lab. Lithium is a naturally occurring salt that just happens to reduce a number of mood symptoms when safely managed under a doctor's care. Downsides include thyroid and kidney problems that may develop with longer term use of lithium.

No one yet fully understands how lithium works in the brain to treat bipolar disorder, but researchers continue to explore a number of possibilities, including effects on cellular *signaling* (electrochemical messenger systems between and within cells), effects on how genes express different proteins, and *neuroprotective* effects (improving cells' recovery from damage). See Chapter 2 for more about brain structure and function. Table 7-1 provides a quick rundown of the potential benefits and side effects of this rock star of bipolar disorder medications.

Table 7-1		Potential Benefits and Side Effects of Lithium			
Generic Name	Brand Names	Typical Adult Dose	Therapeutic Blood Level	Potential Benefits	Some Possible Side Effects*
Lithium carbonate Lithium citrate (oral solution)	Eskalith Cibalith-S Lithane Lithonate Lithotabs Lithobid	600 to 1,800 mg/day, but varies from person to person; blood level is the more important target.	0.8 to 1.2 mEq/L for acute mania; may be lower for maintenance dose; more than 1.5 mEq/L is considered toxic.	Antimanic; antidepressant; reduces mood cycle frequency; reduces frequency of suicide. May reduce long-term cognitive deficits related to bipolar disorder.	Stomach problems; weight gain; frequent urination; kidney damage; thyroid damage; foggy thinking; fatigue; tremor; dry mouth

mg/day = milligrams per day; mEq/L = milliequivalents per liter.
*Other side effects may occur that aren't listed.

You must keep lithium blood levels in a very narrow range, so always take the prescribed dose. Your doctor will test your blood levels every few weeks when you first start taking it and then every several months after the dose is stable. She'll monitor additional blood and urine tests regularly as well. If lithium dips below its therapeutic level, it may not be effective. If it rises too high, the substance can become toxic, and lithium toxicity can lead to death.

Lithium levels can rise as you lose fluid, so be wary of hot weather and vigorous exercise and limit your consumption of diuretics, including coffee, and alcohol, which can also amplify the sedative effects of lithium. Non-steroidal anti-inflammatory medications (like ibuprofen) can increase lithium levels, too, so check with your doctor before taking any of those meds along with lithium. Also, don't make dramatic changes to your salt intake, such as starting a low-salt diet, without consulting your doctor when taking lithium. If you experience diarrhea, vomiting, dizziness, lack of coordination, shakiness, blurred vision, or other signs of lithium toxicity, contact your doctor immediately. If you can't reach your doctor, head to the nearest emergency room.

All that said, long-term use of lithium provides excellent management of bipolar for some people. Lithium actually prevents the onset of symptoms, so keep taking it even if you're feeling better. After all, taking lithium is likely what's making you feel better. Continue to see your doctor regularly to discuss your options in terms of how long you should stay on lithium.

Some studies suggest that if you stop taking lithium, it may not be as effective for you if you resume taking it later, although this theory hasn't been clearly proven.

On the web or at your local health food store, you may hear about *lithium orotate,* which is purported to be safer. But no reliable studies currently support the claim that lithium orotate is safer than or as effective as lithium carbonate. With any form of lithium, you and your doctor need to carefully monitor your blood levels throughout treatment.

Anticonvulsants

Your brain and central nervous system form an intricate power grid that carries very low-level electricity. With serious central nervous system malfunctions, as in epilepsy, neurons misfire to such an extent that they can cause seizures. *Anticonvulsants* — including valproate, commonly known as valproic acid (Depakote) — appear to reduce seizures, at least in part by regulating neuron firing.

The mechanisms of bipolar aren't the same as seizures, but a number of anticonvulsants are effective in treating some symptoms of bipolar disorder. Stabilization of neuron cell firing may play a role, but researchers are studying other potential mechanisms of action, including effects on genetic expression. (See Chapter 2 for more discussion of medication mechanism of action.)

Table 7-2 lists the main medications in the anticonvulsant class, along with their doses, benefits, and possible side effects.

Valproate is commonly used as a first-line treatment for acute mania, as well as for maintenance therapy. Carbamazepine (Tegretol) has also proven effective for mania and maintenance care. Oxcarbemazapine (Trileptal) is a medication closely related to carbamazepine but with fewer side effects. It's being used in place of carbamazepine, but the research on its effectiveness is still limited. Lamotrigine (Lamictal) is growing in popularity because of its effectiveness in mood maintenance and potential for helping to alleviate depression, but it's not effective in treating acute mania.

Topiramate (Topamax) is an anticonvulsant that was sometimes used to treat bipolar disorder, but studies have shown that it to be ineffective. It often reduces appetite, though, so doctors sometimes use it to help reduce weight gain associated with other medications for bipolar disorder. Gabapentin (Neurontin) is another medication used for seizure that was once thought to be helpful in bipolar disorder, but studies have shown it to be ineffective. It's sometimes used to treat anxiety (see the later section on anti-anxiety medications).

Table 7-2   **Potential Benefits and Side Effects of Anticonvulsants**

Generic Name	Brand Names	Average Adult Dose	Therapeutic Blood Level	Potential Benefits	Some Possible Side Effects*
Carbamazepine	Tegretol Carbatrol Epitol Equetro	400 to 1,600 mg/day or 10 to 30 mg/kg/day	4 to 12 mcg/mL is the range for seizures; therapeutic level for mania is less well established; more than 15 mcg/mL is considered toxic	Antimanic; third choice after trials of lithium and valproate; doesn't cause significant weight gain in most patients; may help control aggression and violent outbursts.	Can reduce effectiveness of birth control pills; blood cell problems; reduced B-12 and folate levels; liver problems; blurry vision; dizziness; nausea; risk of Stevens-Johnson syndrome, a severe skin and mucus membrane reaction that can be lethal (much higher in individuals of Han Chinese descent due to a genetic effect on metabolism); effects on liver enzymes cause interactions with many other medications.
Divalproex sodium Valproate Valproic acid	Depakote Depakene	1,000 to 2,000 mg/day or 25 to 60 mg/kg/day, but upper limit varies according to amount needed to establish therapeutic blood level.	50 to 125 mcg/mL (risk of toxicity increases above this level).	Antimanic; may prevent or reduce recurrent episodes; possibly some weak antidepressant activity.	Pancreas and liver problems; weight gain; sedation; nausea; possible fertility problems in females; hair loss; elevated ammonia levels.
Lamotrigine	Lamictal	25 to 200 mg/day; must ramp up very slowly to reduce likelihood of Stevens-Johnson syndrome; dosing must start lower and go slower if given with valproate.	N/A	Reduces mood cycle frequency; strong antidepressant properties; not usually associated with weight gain; doesn't reduce acute mania.	Stevens-Johnson syndrome; may reduce effectiveness of some types of birth control pills; nausea and vomiting; dizziness; blurred vision; headache; insomnia or other sleep changes; if taking with valproate, must start with much lower doses of lamotrigine and increase even more slowly than usual.

mg/day = milligrams per day; mg/kg/day = milligrams per kilogram of body weight per day; mEq/L = milliequivalents per liter.
*Other side effects may occur that are not listed.

Researchers are looking into other anticonvulsants such as zonisamide (Zonegran), levetiracetam (Keppra), and tiagabine (Gabitril) for use in bipolar disorder, but at this time the research is scanty with no support for their use.

Withdrawing an anticonvulsant too quickly can cause seizures. Always consult your doctor before you stop or decrease a medication.

Antipsychotics

Atypical antipsychotics (atypical neuroleptics or *second-generation antipsychotics)* were originally formulated to treat psychosis in schizophrenia, but this class of medications has also proven effective in reducing mania and augmenting antidepressant treatment. The *atypical* or *second-generation* moniker stems from the fact that this newer breed of antipsychotics works differently than the older *standard* or *first-generation* neuroleptics, such as chlorpromazine (Thorazine) and haloperidol (Haldol). Table 7-3 lists the most common atypical antipsychotics used to treat bipolar and their benefits and potential side effects.

Paliperidone (Invega) and iloperidone (Fanapt) are two additional antipsychotics that don't have indications for use in bipolar disorder. Invega is indicated for use in treating schizophrenia and schizoaffective disorder, and iloperdione is indicated only for use in schizophrenia. Given that they're in the same family, some prescribers may use these medications in bipolar disorder. They carry the same overall side effect risks as other atypical antipsychotics presented in Table 7-3.

Second-generation antipsychotics share the following possible side effects:

✔ Sugar metabolism problems and increased risk of developing type 2 diabetes (The FDA requires atypical antipsychotic medications to include a label warning for people at risk for hyperglycemia and diabetes.)

✔ Weight gain and increases in cholesterol and other fats

✔ Reversible movement problems, similar to those associated with Parkinson's disease (tremors and stiffness), which go away when the dose is decreased or the medicine is stopped

✔ Irreversible uncontrolled movements called *tardive dyskinesia* (facial twitches or uncontrolled movements of the tongue, lips, arms, and so on), which usually don't go away when the medicine is stopped

✔ *Akathisia,* a feeling of extreme restlessness, commonly described as the overwhelming desire to jump out of your skin

✔ Changes in cardiac rhythms

Table 7-3		Potential Benefits and Side Effects of Atypical Antipsychotics		
Generic Name	Brand Name	Average Adult Dose	Potential Benefits	Some Possible Side Effects*
Aripiprazole	Abilify (also available in quick-dissolving tablets and long-lasting injectable)	15 to 30 mg/day	Antimanic; may prevent or reduce recurrent episodes; antipsychotic.	*Akathisia* (severe restlessness); weight gain; increased blood sugar and cholesterol levels; increased risk of diabetes and heart disease; reversible movement disorders; sedation or insomnia; headache.
Asenapine	Saphris	10 to 20 mg/day	Antimanic; antipsychotic.	Weight gain; increased blood sugar and cholesterol levels; increased risk of diabetes and heart disease; reversible movement disorders; sedation or insomnia; nausea.
Lurasidone	Latuda	20 to 80 mg/day	Approved to treat bipolar depression; unknown as to whether it has benefits in mania or preventing/reducing recurrent episodes; antipsychotic.	Weight gain; increased blood sugar and cholesterol levels; akathisia; nausea; reversible movement disorders.
Olanzapine	Zyprexa Relprevv (injectable) Zydis (oral disintegrating tablet) Symbyax (a combination of olanzapine and fluoxetine); see the later discussion on antidepressants	5 to 20 mg/day	Antimanic (FDA labeled); may prevent or reduce recurrent episodes; antipsychotic. Used in combination with fluoxetine as Symbyax to treat bipolar depression (see Table 7-4).	Weight gain, increased blood sugar and cholesterol levels; increased risk of diabetes and heart disease; elevated prolactin levels; reversible movement disorders; akathisia; sedation or insomnia.

(continued)

Table 7-3 *(continued)*

Generic Name	Brand Name	Average Adult Dose	Potential Benefits	Some Possible Side Effects*
Quetiapine	Seroquel	50 to 800 mg/day	Antimanic; may prevent or reduce recurrent episodes; antipsychotic; treats bipolar depression; augmentation of antidepressants in unipolar depression.	Sedation; weight gain; increased blood sugar and cholesterol levels; increased risk of diabetes and heart disease; dry mouth; constipation.
Risperidone	Risperdal (also available in quick-dissolving tablets and long-lasting injectable)	2 to 6 mg/day for mania	Antimanic; may prevent or reduce recurrent episodes; antipsychotic.	Weight gain; increased blood sugar and cholesterol levels; increased risk of diabetes and heart disease; elevated prolactin levels; reversible movement disorders; akathisia; sedation or insomnia.
Ziprasidone	Geodon	40 to 160 mg/day split into two doses and always given with food	Antimanic; may prevent or reduce recurrent episodes; antipsychotic.	Heart rhythm changes; may need EKGs before starting and during treatment; minimal risk of weight gain; increased blood sugar and cholesterol levels; increased risk of diabetes and heart disease; reversible movement disorders; sedation.

mg/day = milligrams per day.
*Other side effects may occur that are not listed.

> ✔ Some can increase levels of the hormone prolactin, which sometimes causes breast enlargement in men and lactation or menstrual problems in women
>
> ✔ Impaired sexual function
>
> ✔ Other general side effects, including sedation, dizziness, constipation, and headaches

Clozapine (Clozaril)

Clozapine (Clozaril) is an atypical antipsychotic that psychiatrists often consider to be a medication of last resort due to its severe negative side effects. Clozapine is most commonly used for treatment-resistant schizophrenia, but it's used off-label for severe bipolar mania or psychosis that isn't responding to other treatments. Clozapine also has an *indication* (that is, licensed approval for a particular use in the United States by the FDA or in Europe by the EMA) as a treatment for "recurrent suicidal behavior," regardless of diagnosis.

Clozapine has a high risk of causing a severe reduction in white blood cells, a condition called *agranulocytosis.* People taking this medication must get their blood drawn every week for the first six months of treatment and every other week after that. Clozapine also tends to cause significant weight gain.

Typical, first-generation antipsychotics

First-generation antipsychotics include haloperidol (Haldol), perphenazine (Trilafon), molindone (Moban), and thiothixene (Navane). These medications were developed to treat schizophrenia and then expanded into use for other conditions, including bipolar disorder and agitation. The first-generation antipsychotics have fallen out of use now that newer ones are available.

One reason for the reduced use of the older antipsychotics is the higher risks they carry for triggering movement disorders, including tardive dyskinesia (often irreversible, involuntary muscle movements especially around the face and jaw). But one of the benefits that these medications have over their second-generation counterparts is that they carry a lower risk of metabolic changes associated with weight gain and diabetes.

Some large studies suggest that the older medicines are just as effective in treating schizophrenia at lower cost and without significantly more side effects than the second-generation antipsychotics. However, no systematic large studies compare the first- and second-generation antipsychotics in treating bipolar disorder. Therefore, first-generation antipsychotics are used only as a second choice for treating bipolar when the newer antipsychotics or other alternatives are ineffective or not tolerated by an individual.

Mood-boosting antidepressants

Although mania grabs all the bipolar headlines, recurrent and severe depressive episodes interfere with people's lives at least as severely as mania, and often cause more of the day-to-day devastation for people living with bipolar disorder. Depression is often the first type of mood episode to show up before any manic symptoms, and therefore antidepressants are often the first medications prescribed. But bipolar depression is different from unipolar depression. Particularly in bipolar I, antidepressants are often less effective and can cause serious negative effects, including triggering mania. Using antidepressants in bipolar depression is tricky business.

If you (or your doctor) have any suspicions that your depression is related to an underlying bipolar disorder, your depression treatment will be a complex process and will require close monitoring. See the later section "Lifting bipolar depression" for a more detailed discussion.

The following sections describe the various types of antidepressants and the specific medications that fall within these groups.

SSRIs

Serotonin is a brain chemical that helps regulate mood, anxiety, sleep/wake cycles, sexual behaviors, and many other brain and body functions. *Selective Serotonin Reuptake Inhibitors (SSRIs)* increase the level of serotonin in the *synapses* — the spaces between brain cells *(neurons)* — in the brain. However, the mechanisms of action of SSRIs are more complex than simply increasing serotonin levels. Understanding of the circuits in the brain that regulate mood is still limited, but ongoing research will reveal more over time. Table 7-4 lists the most common SSRIs along with their potential pros and cons. The table also includes olanzapine fluoxetine combination (Symbyax), which is a combination medication that includes the atypical antipsychotic olanzapine and the antidepressant fluoxetine. This medicine was specifically formulated to treat bipolar depression.

SSRIs may take several weeks to become fully effective, so keep taking the medication even if you don't experience immediate relief.

SNRIs

Selective Serotonin and Norepinephrine Reuptake Inhibitors (SNRIs) increase the levels of two brain chemicals — serotonin and norepinephrine — in the synapses between brain cells. As with SSRIs, the full mechanism of action of SNRIs is poorly understood. But researchers know that, like serotonin, norepinephrine plays an important role in regulating mood and anxiety. It also contributes to regulating alertness and concentration. Check out Table 7-5 for a list of the most common SNRIs available and the potential side effects for each one.

Table 7-4 **Potential Benefits and Side Effects of SSRIs**

Generic Name	Brand Name	Average Adult Dose	Potential Benefits	Some Possible Side Effects*
Citalopram	Celexa	20 to 40 mg/day	Antidepressant (approved for treatment of unipolar depression). Not approved but often prescribed for use in bipolar depression. Also used to treat many anxiety disorders but can present challenges in someone with bipolar disorder.	Suicidal ideation; insomnia; sedation; agitation; mania; change in sexual function; nausea or diarrhea; weight gain; night sweats.
Escitalopram	Lexapro	10 to 20 mg/day; sometimes more		
Fluoxetine	Prozac	20 to 60 mg/day		
Fluvoxamine	Luvox Luvox CR	50 to 300 mg/day		
Paroxetine	Paxil Paxil CR	10 to 60 mg/day; sometimes more		
Sertraline	Zoloft	50 to 200 mg/day		
Olanzapine + fluoxetine	Symbyax (Zyprexa + Prozac)	3/25 to 18/75 (Tablets are labeled with the olanzapine dose on top and the fluoxetine dose on the bottom, so a Symbyax 3/25 tablet contains 3 mg of olanzapine and 25 mg of fluoxetine.)	Treats bipolar depression.	Weight gain; increased blood sugar and cholesterol levels; akathisia; sedation or insomnia; reversible movement disorders; suicidal ideation; nausea/ diarrhea.

mg/day = milligrams per day.
*Other side effects may occur that aren't listed.

Table 7-5		Potential Benefits and Side Effects of SNRIs		
Generic Name	Brand Name	Average Adult Dose	Potential Benefits	Some Possible Side Effects*
Desvenlafaxine	Pristiq	50 to 100 mg/day	Antidepressant (approved for use in unipolar depression). Also used to treat many anxiety disorders, but this can present challenges in someone with bipolar disorder.	Suicidal ideation; agitation; disinhibition; mania; insomnia; sedation; elevated blood pressure; change in sexual function; nausea or diarrhea; weight gain.
Duloxetine	Cymbalta	60 to 120 mg/day	Antidepressant (approved for use in unipolar depression). Also used to treat many anxiety disorders, but this can present challenges in someone with bipolar disorder. Treats some pain syndromes.	Suicidal ideation; agitation; disinhibition; mania; insomnia; sedation; elevated blood pressure; change in sexual function; nausea or diarrhea; weight gain; affects the liver, so alcohol intake should be limited.
Venlafaxine	Effexor Effexor XR	75 to 375 mg/day; 75 to 225 mg/day (extended release)	Antidepressant (approved for use in unipolar depression). Also used to treat many anxiety disorders, but this can present challenges in someone with bipolar disorder.	Suicidal ideation; agitation; disinhibition; mania; insomnia; sedation; elevated blood pressure; change in sexual function; nausea or diarrhea; weight gain; has severe withdrawal symptoms with missed doses.

mg/day = milligrams per day.
*Other side effects may occur that aren't listed.

SNRIs may take several weeks to become fully effective, so keep taking the medication even if you don't experience immediate relief.

Other serotonin-related antidepressants

Table 7-6 lists several other antidepressants that also affect serotonin but differ structurally from the SSRIs and SNRIs. Two of the medications in the table are used commonly as sleep aids because they're so sedating, and some affect other neurotransmitters as well (see Chapter 2 for info on neurotransmitters).

Bupropion (Wellbutrin)

Marketed as the antidepressant Wellbutrin and the smoking cessation product Zyban, bupropion increases the levels of dopamine and norepinephrine in the brain synapses (see Chapter 2). It has an unknown mechanism of action but is clearly different from antidepressants in other classes, such as SSRIs, SNRIs, and tricyclics (we describe them in the next section); therefore, bupropion belongs in its own category. It's sometimes used off label to treat ADHD, sexual dysfunction from SSRI/SNRI, and weight gain from other medications, and possibly ADHD. Table 7-7 lists the potential pros and cons for this popular medication.

Tricyclics and MAOIs

Tricyclics and *monoamine oxidase inhibitors* (MAO inhibitors or MAOIs) are older classes of medications that work differently from the antidepressants discussed previously and even differently from one another. These meds are used much less often than many of the other treatments for bipolar that we describe in this chapter because the side effects of tricyclics and MAOIs can be difficult to manage:

- ✔ **Tricyclics:** Tricyclics affect norepinephrine and serotonin levels primarily, but they also touch a number of other brain chemicals, including histamine. These "extra" chemical events cause many side effects, which may include sedation, dry mouth, constipation, and dizziness, as well as cardiac rhythm changes.

- ✔ **Monoamine oxidase inhibitors:** MAOIs prevent the action of an enzyme that breaks down norepinephrine, serotonin, dopamine, and a number of related brain chemicals, which increases the levels of these chemicals in the brain. People taking MAOIs are restricted from eating certain foods, including but not limited to aged meats and cheeses and certain types of beans, to prevent a dangerous spike in blood pressure. MAOIs can also have severe interactions with many other meds and, in particular, are very dangerous with SSRIs and SNRIs. If you're changing to or from MAOIs to an SSRI or SNRI, you must have a complete two-week washout of one medication before starting the other. When changing from fluoxetine to an MAOI, the washout period between medicines should be five weeks.

Table 7-6			Potential Benefits and Side Effects of Other Serotonin-Related Antidepressants	
Generic Name	Brand Name	Average Adult Dose	Potential Benefits	Some Possible Side Effects*
Mirtazapine	Remeron	15 to 25 mg/day	Antidepressant (approved for use in unipolar depression); very sedating (often used as a sleep aid).	Suicidal ideation; agitation; disinhibition; mania; sedation; weight gain; dry mouth; increased cholesterol.
Nefazodone	Serzone	300 to 600 mg/day	Antidepressant (approved for use in unipolar depression); antianxiety.	Suicidal ideation; agitation; disinhibition; mania; liver abnormalities (liver function should be monitored); sedation; insomnia; headache; dry mouth; constipation; muscle weakness; sexual dysfunction.
Trazodone	Desyrel	150 to 600 mg/day	Antidepressant (approved for use in unipolar depression); sedative (often used as a sleep aid).	Suicidal ideation; agitation; disinhibition; mania; sedation; dry mouth; headache; dizziness and nausea; sexual dysfunction; *priapism* (an erection that doesn't stop, which can be a medical emergency).
Vilazodone	Viibryd	20 to 40 mg/day	Antidepressant (approved for use in unipolar depression).	Suicidal ideation; agitation; disinhibition; mania; belly and gastrointestinal problems; sexual dysfunction.
Vortioxetin	Brintellix	5 to 20 mg/day	Antidepressant (approved for use in unipolar depression).	Suicidal ideation; agitation; mania; nausea; sexual dysfunction.

mg/day = milligrams per day;
*Other side effects may occur that aren't listed.

Table 7-7   Potential Benefits and Side Effects of Bupropion (Wellbutrin)

Generic Name	Brand Name	Average Adult Dose	Potential Benefits	Some Possible Side Effects*
Bupropion	Wellbutrin	20 to 450 mg/day	Antidepressant (approved for treating unipolar depression); reduces cravings for nicotine; no sexual side effects; may improve attention and focus; does not cause weight gain.	Suicidal ideation; agitation; disinhibition; mania; jitteriness; insomnia; anxiety; decreased appetite; weight loss; seizure; can't be used in people with current or previous eating disorders or seizures.
	Wellbutrin SR	150 to 400 mg/day		
	Wellbutrin XL	300 to 450 mg/day		
	Zyban (for smoking cessation)			

mg/day = milligrams per day.
*Other side effects may occur that aren't listed.

Calming anxiolytics and sleep agents

Anxiety and sleeplessness often accompany bipolar disorder. If you don't address them effectively in treatment, they can worsen mood episodes and other bipolar symptoms. To help you calm down and get some sleep, your psychiatrist may prescribe one or more antianxiety medications or sleep aids, which we describe in this section.

SSRIs or SNRIs are powerful antianxiety medications and are the first line of treatment for anxiety for many people. But given the risks of agitation or mania that accompany these meds, they can be hazardous for people with comorbid bipolar disorder. Still, this class of medications is important and offers primary treatment for anxiety either alone or in combination with other meds, depending on your particular situation and symptoms. See the earlier sections "SSRIs" and "SNRIs" for details.

Benzodiazepines

The most commonly used purely antianxiety meds are *benzodiazepines* (also known as *anxiolytics* or *tranquilizers,* or *benzos* for short). These medications slow down the whole nervous system, thus reducing agitation and anxiety levels, both of which can be problems in bipolar disorder. Benzos appear to affect a brain chemical called *GABA (gamma-aminobutyric acid),* which has a calming effect on neurons. For many people, just knowing they can take a medication to stop a panic episode helps reduce the secondary fear of having an episode. These medications can also be used as sleep aids when taken at night. Table 7-8 lists the pros and cons of benzos.

Table 7-8		Potential Benefits and Side Effects of Benzodiazepines			
Generic Name	*Brand Name*	*Average Adult Dose*	*Duration (hours)*	*Potential Benefits*	*Some Possible Side Effects**
Alprazolam	Xanax Xanax XR	0.75 to 4 mg/day divided into several doses; 0.5 to 10 mg/day (XR)	4 to 6	Antianxiety; sedation	Severe sedation; dependence/addiction; lethal combination with alcohol; may reduce ability to drive or complete tasks
Clonazepam	Klonopin	1.5 to 4 mg/day divided into several doses	10 to 12	Antianxiety; sedation	
Diazepam	Valium	4 to 40 mg/day divided into several doses	10 to 12	Antianxiety; sedation; anticonvulsant; reduces muscle spasms.	
Lorazepam	Ativan	1 to 10 mg/day divided into several doses	6 to 8		

mg/day = milligrams per day; other side effects may occur that are not listed.

Benzodiazepines are often useful at the beginning of treatment because they take effect much faster than other medications — within 20 to 30 minutes. They provide immediate relief during the two to six weeks or more you're waiting for another medication such as an SSRI to take effect. But as soon as the SSRI takes effect, your doctor may wean you off the benzo.

In choosing a specific benzodiazepine, your doctor considers a wide range of issues related to your condition. Check out the section "Selecting the best medications for you," later in this chapter, for details. With benzos in particular, some options are better tolerated with certain antidepressants or antipsychotics than others because the two types of medicines are metabolized by the same enzymes in your body.

Approach benzodiazepines cautiously. If the dose is too high, benzos can shut down various brain functions, causing severe sedation and stupor and eventually slowing a person's breathing, which can be fatal. Also, benzos work on the same receptors that alcohol affects, so combining benzos and alcohol vastly increases the risk of a serious central nervous system shutdown. Another big problem with these meds is the potential for addiction and dependence: The body eventually becomes dependent on benzos and then requires ever-increasing doses. Careful monitoring of dose and use of these medications is important.

Other antianxiety medications

Several less commonly prescribed antianxiety medications include buspirone, pregabalin, and gabapentin, which aren't considered tranquilizers:

✔ **Buspirone (Buspar):** This medication affects serotonin, like an SSRI, but seems to work directly at the receptor rather than affecting re-uptake. Also like an SSRI, buspirone takes time to build up in the bloodstream to have its intended effect. Like benzos, this medication is used specifically for anxiety and has no known antidepressant effect, but unlike benzos, it doesn't have any potential for addiction.

Dosing for buspirone ranges from 20 to 60 mg per day, split into two doses. Many prescribers find minimal benefit with buspirone alone, so they often prescribe it as an add-on to other medicines. Buspirone can be a good option for people with a history of alcoholism or abuse of benzodiazepines, but its effectiveness is inconsistent.

✔ **Pregabalin (Lyrica):** This medication is approved for the treatment of several types of pain syndromes and as an add-on agent for treating seizures. Although it's not currently formally approved for treating anxiety, several studies have shown it to be helpful in treating some anxiety disorders. Side effects may include dizziness, sedation, tremors, and weight gain.

✔ **Gabapentin (Neurontin):** This antiseizure medication is also used to treat some pain syndromes. Some studies have looked at its use in anxiety, but the results have been inconsistent. However, it's used sometimes in people with anxiety who aren't responding to more traditional medications, such as SSRIs, especially if using benzos because of addiction risk is a concern.

Sleep aids

Doctors commonly prescribe sleep aids for the short-term treatment of insomnia, which is often associated with depression and mania. The benzodiazepines listed in the previous section are often used to help with sleep, but a number of sedative hypnotic medications similar to benzos are used exclusively for insomnia and aren't used to treat anxiety. These medications aren't usually combined with benzos because the combined sedative effects can be dangerous. Like benzos, these sedative hypnotic agents carry risks of addiction and dependence. Table 7-9 lists the pros and cons of some common sleep aids.

In addition to the benzos and sedative hypnotics, doctors use a variety of other medications to reduce insomnia, especially if they're concerned about issues of dependence and addiction. The antidepressants trazodone, amitriptyline, and mirtazapine are often used in low doses for sleep because they're extremely sedating (see the prior section on antidepressants for more details). One antidepressant, doxepin, has been repackaged, in low doses, as a sleep aid called Silenor, and the FDA formally approved it to treat insomnia. Antihistamines, medications that are used to treat allergies such as diphenhydramine (Benadryl), are also used to treat insomnia because of their extremely sedating side effects.

Table 7-9		Potential Benefits and Side Effects of Sleep Aids		
Generic Name	*Brand Name*	*Average Adult Dose*	*Potential Benefits*	*Some Possible Side Effects**
Nonbenzodiazepine sleep aids				
Eszopiclone	Lunesta	1 to 3 mg	Improved ability to sleep.	Dependence; headache; unpleasant taste; grogginess or hangover effect the next day.
Zaleplon	Sonata	5 to 10 mg/day	Improved ability to sleep; short acting so it can be taken in the middle of the night if waking is a problem.	Dependence; grogginess or hangover effect the next day.
Zolpidem	Ambien Ambien CR	5 to 10 mg/day for Ambien 6.25 to 12.5 mg/day for Ambien CR	Improved ability to sleep.	Dependence; odd or dangerous behaviors while sleeping, including sleepeating, sleepwalking, and sleepdriving; memory loss; grogginess or hangover effect the next day.
Benzodiazepine Sleep Aids				
Flurazepam	Dalmane	15 to 30 mg/day	Improved ability to sleep.	Dependence/addiction; sedation; dizziness; respiratory suppression at high doses or when combined with alcohol; grogginess or hangover effect the next day.
Temazepam	Restoril	7.5 to 30 mg/day	Improved ability to sleep.	

mg/day = milligrams per day.
**Other side effects may occur that aren't listed.*

A brand new medication on the market called suvorexant (Belsomra) works completely differently than the benzos and related medications. This medication blocks the binding of orexin to its receptors in the brain. *Orexin* is a group of proteins in the brain that promotes wakefulness. Blocking it helps to discourage being awake, therefore allowing sedation to occur. All other medications used to treat insomnia work by increasing sedation, rather than decreasing wakefulness. It remains to be seen how well this medicine will work with large numbers of people and what the most common side effects will be, because it has only been used in studies and is just coming on the market in mid-2015.

Another sleep aid you may want to discuss with your doctor is ramelteon (Rozerem), which may be useful for people who've experienced addiction to benzos. It works through the melatonin system. *Melatonin* is a chemical that the brain releases in response to changing light at the end of the day. It doesn't carry risks of dependence and addiction and therefore isn't a controlled substance like most other prescription sleep medications. It won't make you feel groggy the next day and is safe to use with many prescribed medications. But it may not be safe for individuals who have a history of kidney or respiratory problems, sleep apnea, or depression, or for women who are pregnant or breast-feeding. Ramelteon may interact with alcohol, and high-fat meals may slow the absorption of the medication.

Exploring Bipolar Psychopharmacology

Psychopharmacology is the use of *psychotropic medications* (any prescription meds that affect mood, emotion, behavior, or perception) to treat mental illness. In the case of bipolar, psychopharmacology has four primary goals:

- ✔ Alleviate acute manic symptoms
- ✔ Ease depressive symptoms
- ✔ Eliminate or lessen any psychosis
- ✔ Maintain mood stability and reduce the likelihood or frequency of future mood episodes

The treatment goals are clear, but psychiatrists sometimes have trouble meeting these goals for the following reasons:

- ✔ **Symptoms vary dramatically.** Depending on the *pole* of the episode — whether it's primarily depressive or primarily manic — the symptoms being treated aren't just different, but they're almost mirror images. When treating bipolar disorder, doctors must target individual poles *and* broader illness itself (the fact that cycles re-occur).

- ✔ **Symptoms change over time.** Someone experiencing a manic episode may quickly begin to experience depression or vice versa. Target symptoms can seem hard to pin down.

- ✔ **Some episodes can have mixed features.** Although someone may be experiencing primarily manic symptoms, she may also experience hopelessness or other depressive symptoms; people in a bipolar depression may be quite agitated and irritable. These mixed features further complicate treatment planning.

- ✔ **Symptom stories differ from person to person.** One person's mania may be primarily irritable whereas another person may seem quite euphoric. Sometimes depression presents with a lot of irritability.

✔ **Other conditions may impact diagnosis and treatment.** An individual may have bipolar disorder coupled with anxiety or substance use disorder, for example. Having a coexisting condition may affect how the bipolar disorder presents and progresses. Treatment for each of these conditions can interact, causing negative physical responses or making treatment ineffective.

✔ **Effectiveness and side effects differ for each individual.** A medication that works for one person may have no effect or the opposite effect on another. One individual may feel fine taking a particular medication, whereas another may feel groggy or gain weight.

✔ **Medications can worsen symptoms.** For example, some antidepressants can induce mania or increase anxiety or agitation in certain individuals.

✔ **Medications can interact with each other.** Treatment often requires the use of two or more medications at the same time, which can affect the efficacy or side effects of either or both medications. See the later section "Juggling meds for comorbid conditions" for more on this complex topic.

In this section, we explain how to work with your prescriber to select the best medications for you and effectively manage your meds.

Selecting the best medications for you

When your doctor is deciding which medication(s) to prescribe, he considers numerous factors, including the following:

✔ **Current symptoms:** If you're experiencing acute mania, for example, your doctor may withdraw any antidepressant and prescribe one or more first-line antimanic medications, such as lithium or olanzapine, which act quicker than lithium. When treating acute depression, your doctor may start by prescribing an antimanic that has antidepressant properties, such as lithium or quetiapine and maybe layer an antidepressant on top.

✔ **Medications you're already taking:** If you're already taking medications to treat symptoms for bipolar or a different condition, your doctor may check the dosage or (for some meds) the level of the medication in your bloodstream, adjust the dosage, and add another medication to supplement the one you're currently taking or prescribe a different medication entirely.

✔ **Response to previous medications and treatments:** If you've tried certain medications in the past and found that they were ineffective or produced intolerable side effects, then your doctor is likely to avoid those options this time around.

✔ **Risk of relapse or shift to the opposite pole:** When adding or withdrawing a medication or adjusting dosage, your doctor considers whether the change may trigger the onset of depression or mania or other emotional/behavioral side effects.

✔ **Side effects and other health risks:** All medications have side effects, and some meds are known to contribute to other health problems. Your doctor can help you evaluate side effect profiles for different medications and avoid certain options If he thinks the risk of developing other serious health issues is too high.

✔ **Gender and age:** Gender is a major factor in choosing the right meds, especially in women of childbearing age or those who are pregnant or breast-feeding. Doctors also give special consideration to older patients who may be at a higher risk for cognitive side effects or are more likely to have other health issues. (See Chapter 10 for details on treatment considerations for women and other specific populations.)

✔ **Patient preference:** As you discuss medications and their possible side effects with your doctor, do your own cost-benefit analysis and provide your doctor with input.

✔ **Cost:** Depending on your health insurance coverage, different meds may have very different costs to you. Your doctor may not know this, and you may need to do some research on your own to find out. Don't be embarrassed to talk to your doctor about medication costs. You can sometimes save a significant amount of money with a simple change (like choosing a generic over a brand name).

We encourage you to work closely with your doctor whenever you consider treatment options, including medications. If you think a particular medication may be effective, ask your doctor about it. If you're not comfortable with the potential side effects of a medication being prescribed, say so.

If a family member has bipolar disorder and is responding well to a particular medication or combination, the same medication(s) may work well for you. This is particularly true for lithium, because research suggests that a specific subgroup of people with strong family histories of bipolar have a higher likelihood of excellent response to lithium.

Knowing what to expect

When your doctor prescribes a certain medication, the assumption is that it'll work — it'll treat the symptoms that brought you to the doctor in the first place. If your doctor offers little more information than that, ask some questions, including the following:

✔ What is the medication likely to do?

✔ When can I expect to notice an improvement?

✔ What are the possible side effects? (For tips on managing side effects, see Chapter 8.)

✔ What side effects need immediate medical attention?

✔ What should I do if I miss a dose?

✔ Should I avoid mixing any other medications or substances with this?

The more you understand about your medications, the better equipped you are to truly partner with your doctor to find effective medications with side effects that you can tolerate.

Testing for med levels and health issues

Many medications require regular medical tests to ensure that they meet but don't exceed their recommended therapeutic levels (the levels at which they work) and that they're not causing any other medical problems. Common tests include the following:

✔ **Blood levels:** To test the concentration of the medicine in your blood

✔ **EKGs (electrocardiograms):** To monitor heart rhythms and evaluate for evidence of heart disease

✔ **Thyroid function:** To ensure your thyroid gland is working properly

✔ **Liver function:** To ensure that your liver is functioning properly

✔ **Blood sugar and insulin levels:** To make sure your blood sugar levels are where they should be, especially if you're taking a second-generation antipsychotic medication (see Chapter 8 for details)

Note: Throughout this chapter, we don't mention the tests required for specific meds unless a medication has a unique side effect that generates significant concern. Ask your doctor if tests are required for any of the medications you're currently taking or considering.

Mixing your pharmaceutical cocktail

The key to finding the right medication or combination of meds is to remain persistent and in regular communication with your doctor. By providing detailed feedback about how you're feeling and whether you've noticed any changes in your routine or behaviors, you can help your doctor more expertly mix a pharmaceutical "cocktail" that's both safe and effective for you. (Chapter 11 features a mood chart designed specifically for this purpose.)

Finding the right medication: An ongoing journey

I was diagnosed with bipolar disorder in 1997 when I was 12 years old. I spent time in the children's psychiatric hospital while doctors tried to find medications that would stabilize me. Being diagnosed with bipolar disorder at such a young age was rare at the time, making it much more difficult to find the right medication. All I wanted was to go to school and play sports on the weekends just like my two siblings! I wanted to be like other kids my age.

I was too young to understand what bipolar disorder was, but I did understand that I needed to find medication that would make recovery possible. It took a long time — three years — to find a combination that worked for me. And the process was like searching for a needle in a haystack. But it was, indeed, a journey to find stability in my life. At the age of 15, I became well enough to go back to school; a year later, I was in college.

Now, at the age of 30, I still need to change my medication from time to time. My moods often cycle with the seasons. So my journey to find the right medication is a road I keep walking. When the road becomes a bit bumpy, my psychiatrist and I make little changes. When you're first diagnosed with bipolar disorder, it can feel as if you'll never find the right medication, but it just takes time.

— Natalie Jeanne Champagne, an advocate for mental health and author of *The Third Sunrise: A Memoir of Madness*

Practicing safety first

Always make sure that any medication you add to your regimen is safe to use with any medications you're already taking, including over-the-counter remedies and "natural" or herbal supplements. Most prescription medicines include a list of *contraindications* (advisories against using a particular medication if you have a certain medical condition) and drug interactions, which your doctor uses to determine one of the following degrees of safety:

- **Dangerous:** Some combos can be toxic. For example, never combine an MAOI with an SSRI.

- **Very risky:** Some combinations may be dangerous to some people, but the potential benefits outweigh the risks. For example, taking lithium with some diuretics or older antipsychotics is risky but may improve symptoms for some individuals.

- **Risky:** A combo with minimal risk may be reasonable when the potential benefits outweigh the risks. For example, mixing valproate and lamotrigine is risky, but this can be an effective mix if it's well managed.

- **Safe but with possible changes in medication effectiveness:** Some medications may change the effectiveness of other medications.

- **Safe:** Frequently, two medications have a very low risk of negatively interacting with one another, making them safe to combine.

Consult your doctor if you have any questions about the effectiveness or safety of a medication or combination. Inform your doctor of any meds, supplements, herbs, or natural remedies you're currently taking. If you're seeing several different doctors for different conditions, make sure they all know which medications you take. Communication among your prescribers may be important at certain times, and you can ask one doctor to contact another if you think it'll help in managing medications.

Taking a gradual, systematic approach

Few psychotropic medications act as quickly as aspirin. And your doctor may gradually ramp up your dosage over time to reduce the occurrence of some side effects, even though the medicine itself may take several weeks to achieve full effectiveness. Furthermore, whenever you add a medication to the mix, you and your doctor need some time to observe the effects, side effects, and interactions. Under psychological distress, your patience may be strained, but following a steady course is critical.

Because so much can change with each medication adjustment, we strongly recommend that you make changes in only one medicine at a time. Such patience isn't always possible — particularly in emergencies — but when you have the time, a systematic, scientific approach can reduce the number of variables at play and make it easier to track down the cause of any specific side effect or benefit. If you introduce two or more new meds at the same time and experience a negative side effect or a great benefit, you may not be able to tell which medication is causing it.

Staying abreast of the changes

Over the course of your life, your brain physiology and chemistry change, your symptoms change, and your environment and relationships change. To remain in sync with these changes, check in with your doctor regularly, even when you're feeling fine, to determine whether you can make any of the following adjustments:

- Change a medication dosage to reduce any undesirable side effects
- Change dosage or switch a med to address a new or nagging symptom
- Eliminate or reduce a medication to minimize long-term risks

A common trap is to start taking a combination of meds during a period of crisis and then continue on the same regimen after you resolve the crisis. During a period of stability, ask your doctor when it's reasonable to consider scaling back or eliminating some of your meds. Most people with bipolar require some medication throughout their lives, but you and your doctor should seize any opportunity to strip away unnecessary layers of medication.

Juggling meds for comorbid conditions

As you weave your way through the brambles of bipolar, you're likely to pick up a few burrs — diagnoses of comorbid conditions. *Comorbid* is a fancy word for any psychiatric or medical condition that accompanies another diagnosis. Of course, the bipolar category already assumes two coexisting conditions — depression and mania or hypomania; comorbidity doesn't apply to that. It applies to other distinct illnesses, such as the following:

- **Attention deficit hyperactivity disorder (ADHD):** This disorder can coexist with bipolar, sharing symptoms such as hyperactivity and impulsivity. Amphetamines often treat ADHD effectively but can jump-start mania or psychosis in people with bipolar. Certain antidepressants may be effective in treating ADHD, but you need to use both stimulants and antidepressants with care when bipolar is also in the picture.

- **Anxiety disorders (panic, obsessive-compulsive disorder, generalized anxiety, or social anxiety):** These disorders show up in about 25 percent (or more) of people with bipolar. Some medications used for bipolar (such as the second-generation antipsychotics) can reduce anxiety, but they may not be adequate and the anxiety may shut you down and prevent a return to daily life. SSRI antidepressants reduce anxiety and OCD symptoms in many cases, but they may not be safe to use without an antimanic agent. Benzodiazepines, such as clonazepam, may be quite useful for anxiety, but they carry risks of sedating you and requiring higher doses over time to get the same effect. Benzos can also lead to dependency and addiction.

- **Substance use disorder:** Substance use disorder, particularly alcoholism, occurs in one-third to one-half of people with bipolar disorder. Many bipolar meds, including lithium, are dangerous with alcohol. Benzos, such as diazepam, are chemically similar to alcohol, and people with alcoholism are more likely to become addicted to them. In combination, alcohol and benzodiazepines can cause death.

- **Memory and thinking problems:** Cognitive problems commonly accompany bipolar disorder. Adding insult to injury, some of the meds used for bipolar can cloud your thinking. Of course, depression and mania can cloud thinking, too, so treating them effectively often helps these issues. Lithium, in particular, may protect brain cells over time and may prevent or reduce cognitive decline. Work with your doctors to find a medication combination and dosage level that can stabilize your mood without clouding your thinking.

- **Personality disorders:** Disorders such as borderline personality disorder or narcissistic personality disorder may coexist with bipolar. This layering of conditions increases the likelihood of impaired function between mood episodes, and it complicates recovery. Personality disorders typically respond poorly to meds and can actually work against them. Psychotherapy is crucial to managing these issues (see Chapter 11 for details on therapy).

Treating Mood Episodes and Preventing Future Episodes

Treatment for bipolar disorder involves managing manic and depressive episodes and trying to prevent future episodes. The following sections give you an idea about how a doctor approaches each challenge. In this section, we focus on bipolar I, the classic form of bipolar, which involves alternating periods of mania and depression. (For more about the different types of bipolar disorder, turn to Chapter 1.)

Muffling mania

Full-blown mania is a medical emergency. Often, especially during the first episode, hospitalization is necessary. The medical interventions often include

✔ Starting lithium along with an atypical antipsychotic, such as olanzapine

✔ Adding an anticonvulsant, such as valproate, if the lithium and atypical antipsychotic aren't effective

✔ Changing the antipsychotic if it's not effective or if the side effects aren't tolerated

✔ Trying other medication combinations, with the core combination usually being a mood stabilizer, such a lithium or an anticonvulsant, plus an antipsychotic

Whatever medication combination is used often takes some time to work — a week to ten days at least, sometimes longer. Figuring out the best medication or combination of medications for a specific individual may add to the recovery time. Numerous medication combinations are possible and finding the combination that produces the best results requires close collaboration between patient and doctor.

Lifting bipolar depression

Bipolar depression looks like unipolar depression; the same diagnostic criteria are used to identify both types of depression. But the two conditions are different and they respond differently to treatment. (Refer to Chapter 1 for a comparison of unipolar and bipolar depression.) The routine treatment of unipolar depression includes antidepressants such as the SSRIs, but they often work less effectively and/or cause serious negative effects in bipolar depression, particularly in bipolar I.

Right now the FDA has approved only three medicines specifically for bipolar depression:

- ✔ Olanzapine/fluoxetine combination (Symbyax)
- ✔ Quetiapine (Serqouel)
- ✔ Lurasidone (Latuda)

These are all in the atypical antipsychotic family, carrying the significant risks of those medications — in particular, risks of weight gain and metabolic changes that increase risks of diabetes and heart disease. Often, doctors try to find other combinations that may work, such as:

- ✔ Lithium alone or lithium plus lamotrigine (Lamictal)
- ✔ Careful doses of antidepressants plus lithium or plus an anticonvulsant such as valproate or lamotrigine

The option of an antidepressant plus an antipsychotic is also common — basically similar to Symbyax. Combining an antidepressant and antipsychotic still exposes you to the side effects of the antipsychotic, but you may be able to take less of the antipsychotic, reducing the overall risk. Some of the antipsychotics, such as quetiapine and olanzapine, are better studied and have better effects in bipolar depression.

Many potential medication combinations can be tried, so working closely with your prescriber is critical in arriving at what's best for you.

Keeping mania and depression at bay: Maintenance treatment

The most common plan for *maintenance* — prevention of future mood episodes — is to continue what worked for you during the acute episode. However, one goal is usually to peel away some medications and, if possible, find a single medicine (a *monotherapy*) that can effectively do this for you. Some of the most common monotherapies for bipolar disorder include lithium, valproate, quetiaepine, olanzapine, aripiprazole, and lamotrigine.

Although the ultimate goal is monotherapy, many people continue to need a combination of medications for maintenance, because one medication alone is insufficient, fails to treat all symptoms, or produces side effects that must be addressed with another medication. Avoiding long-term use of antidepressants for maintenance in bipolar I disorder is generally considered best. Maintenance treatment for bipolar II may be slightly different; the research is less clear.

Treatment-resistant bipolar disorder

The term *treatment resistant* is used to describe situations in which two to three of the standard medications or combinations have been tried for long enough and at high enough doses, but the symptoms aren't *remitting* (going away). When this happens, doctor and patient usually discuss some of the most common reasons that treatments aren't working as well as expected, which include the following:

- **Not taking the medication regularly or correctly:** The most common reason a prescribed medication doesn't work as effectively as expected is that the person stops taking it, takes less of it, or takes it less often than prescribed. Communication with your doctor is essential; if you're not comfortable with your medications, talk to your prescriber to address your concerns. (See Chapter 8 to find out more about dealing with medication issues.)

- **Incomplete diagnosis:** Maybe something else is going on medically and/or psychiatrically that is causing the symptoms. Going back to the drawing board diagnostically, getting a second opinion, and involving a neurologist or other specialist are some common ways of approaching this problem.

- **Substance use disorder:** Using alcohol, marijuana, or other drugs actively while trying to find medications to treat bipolar disorder can interfere with the success of the treatment. Even something simple like excessive caffeine use can be a problem.

- **Genetic differences:** People differ in how their bodies respond to medication and how their bodies break down and eliminate the medicine. For example, some people may be *rapid metabolizers* of certain medicines because of the genetics of particular liver enzymes that break down the medicine, so they may have trouble keeping a high enough concentration of the prescribed medication in their blood. Or a very slow metabolizer may have a high risk of side effects even at low doses. (This type of metabolism has nothing to do with your metabolism of food.) Some easy genetic tests can look at some of these possibilities and may help in making decisions about medications in treatment-resistant situations. These tests aren't standard yet, but they'll be used more and more in the future.

- **Differences in the presentation of bipolar disorder:** Chapter 2 discusses the brain science of bipolar disorder, pointing out that it's not really one illness but a collection of different underlying brain disorders. Likely, some forms of the illness don't respond as well to the medications that are currently available. Working carefully with your doctor and/or getting a second opinion to determine other options, including possibly adding or trying newer or less well-studied medicines or supplements, may be valuable. If you live near a medical school, you may be able to participate in a research study that provides access to medications that aren't yet widely available.

If medications aren't tolerable or as effective as desired, you and your doctor may look into other options such as electroconvulsive therapy (ECT; see Chapter 9).

Peering into the Promising Future of Bipolar Medications

The medications that are available now to treat bipolar disorder work well in many, less well in some, and not well in a few. Scientists are exploring the underlying brain and body changes that are part of bipolar disorder with a long-term goal of identifying new ways to treat it. In the following sections, we introduce and describe several medications that have shown some promise in the treatment of various aspects of bipolar disorder.

Meds that target the glutamergic pathways

One of the hottest areas of research is in the glutamate system that we discuss in more detail in Chapter 2. *Glutamate* is a neurotransmitter related to excitatory or energizing circuits in the brain. Research increasingly shows a strong correlation between glutamate systems and depression and bipolar disorder. Researchers are looking closely at three meds and a naturally occurring amino acid that affect this system, and preliminary studies show positive results:

✔ **Ketamine:** This medication is an antagonist of a particular type of glutamate receptor — N-desmethyl aspartate (NDMA). Several studies show that intravenous infusion of ketamine in people with treatment-resistant depression almost immediately reduces depressive symptoms, making it very different from all other antidepressants in use, which take time to work. How long the antidepressant effects of ketamine last is unclear, but rapid loss of the benefit over the course of one to two weeks is typical. The pattern of response to ketamine seems to be different in bipolar depression compared to unipolar depression. Ketamine has serious downsides though. For one, it's very sedating and can trigger psychotic responses and changes in perception of reality. It also has potential for abuse; it's been used as a street/club drug for many years. So while ketamine's antidepressant benefits are exciting, this medication won't be readily available for clinical use in the immediate future.

✔ **Memantine (Namenda):** This medicine helps reduce some of the symptoms of early dementia. Like ketamine, it works at the NMDA type of glutamate receptor, reducing glutamate activity there. In some preliminary studies of people with bipolar depression who haven't responded well to more traditional medications, the addition of memantine appears to have been helpful in reducing symptoms. Side effects seem to be minor so far. Further research is needed.

✔ **N-acetyl cysteine (NAC):** This amino acid has long been used to treat overdoses of acetaminophen (Tylenol). It plays many roles in the body and brain, being a part of at least two biochemical pathways that are thought to be affected in bipolar disorder. It's involved in glutamate transmission and also plays a key role in the synthesis of *glutathione* — a chemical that helps to reduce *oxidative damage* to cells. Impaired glutathione function has been found in bipolar disorder. NAC has been studied in mania and bipolar depression and has shown some promising results. Although it's an over-the-counter nutritional supplement, its use for bipolar disorder is best discussed with your prescriber to determine doses and patterns of use that would be right for you. (See Chapter 9 for more discussion.)

✔ **Riluzole (Rilutek):** This medication is currently approved to treat amyotrophic lateral sclerosis (ALS, commonly known as Lou Gehrig's disease). It modulates glutamate transmissions and enhances *neuronal plasticity* — a variety of cellular events related to the strength and development of circuits between brain cells. In some early studies, riluzole was shown to reduce symptoms in bipolar depression, but it has severe side effects, so it hasn't been considered for use outside of research.

Protein kinase C inhibitors

Researchers have started looking closely at *protein kinase C (PKC)* as a possible target in treating bipolar, particularly for mania. PKC is actually a group of *enzymes* (proteins that trigger chemical reactions in the body) that has many functions in the body. In the brain, PKC plays a vital role in coordinating and translating chemical messages from neurotransmitters on the outside of cells into particular chemical reactions inside of cells. Many studies suggest that over-activation of PKC pathways may be related to manic symptoms, and inhibiting the pathways (with PKC inhibitors) reduces mania.

Even though lithium and valproate are very different medications, they're both known to inhibit PKC activity. Exactly how reducing PKC activity reduces manic symptoms is unknown, but some working theories suggest that the process may be related to changing the excitability of neurons and/or to improving the growth and health of neurons over time.

The estrogen inhibitor tamoxifen, used in treating breast cancer, is another potent PKC inhibitor. Increasing evidence indicates that tamoxifen can be used in combination with lithium to reduce manic symptoms if other, more traditional medications aren't working for an individual. Tamoxifen isn't included in the U.S. practice guidelines at this time, but it is included in the Canadian practice guidelines. In studies that tested tamoxifen for treating acute episodes of mania, the treatment was well tolerated, but the studies didn't account for long-term risks and potential side effects of blocking estrogen receptors. These risks and side effects need to be better researched before tamoxifen can be considered a viable option for treating bipolar on a long-term basis.

Verapamil, a medicine used to treat high blood pressure, also inhibits the PKC pathway and has been researched for treating mania with mixed results. It's not considered standard treatment at this time.

Other meds worth mentioning

Here are some other medications that are still quite a way from any regular use, but they give you an idea of the wide range of research being done in this area:

- ✔ **Pramiprexole:** This medication is used to treat Parkinson's disease by increasing the effects of dopamine in the brain. Dopamine is one of the neurotransmitters (see Chapter 2) that may be involved in bipolar symptoms. Some studies have looked at this medicine for the treatment of bipolar depression that hasn't responded well to more typical medications. The results of the studies have been inconsistent; more work still needs to be done.

- ✔ **Allopurinol:** This medicine is primarily used to treat *gout* — a disease in which the body produces too much *uric acid,* which is then deposited in the joints causing severe swelling and pain. Allopurinol treats gout by reducing uric acid levels. People in a manic episode have elevated uric acid levels, so some studies have looked at adding allopurinol to other mood stabilizers to improve symptom relief. Some studies have been positive whereas others have shown no benefit so more research is needed to clarify whether allopurinol may be a valuable addition to the bipolar medicine cabinet.

✔ **Scopolamine:** Scopolamine is a popular medication on cruise ships, used primarily to treat motion sickness. It works in the *cholinergic* system (choline is another neurotransmitter), targeting a specific type of choline receptor called the *muscarinic receptor.* Some research has suggested that depression (both bipolar and unipolar) may have some roots in this system. Studies have looked at using the scopolamine *intravenously,* injecting it directly into the blood rather than taking it orally, and some evidence shows that it rapidly reduces depressive symptoms. However, the research remains incomplete, and more work needs to be done.

Chapter 8

Coming to Terms with Medications and Their Side Effects

In This Chapter

▶ Recognizing common responses to long-term medication

▶ Playing an active role in choosing the medications you take

▶ Discovering strategies to reduce unwelcome side effects

▶ Changing and stopping medications under a doctor's supervision

*F*or most people with bipolar disorder, the most effective treatment plan includes medications. It's truly amazing to witness someone in acute depression or mania enter a hospital — unable to think clearly and function normally and perhaps even hallucinating — and then see that same person able to think, speak, and interact normally after just six or seven days on effective medication.

Unfortunately, the need for medication doesn't stop when the person leaves the hospital. A maintenance dose of one or more medications is almost always needed to ward off future episodes. But when the person is feeling better, she may start to think that she doesn't need the medication to remain healthy, and perhaps she's so fed up with a certain medication side effect that she can't tolerate it any longer. Such feelings are normal and common, and they're important to recognize as part of the process of coming to terms with a chronic illness and the prospect of long-term medication.

In this chapter, we confront some prevailing reasons for not taking medications, help you assess the pros and cons of taking versus not taking your meds, offer guidance on how to alleviate the most common annoying side effects, and walk you through the process of making safer medication changes.

Facing Your Emotional Reactions

Nearly all healthcare professionals will tell you that a major challenge in treating any long-term illness is getting patients to follow their doctor's instructions and take medications as prescribed. With bipolar disorder, the challenge is compounded when patients lack *insight* (when bipolar disorder, especially mania, convinces them that absolutely nothing is wrong).

Acknowledging the common objections to long-term medication and realizing that resistance is normal are important first steps toward treatment success for people with bipolar. Understanding the resistance can also comfort friends and family who often become exasperated by their loved one's lack of medication *compliance* (following doctor's orders).

Examining objections to taking meds

People often have valid and reasonable reasons for not wanting to take or continue their medication. Here we explore some of the most common reasons that people with bipolar stop taking their meds, as well as different perspectives to consider as you engage in your own internal debate over the pros and cons of medication.

I'm not sick

Denying that anything is wrong is actually a common symptom of bipolar disorder, making treatment especially difficult, particularly in the early stages of illness. When you're manic, in particular, your brain is distorting thinking, perception, and mood. You feel like everything is fine — in fact, more than fine — you feel the best you've ever felt. You feel like you know things, special things, that other people don't know. Given that this is how you're thinking, why would you listen to people who are telling you something is terribly wrong? A core paradox of bipolar disorder that being unaware of the illness, lacking *insight,* is a key symptom and gets in the way of starting and sticking with medications.

Although depressive episodes don't make you feel so good and all-knowing, they often have profound thoughts of hopelessness, guilt, and self-loathing that convince you not to take medicine because you'll never get well or because you don't deserve to get well, for example. And if psychosis accompanies the depression, your thinking becomes even more disorganized and disconnected from reality, and decision-making about medications gets caught up in the illness itself.

However, even as your mind comes back to itself, and you can think more clearly again, denial is a powerful initial response to serious illness of all kinds, and mental illness is no exception. In fact, mental illness is particularly vulnerable to this type of thinking. As members of the National Alliance on Mental Illness (NAMI) often remind themselves, everyone passes through several emotional stages when dealing with mental illness; the first stage is denial. And when you're in denial, the last thing you want to do is pop a pill, admitting that you have an illness — a highly stigmatized *mental* illness. Talk about a tough pill to swallow! For some people with bipolar disorder and their loved ones, denial may last several years. It may go away only to return later.

We can't provide a good rebuttal for this particular objection; no one can talk you out of symptomatic denial or even of the emotional denial that follows. Paradoxically, you can't get to that first emotional stage of denial until you take medication for the disordered mood and thinking that convinces you that you're not sick or not worthy of help. People with bipolar disorder often must experience several major mood episodes and perhaps even a few hospitalizations before they come to accept that this illness is real and requires medication. This can be a long process. Caregivers, therapists, and doctors must recognize that *acceptance of the diagnosis* is a critical first goal in the treatment process; without this, treatment is unlikely to succeed. Those people around you can do their best to offer unconditional acceptance, strong shoulders to cry on, and active, empathic listening, but this journey will take some time for almost all people receiving a diagnosis of bipolar disorder.

They don't work

Aspirin and acetaminophen (Tylenol) can alleviate pain in a matter of minutes. Decongestants take less than an hour. Lithium, however, which is a very effective antimanic, takes about seven days to start working. SSRI (Selective Serotonin Reuptake Inhibitor) antidepressants commonly require three to six weeks to achieve their full therapeutic effects. And the side effects often appear long before the benefits do. No wonder people suffering from depression or mania get discouraged and stop taking their meds! Having to wait more than a week for relief feels more like torture than treatment.

These suggestions may help you endure the delay and even shorten it:

- ✔ **Ask your doctor upfront how long each medication should take before it begins to work.** Sometimes, knowing that a medication may take a week or three weeks rather than 15 minutes or an hour to start working can reduce your anxiety. Mark the days on your calendar to keep track.

- ✔ **Ask your doctor what to expect when the medication starts working.** Doctors sometimes prescribe medications without explaining how they're supposed to help. Don't be afraid to ask! Knowing the potential long-term benefits of a medication can often encourage you to keep taking it, even when you don't see immediate results.

✔ **Expect some ups and downs during the initial recovery.** You probably won't wake up one day feeling cured. Expect to have good days, not-so-good days, and bad days. The goal is to string together more good days than bad.

✔ **Ask your doctor if there's anything you can take to feel better faster.** Your doctor may be able to add a medication to the mix on a temporary basis and then pull it back when you begin to feel better. For example, antianxiety or sleep meds are often useful for short-term relief.

✔ **If you don't feel better in the time period that your doctor specifies, let your doctor know.** You may need a medication change, extra time, or a higher dose.

I'm fine now

Taking medication when you feel fine may seem about as rational as wearing a raincoat on a sunny day; what's the point? The point is actually twofold and centers around maintenance and prevention.

Maintenance means that the medicine has to stay in your system for you to continue feeling better. When you treat a mood episode, the episode doesn't just melt away; the medicine suppresses it. The episode has its own lifespan, and if you stop the medication too soon, the symptoms will bubble back up to the surface. Basically, you feel better because of the medicine; stop the medicine, and you stop feeling better.

The other primary goal of medication is *prevention.* Doctors often prescribe medications that function as *prophylactics,* meaning they don't just make you feel better when you become ill; they also reduce the likelihood that symptoms will return. And preventing symptoms has some solid benefits:

✔ Avoid potential fallout from mood episodes, such as broken relationships or loss of employment.

✔ Reduce the frequency and intensity of mood episodes.

✔ Improve the course of your illness. Every episode subjects the brain to additional trauma.

✔ Avoid a stay in the hospital.

The side effects are unacceptable

Medication advertisements in magazines often consist of a few words in big print that tout the benefits. These few alluring words are followed by a full page of tiny print that lists possible side effects. The choices these ads present are often absurd. For example, celecoxib (Celebrex) relieves arthritis pain and inflammation but may increase the risk of heart attack and stroke. When deciding which medication to take for bipolar, you face similar lousy choices:

✔ Valproic acid (Depakote) controls mania but can result in weight gain, pancreatitis, and/or hair loss. It can also cause changes in young women's reproductive systems, as we explain in Chapter 10.

✔ Lithium stabilizes moods but may also cause weight gain, kidney damage, and/or thyroid dysfunction.

✔ Fluoxetine (Prozac), paroxetine (Paxil), sertraline (Zoloft), and other SSRI antidepressants alleviate depression at the risk of causing agitation or other emotional side effects and negative sexual side effects.

✔ Lamotrigine (Lamictal) helps control depression but may cause a potentially lethal skin reaction.

✔ Antipsychotics can cause weight gain, sedation, changes in sugar or fat metabolism, and other undesirable side effects.

Potentially negative side effects accompany all medications, even aspirin. If the medications are powerful enough to work, then they're powerful enough to cause problems. Always discuss potential side effects with your doctor so you know what to look for and what to do if you experience one or more negative side effects.

I forget to take them

When you feel well, you have better, more important things to do than think about your medications; and work, relationships, kids, and golf are much more fun. But when you have bipolar disorder, managing your medications needs to be a priority or at least a well-ingrained habit.

To stay on top of your daily medications, try the following tips:

✔ **Record your medications on an index card.** Keep the card in your wallet or purse or stick it to the side of your refrigerator for quick reference. Or keep your list of meds on your favorite mobile device. Bring your list with you to every doctor visit and update it whenever your doctor adjusts your medications.

✔ **Use a seven-day pillbox.** A seven-day pillbox has a compartment for each day of the week so you know exactly what you need to take each day. You can even add a sticker to the box that lists the times of day for taking each medication, or you may want a separate pill box for each time of day that you take medications.

✔ **Store your medications where you can see them.** Doing so gives you a visual reminder to take them.

✔ **Link your medication to daily meals or events.** Remembering to take your medications when you wake up, before you go to bed, or at mealtime may be easier than setting a specific time, such as 10 a.m. Put a note on your toothbrush or near your contact lenses, for example, to remind you to take your medicine each day.

✔ **Assign the task of remembering to a responsible family member.** If you simply can't remember to take your medications on time, ask a family member to remind you. In some communities, service organizations have volunteers who can fill this role.

✔ **Go hi-tech.** Alarms on your mobile device can serve as reminders. Just be sure to change the alarm sound regularly so it doesn't become background noise that you ignore. Also, you can download medication reminder apps that tell you it's time for medication. If you don't indicate to the app that you took your medicine, it will let someone else know (you identify a medication buddy when you set up the app). This person can then reach out to you directly to see what's up.

Having a family member or friend remind you to take your medication works for some people, but it isn't always the best idea. If you're the type of person who tends to feel nagged by reminders from others, this system may become a source of conflict. Know yourself and establish a reminder system that works for you in a positive way.

Normal is boring

The alternative to the extreme highs and lows of bipolar disorder is normalcy. How dull is that? You get to be like everyone else — the people who find small talk intriguing, who've never experienced the utter loneliness of depression, and who remain unfazed by a world gone mad. Your mania may have given you new insights and ideas, a vivacious personality, and a high energy level. With medication, you may feel like the color's been washed out of your life and your mind is dull and gray; you may be bored and feel as though time has slowed down; and you may wonder how you'll be able to enjoy life without mood-induced drama and excitement.

If your medications have flat-lined your moods, here are some tactics to try:

✔ **Realize that your muted mood probably is a temporary condition.** You may need several weeks to recover from a major mood episode. And the medications may take several days or weeks to begin working. Some of the flattening may be related to your mood system rebooting back to more typical variations. The good news is that the negative side effects usually wear off as your moods begin to stabilize.

✔ **Consult your doctor.** As your depression or mania settles down, your doctor may be able to tweak your medications so you can experience more acceptable mood variation.

✔ **Work toward accepting that your recovery is a process.** Side effects and medication trials can cause some people to get worse before they get better. Most healthcare providers do everything in their power to prevent this situation, but it does happen. Don't assume that you'll never get better, even if your first few treatments make you feel dull, slow, or sluggish or worsen your mood symptoms. Stay in close contact with your doctors and keep them informed about all your symptoms. Continue asking for more treatment options until you find one or more that work.

I just want to be me

When you've lived with bipolar disorder for most of your life, separating it from your personality can be difficult. Some people are fine with the stabilized version of themselves. They've known all along that something wasn't right, and when the wild mood fluctuations are gone, they finally feel some balance. Other people miss "themselves." They feel as though some essential qualities of their personality have been extracted. They've lost their mojo, and they want it back . . . without the sleepless nights, ruined relationships, unpaid bills, and other inconveniences, of course.

Be patient with yourself as you mourn the losses of the life you used to have and adjust to your current reality. Give yourself time to fully embrace your future prospects — a life without debilitating mood episodes. Treatment for bipolar disorder can trigger genuine grief that takes time to resolve. You're still you. Medication doesn't take away your creativity or zest for life. With a stable mood, you have the power and control to discover things you really enjoy and pursue them. Therapy can help you through the transition (see Chapter 11 for info on therapy options).

I can control my moods without medication

Some people claim that they can successfully control their bipolar symptoms through diet, exercise, therapy, and the cooperation of family and friends — just as some people can control some types of diabetes by making dramatic lifestyle changes. Is this really possible? Think of it this way: You can survive a free fall from 100 feet, but you have a much better chance of doing so if you're strapped to a well-anchored, 50-foot bungee cord. Controlling bipolar symptoms without medication is extremely risky. In fact, the medical community advises against it, and we don't recommend that you try it either.

That said, bipolar disorder does have several degrees of severity, and everyone is different. Some milder forms can be amenable to *less* medical intervention, just as you can manage some types of diabetes with lifestyle changes (whereas severe cases require insulin treatment).

Never attempt to reduce or eliminate your medications without discussing the situation with your doctor. (For more about tapering off or stopping a medication, see the section "Switching, Reducing, and Stopping Meds.")

I want to drink alcohol or use other substances sometimes

Many people enjoy drinking alcohol or using recreational drugs, such as marijuana. Both of these substances affect mood and brain function and may interact negatively or even dangerously with psychotropic medications. For example, combining alcohol with antianxiety medications — such as alprazolam (Xanax) or diazepam (Valium) — is dangerous because the combined effects of these central nervous system (CNS) depressants can lead to unconsciousness and death.

The best approach is to stop any recreational drug use entirely when taking psychotropic medications. As for alcohol, consult your doctor. With certain medications, alcohol consumed in moderation may be okay. In other cases, combining alcohol and medication is ill-advised or prohibited.

They cost too much

Many medications used to treat bipolar disorder are inexpensive, but some are quite costly. Depending on your insurance coverage, your out-of-pocket costs can be a real barrier to long-term medication treatment. If the cost of medication is an issue for you, don't be embarrassed to ask your doctor about options. Your doctor may be able to prescribe a less-expensive medication or even a different form of the same medication. (See Chapter 18 for possible ways to overcome this obstacle.)

Accepting that your reluctance is normal

Head over to the nearest all-you-can-eat buffet and ask the diners waddling back to their tables with heaping portions whether they're following their doctors' orders and acting in the best interest of their overall health. Or dig through any medicine cabinet (just don't get caught!) and count the unused portions of medications that have specific instructions to take until gone. The point is that the tendency to ignore doctors' orders and avoid taking medication doesn't apply only to people with bipolar disorder; the rebellion is universal. People just want to enjoy their lives, unfettered by dietary restrictions, medications, and other health regimens.

In other words, reluctance to taking long-term medication is normal and perfectly understandable. Ultimately, perform a cost-benefit analysis, so to speak, and decide whether the benefits of taking medications outweigh the costs of not taking them (and vice versa), as we explain in the next section.

BIPOLAR BIO

Coming to peace with my meds

When I was first diagnosed with bipolar disorder at age 22 — young, wild, and free — the last thing I wanted to hear was "take these pills." I had a desperate need to feel normal, and the idea of taking medication every day did not sit well with this rebellious girl. Then they told me I couldn't drink, and I *really* hated the idea. At every turn, I analyzed and argued the necessity of following my doctor's instructions. And when I felt better, I'd stop taking my meds because I thought I was okay. It was a dangerous tug-of-war game I played until my late 20s.

Eventually, my attitude changed, and acceptance emerged. Compliance shifted from being a chore I loathed to becoming part of my daily routine. Each day I opened my trusty pill tray and down the hatch it went! Finding the right doctor was a pivotal part of this change. I turned a corner when he finally found that magic combo of meds for me; I was 30.

I'm 40 now. Thankfully, my medications and eight hours of sleep each night have kept me out of the hospital for nearly ten years. And though I'm aware that a bed is always available (if I need it), I'm not anxious to check in. When the road gets bumpy, as it can, my doctor tweaks my meds to smooth it. I shudder to think about where I'd be now without my medication, and I'm grateful for it.

I no longer view bipolar as an impossible illness to treat. Rather, it's one that requires vigilance. My medications are my life jacket. I'm a V.I.P. at my local pharmacy, and that's a place where I'm *glad* everyone knows my name.

— Wendy K. Williamson,
author of *I'm Not Crazy Just Bipolar*
and *Two Bipolar Chicks Guide to Survival:
Tips for Living with Bipolar Disorder*
(www.wendykwilliamson.com)

Performing a Cost-Benefit Analysis

Every major decision involves a *cost-benefit analysis*. Whether you're deciding to change jobs or careers, get married, or buy a new car, you weigh the potential benefits of each choice against the drawbacks to decide which option will ultimately provide you with the most of what you want while requiring you to sacrifice the least. The same is true of your decision to take medication voluntarily to treat the symptoms of bipolar disorder — or not. The following steps lead you through the analysis process:

1. **List the potential benefits.**

   Potential benefits to medication may include achieving more stable moods, staying out of the hospital, avoiding financial and legal problems, improving relationships, getting and keeping a job, increasing control over your own mental health, and reaching a place where you can pursue nonmedication treatments (such as psychotherapy).

2. List the possible costs.

What do you have to lose by taking medication? Some drawbacks may include cost of medication, undesirable side effects, and the hassle of remembering to take it. Plus, you may miss the highs. Jot down why you don't want to take medication.

3. Recognize the emotions in your thinking.

Review the list of possible costs you came up with in Step 2 and flag any that are more emotional than rational. Are you afraid of specific side effects? Does taking medication mean admitting that you have a mental illness? Does a need to take medication seem unfair? Acknowledging emotional thinking is just as important as listing your rational concerns because both parts are going to factor into your ultimate decisions. Fully owning the emotional components also helps make the decision-making process more transparent. You retain more control over your outcome when you're aware of the emotions at play than when you allow them to operate silently in the background.

4. Bounce the idea off someone you trust.

Review your list of pros and cons with your doctor, therapist, or a close friend or relative to get a trusted third-party perspective. This other person may point out something you haven't considered or help you realize that a certain factor is really more or less important than you initially thought.

5. Decide.

Weigh the costs against the benefits and make the call.

 Not taking prescribed medicine carries risks that can be quite serious, so carefully weigh the costs of not taking your prescribed medications against the costs of taking them. If you don't take the medications your doctor prescribes, what's likely to happen?

The decision of whether to take medication to treat bipolar symptoms may initially seem like an either-or choice, but it doesn't have to be. As we emphasize in Chapter 7, numerous medications are available, and each one has its own cost-benefit profile. The same medication may have different effects for different individuals. Also, as we explain in the next section, solutions may be available to minimize unwelcome side effects.

Alleviating Undesirable Side Effects

Every medication, even over-the-counter medications generally considered safe, cause negative side effects; for example, aspirin may cause indigestion and stomach bleeding, and it increases the risk of stroke. Likewise, psychotropic medications have both desirable and undesirable effects. Sometimes the undesirable side effects lessen or even disappear over time. In other cases, people may decide to live with the negative side effects because they figure that a medication's benefits outweigh its drawbacks.

However, you don't necessarily have to live with undesirable side effects. Your doctor may have suggestions on how to reduce or eliminate certain negative effects of a medication you're taking. In the following sections, we describe a few approaches to discuss with your doctor.

Tweaking your doses and times

You may be able to reduce or eliminate undesirable side effects without changing medications by doing any or all of the following:

- ✔ **Gradually ramp up dosages.** Many negative side effects occur when you first start taking a medication. Your doctor may be able to increase the dosage gradually to avoid or diminish the intensity of the effects.

- ✔ **Change medication times.** If you typically take a medication in the morning, for example, and it makes you too drowsy for work, your doctor may recommend that you take it in the afternoon or evening or take more of it in the evening and less of it during the day.

- ✔ **Switch to an extended-release version of a medication.** Many medications come in extended-release tablets that gradually deliver treatment to your bloodstream. Ask your doctor if this type of med is an option for you.

- ✔ **Reduce the dose.** With your doctor's approval, try reducing the dose to see if you can get the same benefits at a lower dose that may have fewer side effects.

 Many medications are available in generic form, which has the same active ingredients as the associated name brand, but generics can have a range of *bioavailability* (how much medicine is available to your body) that is different from the name brand product. Generic products typically produce the same positive effects and side effects but not always. People may experience a better or worse response to the brand or generic version of a medication, so switching to the other form may be worth a try.

Trying different meds in the same class

A medication that's in the same class as the one you've been prescribed (and that's giving you trouble) may be just as or more effective and offer a better side effect profile for you. For example, if you start taking olanzapine (Zyprexa) and experience weight gain that you can't tolerate, switching to another atypical antipsychotic such as aripiprazole (Abilify), which sometimes has less weight gain associated with it, may be a good move. See Chapter 7 for medications by class as well as their side effect profiles.

Another option is to try a medication in a slightly different class. Antipsychotics, for instance, come in two classes:

- **First generation (older):** Are more likely to cause movement disorders, including *akathisia* (severe restlessness) and *tardive dyskinesia* (involuntary movement of the face and jaw)
- **Second generation (newer):** Are more likely to cause weight gain and changes in metabolism but have lower risk of movement disorders

Exploring other options

Your doctor may have other tricks up his sleeve for alleviating unwanted side effects, including the following adjustments:

- Add a medication to counteract the side effect; for example, if you experience weight gain on risperidone (Risperdal), your doctor may prescribe topiramate (Topamax) to reduce weight gain.
- Replace the medication with a different type of biological intervention, such as a nutritional supplement, light therapy, or electroconvulsive therapy (ECT).
- Suggest lifestyle changes, such as dietary changes or exercise routines, to counteract the side effects.

Dealing with specific side effects

Certain side effects are more common and bothersome than others. In the following sections, we offer specific suggestions for alleviating or minimizing common side effects of bipolar medications.

Fatigue and drowsiness

If your medication is making you feel tired during the day, talk to your doctor about the following options:

- Taking the medication later in the day or at bedtime
- Scheduling a nap for the time of day when you typically feel most tired or drowsy

✔ Consuming less sugar and simple carbohydrates and more protein and complex carbohydrates

✔ Engaging in light to moderate exercise (such as walking) at least every other day

Weight gain

Many antidepressants, almost all atypical antipsychotics, many anticonvulsants, and lithium have weight gain as a possible side effect; in fact, it's one of the main reasons people stop taking these medications. The best way to monitor and manage weight gain when you're on one of these meds is to take a proactive approach such as the one we outline here:

1. **Monitor weight and appetite from the start so you can take action before the weight gain becomes a big problem.**

   You needn't jump on the scales every day; just weigh in during your regular doctor visits. Keeping a food/appetite journal can be helpful for many people, but some find it makes them overly focused on food and eating and is an overall negative intervention.

2. **Ask your doctor to order regular lab tests (every six months or annually) to keep an eye on your blood sugar and lipid profiles.**

   Doctors have their favorite lab panels that include fasting blood glucose and lipid levels. They'll also usually order a *hemoglobin A1C,* which gives them a picture of the average range of blood sugar levels over the previous three months. This level is important in monitoring trends of glucose metabolism. If doctors have specific concerns, they may also order insulin levels to see whether the insulin is no longer as sensitive as it used to be; lowered insulin sensitivity is key to developing type 2 diabetes. The range on the lab slip shows the cutoffs, but noting significant shifts from your baseline levels is more useful. If results from these routine tests change dramatically or you're experiencing other symptoms or problems, your doctor may order more comprehensive lab work and/or refer you to a specialist.

3. **When starting a new medication or changing medications, work with your doctor to make food and movement choices that encourage healthy energy production and metabolism.**

   Find movement that you enjoy and do some every day. Even one minute of vigorously elevating your heart rate several times per week can change your health profile. Eat more vegetables and low-glycemic fruit (such as berries and melon), and try to pay attention to hidden added sugars in food, especially bread, crackers, and bakery items. Opt for whole-grain products and consume them in moderation. Avoid hydrogenated oils in processed foods. Eat whole food more than processed food. Focus on health rather than weight.

4. **If you're taking an atypical antipsychotic, keep your primary-care doctor in the loop.**

   Your primary-care doctor can keep a close eye on health issues related to these meds and offer suggestions to limit your weight gain, but beware of overly punitive approaches to diet and exercise or any judgments about the weight gain. You're trying to perform a balancing act of getting your brain and body healthy from bipolar disorder while trying to limit health risks of the medications that are helping you. Don't interpret it as a matter of willpower or strength; it's a difficult process. Support and compassion from others and from yourself are most effective in helping you navigate these difficult waters.

If you're currently experiencing weight gain, discuss the following options with your doctor:

- ✔ Switching to a medication in the same class that's less likely to cause weight gain. Ziprasidone (Geodon) has been studied in this regard and can be an effective alternative if other atypical antipsychotics are causing significant weight gain.

- ✔ Making lifestyle adjustments, including dietary changes and increased physical activity as previously described.

- ✔ Adding metformin (Glucophage) to the mix. Metformin, a medication used to treat diabetes, is being studied to see if it can reduce weight gain and/or the risk of developing diabetes associated with some psychiatric medications. If a doctor is considering metformin, he often starts by ordering lab tests to assess your glucose levels and insulin function.

- ✔ Adding topiramate (Topamax), an anticonvulsant associated with some mild weight loss in many people. It can carry important side effects, including hair loss and cognitive dulling. Discuss these pros and cons in detail with your doctor if she is considering this option.

- ✔ Considering other medications to assist in weight loss. Your doctor can consider them if the weight gain is severe. These medications are best managed in consultation with your primary care doctor because they have a number of restrictions on their use due to high rates of side effects and low rates of desired effect.

In severe situations related to weight gain, especially if you have longstanding obesity concerns that are complicated by psychiatric medications, you can talk to your doctor about *bariatric* (weight-loss) surgery. Some studies link obesity with major depression and bipolar disorder, and weight loss often isn't going to happen with an eat-less-exercise-more approach. Several studies suggest that some people with bipolar and obesity respond well to bariatric surgery, improving both in mood and overall health.

Bipolar disorder itself may cause problems with metabolism and weight, so medications aren't the only factor in this situation. Body weight and metabolism are highly complex processes, affected by many things including medications. A balanced approach to factors that can be controlled along with careful monitoring and proactive management are extremely valuable tools for solving these complicated problems.

Sexual dysfunction

SSRIs and some antipsychotics are notorious for causing sexual dysfunction, including reduced desire, erectile dysfunction, and inability to orgasm. If you experience sexual dysfunction while taking a prescribed medication, consult your doctor about the following possible remedies:

- Reducing the dose of the medication to a point where it still helps maintain mood stability without contributing to sexual dysfunction.

- Switching to a medication in the same class that's less likely to cause problems; for example, switching from an SSRI antidepressant to something like bupropion (Wellbutrin), which is much less likely to cause sexual dysfunction.

- Adding a medication to treat the sexual dysfunction. Some medications for sexual function are taken just for sexual activity; others are taken every day, just like an SSRI. Adding bupropion to an SSRI can improve sexual function for some people.

- Taking a medication holiday — skipping the medication a day or so during the week. Doing so may help improve sexual function without risking a mood episode.

Memory and cognitive difficulties

While some medications have neuroprotective properties that seem to help memory and cognition over the long term, others may cause difficulties. If you feel that a medication is negatively affecting your memory or ability to think clearly and sharply, consult your doctor about the following options:

- Changing the dose or time of day you take the medication

- Switching to a medication in the same class that's less likely to cause memory and cognitive difficulties

- Engaging in social and mental activities to stimulate your brain

- Engaging in physical activity to maintain mental sharpness

Switching, Reducing, and Stopping Meds

With bipolar disorder, medication adjustments are common. You and your doctor may decide to switch medications, increase or decrease the dosage, or perhaps even withdraw all medication at various points in your treatment journey. Whatever the case may be, some ways of making these medication changes are safer than others.

Don't stop a medication abruptly unless your doctor specifically instructs you to do so. If your doctor believes that a medication is causing a serious and acute medical problem, she may remove it abruptly. However, the safer approach to medication adjustments usually involves making small changes over measured periods of time. Going cold turkey with certain medications may cause seizures or other withdrawal symptoms or increase the risk of relapse.

Here are some general guidelines to discuss with your doctor before you make any medication adjustments:

- **Taper doses gradually.** When reducing or stopping a medication, reduce the dosage slowly — usually over at least several weeks or sometimes a number of days; your doctor will discuss the details with you. This type of tapering is especially important if you've been taking a large dose for a long time. When going from a small amount to nothing, you may need to split a pill in half, but be careful because some pills are designed only to be swallowed whole, not cut or crushed.

- **Change one medication at a time.** By changing the dosage of only one medication at a time, you have a better chance of identifying the cause of any problems or benefits that arise.

- **When switching medications, gradually ramp up the new medication while tapering off the old one.** This is opposite to the previous guideline, but it's not an uncommon practice when changing to a different medicine in the same category. Sometimes you can move a little faster in tapering off a medication when introducing another one in the same class to take its place. If you're changing to a medication in a different class, your doctor may want you to continue taking the old medication with the new one for some time before tapering off the old medication.

People with bipolar may suddenly decide to stop taking the medications they've been prescribed, which is a really bad idea. Under certain circumstances, however, carefully discontinuing some or all medications in consultation with your doctor may be worth the risk. For example, if your moods have been stable for a long time and you and your doctor have good reason to believe that you experienced a one-time manic episode that was probably drug or medication induced, then it may be time to try living medication-free. This may also be the case if you're doing well on very low doses of medication and have made lifestyle adjustments and significant progress in therapy; these other supports may be sufficient for maintaining your mood stability.

If you're considering the possibility of stopping your medications, complete the following checklist and talk to your doctor to determine whether you're in a good position to make the attempt:

- ✔ Your moods are currently stable and have been stable for a sustained period of time — typically for one year or longer.

- ✔ Your doctor approves and agrees to supervise your attempt — _slowly_ decreasing doses of your current medications.

- ✔ You're not currently experiencing (or have plans for) any major life events or changes, such as getting married or divorced, changing jobs or careers, or returning to school.

- ✔ You have a solid routine in place that ensures sufficient sleep.

- ✔ You're not using alcohol or other drugs regularly or excessively.

- ✔ Your support network is cooperative and well informed.

- ✔ You and your support network have a system in place to carefully monitor your moods (see Chapter 11).

- ✔ You have a solid backup plan in case things go wrong (see Chapter 15).

Even under these conditions, withdrawing mood medications entirely is extremely risky. Consider working out compromises with your doctor and therapist. With additional therapy and lifestyle changes, you have a chance to manage your moods with _less_ medication rather than _no_ medication. Think in terms of making minor changes over several months or years rather than major changes in a short period of time. Proceed only with your doctor's approval and under your doctor's careful supervision.

Chapter 9

Expanding Your Biological Treatment Options

In This Chapter

▶ Supplementing treatment with all-natural ingredients

▶ Brightening your moods with light therapy

▶ Rebooting your brain with ECT, rTMS, and DBS

Medication along with therapy and self-help strategies are usually sufficient to keep most bipolar symptoms at bay, but sometimes medication is ineffective or provides only partial relief. Medication may produce side effects that you can't or won't put up with, or you can't tolerate a high enough dose to get full symptom relief. In specific cases, especially if you're pregnant, the potential risks of medicine may outweigh the benefits or may warrant decreasing doses or the number of medications you take. In situations such as these, you and your doctor may want to consider expanding your treatment options. In this chapter, you have the opportunity to explore these other options and weigh the potential benefits against the possible risks.

Treating Your Moods to Supplements

This section explores the pros and cons of some of the more promising "natural" treatments (or interventions) for depression and mania and lists some of their potential risks and side effects. Researchers refer to these types of interventions as *complementary and alternative medicine (CAM)*. A growing body of medical research explores complementary and alternative strategies for treating a variety of illnesses, including bipolar disorder. Some interventions clearly seem to be helpful without causing unacceptable risks. Others, however, seem to have more anecdotal than clinical evidence to support their usefulness and may not be effective or safe.

Don't assume that your doctor is ignorant or averse to trying alternative treatments. Most doctors know something about them, are quite willing to discuss them with you, and can help guide you in making informed and safe decisions for managing your health.

Fishing for a cure: Omega-3 fatty acids

Studies have shown lower rates of depression in countries where people eat a lot of seafood. Over the last decade, researchers have tried to understand this connection and have focused on *omega-3 fatty acids* — nutrients that the body can't manufacture itself and must take in through diet. Omega-3 fatty acids are necessary for healthy brains and cardiovascular systems, and you find them in high concentrations in many types of seafood. They may work through reducing inflammation in the nervous system and improving brain cells' ability to recover from stress and damage (see Chapter 2 for a discussion of how these processes relate to bipolar disorder).

Recent reviews of medical research indicate that supplementing standard treatments with omega-3 fatty acids reduces the symptoms of bipolar and unipolar depression. Research hasn't found any particular benefit to omega-3 fatty acids in mania. Additionally, studies suggest that omega-3 supplements may reduce symptoms of anxiety in healthy young adults.

Omega-3s aren't a replacement for your antimanic or antidepressant, especially if you're treating extreme mood episodes, so don't ditch your meds.

You can obtain omega-3 fatty acids from any of the following sources:

- Cold-water fish, including salmon, mackerel, herring, tuna, anchovies, and sardines
- Wild animals (including deer, buffalo, and free-range chickens)
- Omega-3 enhanced eggs
- Dark-green leafy vegetables (such as spinach, arugula, and purslane)
- Flaxseed oil
- Walnuts
- Omega-3 supplements

Unless you literally chew the fat with Eskimos, you may have a hard time getting enough omega-3s in your diet to produce the desired effects, so you probably need to take a supplement. Over-the-counter (OTC) fish oil supplements contain two types of omega-3 fatty acids:

✔ **Eicosapentaenoic acid (EPA):** EPA is generally thought to play more of a role in the antidepressant effect than the other omega-3 (DHA). To get the full antidepressant benefits, most doctors recommend that you get 1 to 2 grams daily of EPA.

✔ **Docosahexaenoic acid (DHA):** DHA may play a lesser role in depression than EPA, but it does affect overall brain health. Evidence suggests that DHA has protective properties in relation to Alzheimer's.

Unfortunately, the U.S. Food and Drug Administration (FDA) doesn't control what goes into omega-3 supplements, so review dosage recommendations with your psychiatrist or primary-care doctor, ask for product recommendations, and check the label to make sure the supplement is consistent with what your doctor recommends in terms of concentration and dosages of EPA and DHA. Look for a product that has a high purity rating — with the fewest possible contaminants. You may need to try a few different brands to find one with the least fishy aftertaste.

Taking high doses of omega-3 may be associated with increased bleeding, so consult your doctor before ingesting large amounts of omega-3.

Pumping up your brain with vitamins and minerals

In Western countries, where food is plentiful and enriched, true vitamin and mineral deficiencies are rare, but low levels of these nutrients, even when they don't qualify as a deficiency, may be related to some depressive symptoms. Although we wouldn't suggest that any vitamin or combination of vitamins is effective for treating depression or mania, several vitamins and minerals, including the following, can have a significant effect on brain development and function:

✔ **B-complex vitamins:** Your body uses the B-complex vitamins in a variety of ways to build and maintain a healthy nervous system. Taking them together in the appropriate relative concentrations is important because too much of one may lead to a deficiency of another. No reliable or replicated studies indicate specific benefits of B vitamins (other than folic acid) in treating bipolar disorder or depression. Here's what you need to know about the B vitamins:

• **B-1:** B-1 (or thiamine) deficiencies can cause severe neurologic problems. Diet-related thiamine deficiencies are rare in the U.S., but deficiencies due to alcohol abuse aren't uncommon.

- **B6:** Isolated B-6 deficiency is rare, but old age, alcohol abuse or dependence, autoimmune disorders, renal failure, and medications such as valproate (Depakote), carbamazepine (Tegretol), and the anti-asthma medication theophylline (Aerolate) increase the risk of low B-6 levels. B-6 can be dangerous in high doses, so don't take B-6 beyond a traditional supplement unless prescribed by a physician.

- **B-12:** B-12 deficiency can cause symptoms of depression or other psychiatric illnesses. It's uncommon, but strict vegetarianism (vegan diets), old age, certain stomach and intestinal illnesses, weight-loss surgery, and certain medications, including those used to treat acid reflux and peptic ulcers and the diabetes medication metformin (Glucophage) increase the risk for B-12 deficiency. Doctors often check B-12 levels in people with acute depression. (Research has discovered a genetic link between B-12 deficiency and bipolar disorder in some families.)

✔ **Folic acid:** Folic acid is one of the B vitamins, but it isn't always included in B-complex supplements. It's critical in the development of the human nervous system, so pregnant women must take folic acid supplements. People who abuse alcohol, have certain illnesses, or take a number of different medications are at risk for folate deficiencies, which can present with a variety of cognitive, emotional, and behavioral symptoms. A prescription strength version of folic acid — L-methylfolate (Deplin) — is now approved as an augmenting agent for people who aren't responding to antidepressant therapy alone. Doctors may check for folic acid levels as part of an initial work-up of depression.

Make sure your doctor checks for both folic acid and B-12 levels before supplementing with folic acid. High folic acid levels may mask a vitamin B-12 deficiency. Both folic acid and B-12 deficiencies cause anemia — low red blood counts. If you start taking a folic acid supplement when you also have a B-12 deficiency, the anemia may get better, but the nervous system damage from the B-12 deficit will still occur.

✔ **Vitamin D:** Several studies indicate a link between low levels of vitamin D and depression, but as of the writing of this book, no clear evidence shows that low levels of vitamin D cause depression. Even so, your doctor may want to check your vitamin D levels to determine whether supplementation may be useful to you.

✔ **Magnesium:** A magnesium deficiency is rare, but high-risk groups include older adults and people who abuse alcohol, have diabetes, or are afflicted with a number of other medical conditions that require a variety of medications. Low body stores of magnesium may be related to a number of health problems, including mood regulation and migraine headaches. Magnesium is part of one of the pathways that lithium affects, so many doctors are intrigued to consider its possible relationship to bipolar disorder. A couple of small studies have suggested that magnesium may be a useful add-on in the treatment of mania.

✔ **Zinc:** Zinc is a trace element that plays a key role in managing the oxidative stress (cell damage) process, which has been associated with bipolar disorder. Some recent data confirm a strong association between lower zinc intake and depressive symptoms, but only in women — not in men. People who abuse alcohol or have gastrointestinal disorders, especially if chronic diarrhea is present, and people who've had weight-loss or other intestinal surgery are at risk of zinc deficiency. People with sickle cell disease, pregnant and nursing women, and vegetarians are also at risk of lower zinc levels.

Investigating herbs and other supplements

Nature provides a host of effective cures and treatments for common ailments, but does it serve up anything for bipolar disorder? Medical research suggests that some of the supplements we list here may provide benefits to people with bipolar disorder:

✔ **Coenzyme Q10:** This substance plays a key role in energy metabolism within cells, which may be disrupted in bipolar disorder. One very small study showed some antidepressant effect to high doses of Coenzyme Q10 in elderly patients with depression. More research is needed.

✔ **5-HTP:** This supplement provides your body with the building blocks it needs to assemble *serotonin* (a key mood-related neurotransmitter), and some studies suggest that 5-HTP is helpful in enhancing mood, decreasing anxiety, and improving sleep. The studies aren't strong or consistent. Potential risks include inducing *serotonin syndrome* — a potentially deadly effect of very high serotonin levels in the body — if combined with antidepressants such as SSRIs or MAOIs. This risk seems to be low, but talk to your prescriber before taking this in addition to an antidepressant.

✔ **GABA:** GABA (gamma-aminobutyric acid) has been touted as a treatment for mood disorders because it's a neurotransmitter related to depression, anxiety, and mania. However, GABA taken as an oral supplement doesn't cross the blood-brain barrier, so it's useless. This particular "natural" cure is a fraud.

✔ **Glutathione:** Glutathione, one of the most common antioxidants in the human body, may reduce *oxidative stress* (literally, cell damage), which may be related to bipolar disorder. Glutathione also modulates the effects of *glutamate,* another important mood-regulating neurotransmitter. Taken orally, glutathione doesn't significantly raise the levels in the brain, but you can raise glutathione levels by taking N-acetyl cysteine, as explained later in this list.

✔ **Inositol:** This chemical plays an important role in the messenger systems within cells and has long been discussed as having a relationship to manic and depressive symptoms. Lithium and valproic acid, both used to treat bipolar disorder, help to stabilize inositol signaling in cells. Some studies support the use of inositol as an add-on medicine in bipolar depression that hasn't responded fully to typical medications. It can potentially trigger manic symptoms. Pregnant women shouldn't use it because it may trigger uterine contractions.

✔ **Kava:** This plant/herbal product purportedly reduces stress and anxiety, but some reports link it to liver damage. As a result, it's banned in many places. Don't use kava without a doctor's permission and supervision.

✔ **Melatonin:** Melatonin is a hormone that the brain produces in response to light and dark; it's part of the body's sleep/wake machinery. Supplements may reduce insomnia for sufferers of some types of sleep problems. Melatonin is safe for short-term use, even in children. But check with your doctor before you use melatonin, because it can interact with some psychiatric medications.

✔ **N-acetyl cysteine (NAC):** This chemical is part of the system that produces glutathione (mentioned earlier in this list), which is important as an *antioxidant* (helping cells recover from various kinds of stress and damage) and as a key factor in the glutamate receptor system, helping to regulate how glutamate communicates between cells. A number of studies have found NAC supplementation to have some benefit in bipolar depression. It takes a long time (several months) to show benefit, and the effect wears off quickly after stopping the supplement. But this chemical may be an important building block of next-generation treatments for bipolar disorder and other psychiatric illness.

✔ **SAMe:** Short for S-adenosylmethionine, SAMe is a natural substance found in your body that has been proved to function effectively as an antidepressant in some studies, but inadequate data are available to support its regular use as an antidepressant. Some research also supports using SAMe along with a traditional antidepressant when the antidepressant isn't effective enough. SAMe carries the risk of side effects similar to those of antidepressants, so consult your doctor before trying it. Another drawback: It isn't cheap.

✔ **St. John's wort:** Reviews of medical literature suggest that St. John's wort (a medicinal herb called *hypericum*) is effective in treating mild to moderate unipolar depression, but inconsistencies in the data remain. Some doctors continue to recommend it, particularly in Germany, and some people with depression continue to sing its praises. Be careful, though; like most antidepressants, St. John's wort may carry the risk of inducing mania. It can also interact with a number of meds.

✔ **Taurine:** Taurine is one of the most abundant amino acids in the brain. It increases activity at GABA receptors. Studies in animals have shown little, if any, support for its use in anxiety and depression. Taurine is found in all of the so-called energy drinks but has been poorly studied in humans. Taken in very high doses on a frequent basis it may carry some risk of toxic effects in the brain.

✔ **Valerian:** Valerian is an herb commonly marketed for the treatment of insomnia. Although studies are currently deemed inconclusive, some report positive results. Valerian appears to be relatively safe, but be cautious, especially if you're pregnant, nursing, or taking other meds.

Before ingesting any of these natural substances, check with your doctor and do your own research. A reliable information source is the National Institutes of Health's Office of Dietary Supplements (www.ods.od.nih.gov).

Assessing the safety of all-natural ingredients

People often think that vitamins, herbs, and supplements are "worth a try." If you can get them at the store without a prescription, they must be safe, right? Well, not exactly. These nutraceuticals carry their own potential risks and drawbacks, including the following:

✔ **Unconventional treatments may cause you to forgo more effective treatments.** The most serious risk associated with trying alternative remedies is that they may keep you from obtaining the best treatments currently available.

✔ **Unconventional treatments may not be cost-effective.** All-natural remedies and supplements can cost hundreds of dollars. A prescription for lithium or a generic mood medication may be more affordable and much more effective.

✔ **Insurance may not cover unconventional treatments.** If you load up your cart at the local health food store with megavitamins, nutritional supplements, and herbal remedies, your insurance company is unlikely to help pay the bill.

✔ **Unconventional treatments can require a lot of extra work.** Some treatments require you to perform extensive colon-cleansing and liver-cleansing routines and then take high doses of dietary supplements and herbal mixtures. Even worse, drastic body-cleansing routines can raise the concentrations of some medications, particularly lithium, to dangerous and potentially lethal levels.

✔ **Unconventional treatments have negative side effects, too.** Like prescription medications, "natural" substances work by changing your brain chemistry. Although natural substances may seem to be safer, that's not always the case.

✔ **Unconventional treatments are less strictly regulated.** In the U.S., dietary supplements and herbs are classified as food products, so they don't have to meet the same stringent FDA standards of efficacy, safety, quality, and content regulation that prescription medications have to meet. As a result, in many cases, you may not know what you're really taking or what it may or may not do to you.

✔ **Your doctor may not be well versed in unconventional treatments.** Most physicians and psychiatrists invest their time and research treating their patients with the most effective and safest medications supported by medical research. They may not have as much expertise with less mainstream approaches, but some do.

Well-done scientific research remains the best tool available to assess the risks and benefits of any treatment or medication. CAM may be valuable for many people, but clarity about the potential risks is just as important with these products as it is with traditional medications.

Treating Depression with Light Therapy

Some moods, especially those of people with bipolar, are very responsive to light: Too little light leads to deep depression, and too much light sparks mania. In fact, a distinct disorder called *seasonal affective disorder (SAD)* is a condition in which depressive episodes are predictably associated with the shortening of the days and decreased daylight time. (Check out *Seasonal Affective Disorder For Dummies* by Laura L. Smith, PhD, and Charles H. Elliott, PhD, published by John Wiley & Sons, Inc.)

Light therapy, also called *phototherapy,* can often boost mood, but not just any light will do. For safe, effective phototherapy, follow these guidelines:

✔ Consult your doctor first.

✔ Proceed with light therapy only under the direction and supervision of a qualified professional. Time of day, frequency, and duration of treatment are critical factors.

✔ Use a device designed specifically for the purpose of providing phototherapy. Most phototherapy light boxes use special fluorescent or LED bulbs rated at 10,000 lux.

Light therapy with a 10,000-lux white light source consists of sitting for about 30 minutes a day (the time needed can range from about 15 minutes to an hour, but 30 minutes is typical), facing the light box, but you don't need to stare directly into the light. You can read the morning paper or do whatever you normally do, as long as you face the light.

Too much light can cause hypomania and mania, especially during seasonal changes when you receive more light from natural sources. You and your doctor need to monitor your light intake just as carefully as you monitor doses of medication.

Stimulating Your Brain with Electricity and Magnetism

Doctors have various ways to reboot the brain by stimulating it with electricity or magnetism. Many people with bipolar disorder have found that of all the treatment options currently available, electroconvulsive therapy is one of the safest and most effective options.

However, you need to approach every treatment with a healthy dose of skepticism and understand its potential risks and benefits. In the spirit of keeping you informed, the following sections describe four non-medication-based treatment options: electroconvulsive therapy, repetitive transcranial magnetic stimulation, vagus nerve stimulation, and deep brain stimulation. These options are usually reserved for more severe, treatment-resistant cases — when medications don't work.

Zapping your moods with electroconvulsive therapy (ECT)

Electroconvulsive therapy (ECT) is based on an observation made many years ago that seizures seemed to reduce depressive and manic symptoms in some people. Contrary to what you may think, the therapeutic mechanism of ECT isn't the electrical "shock" but rather the series of controlled seizures it induces. ECT is a very effective technique that can be life changing for some people . . . in a good way, that is.

Modern techniques have significantly reduced the trauma and the drama of ECT. Nowadays, the doctor uses sedatives to keep you sleeping through the procedure along with neuromuscular agents to temporarily paralyze your muscles so you don't shake or move during the seizures. The repeated seizure activity, usually three times a week for about 12 weeks, relieves mood symptoms. About 80 percent of people who undergo ECT experience significant relief from symptoms of both depression and mania and report relatively mild side effects, such as temporary memory loss and blood pressure changes.

If you have bipolar, you may consider ECT under the following conditions:

- ✔ Nothing else works for you.
- ✔ Your depression or mania is severe and requires fast relief of acute symptoms.
- ✔ You can't or don't want to take medicine.
- ✔ You're pregnant, nursing, or plan to become pregnant, and you're concerned about the effects of various medicines on the fetus.

Doctors commonly use ECT in elderly and frail individuals who can't tolerate antidepressants and antimanic medications. In these people, ECT has proven very effective.

BIPOLAR BIO

ECT: Not as shocking as it sounds

The term *ECT,* formerly known as electroshock treatment, may send a chill down your spine. When my doctor recommended it, the horrifying images of *One Flew Over the Cuckoo's Nest* flashed in front of me. I resisted the treatment for three years. After yet another severe manic-depressive episode, I attempted suicide and was hospitalized. The doctor recommended ECT again. This time I accepted, and it was one of the best decisions I ever made. With my first treatment, I felt 50 percent better. With every treatment after, the heavy weight of depression lifted a bit more.

Yes, ECT has some drawbacks. I experienced disorientation, a lack of sense of direction, and forgetfulness regarding names and conversations, but my short-term memory returned soon after treatment ended. Unfortunately, I also lost some long-term memories. Because I was in such a critical state, I opted for intensive treatment given over the course of nine months. Most of the long-term memories I lost were within the ten years prior to treatment. The procedure didn't erase all my memories. It was more like someone pulled files randomly from my memory bank. But that was a risk I was willing to take. I sacrificed both good and bad memories in exchange for my peace of mind. I've been episode-free for ten years. I believe that going through ECT, along with staying on a medication regimen, played a big role in restoring my mental health. It may not be the best treatment for everyone — and everyone who has ECT experiences different side effects to varying degrees — but the trade-offs were well worth it for me.

— Janine Crowley Haynes, freelance writer and author of award-winning memoir *My Kind of Crazy: Living in a Bipolar World* (janinecrowleyhaynes@gmail.com)

ECT's main side effect is memory loss, which is usually temporary. Other potential risks include reactions to the anesthetic or muscle relaxant and possible changes to heart rhythm and blood pressure. Your doctor will evaluate your health before treatment and monitor it during treatment for any signs of distress.

Moderating moods with repetitive transcranial magnetic stimulation (rTMS)

Powerful magnets, similar to those used in MRIs, may be able to reset your brain's electrical power grid. Several studies have shown that *repetitive transcranial magnetic stimulation (rTMS)* may be effective in reducing symptoms of depression, but it doesn't have the same powerful effect as ECT. Research so far indicates that rTMS appears to be less effective at treating mania and may induce hypomania and mania in some people.

The course of rTMS treatment typically calls for five half-hour sessions per week for six weeks. No anesthetic is required, and few people report any pain, although some have reported a tightening of the skin, especially around the scalp and jaw, and a knocking sensation in the skull, which may be partially due to the sound of the machine. Very little risk of memory loss or seizure accompanies the procedure.

At least one rTMS device is approved in the U.S. for treatment of depression that hasn't responded to antidepressant medication. But rTMS isn't specifically approved for treatment-resistant depression. At this time, rTMS doesn't seem like a replacement for ECT for the most severe and treatment-resistant depression.

Soothing depression with neurostimulation

Doctors may be able to stimulate your brain with mild electrical currents in various ways to reduce depressive symptoms, particularly in people with *treatment-resistant depression (TRD)* — depression that has failed to respond adequately to four or more medications and/or ECT. The two neurostimulation treatments that have shown the most promise are **vagus nerve** and **deep brain stimulation**, which we describe here.

Stimulating the nervous system with VNS

Vagus nerve stimulation (VNS) has a fairly long history of being used in Europe, Canada, and the U.S. to treat epilepsy and in Canada and some European countries to treat depression. Relatively recently, the FDA approved its use in the U.S. for TRD. The FDA requires that people receiving this treatment be at least 18 years old.

With VNS, an electronic implant that functions as a pacemaker for the brain sends electrical signals to a specific brain region through the vagus nerve (in your neck) for a few seconds each minute. (You have two vagus nerves, one on each side of your body, each of which runs from your brainstem down to your chest and abdomen.) The treatment carries a variety of risks, including voice changes, throat or neck pain, difficulty swallowing, worsening of depression, and risks associated with surgery. Currently, most insurance companies don't cover the procedure.

Targeting parts of the brain with DBS

Deep brain stimulation (DBS) involves implanting electrodes into parts of your brain that are thought to affect mood. After positioning the electrodes, the doctor stimulates them a few times to get the pulse dosing correct. A battery-powered pulse generator, implanted below the skin usually near the collar bone, is then activated and continually sends a small current through the electrodes to the targeted parts of the brain. Implantations are reversible; doctors can remove the pulse generator and electrodes at any time.

DBS has shown some promise in alleviating depression in people who haven't responded to numerous other treatments, but it's considered an experimental procedure and is currently awaiting FDA approval. However, the studies are encouraging. DBS has a long history of use in treating movement disorders, including Parkinson's disease.

Surgical procedures like DBS carry risks. With a DBS implant, you need to consider the possibility of bleeding in the brain or stroke; infection; speech, heart, or breathing problems; seizure or slight paralysis; undesirable mood changes; pain, swelling, or scarring at the incision points; a shocking sensation from the electrical current; and even the possibility of your body rejecting the implant.

Chapter 10

Treating Bipolar Disorder in Women and Other Specific Populations

In This Chapter

▶ Recognizing why women may need different treatment approaches

▶ Addressing medication issues before, during, and after pregnancy

▶ Identifying special medication needs for older people with bipolar

▶ Exploring ethnic, cultural, and sexual identity factors in diagnosing and treating bipolar

*I*n the adult population, doctors diagnose the different types of bipolar disorder based on the same criteria regardless of age, gender, ethnicity, and other distinguishing demographics. Patterns of diagnosis and recommended treatment options, however, may vary considerably among different populations and circumstances, especially for women of childbearing years and older adults dealing with other health issues.

In this chapter, we explore key differences in diagnosis and treatment options for specific populations, including women, older adults, and people who identify as lesbian, gay, bisexual, or transgender (LGBT). We also point out how differences in ethnicity and culture may influence treatment choices and how providers and consumers communicate.

Bipolar Disorder in Women

Medically, women's bodies are different from men's. Women can have babies, which impacts everything — anatomy, physiology, chemistry — you name it. These differences may influence the nature of bipolar disorder and affect the optimal approach to diagnosing and treating it.

In the following sections, we highlight the effects of bipolar in women and describe how hormonal fluctuations throughout a woman's life cycle impact the illness. We also point out vital issues to consider when choosing bipolar medications and other treatment options for women, particularly with regard to pregnancy decisions.

Considering the nature of the illness

Although bipolar disorder doesn't afflict men or women exclusively, differences exist in age of onset, prevalence of certain symptoms, and so on. For example, while bipolar I occurs with equal frequency in men and women, women tend to be more prone to the following:

- **Depression and bipolar II:** Depression seems to be the more prominent "pole" for women, and women may be more prone to treatment-resistant depression. Bipolar II, in which depression is more predominant, is more common among women.

- **Mixed episodes and rapid cycling:** *Mixed episodes,* in which mania and depression are involved at the same time, and *rapid cycling* (four or more mood episodes per year) seem to be more common in women. As a result, women are more often prescribed a combination of medications, including antidepressants and antimanics.

- **Later onset:** According to the Centers for Disease Control and Prevention (CDC), the median age of onset for bipolar disorder is 25 years, with men having an earlier age of onset than women.

- **Comorbid psychiatric conditions:** Women with bipolar disorder seem to have more co-occurring anxiety disorders and eating disorders. Men have higher rates of comorbid substance abuse.

- **Comorbid medical conditions:** Other medical conditions, especially thyroid disease, migraines, and obesity may be more frequent in women than in men. Furthermore, these comorbid conditions often adversely affect recovery from bipolar disorder in women.

- **Medication-induced weight gain:** Some studies suggest that the atypical antipsychotics are more likely to cause weight gain and glucose regulation problems in women than in men, but these findings still need to be confirmed with additional research.

Tracing hormonal changes

Male and female sex hormones interact with other body systems, including the brain. The primary sex hormones involved for girls and women are

✔ **Estrogen:** A female hormone that affects the growth, maintenance, and repair of reproductive tissues. Estrogen is at its lowest level at the beginning of the menstrual cycle and peaks near the time of ovulation (approximately day 14 of the cycle). If pregnancy occurs, estrogen levels remain high. If the egg isn't fertilized, estrogen levels drop.

✔ **Progesterone:** A female hormone that prepares the lining of the uterus for a fertilized egg. If the egg is fertilized, progesterone levels continue to rise; they remain high during pregnancy. If the egg isn't fertilized, progesterone levels drop. The balance of estrogen and progesterone levels and the timing of increases and decreases of these levels appear to play a role in symptoms of depression.

✔ **Testosterone:** A so-called male hormone that also happens to be a critical sex hormone in women. Testosterone is associated with energy, mood, and sex drive in both men and women. Testosterone levels increase in girls during puberty, although not as much as they do in boys. Testosterone levels vary during the menstrual cycle.

A woman's development is characterized by powerful hormonal changes that can be associated with a variety of mood responses and symptoms. These hormonal shifts occur primarily in support of women's ability to have babies at the following key stages of their lives:

✔ **Menarche:** The time period when a girl begins to menstruate. Before puberty, girls and boys have about the same rates of depression, but after puberty, the rate of depression becomes higher for girls. How or why this occurs is unclear, but it certainly suggests a close connection between the female sex hormones and mood.

✔ **Menses:** The medical term for *menstruation*. Women's menstrual cycles occur in response to rhythmic changes in sex hormones that occur in anticipation of pregnancy. If a pregnancy doesn't occur, the woman gets her period, and the cycle begins again. Throughout a monthly cycle, many women experience some level of mood and behavioral symptoms:

- **Premenstrual syndrome (PMS):** PMS is characterized by physical symptoms and emotional irregularities in the days between ovulation and menstruation. Some estimates show that as many as 80 percent of ovulating women experience symptoms of PMS.

- **Premenstrual dysphoric disorder (PMDD):** PMDD presents as premenstrual symptoms — primarily emotional/behavioral rather than physical — that are severe enough to interfere with function on a regular basis. An estimated 3 to 8 percent of ovulating women suffer from PMDD.

- **Premenstrual exacerbation (PME):** PME is a worsening of manic or depressive symptoms that occurs in sync with a woman's menstrual cycle and may be associated with a more chronic, severe course of bipolar disorder. Effective treatment for bipolar disorder, however, may significantly reduce premenstrual mood symptoms.

- ✔ **Pregnancy:** Consistent information about how pregnancy affects bipolar symptoms is scarce. Sleep deprivation and energy changes are certainly important considerations, as are the underlying hormonal shifts that occur throughout pregnancy.

- ✔ **Postpartum:** Women with bipolar disorder are at higher risk for experiencing a mood episode immediately or shortly after giving birth; this is well established. Hormone changes are swift and dramatic and are thought to play a major role in these high-risk times.

- ✔ **Perimenopause/menopause:** Women with depression and bipolar disorder are at higher risk of experiencing an episode of depression during menopause than are women with no history of a mood episode. This higher risk often overlaps with the additional concerns of aging as it relates to bipolar disorder and its treatment.

If you experience severe premenstrual mood symptoms, your doctor may consider prescribing a Selective Serotonin Reuptake Inhibitor (SSRI) antidepressant for you to take only during the week immediately preceding your period. SSRIs may have some specific and immediate effects on sex hormone production and/or metabolism that allow for more rapid reduction of depressive symptoms than typically experienced with SSRIs. (SSRIs often take three to six weeks to become fully effective.) However, if you have bipolar disorder, SSRIs can sometimes cause serious negative effects including triggering manic symptoms. Make sure the doctor treating your premenstrual mood symptoms is aware of your psychiatric diagnosis.

Bipolar disorder and pregnancy

All women of childbearing age being treated for bipolar disorder should discuss contraception and pregnancy with their doctors and have contingency plans in place for an unplanned pregnancy. These discussions must cover the different aspects of reproductive healthcare — both in terms of how bipolar affects pregnancies and how pregnancies affect bipolar. After all, half of all pregnancies are unplanned, and the percentage may be higher for women with bipolar disorder because they're at a higher risk of experiencing irregular menstrual cycles and patterns of impulsive sexual behavior.

In the following sections, we point out important decisions women with bipolar need to make, starting with the question of whether to get pregnant. We also provide important information for making medication choices before, during, and after pregnancy. This section also includes guidance on planning and preparing for pregnancy and managing bipolar during pregnancy.

Deciding whether to get pregnant

Bipolar disorder doesn't exclude you from parenthood. Many parents with bipolar disorder have raised healthy, well-adjusted children. When you're thinking about having children, ask yourself the following questions and discuss them with anyone in your support network who's likely to be involved in or affected by your decision:

- **What are the odds that my child will develop bipolar disorder?** If only one parent has bipolar, the child has a 5 to 10 percent chance of developing the illness. If both parents have it, the risk may be as high as 25 percent. (See Chapter 2 for more about the genetic factors of bipolar.)

- **How will the medications affect fetal development?** Many of the medications used to treat bipolar disorder can be dangerous to a developing fetus. (Check out the next section for details.)

- **How will the pregnancy affect my moods?** Pregnancy and the postpartum period are high-risk times for mood instability. Careful monitoring during pregnancy and at least 30 days after delivery can help you and your doctors identify early warning signs.

- **Can I handle the stress?** Being pregnant, delivering a baby, and raising an infant and child will undoubtedly disrupt schedules, change relationships, and increase stress. Through careful planning, though, you can reduce the disruptions and outsource at least some of the responsibilities and stressors.

Choosing medications before, during, and after pregnancy

If you're pregnant or may become pregnant, you and your doctor should carefully consider the benefits and risks of using medications during pregnancy. The following sections highlight important considerations to discuss with your doctor at various stages of reproduction.

Before pregnancy

All women of childbearing age need to discuss the following factors with their doctors when choosing medications for treating bipolar symptoms — even if they're not planning to become pregnant any time soon:

- Some medications, including carbamazepine (Tegretol), oxcarbazepine (Trileptal), lamotrigine (Lamictal), and topiramate (Topamax), may decrease the effectiveness of some types of birth control pills.

- Birth control pills may affect concentrations of other medications in the bloodstream, particularly lamotrigine, lowering the levels during the three weeks of exposure to estrogen and allowing levels to increase up to 50 percent during the pill-free last week.

✔ Certain antipsychotics may raise prolactin levels and reduce the chances of conception. If you're planning a pregnancy, your doctor may test your prolactin levels and discuss alternative medications.

✔ Valproate (Depakote) increases the risk of *polycystic ovary syndrome* (PCOS), a hormonal imbalance that increases levels of testosterone in women, which disrupts periods, causes acne and *hirsutism* (excessive body hair growth), increases the risks of type 2 diabetes and other health problems, and may cause infertility. Check out *PCOS For Dummies* by Gaynor Bussell and Sharon Perkins (John Wiley & Sons, Inc.) for more information.

During pregnancy

Medication decisions during pregnancy require close collaboration between the woman with bipolar, her psychiatrist, and her obstetrician. Of course, in a perfect world, not having to take medication during pregnancy is best, but research shows that discontinuation of bipolar medications during early pregnancy greatly increases the risk of a recurrent mood episode, especially in women with a history of frequent or severe mood symptoms. Such a mood episode can pose a danger to both mother and baby. Yet, early pregnancy (first trimester) is the period of highest risk for the most severe malformations of a fetus due to medication use, so it's when many women consider stopping all medications.

Medications are assigned to a class regarding potential risks during pregnancy. The following list describes where types of bipolar medication fall in this classification system and describes some of the specific concerns related to each class of medication:

✔ **Pregnancy Class D:** Use in *life-threatening* emergencies when no safer medication is available. Positive evidence of human fetal risk exists.

- **Lithium:** This medication presents a significant risk of cardiac abnormalities as well as risk of premature delivery, neurologic problems, and thyroid or kidney abnormalities in the fetus.

- **Valproate (Depakote):** This treatment comes with a high risk for major malformations of the fetus, especially when used in the first trimester. It also increases risk for stillbirth and miscarriage.

- **Carbamazepine (Tegretol):** Mothers taking carbamazepine during pregnancy face significant risk of fetal malformations.

- **Benzodiazepines:** This class of medication carries some increased risk of fetal malformations when used in the first trimester. When used late in pregnancy, it can cause *floppy baby syndrome,* a neurologic condition associated with weak muscles.

- **Paroxetine (Paxil):** Use in the first trimester has been associated with a higher risk of fetal malformations, especially in the cardio-vascular system. (Most of the currently used antidepressants fall into Class C, as presented next.)

- **Imipramine (Tofranil) and nortriptyline (Pamelor):** These tricy-clic antidepressants are considered Class D medications, while other tricyclics fall into Class C, as listed next.

✔ **Pregnancy Class C:** Use with caution if the benefits outweigh the risks. Animal studies show risk, human studies aren't available, or neither animal nor human studies have been done.

- **Lamotrigine (Lamictal):** This medication presents less risk of major malformations compared to the other anticonvulsants listed previously, but a significant risk of some birth defects still exists — possibly higher risks at higher doses.

- **Atypical antipsychotics:** Little information is available on the pregnancy risks of atypical antipsychotics, but they're thought to present lower risk of major malformations than Class D meds (lithium, valproate, and carbamazepine). Treatment-related weight gain and glucose/insulin changes in the mother may affect fetal development.

- **SSRI and SNRI antidepressants other than paroxetine:** Pregnant women should try to avoid antidepressants during the third tri-mester to reduce serotonin-induced problems in the newborn, including jitteriness, feeding difficulty, and breathing issues. Most antidepressants pose less risk of major malformations than the Class D medications. A rare problem associated with SSRIs is *pulmonary hypertension* — a problem in the heart and lung system — in the baby after lengthy exposure during pregnancy.

- **Other antidepressants:** These include bupropion (Wellbutrin), nefazodone (Serzone), vilazodone (Viibryd), desyrel (Trazodone), fluvoxamine (Luvox), mirtazapine (Remeron), the tricyclics desip-ramine (Norpramin) and amitriptyline (Elavil), and the MAO inhibi-tors tranylcypromine (Parnate) and phenelzine (Nardil).

Don't change your treatment regimen or stop taking medications without consulting your doctor. Relapse rates during and after pregnancy are rela-tively high and increase the risk of impulsivity, poor self-care, and suicide. Work with your doctor to develop a treatment plan that balances your well-being (which is just as important for the baby as it is for you) with security regarding the baby's development. Often such plans include choosing medi-cations that carry less risk in pregnancy, using only one medicine if possible, and keeping the doses as low as possible. (See the section "Planning and prepping for pregnancy" for details.)

Postpartum

The postpartum period is known for its high risks for recurrent mood episodes. Many women and their doctors restart the prepregnancy medications right after delivery to reduce the likelihood of a mood episode occurring. But doing so has the following potential downsides:

- ✔ Many medications are transmitted through breast milk, so if you start taking your meds immediately after giving birth, you may want to bottle-feed rather than breast-feed, which may also help regulate your sleep.

- ✔ Fatigue or other side effects of restarting medication may be especially challenging with a newborn at home; however, these effects may be a small price to pay for preventing a mood episode.

- ✔ Getting medication levels on track can be challenging immediately after delivery, when body weight and fluid levels shift so much.

Planning and prepping for pregnancy

If you're a woman with bipolar disorder and you decide to try to get pregnant, work with your doctor to develop and write a plan to facilitate the pregnancy, minimize risks to the fetus, and prevent mood cycling. Your planning and preparation should target the following goals:

- ✔ **Stabilize your mood for several months prior to conception.** Starting a pregnancy when moods are stable improves your chances for maintaining mood stability throughout the pregnancy.

- ✔ **Monitor your moods more closely.** Recruit a few trusted friends or relatives — ideally those you see a few times or more every week — to help monitor your moods. Make sure your recruits know your early warning signs and know what to do if they notice a problem.

- ✔ **Use the least number of medications at their lowest effective doses.** If medication is necessary, the goal is *monotherapy* (one med).

- ✔ **Avoid medications that have high risks of causing problems with fetal development.** This usually means weaning off valproate, carbamazepine, lithium, and paroxetine and switching to a different preventive medication if possible.

- ✔ **Ramp up non-medication treatments and support.** Proper nutrition (which includes prenatal vitamins with folic acid), getting regular and adequate sleep, psychotherapy, and family support ease the added burden of the pregnancy and help make up for any reduction in medication.

Managing bipolar and pregnancy

If you think you may be pregnant, confirm the pregnancy as soon as possible and schedule a meeting with your psychiatrist and your OB/GYN to plan a course of action that's most appropriate for you and your pregnancy. As part of your plan, consider the following steps:

1. **Schedule more frequent doctor and therapist appointments.**

2. **Discuss and make medication adjustments with your doctor.**

3. **If you're on lithium and decide to stay on it during the pregnancy, take the following precautions:**

   - Discuss with your doctor the possibility of stopping the lithium during the first trimester, when it's more likely to affect fetal development, and restarting it in the second trimester.

   - Talk with your doctor about spreading your daily dose over the course of the day to maintain a steady level of lithium.

   - Ask your OB/GYN about scheduling regular ultrasounds or other tests to monitor the development of your baby's heart.

   - Regulate your fluid intake more carefully. Be especially mindful of dehydration, which can increase lithium levels.

   - Talk to you doctor about gradually and temporarily reducing your dose of lithium by at least 50 percent for the week prior to delivery to avoid lithium toxicity that may result from fluid loss during delivery.

   - Have your lithium blood level checked more frequently — every four weeks until the 36th week and then weekly until the delivery. Check it again within 24 hours after childbirth.

   - Talk with your doctor about reestablishing your full maintenance dose of lithium after your baby is born and discuss any plans you may have to breast-feed.

4. **If you're taking an atypical antipsychotic, have your doctor monitor your weight and glucose levels throughout the pregnancy.**

   Doctors monitor these levels for all pregnancies, but your doctor may choose to be more vigilant if you take atypical antipsychotics.

5. **As always, if you observe the early warning signs of a change in mood, contact your psychiatrist immediately.**

If your mood starts to shift toward mania or depression, you and your doctor may want to reconsider medication or non-medication alternatives, such as electroconvulsive therapy (ECT). ECT is considered a relatively safe option for pregnant women who are experiencing severe mania or depression that's not responding to medication. ECT doesn't appear to be associated with significant fetal malformations; the issues that arise are mostly related to possible cardiac problems in the fetus related to the use of anesthetics. In rare cases, ECT can also trigger uterine contractions. ECT is still a second or third choice after medications, even in pregnancy simply because it's a more invasive and complicated procedure. (For more about ECT, see Chapter 9.)

Dealing with bipolar during menopause

Perimenopause, the years leading up to menopause, as well as menopause and postmenopause are times of significant shifts in hormone levels that can trigger mood irregularity even in women who don't have bipolar disorder. For women who do have bipolar, these fluctuations in hormone levels can seriously exacerbate mood symptoms, especially depression as estrogen levels drop and the ratio of estrogen to progesterone shifts.

If mood irregularities arise or worsen as a result of menopause, your doctor may recommend some form of hormone replacement therapy (HRT) instead of or in addition to prescribing an antidepressant or antimanic medication. HRT isn't for everyone, especially if cardiovascular problems are a concern, but some women with severe mood symptoms respond well to HRT.

Older Adults and Bipolar Disorder

Diagnosing and treating bipolar in older adults poses unique challenges. Here, we highlight some characteristics of this population that don't apply to others, and we offer guidance on choosing and managing medications when bipolar disorder threatens to take the shine off your golden years.

What's so different about older adults?

Only about 10 percent of people with bipolar disorder receive their diagnosis when they're past the age of 50, but whether you've been diagnosed before or after your 50th birthday, aging brings new challenges in managing the illness. The common thread in both situations — new and preexisting diagnoses — is that the changing body and brain in older adults create the following important differences in the presentation and treatment of bipolar disorder:

- Risks of medical and neurologic conditions are much higher in older adults. If someone presents with new symptoms of mania or depression in his later years, a doctor must perform a careful differential diagnosis to rule out other possible causes of the mood symptoms. (See Chapter 5 for information on what constitutes a differential diagnosis.)

- Doctors need to put together a careful medical work-up for people with preexisting bipolar disorder and worsening mood symptoms, especially if the symptoms are inconsistent with previous patterns.

- Older people tend to take more medications, and the risk of side effects increases due to age and the layering of medicines. Some medicines can trigger depression or mania. New manic symptoms or severe depression in older people can be a result of medication toxicity or interactions.

✓ People who've been on medications for bipolar disorder for many years can develop long-term side effects, including kidney damage and thyroid abnormalities, which can trigger behavioral changes. In addition, side effects of bipolar medications, including lithium toxicity, are much more common in older adults. When someone experiences worsening mood symptoms, his doctor needs to carefully consider medication-related problems as possible causes.

Addressing dementia and bipolar

Declining cognitive function — ranging from mild memory issues to severe dementia — can present with mood and behavioral symptoms, including irritability, impulsivity, low energy or motivation, sadness or apathy, and inappropriate emotional responses. A careful evaluation for dementia is critical in someone presenting with new mood symptoms or in someone with bipolar who appears to be getting worse with age. Bipolar disorder is associated with higher rates of dementia in later life compared to the general population. Some of this may be specific to bipolar, and some may be overlap with Alzheimer's and other dementias.

Evaluation for dementia often starts with a Mini Mental Status Examination (MMSE). If this exam suggests evidence of cognitive decline, the doctor orders more detailed cognitive or neuropsychological testing. Medicine, combinations of medicines, and many different medical conditions can cause symptoms of dementia. So just as with mood and behavioral symptoms, after dementia is detected, a full medical work-up is required to rule out treatable causes of the cognitive changes.

Medication issues for older adults

Medication profiles for older adults with bipolar differ from those of younger populations, and doctors must consider these differences when choosing medications and determining the proper dose. In this section, we point out key issues for choosing treatments, especially medication, for older adults.

Treating mania

The same medications are used to treat mania in all adult groups, but the goal of monotherapy (one med) is very important for older people. Note the other differences:

✓ **Lithium:** Kidneys are likely to function less efficiently with age, so lithium levels may build up more quickly, causing toxicity symptoms to occur at lower doses. In addition, nonsteroidal anti-inflammatory drugs (NSAIDs), angiotensin-converting enzyme inhibitors, and thiazide diuretics can raise the lithium level. Your doctor may be less likely to prescribe lithium if you take any of these medications or if you have a cognitive impairment or tremor, which lithium can worsen.

✔ **Anticonvulsants:** Valproate (Depakote) remains in the bloodstream longer in older adults; plus, it interacts with many other medications. Carbamazepine (Tegretol) has been effective in treating mania in older adults, but it has many potentially dangerous interactions with other medications. Lamotrigine (Lamictal) has shown to be effective in maintenance treatment in adults over 55 years old.

✔ **Antipsychotics:** The recommended dose of atypical antipsychotics for older adults is generally one-half to one-third the dose prescribed for younger adults. However, both older (typical) and newer (atypical) antipsychotics are *contraindicated* (recommended not to be used) in elderly people with dementia, because they're associated with increased risk of death most often due to heart problems or infections. These medications must be prescribed carefully for older adults. (See Chapter 7 for more information.)

✔ **Electroconvulsive therapy (ECT):** ECT has proven effective in treating acute mania and depression in older adults with bipolar disorder and may be considered for someone who's not responding to or can't tolerate medications. (For more about ECT, see Chapter 9.)

Treating depression

Treating bipolar depression is always a challenge — no matter how old you are. Options for treating older adults are similar to those for the general population with some variations:

✔ **Antidepressants:** An antidepressant-antimanic combo is a common treatment choice for older adults, but possible side effects, impact on other medical conditions, and drug interactions must be considered.

✔ **Lithium:** This is a standard part of antidepressant care for many people with bipolar disorder, but as previously noted, carries higher risks of dangerous side effects in older people.

✔ **Atypical antipsychotics:** Quetiapine and lurasidone are medications in this family that are used to treat bipolar depression. They carry additional risks (as previously noted) that must be considered when choosing them for the elderly.

✔ **Lamotrigine (Lamictal):** Evidence suggests that lamotrigine is effective in lengthening the time to a depressive episode, and it has some antidepressant qualities in older adults. The risks of developing Stevens-Johnson syndrome, a serious skin reaction to lamotrigine, are actually lower in older adults than in younger populations.

✔ **Psychotherapy:** Psychotherapy and social interventions are often useful in treating depression in older adults, especially if medication isn't an option or isn't fully effective.

✔ **Electroconvulsive therapy (ECT):** ECT has proven effective in treating depression in older adults and may be considered if you're not responding to or can't tolerate available medications.

Treating anxiety and sleep disorders

Because older bodies eliminate medication more slowly, sedating medications (such as those used to treat anxiety and insomnia) can build up over time. This can cause problems with memory and concentration. Because these problems build slowly, the link to medication may not be obvious. It's important to reevaluate the benefits and risks of taking these medications as you get older.

Accommodating Cultural Differences

Rates of bipolar disorder are similar across all populations in every part of the world, but ethnic and cultural factors influence the diagnosis, treatment, and response to medication, so doctors must consider these differences. Here are some of the most significant cultural factors affecting people with bipolar:

✔ **Cultural context:** Thoughts, behaviors, and intensity of emotional expression considered normal in one culture may seem unusual in another. Doctors should consider their patients' thoughts, behaviors, and expressions in context of the patients' cultural identity.

✔ **Language:** When a doctor and a person with a mental illness speak different languages, exchanging vital information can be difficult. To avoid getting a relative's emotionally tainted translation, doctors should use an unbiased interpreter when communicating in this situation.

✔ **Perception of mental illness:** The stigma of mental illness may be stronger in some cultures than in others and result in more resistance to diagnosis and treatment of bipolar disorder.

✔ **Preferences in treatment and support:** Culture influences whether a person is more likely to see a doctor for psychiatric distress or look to religion, folk remedies, or other options. Certain cultures have especially close-knit communities for providing social support, and cultural differences in how people interpret the benefits and side effects of medications affect treatment outcomes.

✔ **Medication metabolism:** Ethnicity may influence dosing requirements and effectiveness of certain medications due to variations in the genetics of enzymes that metabolize medications. For example, people of Asian descent and African Americans tend to be slow metabolizers of many medications, although the genetic variation is different in the two groups. Other groups, including Ethiopians, Sephardic and Ethiopian Jews, and Arabs, tend to be ultra-rapid metabolizers of many medications.

Bipolar in the LGBT Community

Individuals who identify as lesbian, gay, bisexual, or transgender (LGBT) face a host of unique challenges when dealing with a diagnosis of bipolar. Research in this specific area is quite limited, but several issues stand out as considerations for addressing bipolar in LGBT individuals and communities:

✔ **Stigma:** With a diagnosis of bipolar disorder, the stigma of mental illness adds to an already heavy burden for LGBT people and their loved ones. Young people struggling with gender identity and sexual orientation questions are particularly vulnerable to negative and outright hostile attitudes and behaviors in their communities and sometimes in their families. Rejection, taunting, and bullying can cause trauma that further inflames already simmering mood symptoms. Layering stigma around gender and sexuality issues on to stigma related to mental health challenges can feel insurmountable.

✔ **Provider awareness:** Treatment providers vary widely in their knowledge, awareness, and levels of internalized stigma when working with LGBT individuals with bipolar disorder. Sexuality in general is poorly taught in medical school and training, and many doctors don't even bother to ask about sexual orientation or gender identification. If you feel you're not receiving respect and understanding from your doctor, seek help elsewhere or speak to an administrator.

✔ **Other health concerns:** Human immunodeficiency virus (HIV) and acquired immune deficiency syndrome (AIDS) are more common in the LGBT community than in the general population, and these illnesses can complicate the presentation and treatment of bipolar. Neurologic changes caused by AIDS can create emotional and behavioral symptoms that sometimes overlap with symptoms of bipolar, making medical work-ups critical for finding the actual causes of mood symptoms in LGBT people.

Part IV
Developing Essential Survival Skills

Seven ways to improve treatment success

✔ Take your medications as prescribed.

✔ Monitor your moods to identify early warning signs and seek medical help sooner rather than later.

✔ Establish healthy routines, including, most importantly, a regular sleep schedule that ensures seven to nine hours of sleep per night.

✔ Keep regular appointments with a qualified therapist.

✔ Adopt a healthy lifestyle in terms of nutrition and physical activity and avoiding excessive use of alcohol, marijuana, and even caffeine and nicotine, which can disrupt mood.

✔ Team up with loved ones to improve communication skills and reduce misunderstandings and conflicts that may affect mood.

✔ Hone problem-solving skills to more effectively deal with challenges and potential sources of conflict.

Visit www.dummies.com/extras/bipolardisorder for a bonus article on using humor to cope with bipolar disorder.

In this part . . .

✔ Discover self-help strategies for managing your moods, such as mood monitoring and lifestyle adjustments that may help reduce or eliminate triggers that often contribute to mood instability.

✔ Find out about psychosocial therapies that have proven effective in managing bipolar disorder and reducing the frequency and severity of symptoms.

✔ Obtain guidance on how to improve your communication and problem-solving skills to alleviate or reduce the frequency and intensity of interpersonal conflict.

✔ Find tips on how to plan ahead for a major mood episode so that you and the rest of the people on your treatment team are better equipped to reduce an episode's severity and duration and manage the fallout that commonly results from such an episode.

Chapter 11

Exploring Self-Help Strategies, Therapies, and Other Supports

In This Chapter

▶ Keeping track of your moods, sleep patterns, and energy levels

▶ Recognizing what really sets you off . . . and addressing it

▶ Exploring therapies, mindfulness, and other approaches

*I*n the midst of a major mood episode, you may be powerless to help yourself, but after the episode subsides and you feel more like your old self, you can begin to engage in therapy and self-help efforts that have proven useful in maintaining mood stability and warding off future episodes. Simple, free activities include monitoring your moods, sleep patterns, and energy levels and getting involved in a local support group. Professional help is also available in the form of various psychotherapies, mindfulness training, and relationship and family therapy.

In this chapter, we explain different ways you can monitor and manage your moods on your own and with outside assistance. We also encourage you to keep track of how different treatment tactics work for you so you can do more of what works and less of what doesn't.

Monitoring Your Moods

One of the most useful activities you can do to help in your recovery and avoid mood meltdowns is to monitor your moods. Mood monitoring offers the following benefits:

✔ Increases your awareness of your moods and fluctuations

✔ Serves as an early warning of impending mood episodes

✔ Helps gauge the effectiveness of medications and therapies

Go to www.dummies.com/extras/bipolardisorder for a mood chart to help you monitor your moods and track variations over time. You can use it to record your mood every day on a scale of +5 (manic) to –5 (depressed). Normal, baseline is 0. Simply place an X in the box that best represents your overall mood level for each day. The Notes area at the bottom provides space for you to log any medication changes or significant events that affect your moods on any given day. If you already have a calendar, just write a number in every daily block from +5 to –5 to indicate your mood level. Keep in mind that some people experience symptoms of depression and mania at the same time. If that's true for you, be sure to record them both. This means that one day may show a +3 and a –4.

Share your mood charts with your doctor and therapist. The daily information can help you identify your stressors and triggers, manage your medications, and track the success of your treatment. When your doctor or therapist asks you how you've been doing since your last appointment, the charts enable you to answer accurately with data.

If you have a smartphone, consider installing an app for monitoring bipolar moods. The Depression and Bipolar Support Alliance website (www.dbsalliance.org) includes an online wellness tracker you can use to track your mood symptoms. Search online for "bipolar mood app" to find other relevant smartphone and computer apps.

Charting Sleep and Energy Levels

A decreasing need for sleep is an almost universal early indication of an impending manic episode, while an inability to get out of bed is a pretty good indicator of depression. We encourage you to keep a sleep log or at least note on your mood chart or daily calendar how much sleep you're getting and what your daily energy level is.

Simply record the total number of hours you sleep each day, including naps, and record your energy level for that day on a scale of 0 to 5. (You may find that your energy level is a pretty good reflection of your overall mood for the day.) The Notes area at the end of the mood chart doesn't provide much room for notes, but acts more as a reminder to jot down anything that may have affected your mood, sleep, or energy level; feel free to color outside the lines. You can download a larger PDF version of the mood chart at www.dummies.com/extras/bipolardisorder and print as many copies as you need.

If you're tech oriented, consider investing in some type of activity tracker that can measure sleep patterns as well as activity levels during the day — a gadget that syncs to your smartphone or computer or a smartphone app. The new smart watches may be ideal for tracking activity.

You can use your sleep log to identify early warning signs and patterns that you may need to address for optimum mood stability. Monitor your sleep log each day for the following patterns and warning signs:

- ✔ **Increasing need for sleep:** If you're sleeping more and your energy levels are sinking, your mood may be on a downswing.

- ✔ **Decreasing need for sleep:** If your energy levels are climbing and you're sleeping less, you may be working up to a manic episode.

- ✔ **Trouble falling asleep or staying asleep (insomnia):** Most people take about 20 minutes to fall asleep and have some awakenings at night but can fall back to sleep pretty quickly. If you're taking a long time to fall asleep, waking up frequently in the night and can't get back to sleep, or waking up very early in the morning and can't rest again, take note of these red flags, particularly for depression.

- ✔ **Variations in sleep patterns:** If you're sleeping in on weekends, taking long naps during the day, and/or unable to sleep when you normally go to bed, then you may need to work on regulating your sleep patterns.

If you're having trouble falling asleep or sleeping through the night, flip to Chapter 12 for suggestions.

Identifying Stressors and Triggers

People, places, jobs, events, seasons, and even holidays can play a significant role in your mood stability. By identifying your mood triggers and the primary sources of stress in your life, you can begin to remove them or at least diminish the toxic effects they have on your moods.

The body reads all highly charged environmental stimuli as stress whether it's strongly negative or strongly positive. So triggers can range from situations that feel bad or uncomfortable to those that feel especially exciting or stimulating. Some studies suggest that, more often than not, manic episodes actually follow a big positive life event.

Jot down the major sources of good and bad stress in your life, along with situations that seem to trigger depression or mania. Here are some common stressors and triggers that may help you identify your own:

- **Seasonal shifts:** Certain seasons can trigger mood problems for some people. Spring seems to usher in more mania, while the winter months tend to bring on depressive episodes. Daylight saving time may also contribute to mood and sleep irregularities.

- **Holidays:** Holidays often deliver a double dose of dysfunction: They disrupt a carefully structured routine and frequently place you in contact with family members who may be exciting or irritating. Planning for the holidays may include sticking to your daily routines, avoiding or limiting contact with certain people and situations, and consulting your doctor for a short-term medication adjustment or the addition of an antianxiety med.

- **Work- or school-related stress or conflict:** Conflicts with coworkers, irregular hours, unreasonable goals, and unpredictable job responsibilities are just a few of the on-the-job stressors that may contribute to the onset of bipolar symptoms. Promotions, new responsibilities and expectations, and the completion of major projects can also trigger stress reactions, so watch out for those, too. For young adults, back-to-school demands (especially when starting college), and graduation are common triggers.

- **Relationship issues:** Relationship conflict is a common cause of stress. It may arise from numerous sources, and bipolar disorder can contribute to it by seeking out conflict to feed its insatiable appetite for stimulation or simply from the manic and depressive symptoms themselves. The cycle of conflict and symptoms can be difficult to break. Highly positive feelings and events in relationships can also be stressful. If avoiding or ending a negative relationship isn't possible or desirable, then you and the other person may need to work on addressing the challenges together, perhaps with the help of a qualified therapist.

- **Parenting issues:** Raising children is stressful, and it can be even more so when bipolar disorder is part of the family. The birth of a child is a huge life event, and parenting affects your sleep and other life patterns in ways that are often unpredictable. If you find yourself arguing frequently with your children or partner about parenting duties and approaches, then parenting is probably a stressor that you need to address, possibly with the help of a qualified therapist.

- **Financial strain:** Bipolar disorder often strains finances in two ways: It removes sources of income and increases the cost of living. If you're worried or arguing over money, consider finances as a source of stress. In Chapter 18, we provide suggestions on how to overcome the financial setbacks that often accompany bipolar.

✔ **Downtime:** In modern times, having too much to do is more common than not having enough to do; but having too little to do can be a major source of stress as well. In quiet times, the mind may ruminate on worries or negative thoughts. Structuring some of your downtime and keeping your brain and body engaged in tasks or activities can help minimize this source of stress.

Don't try to fix everything at once. Make a list of your stressors and triggers and deal with one issue at a time, in order of importance.

Seeking Out Therapy and Support

Although medication is the first-line treatment for bipolar disorder, several therapies and other supports have proven effective in helping people with bipolar disorder maintain mood stability. In the following sections, we introduce you to these therapies and provide exercises and resources you can use right now to sample each approach.

You may need different types of help depending on the symptoms or problems you're experiencing. If you're struggling with depression, for instance, your focus may be on overcoming negative thoughts, increasing your involvement in positive activities, and finding more support in your important relationships. If your mood is stable, you may want to concentrate on maintaining a healthy routine and keeping an eye on early warning signs of a mood episode. If instead you're experiencing mild symptoms of mania, you may need to explore techniques for managing impulsivity and irritability.

Keep track of your treatment successes and failures in a journal or some other document. In one column, list what has worked for you in the past; in the other, describe what hasn't helped. This record can be very useful for you and the people on your treatment team as you try to find the best tools for maintaining mood stability.

Psychoeducation

Throughout the course of your illness, your ability to accept the fact that you have bipolar disorder may wax and wane. Your ability to objectively observe and evaluate your moods and behaviors may improve or worsen. Your desire to seek treatment may also rise and fall. *Psychoeducation* is a type of therapy that can improve your treatment outcome by educating you about bipolar disorder and making you more aware of symptoms and early warning signs so you can more effectively maintain mood stability. Through psychoeducation, you gain the following benefits:

- ✔ A clearer understanding of bipolar disorder causes and treatments
- ✔ Knowledge of why medication is necessary
- ✔ Insight to how therapy can help
- ✔ Improved ability to recognize symptoms that signal the onset of a mood episode
- ✔ Insight to the stressors and triggers that may contribute to your mood shifts
- ✔ Confidence that proper treatment can improve your condition
- ✔ Strengthened resolve to adhere to your treatment plan

This book is a type of psychoeducation. You can also learn more about how to effectively manage bipolar disorder from doctors and therapists, support groups, group therapy, and websites and blogs that provide accurate information (not all do).

One of the main goals of psychoeducation for bipolar is to improve *insight* (your ability to recognize warning signs) in the early stages of mania or depression, so you can take steps to prevent a full-blown mood episode.

Cognitive behavioral therapy (CBT)

If you've ever beaten yourself up over something you said or did, you're well aware of your brain's power to turn against you and make you feel terrible. *Cognitive behavioral therapy (CBT)* is based on the concept that thoughts are major drivers of emotional responses. CBT is designed to train your brain and body to develop more adaptive thought and behavioral patterns, which then help modulate emotional responses. The other goal of CBT is to modify your physical and emotional responses to stressors through exposure techniques — gradually increasing exposure to uncomfortable situations, such as speaking up when you need something, to make these situations more manageable.

When examined as a step-by-step process, CBT looks something like this:

1. **Develop a list of symptoms or responses and rank them in order of perceived difficulty — most to least difficult.**

2. **Identify distorted thoughts and beliefs that trigger *maladaptive* emotional responses and/or reinforce other symptom patterns.**

3. **Quiet your brain to become aware of distorted thoughts and beliefs.**

4. **Develop and practice new rational beliefs and logical thoughts to replace or "talk back to" the distortions.**

5. **Develop and practice positive and effective behaviors based on the new thoughts and beliefs.**

6. **Work on exposure techniques — being exposed to one of your anxiety triggers at gradually increasing levels of intensity and purposefully triggering controlled anxiety responses that allow the brain and body to change big reactions to smaller ones.**

A qualified therapist can recommend techniques to help you identify and eliminate your distorted thoughts. Approaches vary, depending on your distorted thoughts and the way they impact your behavior and responses in particular situations. Here are some popular approaches:

✔ Journaling to monitor distorted thoughts and identify how they can possibly affect your behavior

✔ Envisioning how an action or event will unfold so you can become comfortable with it

✔ Challenging, in which the therapist acts as a devil's advocate by arguing on the side of your distorted belief while you voice challenges to refute it

✔ Role-playing to enable you to act out an uncomfortable scenario with your therapist before you try it out in the real world

✔ Experimenting with different options that you discuss in therapy

✔ Desensitizing yourself to uncomfortable situations by gradually increasing your exposure to those types of situations

✔ Acting "as if" when you perform the role of someone acting out the new behavior, even if it doesn't feel real or genuine yet

Psychotherapists have used CBT successfully for years to treat unipolar and bipolar depression. CBT is also a primary treatment for anxiety and obsessive-compulsive disorder. Because antidepressants often aggravate mania, CBT is an important tool for helping to alleviate depression without the undesirable side effects of medication. Brain scans have shown that CBT actually changes activity levels in brain regions related to mood and anxiety — decreasing overactivity in some *circuits* (pathways between brain cells) and increasing the activity in underpowered circuits. Like medication, CBT is a powerful modulator of brain activity at its most basic cellular levels.

Theory has it that CBT may also help with early stages of a rising hypomanic or manic episode by toning down overly positive, optimistic beliefs to bring them more in line with reality. Research is less prevalent for this application of CBT than for its use with depression, but the potential benefits of CBT in mania are being explored.

In sports, you practice your skills well before the big game so that they're already second nature when you're under pressure. For similar reasons, do your CBT work daily, when your mind is quiet and life is settled — not during a full-blown mood episode — because the brain has a tough time learning anything new when it's out of control. With new skills firmly in place, when the dust hits the fan, your brain will be poised to keep itself clearer and more focused than it otherwise could.

For more about CBT, check out *Cognitive Behavioural Therapy For Dummies* by Rob Willson and Rhena Branch (John Wiley & Sons, Inc.).

Dialectical behavioral therapy (DBT)

Dialectical behavioral therapy (DBT) is a spin-off of CBT that focuses on building a set of skills for regulating emotions, managing interpersonal relationships and conflict, and tolerating distress. Dr. Marsha Linehan developed DBT as a treatment for individuals with borderline personality disorder (BPD), but it has become much more widely used in practice. Through DBT, people become more sensitive to the ramping up of their emotions, and this increased awareness helps them intercept their emotional arousal and respond to situations in an even-tempered, problem-solving way.

DBT traditionally involves work with an individual therapist every week as well as weekly group sessions that provide participants with opportunities to practice their skills by actually interacting with others, including friends and family members who agree to participate.

In a number of studies, DBT has been proven effective for borderline personality disorder. Evidence of its effectiveness in the treatment of bipolar disorder is evolving and some research supports its use. From a practical standpoint, though, DBT often makes sense as an adjunct treatment, because it helps those living with bipolar

✔ Identify patterns of emotional responses.

✔ Develop skills for tolerating and regulating those emotional responses without paralysis or impulsive actions.

✔ Discover how to effectively navigate interpersonal relationships.

Interpersonal and social rhythm therapy (IPSRT)

Interpersonal and social rhythm therapy (IPSRT) helps you develop a structured routine along with positive personal and social connections. Ellen Frank and her colleagues developed IPSRT at the Western Psychiatric Institute & Clinic at the University of Pittsburgh to reduce the frequency of mood episodes by balancing the stimulation and rest cycles of day-to-day life and resolving interpersonal discord. This therapy typically follows a four-stage process:

- ✔ **Initial:** In this phase, you and your therapist develop a detailed history of your disorder, identifying mood episodes and their severity and any life events, medications, or work history that coincided with each episode. The therapist helps you develop an interpersonal inventory, highlighting important people in your life and the roles they play, and assists you in identifying relationships and social activities that support or undermine stable biorhythms. The therapist also provides psychoeducation about bipolar disorder.

- ✔ **Intermediate:** In this phase, you gradually regulate your schedule and work toward establishing relationships and participating in social activities that are conducive to regulating your biorhythms and less likely to disrupt them. The goal of this phase is to establish a regular schedule of sleep, wake, and meal times.

- ✔ **Maintenance:** Maintaining routines in the midst of discord can be quite a challenge. This phase, which can last for several years, helps you identify events and anticipate and resolve conflicts that threaten your rhythm and routines.

- ✔ **Termination:** When you no longer need your therapist's help to maintain your rhythm and routines, the therapist leads you through a termination phase, essentially weaning you from therapy.

If you want to pursue this type of therapy, teaming up with a therapist who specializes in IPSRT is usually best; but if that's not an option, the following sections offer a basic do-it-yourself guide.

Identify your natural rhythm

The first step toward a more predictable schedule is to determine your current patterns and preferences. Figure 11-1 provides a daily grid that you can fill out to record your activities for a week. For each day, log your activities from the time you wake up until the time you go to bed, including meals, work, social functions, family time, exercise, naps, and anything else you do.

Figure 11-1:
Record your daily schedule on this grid to determine your personal rhythms and needs.

My Daily Activities

Time of Day	Sunday	Monday	Tuesday	Wednesday	Thursday	Friday	Saturday
6 a.m.							
7 a.m.							
8 a.m.							
9 a.m.							
10 a.m.							
11 a.m.							
Noon							
1 p.m.							
2 p.m.							
3 p.m.							
4 p.m.							
5 p.m.							
6 p.m.							
7 p.m.							
8 p.m.							
9 p.m.							
10 p.m.							
11 p.m.							
Midnight							
1 a.m.							
2 a.m.							
3 a.m.							
4 a.m.							
5 a.m.							

Structure your daily routine

After you complete your weekly activity log (refer to Figure 11-1), examine it for the most dramatic variations in your daily schedule and draft a schedule with less variation. Don't make drastic changes that you can't possibly tolerate. Take a gradual approach. You can make additional adjustments later. Part of IPSRT calls for formulating goals and expectations for change. When your expectations are realistic, you're more likely to stay on track.

IPSRT helps you identify your most out-of-sync patterns so you can moderate them. For example, if you go to bed at 10:30 p.m. every night except Friday when you stay out until 3 a.m., IPSRT may help you see the value in going out a little earlier on Friday and getting to bed at 1 a.m.

Regulate your interpersonal and social rhythms

As you work toward regulating your schedule, also strive toward building relationships and engaging in social situations that are conducive for maintaining a regular schedule and a stable emotional environment. Everyone's relationships and interests are different, so we can't provide exact details on how to achieve this, but consider these suggestions:

- ✔ Avoid or *dose* relationships that tend to disrupt your daily routines or are emotionally charged. (*Dosing* relationships is like adjusting doses of medication; you regulate the frequency or intensity of a relationship and make adjustments over time as conditions change.)

- ✔ Identify and address relationship issues that lead to conflict.

- ✔ Team up with the people closest to you to support your efforts toward establishing and maintaining a regular routine.

- ✔ Get involved in a group that meets regularly — a support group, yoga class, volunteer organization, or church group, for example.

Maintain your rhythm in the midst of change

IPSRT recognizes that change is an inevitable part of life. People get married and divorced, have children, change jobs, and so on. Part of IPSRT involves anticipating change and developing strategies to replace certain routines while maintaining others. The following ideas can help you prepare for change:

- ✔ **Plan ahead for holidays.** Don't let your family dictate the routines you follow. Someone else's rhythms may not coincide with yours.

- ✔ **Plan your weekends.** Unplanned weekends can leave you with nothing to do, which can be depressing, or leave you open to unrestrained spontaneity, which can lead to manic impulsivity.

✔ **Seek immediate treatment for any physical ailments.** Coughs, colds, night sweats, incontinence, and other illnesses can really foul up your sleep-wake schedule and other routines. See your doctor for help.

✔ **Resolve conflicts as soon as possible.** Allowing conflicts and relationship issues to fester builds tension, which eventually finds a way to express itself. Seek counseling if necessary.

✔ **Establish 30 minutes of quiet time before bed.** During this time, don't allow any arguments or television shows or video games and avoid stimulating activities that may interfere with your sleep, including work and homework.

✔ **Ban arguments at dinnertime.** If an issue arises during the dinner conversation, take note of it and schedule a time to discuss it later, but not right before bed. Let dinner be a peaceful, restorative time.

✔ **Provide sufficient time to get ready for work.** Keep your mornings as stress-free as possible.

✔ **Allot time at the end of your workday to unwind.** Smooth transitions between work and personal time reduce stress.

Mindfulness and other centering activities

CBT and other therapies we describe in this chapter usually include many strategies for reducing your emotional charge and quieting your brain, including breathing exercises, meditation, and progressive relaxation techniques. One common feature of all these techniques is *mindfulness* — the process of focusing your brain on the moment and being fully present. Mindfulness clears your brain, calms your nerves, and allows you to discover new ways of responding emotionally, cognitively, and behaviorally. In fact, DBT uses mindfulness as a core technique for quieting overpowering emotions and working to balance emotional and rational responses.

Numerous scientific studies support the emotional and behavioral benefits of mindfulness strategies, and imaging studies have demonstrated positive changes in brain and body circuits as a result of mindfulness training. *Mindfulness-based stress reduction (MBSR)* is a form of mindfulness practice directed at reducing distress, improving attention and *cognitive control* (regulating your mental activity), and enriching life. MBSR was developed by Jon Kabat-Zinn at the University of Massachusetts Medical Center and is now being used widely to treat depression and anxiety, as well as other challenges such as attention deficit hyperactivity disorder (ADHD).

Consider including some form of mindfulness training as part of your therapy. Possibilities include

- Breathing exercises
- Visualization techniques
- Progressive muscle relaxation procedures
- Yoga
- Tai chi
- Meditation

A quick and simple mindfulness exercise is to shift awareness to each of your five senses in turn. While you perform a chore, such as folding laundry or pulling weeds, bring your mind to what you're experiencing in the world at that moment. What do you see? Smell? Hear? Touch? Taste? You may be surprised at what you hadn't noticed around you; in the meantime, you're able to focus your brain and get out of the whirlpool of worries, demands, and judgments in your head. Take a deep breath and move forward with fresh mental energy.

For more mindfulness techniques, check out *Mindfulness For Dummies* by Shamash Alidina (John Wiley & Sons, Inc.).

Beyond medication: Taking care of myself

I'm a 38-year-old author and blogger from Slovenia. In 1996, I was diagnosed with schizoaffective disorder, bipolar type — a mixture of schizophrenia and bipolar disorder. Now I'm a rather calm and, for the most part, mentally healthy girl.

Taking my medication is only a part of what I do to stay healthy. I start my day with a Phyllis Krystal (www.phylliskrystal.com) method of meditation called The Maple. While meditating, I burn incense and listen to soft instrumental music. I also do yoga daily, and I love to take long nature walks. Throughout the day, I do various exercises according to the Phyllis Krystal method, such as the Fear Exercise when I'm scared or the Anger Exercise when I'm angry. Occasionally, I also engage in the Cutting the Ties Exercise, which is designed

to free me from control of people, thoughts, and behaviors, including bad habits, addictions, and destructive roles I often get stuck playing. From 2006 until today, I have cut about 20 ties.

Since 2009, my work-at-home job as an author and blogger has relieved a great deal of stress and provides me with a flexible schedule to perform the exercises that help me maintain my health. I'm also an avid runner and find a great deal of solace in drawing and painting in my spare time.

— Helena Smole
(www.helenasmole.com),
author of *Balancing the Beast: A Bright View of Schizoaffective Disorder — Bipolar or Manic-Depressive Type*

Relationship and family therapies

Family therapy can be very effective in helping family members come to terms with bipolar disorder and work together as a team; it also tends to improve the prognosis for the person who has the diagnosis. Therapy that includes psychoeducation, communication skills (see Chapter 13), emotional regulation (see Chapter 12), and problem-solving strategies (see Chapter 14) can help family members acquire much needed knowledge and skills to support one another.

Support groups

Support groups can be useful for obtaining emotional support, information, and solutions to common problems related to bipolar disorder. Some support groups also welcome or are exclusively for family members and significant others. See Chapter 6 for a list of support groups.

Chapter 12

Making Lifestyle Adjustments

In This Chapter

▶ Creating a healthy home environment and getting in a healthier groove

▶ Connecting with supportive friends and relatives

▶ Exercising to alleviate stress

▶ Eating right and avoiding the bad stuff

*W*hen you survive a major mood episode, the whole experience can scrub the sleep out of your eyes and give you a clearer vision of life. You're reborn in a way, baptized by fire. After a period of mourning for the passing of old plans and expectations, you may find this time liberating. It offers an opportunity to start anew — to reinvent yourself, create a life that's more manageable and rewarding, and paint new dreamscapes.

That's what this chapter is all about. Here, we lead you through the process of restructuring your life in a way that helps you maintain your mental health and achieve a meaningful, rewarding existence.

Cultivating a Healthy Home Environment

If you have bipolar disorder, your home becomes your sanctuary, and everyone in your home needs to brush up on bipolar disorder and work together to create an environment that's conducive to your recovery and the mental wellbeing of the entire household. In this section, you discover various ways to tone down the emotional volume and set healthy boundaries.

Educating all household members

Everyone in your home, from Grandma to your toddler, needs to know the basics of bipolar disorder (in developmentally appropriate ways, of course), including how it affects you and what your family can do to help. If your housemates are on a different page, they may work at cross-purposes and undermine any potential progress. For example, if someone in your household "doesn't believe in medication," she may make offhand comments that discourage you from taking your meds.

Sensitivity is important, but be sure that the home environment encourages open communication. Successful management of bipolar disorder is much more likely if everyone is involved in the discussion and has an opportunity to ask questions and voice concerns. Consult your loved ones to determine the best time and the most effective way to open discussions and present information. Having other household members read this chapter is a good way to start the discussion.

Note to family members: A common mistake that family members make is to begin discussing issues without involving the person who has bipolar disorder. Don't create a secret society with the goal of protecting your loved one. Doing so can make her feel as though everyone wants to gang up on her — as if she's the family problem.

Establishing a structured schedule

Some households can function quite well with individual family members following different schedules, but if the person with bipolar disorder relies on the rhythms of other family members, the entire family may need to work together to establish a reasonable schedule and routine.

For example, if Junior likes to have his buddies over on Friday night to play video games until 2 a.m. but that particular activity at that time disturbs the rest of the household, he may need to move the party to a friend's house or reschedule it for earlier in the evening. Sorry, Junior. For more about the importance of structure, see the later section "Establishing Healthy Routines."

Cranking down the volume

You don't want to turn your home into the neighborhood "SHHHH!" zone, but all your housemates should be aware of how their voices, stereos, guests, and televisions affect the other people living in the house. Here are a few suggestions to muffle the noise:

- ✔ **Crank down the stereo, the TV set, the computer speakers, and other noise producers.** Headphones are a must-have. Keeping a few extra sets around the house can be a quick crisis prevention and management strategy.

✔ **Limit the shouting from room to room.** This is actually a good basic rule: Have conversations only when you're within speaking distance and preferably having already made some eye contact. Surprise commentary, questions, or demands, especially delivered loudly and facelessly, can push buttons for everyone, but especially for those individuals working hard to regulate moods and reactions.

✔ **Avoid slamming doors, banging pots and pans, and stomping from room to room.** If you're angry and need to move forcefully, try walking or running around the block, hammering away at a project in your garage, or energetically moving your body in other ways that can defuse your emotions without setting off anger/fear alarm bells in the home.

Reducing conflict and criticism

Some studies show that in families with high levels of conflict and criticism, people who've had a major mood episode are much more likely to suffer a relapse. Researchers use the term *expressed emotion (EE)* to refer to the levels of criticism, hostility, and emotional over-involvement or over-protection. Although *expressed emotion* sounds as though it refers to the expression of all emotions, it doesn't. The term comes from research that associates high levels of negative patterns of emotional communication with higher rates of relapse into episodes of mental illness, including depression and possibly mania, although the connection to mania is less clear.

Any emotional expression that can make a loved one feel nervous, anxious, angry, frustrated, or guilty (for having the disorder or for not meeting some expectation) falls in this category. A high level of conflict and criticism in the home — even if it's indirect — can destabilize someone with a mood disorder. Every family member must be a caregiver to some degree, so all family members must work together to establish a healthier emotional tone. The following three approaches can contribute significantly to dialing down expressed emotion in your home:

✔ Learning more about bipolar disorder typically increases empathy for the diagnosed family member, thus reducing expressions of criticism, blame, and emotional over-involvement. Discovering how to focus anger and frustration on the illness and not the person with the illness is a critical starting point.

✔ Improving communication skills helps family members express themselves in healthier ways. (See Chapter 13 for more about communication.)

✔ Enhancing problem-solving skills enables you to resolve issues logically and rationally. (See Chapter 14 for problem-solving strategies.)

Establishing expectations

You can eliminate many areas of conflict by having family members specifically identify acceptable and unacceptable behaviors. Agreeing on a set of house expectations (or *boundaries*) focuses on what everyone wants to happen and also clearly outlines the downsides to not meeting expectations. Doing so offers several advantages, including the following:

- ✔ **Reduces confusion:** All parties know what's expected of them, the benefits of meeting expectations, and the drawbacks of not meeting them.

- ✔ **Eliminates the need to nag:** You and your loved ones know what everyone expects, and everyone has bought into the benefits of meeting these expectations, so constant reminders are unnecessary.

- ✔ **Helps reduce criticism:** If an expectation is met, the positives outcomes are spring-loaded (they occur automatically). Additional reinforcement and praise generates goodwill and positive energy. Criticism only generates bad will and negative energy, so bypassing it is valuable. If an expectation isn't met, the negative outcomes are also spring-loaded and can occur without adding criticism or judgment to the mix.

- ✔ **Eliminates the need for arguments:** If someone doesn't meet an expectation, the identified outcome follows — period.

- ✔ **Settles your mind:** You don't constantly wonder what you can put up with and how much you can take. It's already established. And you can continue to try to focus on encouraging the positive behaviors without wondering about how to handle the negative ones.

- ✔ **Enables unconditional love:** You can control your personal space and your responses without taking unacceptable behaviors personally. You can respond in previously agreed-upon ways. And you can put in as many reinforcements as you want when expectations are being met.

- ✔ **Encourages independence:** Unclear expectations lead to endless conflict — constant discussions about how to handle every situation — often repeating the same cycles over and over again. Given clear guidelines, individuals can make choices about their behaviors independently with full awareness of the outcomes they can expect.

Approach boundaries and consequences in a spirit of compassion and encouragement without shame or humiliation. Consequences must allow an individual to recover her appropriate behavior patterns, get back on track, and return to the fold. The following suggestions can help you establish effective boundaries and consequences:

✔ **Identify one or two of the most important expectations and how they may not be met:** Pick one or two responses that you simply can't tolerate. If you have bipolar disorder, you may identify the expectation that your caregiver uses positive language and that disrespectful or insensitive comments are unacceptable. If you're a caregiver, a positive expectation may be that your loved one keeps better track of how and where he spends money and that withdrawing money without keeping a written record of it is unacceptable.

✔ **Pick behaviors that you can easily define.** Expectations should be specific and concrete. For example, an expectation "Cleaning up the kitchen" is too broad, especially for someone struggling with focus, attention, and planning as many people with bipolar disorder do. Try something like, "Clearing dishes from the table and emptying the dishwasher after dinner" as a more specific and defined expectation. It's also more limited, encouraging success. Mastery of a task is a much better motivator than failure. Also avoid more subjective expectations. Whether a person arrives home at a specific time is easy enough to determine. Whether a person treats you civilly is a judgment call.

✔ **Assign developmentally appropriate outcomes.** With children, you can limit TV or computer time or withhold allowance. Similar outcomes are inappropriate for adults because such consequences *infantilize* adults, taking away their adult decision-making abilities and making them feel like children. Unless you have a true safety crisis on your hands, you want to optimize the other person's responsible decision making.

For adults, outcomes for not meeting expectations sometimes can be imposed on them; for example, loss of access to a credit card if someone isn't working on more adaptive money management. But often an outcome relates only to the other person's response. For example, if someone isn't meeting the expectation of using supportive language, you can't *force* her; demanding compliance only exacerbates the situation. You only can change your responses, so the outcome in such a situation may be that you disengage from the conversation until the more desired expectations are met. Make sure you can live with these outcomes, so you stick to them.

✔ **Emphasize and define the positive expectation rather than just correcting the unmet one.** When disengaging from someone using unacceptable language, remind her that a more positive approach will be so much more helpful and you'll rejoin her when that's happening. Don't overdo it; say it and then step out of the interaction. You have to give the person some space to make change without you hovering over her.

✔ **Never underestimate the power of positive feedback and encouragement.** Don't get caught up in wondering why you need to award the person for doing what she should be doing. If someone is struggling to meet expectations, positive reinforcements (praise and encouragement especially) are the best tools for building more of the desired behaviors and reducing frequency of the undesired ones.

Consequences should never include withdrawing love or attention. Briefly stepping away from a situation to prevent further escalation isn't the same as withholding love or attention and should be framed in a compassionate, time-limited, and problem-solving way. For example, if your loved one is still asking you about your meds for the umpteenth time and you're both getting agitated, and you had previously agreed that you're managing your medicines and it isn't appropriate for her to be asking all the time, you can remind her of the agreement, remind her that you love her, and then tell her that you're going to take a walk for about 20 minutes so you can both cool down.

✔ **Clearly communicate expectations and the associated outcomes.** You can't expect your loved ones to respect your boundaries if you don't inform them of those boundaries. Go over your expectations and outcomes at a time when emotions are stable, not during times of turmoil. You may need to write them down.

✔ **Apply outcomes consistently.** Without consistently being applied, outcomes become nothing more than idle threats. Being consistent may take a great deal of self-discipline on your part, but it's worth the investment in the long run. The more consistent you are, the less you may need to apply outcomes.

When expectations are first in place and people consistently provide predictable outcomes, sometimes an initial burst of the negative behaviors occurs. Try to be patient and wait it out; it will pass if you persist in the agreed-upon strategies.

Setting boundaries and expectations doesn't mean transforming a person into the ideal human being, whatever *that* is. Rather, it means communicating everyone's expectations for adaptive and appropriate behaviors and language and the unacceptability of not meeting those expectations. You can't control other people's behaviors, but clearly stated expectations and consistent application of outcomes are effective tools to encourage more positive behaviors and discourage negative ones.

Considering the kids

If you have children living with you, they suffer from the fallout of bipolar disorder as well. As a guardian, you may need to physically protect your children from any harm during extreme mood episodes, but shielding them from learning about the disorder is usually a mistake. Perhaps even more than adults, children need to understand what's going on. Otherwise, their developing brains, which are still self-centered, shift into high gear, and they may think that they're the reason why Mommy and Daddy are fighting or why Mommy's crying.

When explaining bipolar disorder to young children, use age-specific language. *Depression* and *mania* may mean nothing to a 5-year-old, so use phrases like "Mommy gets really excited sometimes and can't calm down" or "Daddy can't help getting really sad, even when everything is okay" to help your children understand what's going on. Just be sure to leave some time for questions and answers. Encourage your children to express their perceptions and emotions. Actively and empathically listening to your children and tolerating any and all questions and responses without judgment goes a long way in helping them cope with a parent's bipolar disorder. Using play and other nonverbal expressions such as art, dance, and music can also be wonderful ways to help children express themselves and be part of the family story.

Establishing Healthy Routines

By establishing healthy routines and making efforts to build them up a little at a time, you can improve your hold on your general wellbeing and often prevent depression and mania from establishing a foothold. If you're committed to being in bed only eight hours a night and up and about the rest of the time, for example, no matter how you feel, you may prevent some mood episodes or reduce the severity of them when they do occur. Your routines help keep the sleep and energy changes of depression and mania down to a dull roar.

In this section, you find out how to regulate your sleep and schedule social activities to gain more control over your moods, while giving yourself some wiggle room for a little variety.

Regulating your sleep

Show us a person with bipolar disorder, and we'll show you a person who sleeps too much, not enough, or not deeply enough. The disorder messes with your sleep patterns, and your disrupted sleep patterns often aggravate your moods. To remain healthy, get some sleep. The following suggestions can help you establish a regular sleep schedule:

- **Go to bed and get up at the same time** *every* **day.** Refer to Chapter 11 for suggestions on how to build a structured schedule.

- **Nap only if it's part of your sleep routine.** Napping is like snacking: It can ruin your appetite for sleep. If you're napping and having trouble sleeping at night, try decreasing or stopping the naps as a first step toward getting better nighttime sleep.

Embracing imperfection

Nowadays, everyone needs to be perfect: the super mom, the beauty queen, the sensitive male hunk, the successful investor, the apprentice, the swan. And if you don't stack up to what society and culture expect from you, you'd better get to work. Head to your neighborhood bookstore, load up on all the self-help books and videos you can carry, and pile on a few magazines while you're at it. And don't forget to turn on the TV to get blasted with more messages that you're not good enough, smart enough, or talented enough to make it.

Today's society and media glorify perfection, and people doggedly pursue it, often to the point of self-destruction. Families can't just be made up of loving individuals who hang out together; they have to be "amazing" and achieve some incredible goal. A loving, available mom doesn't quite make the cut unless she has a hot body and the right clothes and makeup to complete the package.

Learning to accept yourself, imperfections and all, is the only key to achieving genuine satisfaction and peace. People with bipolar disorder discover more quickly than others that you can't keep trying to do more and be more. You have to evaluate what you need to do and what you love to do and then carefully sort through everything else that gets piled onto your plate. The word *no* must be become your mantra because people will always ask you to do one more "little" thing. If you're a working mom, you probably can't make it to every school function. If you or your spouse has bipolar disorder, you may have to decline a few dinner invitations. Maybe you can't have your children in organized sports because you don't have the time to get them there. Perhaps you can't take on a promotion that will saddle you with ridiculous hours. Only you can make these decisions and live with them. But whatever you choose to do, don't let society define perfection and set unrealistic goals for you. "Doing it all and doing it well" isn't a realistic option for most people, let alone people living with bipolar disorder.

- ✔ **Don't fight insomnia.** Ordering yourself to sleep is usually counterproductive. Use some of the centering exercises in Chapter 11 to quiet your thoughts, or engage in a quiet activity, such as reading.

- ✔ **Avoid caffeine and other stimulants.** Sleep specialists say that any caffeine after noon influences your sleep. If you have sleep problems, keep this in mind. Also avoid spicy foods, alcohol, nicotine, decongestants, and other enemies of sleep.

- ✔ **Turn off the TV.** If you have a TV or computer in the bedroom, consider moving it out. If you simply can't miss an episode of your favorite show, record it to watch later. If music helps you fall asleep, great; otherwise, turn off the tunes.

- ✔ **Transition to sleep mode.** Avoid all stimulating input, including phone calls, TV shows, work or schoolwork, and computer activities, for one full hour before bedtime. The very nature of phone calls and work wakes you up, and computer and TV screens shine light into your eyes, signaling the brain that it needs to be awake instead of sleeping. Stick to reading, listening to quiet music, and doing other soothing activities instead.

✔ **Turn on a fan or other hummer.** Monotonous noise, commonly referred to as *white noise,* helps some people sleep. It may also block out more disturbing noises, such as dogs barking. Some people like other types of soothing background sounds such as ocean waves, rain, trains, or highway sounds. Track down something you like and download it to your phone or MP3 player for some comforting background noise for sleep.

✔ **Don't exercise before bedtime.** Unless, of course, you consider sex exercise. If you don't have a particular problem with being awake all night after engaging in intimate acts with your significant other, intimacy is usually encouraged. But regular exercise often acts as a stimulant, so try moving your exercise time to earlier in the day.

✔ **Get family support.** If family members keep you awake at night or encourage you to stay up later than you know is healthy, explain how important it is for you to maintain your sleep routines. If that doesn't work, add a new expectation with outcomes and put them into play.

✔ **Work with your doctor.** Ask about changing the time you take your medications, adjusting dosages, or switching/adding medications to help with sleep. If your meds don't put you to sleep soon enough or leave you groggy in the morning, you may need to take them earlier in the evening.

Scheduling social activities

Remaining social as bipolar ravages your life can be quite a challenge. When depressed, you may shun company. After a manic episode, you may hesitate to mix it up with your usual circle of friends, especially if you said or did something embarrassing during your last episode. But maintaining social contact on a regular basis often delivers these and other valuable benefits:

✔ Regulates your schedule and adds activity to your day.

✔ Connects you with others who can often lift your mood.

✔ Offers you a chance to be present for others, which often feels good in moderate doses. Being a friend to someone, just being a good listener, can often bring you satisfaction and a sense of connection to others.

✔ Widens and reinforces your support network.

✔ Provides a social context that enhances your perspective.

✔ Reduces isolation, which may contribute to depression.

Not everyone is a social butterfly, so don't feel as though you need to pack your schedule with social events. Some people value their time spent alone much more than others. But try to get out of the house regularly, even if it feels a little painful at first.

Leaving room for spontaneity

Some people think the perfect vacation is to ride around on a tour bus, visiting roadside attractions. Others prefer to ramble about on their own, searching for hidden gems. And some are content to sit in one place and watch the world go by. Knowing yourself and your own temperament is critical to creating successful outcomes for any activities or plans.

If you enjoy a more freewheeling lifestyle, a rigid routine may feel like too much starch in the collar. To loosen up, program some unplanned time into your schedule. Put regulations on your sleep, work, and meal times, but leave the remainder of your schedule open. Alternatively, people who thrive on structure and predictability may do better with minimal unplanned time.

To ensure successful long-term changes, consider making minor adjustments over an extended period of time. You're unlikely to follow through on dramatic changes that don't align with your temperament.

Serving Healthy Foods

When you're feeling depressed or manic, your diet is likely to suffer. You may overeat to feed your mood, fast because food just doesn't appeal to you, or crave only foods that are high in fat, sugar, and starch. Following some basic nutritional recommendations can improve your overall sense of wellbeing, which is important for long-term management of bipolar disorder:

- ✔ Eat regularly — three full meals a day or several small meals throughout the course of a day.
- ✔ Don't skip meals, especially breakfast.
- ✔ Eat a well-balanced diet, mostly vegetables, fruits, and nuts.
- ✔ Consume coffee and alcohol in moderation, if at all.

Don't skip breakfast, even if you just have a glass of milk or a handful of nuts. Get something into your system before starting your day. Breakfast is essential to wellbeing because the brain doesn't function well on fuel that comes from the breakdown of stored fat or protein. It needs fresh fuel to function; regular food intake is the only way to keep the brain sharp. If you skip breakfast, your brain is operating on "fumes" — the fuel tank is literally running dry, and this impairs all kinds of brain function. A spread of eggs and bacon every day isn't necessary, but try to get a little protein and a little fat into your belly to hold you through the morning. Donuts and sugary cereals aren't the best choice, as we explain in the next section.

Taking care of my brain

For me, the goal of making lifestyle adjustments to manage bipolar disorder is to give my brain what it needs to function well, and that means *everything in moderation,* especially the basics — sleep, diet, and exercise:

✔ **Sleep:** A good night's sleep is essential. I need a solid eight hours each night. When my sleep patterns are off, it's usually my first sign that something's brewing. Too much sleep, and I'm tilting toward depression. Not enough, and I'm getting manic.

✔ **Diet:** A well-balanced diet nourishes my brain. When I'm manic, I tend not to eat much or drink enough water. When I'm depressed, I crave junk food and tend to overeat, which makes me even more lethargic.

✔ **Exercise:** Getting outside and walking is one of my favorite forms of exercise. I also find yoga, breathing techniques, and meditation to be great ways to de-stress and maintain a healthy lifestyle. But too much exercise can send me straight into a manic episode, and too little turns me into a couch potato.

When my brain chemistries are out of balance, even the relatively small challenge of maintaining moderation in all things is difficult. After 20 years of struggling with bipolar disorder, I finally realized that I also needed to adjust my attitude. I needed to come to terms with being bipolar. Once I accepted my diagnosis, I stopped brooding. When I stopped feeling sorry for myself, I took responsibility. And once I owned it, I gained control over my disorder instead of letting it control me. I learned to manage my illness with foresight. If I'm truly honest, I know when I'm slipping into an episode. Identifying the early signs and getting professional help before it gets out of control is a skill worth honing.

— Janine Crowley Haynes (janinecrowleyhaynes@gmail.com), freelance writer and author of award-winning memoir *My Kind of Crazy: Living in a Bipolar World*

Cutting back on simple carbohydrates

Foods such as white rice, potato chips, cookies, crackers, and white pasta are packed with simple carbohydrates that often take your body on a roller coaster ride of sugar highs and lows. You may feel an initial energy surge, but 30 to 60 minutes later, you'll probably crash as your blood sugar drops, leaving you drained and craving your next fix.

A simple carbohydrate buzz doesn't last because it triggers a spike in blood sugar levels that your body responds to as a survival mechanism. As blood sugar levels rise, your pancreas dumps insulin into your system to convert excess sugar to fat for storage. With a large rush of insulin, blood sugar levels drop, making you feel sleepy, cranky, and often hungry for more sweets. And in the long run, high levels of sugar in your diet increase your risk of developing type 2 diabetes and other metabolic problems.

Watch out for hidden sugars in products such as bread, cereals, yogurt, crackers, protein bars, snack bars, coffee drinks, fast food, and many other processed or prepackaged foods. When you start reading labels, you'll be surprised at how much sugar is in some of those products. Even more deceptive, some food companies use a bunch of different types of sweeteners so they can put them farther down the ingredient list. The list always moves from the highest percentage ingredient to the lowest. So although all the sugars together in a cracker may add up to the highest or second highest percentage ingredient, if food companies divide the sugar content into many different sweeteners, the names of all of those sweeteners move down the ingredient list, making it much harder to sort out. Be sure to check out total sugars as well as the ingredient list.

Fruit sugar isn't the same and doesn't carry the same risks as added sugars. When you eat whole, unprocessed fruit, you get fiber and many vitamins and nutrients in addition to the fruit sugar, which help to curb appetite. Fruit juices, even 100 percent fruit juice, reduce the benefits of fruit and create more of a pure sugar rush, so consume them sparingly, if at all. Many "healthy smoothies" are chock-full of both fruit juices and added sugars, so the best advice is to make your own smoothies and juices.

A sugary dessert doesn't have to be the enemy; it can be a wonderful way to end a delicious a meal or take a midafternoon break. Just be sure that you identify your sugar snack as such, and don't take in all the unneeded and hidden sugars in the rest of your diet.

To even out the highs and lows, cut down on junk foods and avoid simple carbohydrates, including most breads and pastas, potatoes, and highly processed foods. Instead, get your fill of vegetables, fruits, and nuts, and moderate amounts of whole grain products, all of which contain complex carbohydrates that enter your system gradually, preventing extreme fluctuations in blood sugar levels. Be careful of tricky or misleading labels such as "multi-grain" or "wheat bread," which may have no whole grains in them at all. Make sure the ingredient list says "whole wheat" or "whole oats" or whatever it is you're looking for and make sure that that ingredient is close to the top of the ingredients list.

Getting your fill of vegetables and fruits

To improve your overall health and wellbeing, increase your daily consumption of fresh or frozen vegetables and fruit, which offer nutritional benefits that are unavailable in most processed foods:

Chocolate, glorious chocolate

Considered by some to be the perfect mood food, chocolate has several ingredients that contribute to mood alteration: a dash of sugar to increase energy and serotonin levels, a pinch of phenylethylamine (a brain chemical that your body releases when you fall in love), smidgens of theobromine and magnesium to enhance brain function, a touch of caffeine to make you more alert, and a few grams of protein to boost the excitatory neurotransmitters. Of course, too much chocolate can give you a bellyache, a definite downer. But a couple squares of dark chocolate, **70** percent or higher in cacao, may be just the treat you need to get over that midafternoon speed bump.

✔ **Fiber:** Improves digestion and cardiovascular health among many other important body functions

✔ **Vitamins and minerals:** Provide the nutrients your body needs to develop and function properly

✔ **Complex carbohydrates:** Provide a steady flow of sustenance and energy throughout the day (instead of the highs and lows associated with refined sugars and starches)

✔ **Antioxidants:** Prevent and slow cell damage

Eating vegetables, fruits, and nuts is also helpful in maintaining healthy populations of beneficial bacteria in your gut. Healthy bacteria in the body, especially in the gut, referred to as the *microbiome,* play vital roles in overall health, including preventing illnesses such as heart disease, type 2 diabetes, gastrointestinal disorders, and autoimmune diseases. As research reveals more about the importance of the microbiome, healthy gut bacteria will likely become a bigger part of the nutrition conversation. High intake of vegetables and fiber is associated with healthier gut *flora* (bacterial collections) and may be one of the connections between a more plant-based food intake and healthier bodies.

Powering up with protein

When you hear the word *protein,* you probably think *muscle.* But protein contributes to many other areas of the body as well. The basic building blocks of proteins are amino acids, several of which act as neurological regulators. When you consume protein, your body immediately breaks it down into amino acids so it can transport them to where your body needs them. One of these amino acids, tyrosine, is a building block of excitatory neurotransmitters — dopamine and norepinephrine — that help the body and brain regulate energy, focus, and concentration, among other things.

Obtaining sufficient protein is necessary for stable energy and moods. Meat provides the easiest way to obtain the nine essential amino acids that comprise complete proteins, but vegetarians can get protein by combining complementary food items, such as beans and rice, beans and corn, and whole wheat and peanuts. Vegetarians should also monitor their intake of essential vitamins and minerals (especially B-complex vitamins and selenium); refer to Chapter 9 for information about supplements.

Feeding your brain healthy fats

Fat has gotten a bad rap over the years, but research is beginning to reveal the vital role of healthy fats in the diet. This doesn't mean you should slather butter on your biscuits, but it does mean that you shouldn't go out of your way to avoid all fats — some are actually good for you! Here's the lowdown on good fats, not-so-good fats, and bad fats:

- **Good fats:** Unsaturated fats, typically labeled polyunsaturated and monounsaturated, are generally good for you. They include olive oil, omega-3 fatty acids, and most vegetable and nut oils, including sesame oil. These oils are typically liquid at room temperature. Many nutritionists add coconut oil to this list, even though it's a saturated fat.

- **Not-so-good fats:** Saturated fats are primarily in the form of animal products, including beef, pork, chicken, eggs, milk, cheese, and butter. Most nutritionists recommend consuming such foods in moderation. By the way, one of the top sources of saturated fat in the United States is pizza.

- **Bad fats:** Trans fats, typically labeled hydrogenated or partially hydrogenated oil, are the fats to avoid. They're typically found in a wide variety of bakery items and other processed foods, fried foods, and all types of butter substitutes. They increase the risk of heart disease and inflammation, which is at the root of many chronic illnesses. Read labels carefully, because manufacturers are permitted to label foods having as much as 0.5 grams of trans fat per serving as having "0 grams of trans fats." (Some animal products contain natural occurring trans fats, but the jury is out on whether they're as bad as manufactured trans fats.) In 2013, the FDA determined that trans fats are *not generally regarded as safe,* and in 2015 the FDA issued a ruling requiring food manufacturers to eliminate trans fats from all food products within three years.

Cholesterol is a naturally occurring fatty substance that your liver makes and is needed to build strong cells and support other important bodily functions. Although the science is continually changing, cholesterol levels and types seem to be important health measurements that affect the risks of heart disease. For a long time, nutritional guidelines have recommended limiting how much cholesterol you eat to maintain healthy levels. However, lowering dietary cholesterol may lower the intake of other important nutrients. And very low cholesterol levels may be associated with depression or cerebral hemorrhage. Because the science is evolving so quickly, you should discuss it with your doctor before making any major changes to your cholesterol intake.

Fat in the diet is key for many reasons: It's essential for building healthy cells, for generating energy, for maintaining stamina, for growing healthy babies, and for numerous other functions. Fat makes food taste good and keeps you full, so a diet that is too low in fat is not only unhealthy directly. A low-fat diet is also deeply unsatisfying and may have indirect effects, such as rebound binge eating to satisfy hunger, filling in the hunger with refined carbs and simple sugars, and feeling generally unhappy about food and eating. Make sure to include healthy fat in your diet and don't forget to enjoy what you eat.

Building Healthy Relationships

Relationships can contribute significantly to stabilizing moods. A friend who's more gregarious than you may encourage you to become involved in activities that lift your moods. A companion who's calm and stable may help set a slower pace that keeps your mania in check. This section offers some tips for considering the state of certain relationships and strengthening important bonds that may be suffering through the course of bipolar disorder and other contributing factors.

Checking relationship vitals

Whether you want to work on improving a current relationship or building a new one, remain aware of the following aspects of relationships that can affect mood stability:

- **Healthy shared interests:** If your shared interests consist of drinking, smoking, or taking drugs, consider structuring the relationship around healthier activities or spending more time with other friends.

- **Acceptance and understanding:** Accepting and understanding bipolar may be difficult for you, but it can be even more so for friends and relatives who don't have first-hand experience with it. If these people criticize you for your illness with words or through body language and behavior, the criticism adds to your burden. By becoming more informed about bipolar disorder, the people in your life can learn acceptance and empathy.

✔ **Appreciation:** The people who love you and find you attractive do so despite your bipolar disorder and also frequently because of it, or at least partially because of it. When building new relationships, look for people who appreciate your attributes and talents. But be careful of people who appreciate your extreme highs and lows too much; they may encourage unhealthy lifestyle choices for their own benefit, even though they may be completely oblivious to the effect of their actions.

✔ **Support:** Stabilizing your moods requires extra work on your part. You need to manage your medications, make lifestyle adjustments, and possibly even face periods of unemployment and diminished cash flow. During times of crisis, you need supportive people around you to meet both your physical and emotional needs.

Every so often, evaluate your current relationships to determine whether any of them are undermining your mood stability. If you spot potentially harmful relationships, decide whether they're valuable enough to save. You may benefit from ending such relationships and investing your time and energy in new, potentially more productive connections.

Criticism, demands, judgment, and abuse (physical, emotional, and verbal) have no place in a healthy relationship. Through therapy, you can often identify some of the harmful elements and root them out, assuming all parties involved are committed to improving the relationship. But if you're in an unhealthy relationship and the other party refuses to negotiate, you face the difficult choice of remaining in the relationship and risking your health or leaving the relationship. If you're in an abusive relationship, make sure to seek counsel from someone familiar with interpersonal violence issues. Traditional couples counseling may not help; it may worsen the situation. And ending the relationship may increase the likelihood of escalating aggression or violence, so if you're ready to end the relationship, do so very carefully, with outside support.

Having some fun

Cultivating healthy relationships means more than just avoiding conflict and "getting along." It requires that you and your loved ones have meaningful discussions and share experiences that increase intimacy and strengthen bonds. When bipolar disorder enters a relationship, you can become so caught up in crisis intervention and damage control that you lose touch with each other emotionally. Encourage your loved ones to become involved in family activities, including meal preparation, physical exercise, games, religious or spiritual programs, family outings, and family meetings to discuss plans.

Mood medication and therapy can do wonders in terms of controlling the symptoms of bipolar disorder, but even a successful combination of medication and therapy is rarely sufficient to return full *functionality* — an ability to carry out all the expected duties as a healthy family member, friend, or worker. Functionality typically improves as you gradually increase your level of involvement and activity in a supportive environment.

Taking breaks from one another

Two people may make for good company for a few hours or days, but after several weeks, even two begins to feel like a crowd, especially when you both have to deal with a long-term health condition. Your loved ones don't need to stand 24-hour watch over you; doing so isn't healthy for you or them. When your moods are cycling, a loved one may need to spend more time and energy as a caregiver, but when your moods stabilize, consider taking a break from each other so you can both recharge your batteries and connect with others. Having outside activities and friendships is healthy for people in a relationship. Maintaining and building these networks of people and interests is especially important in these times of relationship overload.

Relieving Stress through Exercise

You're probably aware that aerobic exercise is good for both body and mind, but you may not know how exercise specifically helps people with bipolar:

- ✔ **Exercise improves depression without inducing mania.** Exercise is a powerful tool for generating and sustaining more positive mood states, and it doesn't carry the risk of triggering mania (although excessive exercise can be a sign of hypomania).

- ✔ **Exercise helps regulate weight and energy.** Bipolar disorder and many of the medications used to treat it commonly lower energy and increase weight. Exercise helps you to reduce the risks of weight gain and lower energy. For more about regulating weight, see Chapter 8.

You don't need to run a 5K and pump iron every day to get in shape. If your primary goal is to regulate your moods, a 15- to 20-minute daily walk is all you really need. With a daily walk, you can immediately begin to reap the mood-stabilizing benefits of aerobic exercise:

- ✔ Increased ability to sleep (in many cases)
- ✔ Improved digestion
- ✔ Increased energy
- ✔ Sense of accomplishment

Consult your doctor before you begin any strenuous exercise program, especially if you're taking lithium. When you perspire, you lose fluids, which can increase the concentration of the medication in your system. In the case of lithium, increased levels can create a potentially fatal condition. Your doctor can recommend ways to reduce the risks.

Avoiding the Bad Stuff

Caffeine, nicotine, diet pills, alcohol, marijuana, and other uppers and downers form a veritable cornucopia of legal and illegal mood manipulators. If you wash down your antianxiety medication with an energy drink and head out for a night of bar hopping with your buddies, you may be doing more harm than you can possibly imagine. Although these substances may seem innocent enough, they can wreak havoc on your carefully crafted medication combination and attempts at improving your diet and exercise.

Following is a list of the most common substances that can cause problems. This list isn't exhaustive, and we don't include plenty of dangerous street drugs, including methamphetamine and cocaine, which are so wrong in so many ways, we've deemed them too obvious to mention.

- **Caffeine:** Monitor your caffeine intake and reduce or eliminate consumption. You may not want to break your habit completely. Just remain sensitive to how it's affecting your energy and mood.

- **Nicotine:** Stop smoking or cut back on the number of cigarettes you smoke. This applies to tobacco chewers and cigar aficionados, too.

- **Amphetamines and other stimulants:** *Amphetamines* are intensified versions of caffeine and nicotine that can easily trigger full-blown manic episodes or psychosis. If you have a problem with amphetamine use, speak to your doctor or seek community support, such as Narcotics Anonymous (www.na.org).

- **Alcohol:** Stick to one or two beers or glasses of wine, if you choose to drink at all, and avoid it entirely if you're taking benzodiazepines. Alcohol can contribute to depression, reduce impulse control, and interact in dangerous ways with some bipolar meds, especially lithium.

- **Marijuana:** Although marijuana can generate feelings of euphoria, it can also trigger paranoia and anxiety, decrease inhibitions, and affect cannabinoid receptors in the brain that are strongly tied to mood modulation. Because marijuana is unregulated in most places, its active ingredient, THC, varies in concentration with each batch, so you may not know how much you're getting. But even if you have a prescription for marijuana, make sure that all your doctors know about it before you stop at the dispensary.

✔ **Weight-loss and energy supplements:** Many diet pills and energy tonics are laced with potentially dangerous stimulants — some that are just as dangerous as nicotine or caffeine. Consult your psychiatrist before taking anything to help you lose weight. Your doctor may suggest other approaches that carry a lower risk of destabilizing your moods.

✔ **Over-the-counter medications:** Consult your doctor before taking any over-the-counter medications, regardless of how safe they may seem. Be especially cautious of the following:

- **Pain relievers such as ibuprofen:** Avoid pain relievers such as ibuprofen and naproxen when you're on lithium. Your kidneys clear these meds, and they can potentially cause kidney damage.

- **Decongestants with pseudoephedrine:** Decongestants such as pseudoephedrine (Sudafed) are stimulants and can exacerbate mania or depression or worsen symptoms, even when calming agents are onboard.

- **Cough suppressants containing dextromethorphan:** Avoid dextromethorphan, a cough suppressant, when you're taking Selective Serotonin Reuptake Inhibitors (SSRIs). In some cases, people abuse this medication and take very high doses to induce euphoria. Read the labels and choose a cough suppressant that doesn't use dextromethorphan.

- **Over-the-counter sleep aids:** Avoid over-the-counter sleep aids unless your doctor gives you the thumbs-up.

✔ **Herbal and all-natural remedies:** Many herbal medications may sound no more harmful than parsley, but they can be quite powerful. Be especially cautious of ephedra, valerian, kava, and St. John's wort. See Chapter 9 for details about herbal and natural products, and always consult your doctor before adding a substance to your medication brew.

Chapter 13

Communicating Effectively

· ·

In This Chapter

▶ Setting a tone that's conducive to positive interactions

▶ Avoiding the top four communication killers

▶ Using "I" statements to dodge the blame game

▶ Reflecting feelings to validate them

▶ Disengaging from lose-lose battles

· ·

*I*n any group of two or more people, effective communication is essential to keeping the peace, maintaining a healthy emotional environment, and facilitating collaboration. When communication breaks down, often due to fear, a lack of empathy, or misunderstanding, emotions heat up and can fuel ferocious interactions in which nobody wins and everyone loses. Add bipolar to the mix, along with the fear, suspicion, irritability, depression, resentment, and lack of impulse control that often accompany it, and even the best efforts of the most well-intentioned individuals fall short.

In this chapter, we offer guidance to help you establish an environment that's conducive to productive communication. We also get you up to speed on applying communication skills and strategies that promote understanding and help resolve conflict.

Setting the Stage

Successful conversations begin with careful preparation and a working knowledge of basic communication skills. In the following sections, we offer tips to help you prepare for productive interactions by explaining how to choose the right time and place, set ground rules, keep emotions and body language in check, and choose words carefully to avoid triggering heated responses.

Choosing the right time and place

Timing and location aren't everything when it comes to successful communication, but they certainly play a big part. Here are some suggestions on how to choose the right time and place:

- ✔ **Wait for a relative calm.** Don't try to resolve differences when emotions are heated or someone in the group is experiencing a mood episode.

- ✔ **Set aside time for discussion.** Schedule time for difficult conversations; otherwise, they may keep getting put off. Choose times that are convenient for everyone so nobody is in a rush to get somewhere else.

Ideally everyone involved is fully focused on the conversation; however, with difficult topics, a less direct approach can be helpful. For instance, the car isn't the best place to talk about something highly emotional, but it sometimes works for addressing sensitive topics because it allows people to avoid direct eye contact while remaining engaged. Counselors often suggest car time for talking with teenagers because it avoids the "face off" that can generate a feeling of being cornered. (However, don't get into or continue a heated conversation while driving; doing so can be dangerous.) Talking while doing a menial task such as drying dishes can also dilute the feeling of a head-on confrontation.

- ✔ **Choose a quiet room free from distractions.** The dining room table is a great place to talk; a table serves as a subtle barrier that gives people a sense of safety and security. Another great place is the living room or den, assuming the TV and computer are turned off and all phones in the vicinity are off or silenced.

Avoid meeting in a public place unless that's the only place you feel you can safely talk. People are less likely to open up when outsiders can listen in, and this hesitancy diminishes effectiveness of a conversation.

Establishing ground rules

With all parties gathered, the first order of business is to work together to establish communication ground rules. Encourage everyone to contribute so each person has some buy-in to the rules that the group eventually settles on. Here are some sample ground rules:

- ✔ Focus on one issue at a time.
- ✔ Stick to observations rather than judgments.
- ✔ Take turns.
- ✔ Converse at a normal volume.

- Try to find ways to express frustration without profanity.

- Collaborate — no threats, intimidation, or violent behavior.

- Anyone can call for a timeout at any time.

- Really listen; try to be an active rather than passive listener.

- Try to see the issue from the other person's point of view.

If you can't seem to communicate without arguing, consider recruiting a therapist, friend, or family member to facilitate. Choose someone with a cool, analytical mind whom everyone respects and whose guidance everyone will follow. The facilitator can help enforce the ground rules and ensure that everyone has a chance to be heard.

Watching what you say

Effective communication calls for clarity, honesty, and accuracy, but you need to be clear, honest, and accurate in a way that keeps people receptive to what you're saying. Here are some tips for choosing words and phrases that listeners are likely to absorb rather than refute:

- **Express yourself with "I" statements, especially when offering an opinion.** Use phrases such as "I think . . . " and "I feel . . . " to begin your sentences. To dive deeper into "I" statements, see the later section "Becoming Less Confrontational with 'I' Statements."

- **Stick to the present as much as possible.** You can discuss the past to learn from it and improve outcomes, but don't get mired in the past because you can't fix it. Don't use past events to blame or launch attacks against someone as a defensive posture.

- **Don't engage in criticism, judgment, demand, or blame.** In short, all discussion participants need to show respect for one another. See the later section "Avoiding the Four Big Tiff-Makers" for details on avoiding criticism, judgment, demand, and blame.

- **Don't exaggerate.** Do your best to accurately depict a situation and avoid absolutes, such as *always* and *never*. Rarely is something always or never the case. If you find yourself saying something like, "You never . . . ," you're committing two no-nos: blaming the other person and speaking in absolutes.

- **Avoid comparisons, especially comparisons between two people.** Telling a wife that she's just like her mother or a son to act more like his father is almost guaranteed to elicit a strong negative reaction. Instead of generalizing a person's behavior through comparisons, focus on specific behaviors or issues to discuss.

Expressing yourself in a positive tone

Sometimes *what* you say isn't as much of an issue as how you say it. A sarcastic tone of voice, for example, can transform the meaning of a phrase into its exact opposite. For instance, if you say something like, "I really appreciate your love and understanding," in a sarcastic tone, it means "I really *don't* appreciate your lack of love and understanding."

Tone of voice can convey a wide range of emotion — from sadness to joy, regret to hope, happiness to anger, and more. Be sensitive to your tone of voice and try to maintain a tone that's positive, upbeat, and encouraging. Avoid negative tones that convey anger, frustration, and bitterness. Striving toward a more positive tone of voice may even encourage you to think more positively. But if you just can't summon positive feelings, work hard to stay neutral.

Being sensitive to posture, position, and body language

Posture, position, and body language all convey meaning and emotion nonverbally. You can read entire books on the topic of nonverbal communication, but when you're communicating with a friend or family member — someone you know pretty well — you probably don't need a detailed study of body language. Just be sure to do the following:

- ✔ Stand or sit at a comfortable distance from the person, remaining sensitive to personal space. Be at the same eye level; avoid one person towering over others.

- ✔ Remain relaxed and nonthreatening. If you feel any muscles, including facial muscles, tensing up, you're probably getting angry, upset, or defensive. Breathe deeply and remind yourself to relax.

- ✔ Be and appear attentive. Maintain appropriate eye contact (not staring or glaring) and use verbal and nonverbal cues, such as nodding and saying "yes" or "okay," to indicate that you're hearing what the person is saying.

    Sometimes indirect attention is more appropriate and can make an exchange feel less confrontational. While walking, washing dishes, driving, or engaging in some other activity, you can still remain and appear attentive nonverbally by nodding, saying "yes" or "okay," and using posture and body language to show that you're listening.

- ✔ If you're addressing more than one person, shift your attention every one or two sentences so nobody feels left out.

How to apologize . . . and how not to

People with bipolar disorder shouldn't have to apologize for what the disorder makes them do, but apologies have the power to heal relationships and liberate everyone involved from guilt and resentment — assuming, of course, that the apologies are sincere and delivered in an appropriate manner. Following are some do's and don'ts for delivering effective apologies:

✔ **Be sincere.** Apologize only if you truly feel that you played a role in upsetting the person and are committed to not making the same mistake again.

✔ **Describe what you're sorry for.** Specifying what you said or did that upset the other person acknowledges your role.

✔ **Validate the other person's feelings.** Describe how you think what you did hurt the other person. Doing so demonstrates that you're aware of the consequences of your words or actions.

✔ **Don't try to weasel out of it.** Don't try to justify what you said or did, and don't

apologize only for how the other person feels. Saying something like, "I'm sorry you feel that way, but . . . " is a self-serving apology. The person you hurt will notice immediately that you're apologizing only to alleviate your guilt and not because of sincere regret for your words or actions.

✔ **Let it go.** Accept the fact that you have no control over whether the person accepts your apology. Remember that you apologized for that person, not for yourself, so don't get bitter if the person refuses to forgive you.

Keep in mind that an apology isn't always what a person really wants or needs. Sometimes when someone expects an apology, what that person really wants is empathy or validation. Your loved one may just need to hear that you know he's hurting and understand that he has good reason to feel that hurt; he's not blaming or expecting you to apologize for something you had no control over. See the section "Validating Other People's Feelings" for details.

Adding mood symptoms to the mix

In the midst of bipolar disorder, you're up against more than your average everyday communication breakdowns. Bipolar symptoms and the emotional fallout they leave in their wake undermine the efforts of the most reasonable individuals in several ways:

✔ **Depression commonly causes loss of confidence and feelings of low self-esteem or worthlessness.** Feeling that way can prevent you from being appropriately assertive when a situation is unfair or hurtful, and you may resent it later. If you're feeling depressed, be alert to how your mood may prevent you from speaking up appropriately; you may need to make special efforts to be appropriately assertive.

✔ **Irritability and anger outbursts are common symptoms of mania and depression.** When you don't feel well, you may be more likely to impulsively say or do things that you later regret. If you're feeling irritable, make a special effort to cool down before responding to others or making statements that may fuel conflict.

✔ **The emotional fallout from having to live with bipolar disorder may lead to persistent relationship issues that surface whenever certain topics arise.** If previous mood episodes resulted in sexual indiscretion, for example, that could fuel future conflict. Resentment over having to take medication or a perceived loss of status in the family can lead to conflict, as well. Fear, suspicion, regret, and other powerful emotional responses can also play a role in destabilizing relationships.

Although medical treatments can help remove the bipolar symptoms from the equation, therapy is often necessary to help those with bipolar disorder and their loved ones deal with the big and small upheavals that contribute to conflict. The emotional damage that bipolar leaves behind is often as difficult to repair as the illness is to treat.

Avoiding the Four Big Tiff-Makers

Conflict often arises when someone feels attacked. When the person who feels threatened goes on the defensive, the exchange can turn ugly and nothing is accomplished. One way to prevent someone from feeling threatened in the first place is to avoid the four major factors that tend to put people on the defensive: criticism, judgment, demand, and blame. These approaches seek to control someone rather than understand them and this shuts down effective communication and problem solving.

Criticism

Criticism (especially if not balanced by positives and empathy) wears people down and triggers anger and/or fear, which immediately shuts down collaboration. So instead of dishing out criticism, work toward fostering a light attitude in which you accept people for who they are. You may be pleasantly surprised at the change in how your loved one responds to you when you take criticism out of the interaction.

For example, parents of an out-of-work adult son who has bipolar disorder may feel compelled to urge him to get a job or move out, because most adult children have achieved these goals. Instead of criticizing his lack of action, the parents may try to ask how he feels about his situation, validate his feelings, and together develop a strategy that reflects his story and not just what they expect.

Judgment

Judgments are often a knee-jerk response when someone doesn't meet your expectations such as "He is so lazy. He sleeps all day." Like criticism, judgment is a tool of power and control that often masquerades as helping someone else to "be better." It triggers strong emotions in the person being judged and reduces the likelihood of effective problem solving.

To reduce the amount of judgment that makes its way into your life and relationships, follow these steps as best as you can:

1. **Recognize judgment in your daily communications.**

   Notice how you feel when you're being judged and how people respond when you're the judge. Notice how your feelings change when you internally judge yourself.

2. **Accept or at least tolerate your differences.**

   Acceptance/tolerance must be mutual for communication to gain traction.

3. **Understand or acknowledge the source of your differences.**

   Every individual has reasons, knowledge, and experience that inform her belief and value systems. Sometimes understanding the source of a person's beliefs and values leads to tolerance, if not agreement.

Demand

Demands go hand in hand with criticism and judgment as ways to try to control another person's behavior. Of course, asking someone to do something for you is perfectly normal and acceptable. In certain formalized relationships (such as between a boss and employee), demands are actually expected. With loved ones, however, issuing demands rather than approaching tasks and problems in a respectful, collaborative way is far less likely to get the desired results. Even if you get what you want, demands typically trigger backlash and emotional fallout as part of a cycle of pain and hurt that only reduces effective problem solving.

Blame

Blame is the natural outcome of criticism and judgment and is, by its nature, a way of issuing demands on others to change their behaviors. Blame is personal and about the past. The keys to overcoming it are to focus on the present and approach every issue as a problem to be solved. Everyone involved should function as a participant in solving the problems that arise. If you have to blame something, blame the illness. But don't blame yourself, and definitely don't blame a loved one who has bipolar disorder — it's not her fault.

Becoming Less Confrontational with "I" Statements

An "*I*" *statement* is a way to express what you're thinking or feeling without putting the other person on the defensive and giving him something to argue about. Here's an example of the bad and better way to phrase a statement:

>**Bad:** *You* stay up too late watching TV, and I can't sleep.

>**Better:** *I* can't sleep with the TV on.

The "you" statement blames the person for staying up late and making it impossible for you to sleep. Blaming puts the person on the defensive, and saying that the person stays up too late gives him something to argue about: "I don't stay up too late!" or "The TV isn't that loud!" or "Maybe you go to bed too early!"

The "I" statement merely says you can't sleep when the TV is on. By omitting blame, you avoid criticism and judgment and don't place a specific demand; more importantly, you leave things open to problem solving. The conversation that begins with an "I" statement has a better chance of developing into a problem-solving session focused on meeting both people's needs — one person needs to sleep; the other needs to stay up and watch TV.

Here are a few more examples:

>**Bad:** (You) Hurry up!

>**Better:** I really don't want to be late.

>**Bad:** You embarrassed me when you started talking about bipolar disorder at the dinner table.

>**Better:** I was embarrassed when the topic of bipolar disorder came up at dinner. I don't like talking about it in public.

>**Bad:** You need to back off and stop attacking me every time I disagree with you.

>**Better:** I feel as though I can't express myself when we have a disagreement without causing a scene.

Bad: You criticize me for everything!

Better: Sometimes I feel as though I can't do anything without being criticized for it.

In the middle of a disagreement, remind your loved ones that you still love them and you still care. During disagreements, when feelings get hurt, remembering the positive connection can be difficult. Being reminded of your bond can help redirect your loved one's emotions to solving the issue at hand and away from the fear and anger that often take over when one person thinks the other has stopped caring or has checked out of the relationship. Reassuring people that you haven't stopped loving them keeps this fear and anger out of the mix, and the whole situation just feels better. (For more about problem solving, see Chapter 14.)

The only thing worse than a "you" statement is a "you always" statement. Rarely does someone *always* behave or react in the same way. Don't exaggerate or make something sound worse than it really is. That tends to derail productive conversation into an exhausting exchange over what exactly was said and how.

Validating Other People's Feelings

Feelings such as fear, anger, bitterness, jealousy, and so on are at the root of most interpersonal conflict. Humans need to express these feelings and have others acknowledge the feelings as reasonable. One of the best ways to release pressure in an emotionally charged interaction is to *validate* the other person's feelings — that is, demonstrate that you understand what the person is feeling and acknowledge that the person's feelings are reasonable.

Validating is one step beyond reflective listening. With *reflective listening,* you merely acknowledge that you've heard and understood what the person said. With *validation,* you're saying it's okay to have that feeling and that the feeling is reasonable given the situation the person described. Here's an example of a typical interaction with three different responses:

Husband: Whenever we're in family therapy, everyone gangs up on me, as if I'm the only one responsible for the problems we're having.

Wife (typical defensive response, bad): Nobody's ganging up on you! Everyone knows this isn't all your fault.

Wife (reflective response, better): Sounds like you're pretty upset about how our family therapy sessions are going.

Wife (validating, best): I'd be pretty upset, too, if I felt as though everyone in the family were ganging up on me.

Unexpressed, unaccepted feelings tend to simmer below the surface and ultimately show up in destructive ways — for example, through sarcasm, anger, and sometimes violence.

Validating someone's feelings certainly sounds easy enough, but doing so runs counter to how most people are wired to respond. In polite society, people tend to hide their emotions or wish they had. If someone expresses a strong emotion, people tend to respond in one of the following counterproductive ways:

- ✓ **Counterattacking:** Big emotions often trigger bigger emotions — fear and anger most commonly. Avoiding the urge to jump into the fray when your own emotions are triggered is a huge challenge. But giving in to an emotional counterattack will quickly regress to blame and criticism, both of which are hurtful and counterproductive interactions.

- ✓ **Discounting:** The listener rejects the other person's emotion as invalid by saying something like, "Why are you so angry? No one is trying to hurt you." Don't try to argue against how someone feels. The fact is, the person feels that way. Accept it by saying something like, "I can see why you might feel that people are trying to hurt you. What can we do to make you feel safer?"

- ✓ **Advising:** The listener assumes that the expressed emotion is a cry for help and begins to offer advice that the speaker never asked for. A good rule of thumb is to avoid offering advice unless the other person specifically asks for it. If you're not sure, ask the speaker something like, "Do you want me to make some suggestions?"

- ✓ **Ignoring:** Another way to reject the validity of someone's emotion is to remain silent about it or to try to change the subject, which is nearly equivalent to ignoring what the person said. If you don't know how to respond to something, at least try to indicate that you heard and understand the person by paraphrasing what she just told you and/or asking her to clarify or help you understand more clearly what she's saying or asking.

Disengaging from Unproductive Conflicts

While no family member is to blame for having or causing bipolar disorder, all family members can work together to try to resolve conflict and keep the tone of unavoidable disagreements to a dull roar. Strong emotions tend to fuel conflicts, which isn't good for anyone involved. If a disagreement begins to heat up, you may need to disengage for a while to let emotions cool. Following are some techniques to help you disengage from heated, unproductive discussions:

✔ **Call a timeout.** Anger comes in waves. Waiting out the worst of it — away from the person or people you're arguing with — allows for the strongest emotions to settle so you can return to the discussion in a more even state of mind. Remember to acknowledge the feelings first, because ignoring them tends to escalate conflict. But everyone needs a chance to disengage. Saying something like, "Don't you walk away from me," is unproductive and an attempt to control someone else's behavior. Taking timeouts or walking away to cool off must always be an option.

✔ **Share some humor.** Humor can be a great defuser, but be careful; it's only funny if everyone laughs. Dismissing someone else's concerns by laughing at her is likely to trigger more conflict. Yet shared humor as a reminder of affection can be great; humor can help everyone remember that these things blow over.

Sometimes it helps to remember something that you fought over before but later laughed at because it was really silly or because you figured out what the miscommunication was. Or bring up a memory of a time when you struggled together over something and then laughed about it later.

✔ **Take a walk.** Walking helps alleviate conflict in a couple of ways. When you walk with someone, you're physically side-by-side, moving in the same direction, which is less confrontational than face to face. Also, the activity of walking tends to act as an emotional release in and of itself, and if you're walking in a public place, you may be more motivated to lower the tone.

These strategies aren't a magic cure for disagreements, but they often help to de-escalate conflict, and reduce its duration. All people in relationships have disagreements and argue at some point. But finding ways to maintain composure and compassion can keep conflicts from becoming toxic.

Disengaging is a temporary fix. After emotions cool down, you still need to resolve the underlying cause of the conflict, which you can often accomplish by practicing the communication techniques we describe earlier in this chapter and engaging in productive problem solving, as we describe in Chapter 14. Disengagement is a temporary cease-fire to prevent casualties while regaining composure.

Using verbal assaults, calling names, making intimidating or threatening movements or gestures, throwing things, damaging property, and being physically aggressive are never acceptable forms of communication. No matter how someone tries to rationalize these behaviors, they're forms of abuse — plain and simple. If you see these patterns in your relationship, talk about it with someone you trust — a friend or family member — and seek support from programs or counselors who work with abuse situations.

Chapter 14

Solving Problems and Resolving Conflict

. . . .

In This Chapter

▶ Preparing for a successful problem-busting session

▶ Focusing on the actual problem at hand and recognizing each person's needs and interests

▶ Coming up with and implementing solutions

▶ Steering clear of actions that worsen problems and letting go of problems you can't solve

. . . .

*P*roblems tend to come and go with an entourage of tension and conflict. The good news is that every problem has a solution, usually more than one, that can help alleviate tension and resolve conflict at the same time.

Many experts and organizations have developed structured approaches to problem solving. In fact, some therapists offer a specific type of psychotherapy called *problem-solving therapy (PST)*. Most structured approaches to problem solving are similar, recommending something like the following steps:

1. **Define the problem.**

2. **Set goals or identify needs.**

3. **Brainstorm solutions.**

4. **Rank solutions and choose the most promising one.**

5. **Implement the solution of choice.**

6. **Evaluate the outcome.**

   If your first choice doesn't work, return to Step 5 to try one of the other solutions on the list or go back to Step 3 and brainstorm more solutions.

In this chapter, we recommend a similar approach to problem solving with other people to address not only the problem but also the interpersonal conflicts that accompany it. We also point out some unproductive problem-solving styles and describe situations when letting go of a problem may be the best course of action.

Setting the Stage for Effective Problem Solving

If you're problem solving a solo situation, then setting the stage for effective problem solving is easy: Go off by yourself to a quiet place and mull it over. Things get more complicated when you're problem solving with others. To set the right tone for a successful — or at least productive — problem-solving session, take the following steps ahead of time:

- **Invite all stakeholders.** Everyone affected by the problem should play a role in solving it. Anyone who's excluded is less likely to follow through on implementing the solution.

- **Set an agenda.** Let all the stakeholders know what you're planning to discuss during the problem-solving session so they can begin formulating ideas. You may have already defined the problem, as discussed in the next section, or you may just sense conflict and want to find out what's at the root of it.

- **Schedule a time block.** Choose a time that's convenient for everyone and after emotions have cooled. Make sure you have at least one hour of uninterrupted time. If you wrap it up in less time, good for you! If you can't solve the problem in an hour, schedule another session.

- **Choose a setting that's conducive to problem solving.** Choose a quiet setting that's free of interruptions, including phones, computers, and TVs. Sitting around a table often makes people feel safe; it also provides a surface for taking notes.

- **Set ground rules.** The first item on your agenda may be to discuss ground rules so everyone feels safe and comfortable. Some good rules to start with remind everyone of basic communication techniques (see Chapter 13):

  - No blaming.

  - No yelling.

  - No dwelling in the past (in other words, staying in the present).

- Stay positive, constructive, and practical.

- Respect one another's opinion, even when you disagree.

- Allow for brief timeouts if a person feels her emotions escalating and needs to step away for a few minutes.

 Don't try to engage in problem solving when you or your loved one is currently experiencing mania, hypomania, or depression. In the midst of the mood episode, the problem you need to focus on is the mood episode. Clear thinking is essential for productive problem solving, and trying to resolve problems during a mood episode is often counterproductive.

Identifying the Problem

The first step to solving any problem is identifying what the problem is. One way to identify a problem is to start with how you feel. Are you angry, frustrated, afraid, hurt? Then ask yourself what's making you feel that way. Try to form a statement that starts with the way you feel and ends with the cause. For example, "I get upset when my family treats me like a child" or "I'm afraid we're going to lose our home because we're spending more money than we're earning."

 Keep in mind that if you're problem solving as a couple or as a family or group, one person's problem is everyone's problem; however, each individual may have a different perspective on what the problem really is. Try to work toward a definition of the problem that everyone can agree on.

 Another way to identify a problem, particularly when the problem is causing conflict with another person, is to exchange stories. This method allows each person to share his perspective on what's going on and perhaps his ideas about the underlying issue. If you can't talk about the problem without arguing, have each person involved write down his story and then exchange the written versions. Exchanging stories is most productive when everyone turns off his judgment response and tries to listen actively and be aware of the other person's experience without criticizing or judging his perspective. (See Chapter 13 for guidance on communicating without judgment.)

 Because different sides of any story invariably diverge and these exchanges often trigger big emotions, sharing conflicting stories is usually best done in the presence of a skilled mediator or family therapist who can ask questions, help regulate emotional responses, and facilitate a productive narrative of what's going on. If you choose to exchange stories on your own, give each party an opportunity to present his story uninterrupted, and then take turns asking each other questions until everyone involved has a clear understanding of everyone else's position. Leave plenty of time and space for emotional reactions to flare and cool down as needed. Try to flesh out what's going on by asking open-ended who, what, when, where, why, and how questions, such as the following:

- Who's usually involved when the problem occurs?
- Whom does the problem affect and how?
- What's happening when the problem occurs?
- What makes the problem better or worse?
- When does the problem typically occur or become most serious? Is the problem more common or serious at a particular time during the day or year or during certain types of events or situations?
- Where does the problem usually occur? At home, work, school, in the car, at a restaurant?
- What are the identifiable triggers — events, words, actions, or emotions — commonly associated with the problem or conflict?
- How have you dealt with the problem up to this point?
- How do other people deal with similar problems? Are their methods effective?

Questions elicit details, and details often deepen people's understanding of the problem and point the way to solutions.

The process of identifying problems often gets clouded by past events, other problems, and emotions, especially when you're dealing with a group of people. Here are three tips that can help you avoid the most common pitfalls associated with this stage of the problem-solving process:

- **Stay in the present.** You can't change the past, so don't ruminate over it. This is tough advice to put into practice, so try to develop a way for the group to mediate when discussion is drifting into past hurts and redirect it back into the present.

- **Focus on a single problem.** Problems tend to come in waves, but if you try to solve them in waves, you'll drown. Pick the single, most pressing issue. Solving problems one at a time can be difficult to do, so develop a plan for noticing when things are moving away from a single problem and a plan for getting back on track.

> ✔ **Remain objective.** Try to view the problem from the perspective of someone who's sitting in the balcony rather than interacting onstage. Doing so can help you develop a more objective perspective and become less reactive and more proactive.

If you're teaming up with others to solve a problem, good communication is crucial. Chapter 13 offers guidance for communicating with loved ones.

Redefining the Problem/Conflict: From Right Versus Wrong to Unmet Needs

People often view problems, especially those that result in conflict, in terms of right versus wrong. In fact, if your problem were to find its way to a courtroom, the entire focus would be on who's right and who's wrong. The legal system revolves around rights, obligations, and *remedies* — relief that's usually in the form of money for the party who's been wronged.

Unfortunately, loved ones often approach problems as legal battles. They try to argue and prove their case to one another, usually in vain. With no judge or jury to decide the case, issues remain unresolved and often fester.

A more effective approach is to redefine the problem in terms of unmet needs or interests. This approach is one that professional mediators often use to resolve conflict. Here, all parties communicate their needs and expectations and then work together to find ways to address concerns and meet everyone's needs. In the language of problem-solving therapy, this step focuses on identifying goals that meet the needs of all involved.

The goal of interest-based problem solving is to make all parties winners. Instead of defending conflicting positions, you communicate interests and then work collaboratively to find resources that address those interests.

To identify needs, ask yourself and any other people involved in the situation what they want — what must happen to make you feel that the problem or issue has been resolved? Answers vary depending on what the problem is and whether you're working alone or collaboratively to solve it. Here are some examples of needs:

> ✔ We really need to stop fighting at dinner.
>
> ✔ I need medications that I can't afford.
>
> ✔ I need transportation to work because I lost my driver's license.
>
> ✔ We need to earn $1,000 more every month or spend $1,000 less.

    ✔ I need to know that you're safe.

    ✔ I need some assurance that you're taking your medications.

    ✔ I need for everyone to stop nagging me about taking my medications.

After you've identified everyone's needs and goals, the process moves to the next step of brainstorming solutions and working to find strategies and resources to meet those needs.

Brainstorming Possible Solutions

Now for the fun, creative part of problem solving — brainstorming possible solutions. The goal here is to come up with as many solutions as possible. If you're problem solving on your own, just start jotting down ideas. If you're collaborating with a group, go around the circle and ask each person to contribute at least one idea. Put one person in the group in charge of writing down all the ideas. (A whiteboard comes in handy for this process.)

Choose the process that works best for everyone involved. Some people do better thinking of solutions on their own and then bringing them to the group, whereas others are most creative in the context of a lively group discussion. The goal is to generate a lot of potential solutions, and there's no single "right way" to accomplish that goal.

Be creative, not critical. You can eliminate less helpful ideas later, but criticism at this stage discourages the creative thinking that often leads to the best solutions. Have fun tossing around ideas and thinking outside the box.

When you've run out of ideas, switch to feedback mode. (You may want to cross out any solutions you tried in the past that didn't work, but keep in mind that a failed solution from the past may be successful with better planning and execution.) For each solution on your list, jot down a list of pros and cons or do a cost-benefit analysis. Ask questions such as the following:

    ✔ How costly is the solution to implement in terms of time, money, effort, emotional investment, and so on?

    ✔ Which solution, if it works, is likely to deliver the greatest benefit?

    ✔ Looking at the pros and cons or costs versus benefits, which solution looks best to everyone?

Rank the solutions to identify the top two or three and choose one. Save the others as backups.

Planning and Implementing Agreed-Upon Solutions

To improve your chances of successfully resolving the problem, develop a plan for implementing the chosen solution. Be sure to include the following elements in your plan:

- ✔ **Resources:** Sometimes resolving problems and conflicts requires additional resources, such as alternative living arrangements, money, or transportation. If you've identified certain needs, make sure your plan includes a list of resources to explore.

- ✔ **Tasks:** If the solution is fairly complex, break it down into tasks to make implementation seem less overwhelming and more doable.

- ✔ **Assignments:** Figure out who's going to perform each task.

- ✔ **Deadlines:** Set a deadline for implementing your plan and perhaps interim deadlines for accomplishing the various tasks.

- ✔ **Signs of success:** Write a short description of what success will look like so you have a point of reference to determine how successful you've been in solving the problem.

Consider adding a way to celebrate your success. For example, if you successfully solve the problem or reach a particular milestone, celebrate together with a dinner out or a movie.

With your plan in place, you're ready to roll. Put that plan into action and monitor the situation. Schedule another meeting to discuss your progress. If you've fallen short of your goal, you may need to adjust your plan or ditch it and try another solution (see the preceding section for details on how to come up with other solutions).

Sometimes solving a problem or resolving a conflict is a simple matter of making trade-offs. For example, to get her dad to stop calling her cellphone to check up on her, Tara agrees to call home once a day to let her dad know she's safe. In other cases, you may need to explore available resources. Suppose a loved one with bipolar can't live at home because the situation is too stressful for his recovery. The family may look into renting an apartment, having their loved one move in temporarily with another family member, or explore alternative living arrangements through their church or community organizations.

Resources are usually available to meet everyone's needs, although finding and securing those resources may require some creative thinking and research. If the required resources cost money, check out Chapter 18 for some leads on where to start looking for assistance.

BIPOLAR BIO

Problem solving through "self" education

I'm a problem solver . . . no, not the mathematician sort and not some thug you hire to rough up a troublemaker. That's not me! I'm a problem solver who likes to use his mind to figure out solutions — whether the problem is mechanical, as with a friend's vehicle, or emotional. I listen closely, question what's really going on, and then try to come up with possible fixes. So when I was diagnosed with bipolar disorder, my very first thought was, "How can I solve this problem?" Not long after that, I started to realize that bipolar disorder wasn't the problem. The real problem was how I viewed it.

For me, education is key. I'm not just talking about education through books, blogs, and websites, although those sources are all valuable, too. I had to get educated about *myself*. That was the only way to solve the problem I was facing. I had to take myself out of the equation as "the victim" and look at bipolar disorder objectively as a chemical imbalance. When I took the time to learn about myself and how bipolar disorder was affecting my life, I was able to map out a course to recovery.

It was important for me to realize that I'm not living with a character flaw. It's a mood disorder caused by chemicals in my brain. The simple solution is never the simplest treatment. So the first part of solving my bipolar problem was open and honest communication with loved ones; the second part was seeking professional help — through therapy, medications, or cognitive approaches. A final element was to find what works and stick to it.

Personally, I use humor as a stepping stone toward wellness as I courageously continue to work toward real recovery. Family members, community organizations, national and local mental health groups, and drop-in centers have also helped me stick to my road to recovery. It took all my faith, love, support, and hope to benefit from my bipolar self-education and take control so that I could solve the problem that is bipolar disorder.

— Chato Stewart, husband, father, and mental health advocate and cartoonist for the Mental Health Humor blog at `blogs.psychcentral.com/humor`. He creates positive, provoking, and sometimes even funny cartoons drawn from his personal experience of living with bipolar disorder.

Avoiding Unproductive Approaches

Everyone approaches problems a little differently — rightfully so. But some approaches are more constructive than others. The problem-solving technique we present in this chapter — identify the problem and take action to resolve it — seems to work well. But others work, too. Just do your best to avoid the following unproductive approaches:

✓ **Avoiding:** If you have an aversion to conflict, you may tend to avoid talking about issues or doing anything to resolve problems because you're afraid that the process will trigger arguments. While that may be true, try to weigh the cost of the short-term pain against the relief you're likely to feel from a long-term fix. Problems often become worse and more entrenched over time, so avoidance typically results in temporary relief and a bigger problem to deal with later.

✓ **Giving up:** Persistent problems can derail even the best attempts at solving them. Fight back by being even more persistent. Every problem really does have a solution if you can get everyone to work together and stick to the goal of achieving a positive outcome. Don't give up!

✓ **Taking charge:** Declaring ownership of a problem isn't necessarily bad or unproductive, especially if you're working on it alone. In a collaborative effort, however, outcomes improve when everyone involved participates in solving the problem. If you're a take-charge person, you may need to step back a bit and let others play an active role.

✓ **Talking without action:** Talking about a problem is helpful, but action is usually required to solve a problem. If you notice yourself or a loved one constantly complaining about the same issue, it's time to start planning and acting to solve the issue.

First do no harm. Sometimes simply sitting with a problem without taking action is best, at least until you have a promising solution in mind and a solid plan for implementing it. "Sitting with" a situation means to try to be more aware of the situation — taking in the problem and your feelings about it — without reacting or taking action. This process allows for more careful problem solving or gives you a chance to just tolerate the difficult feelings and recognize that some things are out of your control. Even the best plans can backfire and make matters worse, but knee-jerk reactions carry a greater risk of disaster. Do your best to avoid undercutting the trust required to deal effectively with current and future problems. Carefully consider the potential fallout of both action and inaction as you determine the best approach to solve the problem.

Letting Go of Problems You Can't Solve on Your Own

Just because every problem has a solution doesn't mean *you* can solve every problem. Some problems simply aren't yours to solve. And although you may be able to convince someone of the benefits of a certain course of action, ultimately you can't control another person's responses or willingness or ability to follow through. If you're working on a problem that requires someone else's cooperation that you're not getting, you basically have four options:

✔ Convince or cajole the person to cooperate through encouragement and support; help him identify the positives of trying something different.

✔ Force the person to cooperate, for example, by contacting law enforcement or working through the courts.

✔ Enlist the assistance of an objective third party whom everyone trusts and respects to mediate and perhaps offer solutions that nobody involved in the situation has thought of. (The third party can be a friend, family member, therapist, or even a professional mediator.)

✔ Let go of the problem and do whatever possible to shield yourself from it. In other words, set and enforce boundaries. (See Chapter 12 for more about setting boundaries and expectations.)

Keep in mind that the problem-solving approach we outline in this chapter is just a starting point. Certain situations call for additional or more specific strategies. For example, financial problems call for an exploration of external resources, as we explain in Chapter 18. For problems that are rooted in ineffective communication, everyone involved may need to build communication skills; see Chapter 13 for details. If you're dealing with work-related issues, turn to Chapter 17 for some solutions that can help deliver positive results.

Chapter 15

Planning Ahead for a Mood Episode

In This Chapter
▶ Keeping all your care providers in the loop
▶ Preventing a mood episode from spinning out of control
▶ Picking a psychiatric facility ahead of time
▶ Jotting down everything your loved ones need to know in an emergency
▶ Signing medical releases to facilitate communication among care providers

Have you given your loved ones consent to talk with your doctor in an emergency? Should they call other family members? If so, whom? When they reach someone who can help, what do you want them to say? Should they freeze your bank or credit card accounts? Do they have power of attorney to do so? Don't wait until an episode is underway to address these questions. By then, you and your loved ones should already have the answers.

If the idea of sitting down with your loved ones to discuss the "what ifs" of bipolar disorder is a little overwhelming, don't panic. This chapter provides information that can help you develop a customized emergency plan so you and your loved ones are prepared if a crisis hits.

Teaming Up with Your Care Providers

Doctors and therapists are helpful when you're not feeling well or you have a specific problem; but when you're doing fine, they rarely bring up the painful topic of "what if?" As in, what if symptoms return or get worse? At your next session with your doctor or therapist, ask the "what if?" question and get details on what to do if you or others start to notice a return or worsening of symptoms. Make sure you discuss the following:

- **What to watch for as early warning signs:** A nearly universal early warning sign is sleep irregularity — sleeping significantly less or more than usual. Here are some other common early warning signs categorized by mania or depression:

    - **Mania or hypomania:** Increased energy, restlessness, or irritability; rapid, pressured speech (can't stop talking); impulsive speech or behaviors, such as being overly honest or open; overspending on shopping sprees, vacations, and so on; grandiose thinking; hypersexuality/promiscuity; flight of ideas or impaired concentration; inflated self-esteem; increased interpersonal conflicts; flamboyant makeup or dress.

    - **Depression:** Loss of interest in pleasurable activities; fatigue or decreased energy; social withdrawal; unexplained aches and pains; weight loss or gain or increase or decrease in appetite; unexplained sadness that won't go away; feelings of guilt, worthlessness, or indifference; lowered self-esteem or increase in self-criticism; a sense of hopelessness or despair; increased focus on death or mortality; suicidal thoughts or ideation (envisioning or planning suicide).

- **What to do when you or others notice your early warning signs:** The first step is to contact your doctor or therapist. She may offer several courses of action depending on the duration and severity of the early warning signs. Actions may include increasing the dose of a medication, changing medications, engaging in more frequent or additional outpatient therapy sessions, or checking you into a psychiatric facility. See the next section, "Thwarting a Mood Episode," for details.

- **Who's in charge if you don't notice the early warning signs:** Lack of *insight* — an inability to notice that something's wrong — is a common symptom of bipolar, so you really should assign one or more trusted members of your treatment team, preferably people who see you every day, to step in when they notice one or more of your early warning signs.

- **How to reach your doctor or therapist during off hours:** If you haven't received emergency phone numbers to reach your doctor and therapist on nights, weekends, and holidays, get them now. Also, ask your doctor or therapist what to expect when you call the number. Will you reach a doctor on call or get an answering service? If you leave a message, how long will it take for someone to call you back? What should you do while you're waiting for that call? What should you do if nobody calls back?

- **Whom to call or where to go if you can't reach your doctor or therapist:** If you end up in the emergency room of a hospital that doesn't have a psychiatric facility, the doctors there are going to want to know which psychiatric facility to take you to. Ask your doctor ahead of time so you know where to go. See the section "Choosing a Psychiatric Facility" for details.

Thwarting a Mood Episode

Ideally, effective mood management hinges on prevention. But even when you're doing everything right, you can experience *breakthrough episodes* — symptoms that occur even when you're taking therapeutic doses of medication and receiving other therapies that had been working. This is why mood management requires ongoing monitoring even when things seem to be okay.

When you or others notice the early warning signs of depression or mania (see the preceding section), consult your doctor for guidance. Your doctor may recommend one of the following courses of action, depending on the severity of your symptoms:

✔ **Discontinue a medication that may be contributing to symptoms.** For example, if you're currently taking an antidepressant and you begin to notice symptoms of hypomania, your doctor may have you temporarily decrease or discontinue the antidepressant.

✔ **Increase the dose of one or more medications you're already taking.** Your doctor may advise you to take more of a medication that you already take. He may send you for blood tests such as a lithium level before making this kind of change.

✔ **Add a medication.** If your moods have been stable while taking a certain medication, your doctor may prescribe an add-on medication to help treat the same symptoms — at least temporarily, until mood stability is reestablished.

✔ **Enroll in intensive outpatient therapy (IOT).** If your doctor believes your symptoms are serious but not a threat to your safety or the safety of others, he may recommend IOT, during which your moods can be more closely monitored while any medication changes have time to take effect.

✔ **Head to the hospital or a psychiatric facility.** If symptoms are serious and your doctor believes they may be a threat to you or others, he may recommend calling 911 or having someone drive you to the nearest emergency room or psychiatric facility.

The earlier you get help, the more input you have in the treatment approach. If you wait so long that you lose control over your mental faculties, decisions may be out of your hands.

Choosing a Psychiatric Facility

One way to reduce some of the anxiety about hospitalization is to choose a mental health care facility before you need one, assuming you have a choice. Insurance restrictions and the shortage of inpatient psychiatric beds (in many places) may leave you with little or no choice when hospitalization becomes necessary. Ask your doctor for a list of facilities in your area or call your local hospital or community mental health center and get a list of options. With this list, start to filter your choices by answering these questions:

✔ Which facility does your doctor or therapist recommend?

She may "do rounds" at only one or two facilities on your list. In many areas, a doctor on staff at the hospital who consults with your outpatient doctor treats you. In other parts of the country, psychiatrists admit their own patients to a local hospital and function as the primary doctor while they're inpatient.

✔ Which mental health care facilities does your insurance policy cover?

✔ If you belong to a support group, which facilities do your fellow members think are best and worst?

After you've trimmed your list to two or three possible candidates, schedule a visit to each facility. Consider inviting one or more close friends or family members (people in your support network) to go with you so they can provide additional input. Visiting a facility can be an emotional experience, so visit only when you feel ready and expect some emotions to well up.

If a psychiatric hospital doesn't allow you to physically tour the actual patient spaces due to confidentiality, you can still inspect the public areas of the facility and/or speak to someone by phone to ask specific questions such as the ones we include in the following list. You can also ask to speak to the Head Nurse or Medical Director of the specific unit. When you arrive at the facility, try your best to obtain answers to the following questions:

✔ Does the facility seem clean and well organized? (Check bedrooms, bathrooms, and common areas, such as the cafeteria and group therapy room.)

✔ Does the staff seem to treat the patients with respect and empathy?

✔ Does each patient have her own bedroom?

✔ Does the facility provide outdoor access? If so, for how much time each day?

✔ Will you be able to see your doctor, or does the facility have its own doctor who will manage your inpatient care?

✔ How often will you see your doctor or the doctor on staff?

✔ How long is an average stay?

✔ What is the phone call policy for patients?

✔ What can you take with you, and what is prohibited?

✔ Does the facility allow smoking — where and when?

✔ Which days and times are visitors allowed? (Be wary of visiting hours that are highly restrictive.)

✔ What types of therapy are offered?

✔ How much time each day can you expect to be in therapy sessions?

✔ What is the policy on "seclusion and restraint"? (See Chapter 16.)

Documenting Essential Information

Digging through someone's purse or wallet for doctor names and phone numbers or rummaging through the medicine cabinet to piece together prescription information during a crisis is frustrating and often produces a wealth of unreliable information. Fortunately, it's also unnecessary. You should keep a list of all pertinent information in a single document, store it on a computer or smartphone in a format that's confidential but accessible to loved ones, and print a copy for each member of your team. This document should include the following information:

✔ Current medications, doses, and instructions

✔ Doctor's name and office and emergency phone numbers

✔ Therapist's name and office and emergency phone numbers

✔ Name, address, and phone number of preferred treatment center, hospital, or emergency room, along with backup choices

✔ Insurance information, including customer service number and the policyholder's group number and member ID

✔ Names of people to contact (and not to contact)

✔ Description of what has and hasn't worked in the past

With the help of your loved one, fill out the Crisis Information Sheet shown in Figure 15-1, distribute it to all the people on your support team, and keep it handy at all times.

Keep several copies of the Crisis Information Sheet on hand: one at home, one at work, one in your purse or briefcase, and one on your computer or smartphone. Also make sure to keep the information up to date.

Contact Information		
To Call	**Name**	**Phone Number**
Psychiatrist		
Therapist/Social Worker		
Primary Care Physician		
Preferred Hospital/Psych Facility		
Backup Hospital/Psych Facility		
Local Mental Health Crisis Team		
Local Support Group Crisis Responder		
Local Police		
State Police		
Friend/Relative		
Friend/Relative		
Friend/Relative		

Medication		
Medication	**Dose**	**Times Per Day**

Insurance Information	
Insurance Company	
Member Services Phone Number	
Mental Health Services Phone Number	
Member ID	
Group ID	

Figure 15-1:
A sample
Crisis
Information
Sheet.

Work/School Information	
Employer/School Name	
Employer/School Phone Number	
Contact Person Name	
Contact Person Phone Number	

© John Wiley & Sons, Inc.

Signing Releases . . . Or Not

Sometimes laws intended to protect an individual's rights undermine the efforts of others to do what's in the person's best interests. For example, the Health Insurance Portability and Accountability Act (HIPAA) Security Rule may discourage a doctor from discussing a patient's condition with a family member — even if doing so would help the family member deal with a particular situation more effectively.

Your loved ones usually find out about rules like HIPAA when you're in crisis mode and they can't get the doctor to speak with them about what's going on. Don't wait until a crisis occurs. Consider getting legal documents signed in advance so your loved ones can obtain information and act on your behalf when necessary. The documents you may want to sign are a release of information authorization, power of attorney, and advanced directive, as we explain in the following sections.

You don't have to sign any of the legal documents described in the following sections. Do so only if you fully trust the people named in the documents to use their authorization only when necessary and to serve your best interests.

Release of information authorization

A *release of information authorization* enables your doctor or therapist to share information about your condition with others. The type of information and the people authorized to receive it are entirely up to you. You can stipulate restrictions in the release itself. Figure 15-2 provides an example of a release of information authorization, though your doctor may have a release she wants you to use instead. (In the U.K., the release of information authorization is more likely to be a part of the advanced statement or directive. See the section "Advanced directive," later in this chapter.)

Provide signed copies of the authorization to your doctor, therapist, and the person (or people) you're authorizing to receive information. Advise each person to store the document in a secure location.

Laws, rules, and regulations may vary from one jurisdiction to another. In addition, people may interpret them differently. Don't assume that just because someone claims that the law prohibits her from sharing information or talking with you that what she's telling you is correct. Check with other reliable sources, such as an attorney who has experience and expertise in healthcare privacy laws in your area.

TIP

Even without a release of information authorization, a doctor or therapist can receive input from a loved one, so if you're concerned about a loved one with bipolar to the extent that you think her doctor or therapist needs to know about it, you can call, email, text, or send a letter to the doctor or therapist expressing your concerns. Just keep in mind that the doctor or therapist may be required or feel obligated to share what you say with your loved one.

Release of Information

Dr. or Therapist's Name: _____

Address: _____

City: _____ State: _____ ZIP: _____

Phone Number: _____

Consent to Release Information

I hereby give _____ (doctor/therapist) permission to share information — verbal or written — with the following individual/organization:

Individual/Organization Name: _____

Address: _____

Telephone: _____

... regarding:

Myself or My Child (circle one)

Name: _____ DOB: _____

Patient Name: _____

Patient/Guardian Name/Relationship: _____

Patient/Guardian Signature: _____

Dated Signed: _____

This consent expires within one year of date of signing unless otherwise specified here:

_____

Figure 15-2: Sample release of information authorization.

Power of attorney

Power of attorney (POA) enables you to designate another person to act on your behalf in a range of matters including financial, legal, and medical — you specify which areas are covered. In the world of bipolar disorder, POA can come in very handy, especially when overspending and impulsive financial and business decisions accompany mood episodes. While the specifics of POA vary by state and jurisdiction, four basic forms are available in most places:

✔ **Durable power of attorney:** This type of POA stays in effect even if the person who signed the POA (the *principal*) becomes incapacitated.

✔ **Medical power of attorney:** Also known as *healthcare proxy,* this POA enables you to designate another person to make medical decisions on your behalf when you're unable to do so for yourself.

✔ **Springing power of attorney:** Available in some states, this POA becomes effective only when something happens, such as the principal becomes incapacitated. The criteria for what qualifies as incapacitation and who makes that determination are spelled out in the POA. Although the determination is usually left to the principal's physician, legal and privacy challenges may complicate the process.

✔ **Nondurable power of attorney:** This type of POA is effective immediately and terminates if the principle becomes incapacitated, which totally defeats the purpose of using a POA for help during a mood episode.

Consult an attorney for guidance in choosing a POA that's best for you.

A power of attorney relationship is serious and can lead to bitterness and resentment even when it's used in the best interest of an ill friend or relative. Be very specific in describing conditions under which power of attorney may be granted and terminated and specifically identify which matters the person with power of attorney is permitted to manage and which ones she may not.

Advanced directive

Alternatively or in combination with a general or medical power of attorney, a person with bipolar disorder may draw up an *advanced directive* or *advanced statement,* in which she spells out her treatment preferences ahead of a crisis. Two types of advanced directives are commonly used:

✔ **Instruction directive:** Like a living will, the *instruction directive* enables you to specify which facility you want to be taken to, which medications you want and don't want to take, who's allowed and not allowed to visit you, and so on.

✔ **Proxy directive:** Like a medical power of attorney, the *proxy directive* allows you to authorize someone to make medical decisions on your behalf in the event that you become incapacitated.

Laws authorizing advanced directives have been enacted in all 50 states in the U.S. and in the District of Columbia, but specific legislation varies from state to state and only a few states have enacted laws that govern psychiatric advanced directives specifically. For additional information and guidance about advanced directives, consult a local attorney. You can find additional information on the web at www.dbsalliance.org and www.nami.org. Visit www.bristolmind.org.uk/files/docs/info/advance-statement.pdf for a good summary of advanced statements in the U.K.

Advanced directives have several qualities that can be good or bad depending on the situation: They can be used to try to refuse all psychiatric treatment, revoked at any time, and challenged on the grounds that they were signed under duress or that now, when the advanced directive is about to be enforced, the person who signed it claims that she isn't incapacitated. In addition, the treating physician may override a directive if she feels that doing so is in the best interest of her patient's health and safety. Yet, advanced directives can be helpful in getting the treatment you need and avoiding treatments that haven't worked or that caused problems in the past.

Part V
Dealing with the Fallout

Seven ways to respond to financial setbacks

✔ Contact your state or county mental health department to find out about affordable treatment options and other services.

✔ Call the Mental Health America at 800-969-6642 or visit www.mentalhealth america.net to find a local branch and ask about available services.

✔ File for disability benefits.

✔ Explore government programs, including food assistance, cash assistance/welfare, housing programs, and health insurance plans.

✔ Call the Partnership for Prescription Assistance website at www.pparx.org or call 888-4PPA-NOW (888-477-2669) to find out about prescription assistance programs.

✔ If you own your home, and it won't put you into a financial danger zone, consider taking out a home-equity line of credit to get through a period of low or no income while you explore other options.

✔ Reach out to family members or friends for temporary financial assistance or a place to live.

Visit www.dummies.com/extras/bipolardisorder for more information on how to tell the difference between bipolar disorder and borderline personality disorder, two conditions that are often confused.

In this part . . .

- Find out how to deal more effectively with hospitalization and get the most benefit out of the time you spend there.

- If your loved one is hospitalized, find out what you can do to help. (*Hint:* It's not much different from what you would do if your loved one were hospitalized with any other illness.)

- Weigh the pros and cons of returning to work and, in the process, decide what recovery means to you. Does it mean returning to the life you had or exploring new opportunities?

- Deal more effectively with financial setbacks by tapping into government programs, filing for disability, accessing sources of free or cut-rate medical treatment and pharmaceuticals, and more.

Chapter 16

From Hospitalization to Recovery

In This Chapter

▶ Considering the benefits of hospitalization and developing realistic expectations

▶ Brushing up on patient rights

▶ Staying comfortable while in the hospital and keeping your doctors in the loop

▶ Pacing yourself during your recovery

Despite your best efforts and those of your mood-management team, breakthrough mood episodes may land you in a hospital or psychiatric facility, perhaps against your will. Hospitalization may be traumatic, but it's also the first step toward regaining both your mental health and your freedom from the debilitating symptoms of bipolar disorder.

In this chapter, we provide information to help you make the most of a stay in a hospital or psychiatric facility. We describe standard operating procedures so you know what to expect; offer tips on how to make your stay more comfortable; encourage you to keep loved ones in the loop; and offer suggestions for healing to minimize chances of a relapse soon after your release.

Coming to Terms with Hospitalization

Few people enjoy spending time in a hospital, but there is an upside. In addition to being a possible lifesaver, hospitalization gives you an opportunity to achieve some important goals. In a hospital setting, you have the opportunity to

✔ Recover in a safe place.

✔ Find relief from daily responsibilities, stressors, and triggers.

✔ Focus your energy on getting healthier.

✔ Stabilize your medications or switch to more effective medications.

- ✔ Engage in therapy to develop better coping skills.
- ✔ Find out about community-based services and supports that can help you after you're released.
- ✔ Give your loved ones time and space to seek help for themselves.

Think of hospitalization as a way to reboot your brain after a crash. Try not to worry about letting other people down or falling behind at work or school. Care first for yourself so you can get to a place where you're able to help yourself and function better when you're released.

Knowing What to Expect

Knowing how a psychiatric facility operates *before* you're admitted to one can help alleviate the anxiety that accompanies hospitalization, especially if you're hospitalized against your will. In the following sections, we describe what to expect when you're hospitalized. Keep in mind that every facility is different and every experience is unique.

Seeing the doctor

Waiting to see the doctor, especially when you're first admitted and when you're about to be released, is probably the most frustrating part of a hospital stay. Doctors normally make their rounds once every 24 hours, but on weekends you may only visit briefly with an on-call doctor, who will likely keep you in a holding pattern rather than developing a comprehensive treatment plan. Friday afternoon admissions sometimes mean waiting until Monday morning to see your assigned doctor and making plans for major medication changes. That can seem like an eternity when you're locked up, manic or depressed, and not thinking clearly.

Adjusting your medications

The doctor's first order of business is to evaluate your condition and prescribe medication. Because your symptoms were serious enough to land you in the hospital, you may need increased doses of first-line medications. If you were taking medications that have a relatively poor track record for treating acute mania or depression or that may be worsening your symptoms, the doctor may discontinue them and try something else. (See Chapter 7 for more about medications.)

The doctor's goal is to extinguish your mania or depression as quickly as possible. Because the inpatient stay is usually quite brief — one to two weeks at most — you'll complete your recovery from your acute mood episode in some type of outpatient setting. After you recover from the episode and experience several weeks of stable moods, you and your regular doctor can discuss the possibility of scaling back or stopping certain medications.

Engaging in therapy

Most facilities provide individual and group therapy sessions that begin at about 9:00 a.m. and continue into the early evening. In short, expect a fairly full schedule. Therapy sessions may include patient education, coping skills, reflection, spirituality, pet therapy, group or community sessions, mindfulness training, and other individual adjunctive therapies. Most facilities offer some form of family support, too, to help your loved ones better understand what's going on and strengthen their communication and problem-solving skills.

Looking into seclusion and restraint policies

Federal regulations mandate that hospitals use seclusion and restraint only when "absolutely necessary" using the "least restrictive alternative." Some facilities and personnel are better than others in using de-escalation skills (such as listening closely to patients, responding to their concerns and needs, and staying calm while encouraging patients to use self-soothing strategies) to manage aggressive and violent behaviors without the use of restraint or seclusion, but when these efforts fail, facility staff may restrain patients by using one or both of the following means:

- ✔ **Physical restraint:** Immobilizing a patient, perhaps by holding him a certain way or securing him to a hospital bed
- ✔ **Seclusion:** Isolating a person in a quiet, safe room, for example
- ✔ **Chemical restraint:** Sedating psychotropic medication, given acutely, often as an injection, that's not part of the standard treatment for the person's condition

Hospitals should use seclusion and restraint rarely and only as a last resort, when all other interventions have failed, and only when necessary to protect everyone's safety. Hospital personnel should use seclusion or restraint only with compassion and cool tempers — not in anger and in no way to punish or shame the patient. When you're the one being restrained, you'll likely have a hard time remembering that restraint is being used to keep you and those around you safe — to prevent unintentional harm that can arise from extreme symptoms. But that's always the goal . . . or should be.

You should have an opportunity to discuss a seclusion or restraint incident with your treatment team when things calm down. Hospital staff often debrief after a situation involving restraint, and you should have a similar opportunity. The post-restraint interaction with staff should be about healing and recovering from the event as well as offering feedback to staff about how you felt during the process.

 Having a family member or loved one review the seclusion and restraint policy with the treatment team or unit staff when you're first admitted gives your family important insight to the unit's policies and procedures. A preemptive review of this policy also gives the hospital staff the heads-up that you and your support team are paying close attention to seclusion and restraint procedures and that you expect potential conflicts to be handled in the safest, most humane, and clinically appropriate way.

Exploring variations in visiting hours

Visiting hours at psychiatric facilities vary considerably. At some facilities, you can have visitors only on specific days. Others have daily visiting times that include one or more hours in the evening. Some of the more liberal facilities have two visiting sessions — one in the afternoon and one in the evening. Visitation policies that allow visitors to drop in any time are rare.

 If you want to have visitors, call and ask certain loved ones to visit, or call your main contact on the outside and ask that person to contact others you'd like to have visit you. In many cases, loved ones avoid visiting because they assume you don't want visitors or don't want anyone to know that you've been hospitalized for a mood disorder. They just need to know that you're okay with them stopping by.

 If you're planning to visit a loved one in a psychiatric facility, call ahead to see if there's anything she needs or wants and then check with the facility to find out what you're allowed to bring. Other than that, approach your loved one's hospitalization as you would a hospitalization for any illness. If you'd normally bring flowers, bring flowers (in a plastic vase). If you'd send a get-well card, send a card. Try to make the hospitalization feel as normal as possible for your loved one.

Knowing about how long you'll stay

According to the American Psychiatric Association, the average stay for adults in psychiatric facilities in the U.S. is 12 days. For many adults, their stay lasts just a few days — just long enough to intervene in the crisis, give the medication time to take effect, and schedule outpatient treatment for the day following discharge. In short, the days of three- to six-month hospital stays are over.

Some insurance carriers cover home healthcare or visiting nurse services for psychiatric care; ask your hospital team to look into this option, especially if you live alone.

Getting released

When your doctor at the facility thinks you're well enough to leave, she meets with you for a final evaluation and to provide you with prescriptions for any medications you may need to take. If you provide the doctor with your pharmacy's phone number, she can call in or *electronically prescribe* most of your medications so you can pick them up on your way home. Some medications, such as benzodiazepines, are controlled substances with special prescribing requirements. Depending on where you live, the doctor may have to give you a written prescription for them, but many states allow them to be electronically prescribed. Check with your doctor for details in your area.

The doctor, not the hospital staff, decides when you're discharged. Pleading with nurses and other staff members won't shorten your stay.

Knowing Your Patient Rights

Most jurisdictions mandate rights specifically for patients in mental health facilities. In most places, you have the right to

- ✔ Refuse to submit to treatment, including medication, if you're a voluntary adult patient
- ✔ Petition the commitment court for consideration of the treatment program if you're an involuntary patient
- ✔ Be free from harm, including unnecessary or excessive seclusion or restraint, emotional or physical abuse, and neglect

✔ Receive information about your diagnosis and treatment and participate in treatment planning

✔ Keep and use your own personal articles, including clothing and toiletries, with some restrictions

✔ Access individual secure storage space for your private use

✔ Keep and spend a reasonable sum of your own money for small purchases, if necessary

✔ Make and receive confidential phone calls

Patient rights vary according to the jurisdiction you're in and whether you're voluntarily or involuntarily admitted to the facility. In the U.S., you can find a mental health patient rights manual for nearly every state online. Use your favorite search engine to search for "mental health patient rights" followed by the name of the country, state, or other jurisdiction in which you live. You may also have access to mental health patient rights advocates.

Making Your Stay More Comfortable

The following survival tips can make your stay in the hospital a little more pleasant and productive:

✔ Bring any medications you're currently taking, including nonpsychiatric medications and any over-the-counter medications, supplements, or complementary/alternative products, or a complete list of your medications and the doses.

✔ Tell the nurse and doctor if you've been drinking alcohol or taking any other nonprescribed drugs. A withdrawal reaction can be dangerous, especially if no one knows what's happening to you.

✔ Bring your doctor's and therapist's contact information.

✔ Leave valuables at home.

✔ Leave your belt, pocketknife, and any other potentially harmful accessories at home. The hospital won't let you have anything that you or another patient could use to harm yourself or others.

✔ Bring slippers or loafers or some other footwear without shoelaces.

✔ Bring comfortable but modest clothing.

✔ If you can, bring your own pillow and a comfortable blanket.

✔ Bring a journal without spirals or wires to record your thoughts and feelings and to jot down any useful information you pick up from the staff, therapy groups, or other patients.

✔ Cooperate with the staff as much as your mental state allows.

✔ Get to know your fellow patients. Psychiatric hospitals are populated with interesting and intelligent individuals who understand your experience better than most people on the outside.

✔ If you smoke, bring an ample supply of cigarettes. (If your hospital is nonsmoking, you may receive a nicotine patch.)

✔ Bring books, magazines, and a deck of cards if you play.

✔ Pack one or two photos of family, friends, or pets — without glass frames — to warm up your space.

Find out your visiting and phone privileges as soon as you can process the information. You can then plan a schedule to communicate with your family and other support team members. Continued contact and support from the outside world can be very beneficial, but avoid potentially dangerous or toxic interactions as much as possible. Use phone and visiting time to build an outside support network of healthy relationships and a firm foundation on which to build your recovery.

Keeping Your Team in the Loop

Communication is an important part of building and maintaining your support network and getting what you need to facilitate your recovery both during your hospitalization and beyond. Be sure to keep your doctor, therapist, and loved ones in the loop:

✔ **Notify your doctor and therapist.** If you didn't notify your doctor and therapist that you were heading to the hospital, let them know where you are as soon as you can. Confirm that your inpatient team has contacted your outpatient caregivers to get past history and information on current medication/therapeutic interventions and to collaborate on your inpatient treatment plan and your transition from inpatient to outpatient status.

✔ **Stay in touch with loved ones.** Your support network of loved ones can contribute to easing your transition back to the real world after your hospital stay, so if you're feeling up to it, keep friends and family members in the loop, especially if this is your first hospitalization.

Some facilities offer family education and therapy, which can help family members start to develop understanding, empathy, and realistic expectations for your recovery. If the facility offers it, encourage your family to do their best to take advantage of it.

Making Recovery Your Top Priority

Leaving the hospital doesn't necessarily mean you're ready to get back to your daily routines. A severe mood episode can leave you exhausted, and you may not regain your bearings for several months. No matter how much you want to get back to your normal routines, we encourage you to take it slow and make full recovery your number-one priority.

In the following sections, we help you come to terms with the aftermath of a major mood episode and deal with the fallout. We also reveal the importance of focusing on your health and wellbeing and offer ideas for how to retreat to a place that's conducive to convalescence.

You may be tempted to try solving everything at once, especially if you're coming down from a manic high. In most cases, however, your overall health is better served by taking small steps and focusing on your own wellbeing, a process we discuss in this section.

Anticipating the aftershock

How fast and fully you recover from depression or mania depends primarily on how severe your mood episode is and how well you respond to treatment. You may be one of the lucky few who respond within days of treatment, or you and your doctor may spend weeks or longer trying to find the right mix of medicines and therapy. As your body adjusts to the meds and your mood begins to stabilize, you may experience one or more of the following effects:

- **Memory difficulties:** You may not recall periods of time during the mood episode, especially during a manic episode.

- **Increased/decreased energy levels:** Don't be surprised if you need significantly more sleep after a manic or depressive episode; your body and brain need time to recuperate.

- **Anxiety:** You may become anxious after a mood episode due to certain medications or worries about family, work, relationships, bills, and other facets of your life that may be in upheaval.

- **Confusion:** A major mood episode and the medications used to treat it can muddle your thinking. You may wonder who you really are and how the medications will affect you. Until you know more about bipolar disorder, you may realize that something's not right, but you may not know exactly what's wrong.

Many of these symptoms, if they're related to medication changes, are most prevalent when you begin taking a medication, but they diminish over time. If the symptoms are intolerable, contact your doctor. General body and brain recovery takes quite some time, so be gentle and patient with yourself and ask others to be as well.

Mastering the art of selfishness

If you're one of those overachievers who puts everyone else's needs in front of your own, a mood episode may signal the time for a change — for you to become more aware of your own needs and more assertive in meeting them. This change may prompt you to begin working on developing the fine art of selfishness. During your recovery, you need to look out for yourself.

Assessing your needs and asking for and accepting help

The first step in mastering selfishness is to figure out what *you* need and how to ensure that *your* needs are met (either by you or someone else). Asking people to help you or accepting help that's offered may feel foreign and uncomfortable, especially if you're usually the *caregiver* and not *care receiver*. But defining your needs, asking others directly to help you, and letting them help when they offer are all important parts of recovery.

To assess your needs and get them met, try the following exercise:

1. **Write down five to ten needs, starting with the biggest one.**

   For example, "I need help getting the kids ready for school."

2. **Brainstorm ways to have each need met, including the names of people who can help, such as friends or family members.**

   You may be able to meet some needs on your own, by taking an hour at the end of the work day to wind down, for example. But for many situations you'll need help, so think about whom to ask.

3. **Draw up a plan for executing the best idea for meeting each need.**

4. **If you need assistance, write a detailed description of the type of help you need and the amount of time required to provide it.**

5. **Contact the people who can help and request their assistance**.

   If someone has asked, "What can I do to help?" encourage him to look over your plan with you to see what needs he can help with.

6. **Put your plan into action.**

Getting used to saying no

Mastering the art of selfishness requires you to become sensitive to your own needs and to avoid overcommitting your time and energy. In short, you have to learn how to say no. If you have trouble saying no, try the following lines:

- ✔ "I would love to help, but I really have too much on my plate right now."

- ✔ "I'm sorry, but I really want to spend more time with my family."

- ✔ "I'm sorry, but we've experienced some financial setbacks and can't donate anything at this time."

 Use the caller ID on your home phone or cellphone to screen out the most annoying callers. Or let your voicemail pick up and then return calls later. If telemarketers are infringing on your peace and tranquility, consider having your number added to the National Do Not Call Registry. You can do this online at www.donotcall.gov.

Retreating to a safe, quiet place

The most obvious place to recuperate from a major mood episode — your home — isn't always the best. If you live alone, the solitude may aggravate your symptoms, and without the watchful eyes of a support person and some human interaction, you may slip back into depression or mania. On the other hand, if your home is tense or you live with unsupportive family members, the environment can be downright toxic. The best place for your recovery is a safe and quiet place, a structured environment with the right combination of the following elements:

- ✔ **Tranquility:** Peace and quiet are essential in relieving anxiety, especially after a manic episode.

- ✔ **Activity:** Rest is important, but too much rest can lead to depression.

- ✔ **Interactivity:** Remaining connected to friends, family members, and colleagues provides additional social support.

- ✔ **Support:** Having somebody available to help you follow your treatment plan and remain on call if you need assistance can be a lifesaver.

- ✔ **Routine:** A structured routine with regular wake times, bedtimes, meals, and activities can help recovery.

Living arrangements that meet these criteria may include staying with a friend or family member or, if necessary, going into another type of temporary residence. Having a friend stay with you can sometimes provide support and companionship if you live alone or supply an ally and advocate if you live with family members who don't get it. Just remember not to stray too far from your medical and personal support networks when looking for places to stay.

If your family situation has deteriorated, avoid the impulse to move out on your own. Solitude can often deepen depression and unleash your manic impulses. Living alone sets up many new demands that you may struggle to meet. Some degree of personal support almost always improves the treatment outcome.

If you decide to return home with family members, we strongly encourage your family members to learn more about bipolar disorder and make any necessary adjustments to ease your transition. Family therapy can play a critical role in your successful recovery, as we explain in Chapter 11. Turn to Chapter 12 for additional guidance on how family members can help create a healthy emotional environment.

You don't necessarily have to move to cultivate a safe, quiet place. With the support of friends and family, you may be able to create such a place at home.

Following your doctor's orders

Your doctor will give you an earful about the importance of taking your medications as directed and sticking with your treatment plan, so we won't bore you with another lecture. What your doctor may omit, however, are instructions about what to do if your medications don't work or if they produce undesirable side effects. Here are four rules for sticking with your treatment plan and making adjustments if the plan doesn't produce the desired results:

- ✔ **Give it time.** Some medications take several days or even weeks to become fully effective. During this adjustment period, many negative side effects taper off.

- ✔ **Keep a record.** Using the mood chart in Chapter 11 or a mood-tracking app for your phone, you can follow the medication changes and your emotional, behavioral, and physical responses to those changes.

  You can find a sample mood chart and instructions about how to use it at www.dummies.com/extras/bipolardisorder.

- ✔ **Communicate your concerns.** Feeling just okay is unacceptable. If you experience negative side effects, contact your doctor for suggestions on how to minimize them. If your doctor seems insensitive to your concerns, find a doctor you can work with.

- ✔ **Consult with your doctor before making any changes.** Don't play doctor or stop taking a medication without your doctor's approval.

Treatment for bipolar is highly individualized; what works for one person doesn't necessarily work for another. Team up with your doctor to discover the most effective treatment plan for you. Your job is to tell your doctor how you feel so he can make well-informed treatment decisions and adjustments.

Reclaiming Your Life

You found the perfect place to recover — a private little beach in Aruba, two blocks from your psychiatrist's grass hut. You're resting in your hammock and reading this book without a care in the world. We hope you have a good vacation, but eventually, you need to sail back to reality — return to your family and friends, deal with your problems, and figure out how to support yourself financially, which typically includes finding some gainful employment that's not too stressful.

In this section, we help you determine when you're ready to board the cruise ship home, and we provide tips to ease the transition. For guidance on returning to work, see Chapter 17.

Knowing when you're ready

Recovering from a major mood episode calls for a slow and steady approach in which you first stabilize your medications and moods and then slowly transition back to normal activities. To prevent relapse and ensure a smooth transition, make sure you meet or exceed all the criteria in the following checklist before you head back to your normal life:

- ✔ Your medications are stable.
- ✔ Your moods are stable.
- ✔ You're getting sufficient sleep.
- ✔ You're thinking clearly.
- ✔ Your support group is in place.
- ✔ Your doctor/therapist believes you're ready.

Don't divorce your spouse, quit your job, or make any other major life decisions while your moods are unstable. Mania, depression, and anxiety can often push you to make rash decisions you later regret. We're not advising you to stay in a toxic relationship or in a job that stresses you out. Our advice is to make these major life decisions when your brain is functioning properly and you're in the right frame of mind.

I should've stayed longer the first time

In May, 2008 our daughter, Ali, was about to graduate high school. While I was wrapping up my school year (as a teacher), Joe (my husband) and I planned Ali's graduation party, and Ali and I prepared for a two-week excursion to Spain.

Unfortunately, mania kicked in. Family tension sparked, and I wasn't sleeping well on the nights I slept at all. We knew the warning signs, so I doubled up on my therapy visits and checked in with my psychiatrist. With each visit, he adjusted a medication or added something like pregabalin (Lyrica) to help me sleep. He failed to fully grasp the severity of my condition.

Soon I was experiencing severe paranoia along with audio and visual hallucinations. When I'm manic, one of the nice side effects is that I see a crystalized version of the world. Because I couldn't sleep, I walked around outside enjoying the beauty of nature. On one of these excursions, I decided to feed Cheerios to the carp and catfish in the lake behind our house. As I fed them, I could've sworn the catfish were jumping out of the lake and turning into cats.

Finally, I had no option but to head to the hospital, where Joe and I were led to a waiting room. I wasn't in a waiting state of mind, so I went out to the lobby and struck up a conversation with a nice family, mistakenly thinking that their daughter had been one of my students. They played along until security personnel arrived and ushered me to the psychiatric unit, where a social worker handed me a stack of legal forms to sign myself in. I couldn't focus, so without reading the forms, I angrily scrawled a big X across each page as my signature. Later in the evening, I had wrestled with a couple of orderlies and awoke the next morning with a few nasty bruises.

After just three days, I convinced the doctor to release me because my daughter and I had travel plans. Unfortunately, my mania had other plans. Two days after leaving the hospital, I had a severe attack of paranoia and I flushed some of my medications down the toilet. I had become convinced that I was under surveillance for drug possession and suspected of dealing, so I called the police to turn myself in. Officers showed up at our house, talked to my husband, and drove me to the emergency room. Later I was transferred to a mental health facility, where I spent about ten days recovering.

This time, I emerged from the hospital feeling pretty stable. My daughter and I had to cancel our trip to Spain, but she was able to make last-minute arrangements to travel to Costa Rica later that spring with her Spanish class. Having to cancel our trip was certainly a bummer, but Spain didn't fall off the map; we'll get there someday.

— Cecie Kraynak, teacher and author

Returning to friends and family

A mood episode doesn't always physically remove you from your family and friends, but it almost always drives a wedge between you and loved ones in some way. The first step toward reconciling with loved ones is to forgive yourself for whatever may have unfolded during the mood episode. The only thing you're guilty of is having an illness. The next step is to encourage everyone to work together; this is the tough part, because it takes understanding, empathy, and an ability to forgive. Here are some ways to achieve these goals:

1. **Find out how you may have hurt the people in your family and then apologize or at least acknowledge their pain.**

   It's natural to be unaware that you hurt someone and how you hurt that person, especially during a mood episode. It's also okay to feel that you don't need to apologize for something you did while in the grip of bipolar, but acknowledging that you're not the only victim can help heal the hurt.

2. **Encourage family and friends to learn more about bipolar disorder.**

   The more they know, the easier it is for them to understand that this illness isn't a product of your volition. They can start by reading this book, especially Chapter 19.

3. **Involve family members in your therapy to a degree that you and they feel comfortable.**

   Chapter 11 provides details on how family therapy can help.

4. **Give family members specific instructions on how they can help support you.**

   By becoming involved, family members often feel empowered rather than victimized.

You may meet some resistance from family members or friends who feel as though *you* have somehow victimized *them*. What they need to realize is that bipolar disorder has victimized your entire circle, *you* most of all. You're doing your part by seeking treatment, managing your medications, and attending therapy sessions. Now it's their turn to step up and contribute.

Following your doctor's orders and performing your due diligence in maintaining your health doesn't guarantee that you'll remain symptom-free. Sometimes bipolar disorder has a natural course that defies prediction or preparation, and an episode occurs regardless of treatment and planning. Realizing that setbacks are normal helps you and your family keep them in perspective so you don't feel as though your treatment has failed or that you've done something wrong when breakthrough episodes occur. The key is to remain vigilant, identify problems as early as possible, and address those problems quickly and aggressively.

Chapter 17

Returning to Work . . . or Not

. . . .

In This Chapter

▶ Gauging your return-to-work readiness and easing back in

▶ Choosing whether to disclose your diagnosis

▶ Checking out workplace accommodations that may help

▶ Deciding to do something else or not to work

. . . .

*T*he desire to return to work after a major mood episode can range from high to nonexistent or somewhere in between. You may want to get back in the game even as you feel unsure of your ability to perform and afraid of how your supervisor and coworkers will respond upon your return.

You probably have plenty of questions running through your mind. "Am I ready to return to work?" "Should I tell my coworkers or supervisor what happened?" "Should I ask for workplace accommodations; and if so, what kinds of accommodations are even feasible?" "What should I do if I'm unable to return to work?" In this chapter, we provide information and guidance that can help you make informed decisions and answer important questions about your return to work.

Reality Check: Are You Ready to Return to Work?

Nobody can tell you if or when you should return to work. The answer hinges on several variables, including the severity of your illness, the effectiveness of the treatment you receive, the amount of support you have at work and home, the stress level involved (and your capacity for handling it), and your eagerness to return to work. Instead of trying to answer the complex, all-encompassing question "Am I ready to return to work?," ask yourself what your return might look like:

- ✔ **Full return:** Some people with bipolar take a few weeks or months off work, obtain the medications or other treatments they need, and then return to work as though nothing happened.

- ✔ **Partial return:** Instead of returning full time, you may be able to scale back and work only three or four days a week if your situation allows for it. Some people who take this approach find that they can, over time, build back up to working full time.

- ✔ **Return with accommodations:** The Americans with Disabilities Act (ADA) covers mental illness, so you qualify for reasonable workplace accommodations. Check out the later section "Requesting Workplace Accommodations" for details.

- ✔ **Job change:** Instead of returning to the same job, you may be able to secure a less demanding position with the same employer, seek employment elsewhere, or change careers altogether.

If you're considering not returning to work, ask yourself whether you can afford *not* to work on a long-term basis. This isn't just about money and benefits. Work offers a host of other perks, including the following:

- ✔ **Structure:** People with bipolar often respond well to a structured environment and consistent schedule; work can often meet this need.

- ✔ **Positive self-esteem:** Being productive and receiving a paycheck provides a sense of self-worth.

- ✔ **Camaraderie:** For many people, work includes socializing, and an active social life (albeit not too active) can level out a person's moods and provide support for recovery goals and adaptive habits.

Don't underestimate the value of these benefits when making your decision. But if bipolar prevents you from returning to work, don't assume that you're necessarily missing out on all this great stuff. You can structure your day, establish a healthy social life, and build self-esteem without a job; it just may take a different kind of effort — possibly in the form of volunteerism, new roles within your family, adult education, or hobbies.

When you start to think about returning to work (or not), discuss your options with your doctor and therapist and ask for their input. They can help you weigh the pros and cons of returning and not returning to work, let you know if and when they think you're ready, smooth the transition back to work (if that's what you decide to do), or explore resources you may want to look into if you're unable or choose not to return to work.

Getting Back into the Swing of Things

If you decide to return to work and you and your doctor and therapist agree that you're ready, consider returning gradually instead of taking on a full workload right away. A gradual return may include the following scenarios:

- ✔ Working half days or at least fewer hours per day or week
- ✔ Working a one-day-on/one-day-off schedule
- ✔ Having a coworker assist you with some of your responsibilities
- ✔ Temporarily performing some of your job duties at home

Back to work with bipolar disorder

I had my first manic meltdown a week before Christmas break in 1999. I had been working as a junior high school Spanish teacher for 16 years. People told me that teaching junior high would make anyone crazy, but in my case, it took a few other factors (including bipolar disorder) to do the trick.

I ended up in the hospital, and the doctors put me on valproic acid (Depakote) and a few other meds. After three long months of outpatient therapy, I was improved enough to return to work, or so we thought. Unfortunately, I wasn't fully recovered. The medications I was on made it impossible to think clearly enough to effectively do my job. I was disoriented at school and operating in a fog, surrounded by confused friends and family who had been as blindsided by this illness and the side effects of the medications as I had been.

I'd work a few weeks and then need to take time off. Each time I returned, something would happen to break through my tenuous grasp of reality or "sanity." One day, I had to stop another teacher in the hall because I couldn't find my classroom. Increasingly, I felt guilty about missing work, and I knew that the inconsistency wasn't fair to my students. Finally, I made the difficult decision to take early retirement. A couple of years later, when I had a handle on managing my illness, I landed a low-stress job as an English as a Second Language (ESL) coordinator for another school system. It was just what the doctor ordered. I was good at the job, it structured my days, and I had positive interactions with students and my peers. Every day I was rewarded with a sense of accomplishment.

Over time, I was even able to return to teaching part time, and I've written a couple of books of my own, including *Spanish Grammar For Dummies*. I feel like my meds and moods are stabilized, and I'm functioning near full capacity again. My advice for anyone who's thinking of returning to work is this: Don't be too eager to get back to work. Take it slow. Wait until *you* feel ready.

— Cecie Kraynak, teacher and author

Schedule weekly appointments with your doctor and/or therapist for the first four to six weeks of your return to work so they can help monitor your condition throughout the transition. They can help you decide if and when you're ready to work more hours and take on more responsibilities.

Disclosing Your Diagnosis . . . or Not

The question of whether to disclose a diagnosis of bipolar disorder to an employer often causes considerable anxiety for the person with the illness. Of course, it shouldn't be that way. If you were ill with cancer, diabetes, or heart disease, you'd probably disclose it without reservation. You may even get some sympathy. People with bipolar disorder, however, often fear the real possibility of being stigmatized. In the following sections, we help you decide whether disclosing your condition is in your best interest and then provide guidance on how to proceed if you choose to do so.

Weighing the pros and cons of disclosure

Telling the people you work with and for that you have bipolar disorder carries the risk of being stigmatized in the following ways:

- Getting fired, let go, or subtly forced out
- Getting passed over for promotions
- Being excluded from social gatherings by coworkers
- Worrying about people's perception of you

Discriminating against a person because of a health condition is illegal, but that doesn't mean it never happens.

In the best-case scenarios (with employers who value their employees and understand that good people often have health issues that need to be managed), disclosing your condition can benefit you in several ways:

- You no longer have to carry the burden of hiding your illness.
- You become eligible under the Americans with Disabilities Act for reasonable workplace accommodations. (Your employer must be aware of your disability to be held accountable for providing accommodations. See the later section "Requesting Workplace Accommodations.")

✔ Your supervisor and any coworkers you tell may be more willing and able to offer assistance if they understand what's going on.

✔ In educating others, you may learn more about bipolar and feel empowered.

We can't tell you whether disclosure is the right course of action for you. You may be able to gauge how receptive people will be by considering their past behaviors and comments about mania or depression. If they've demonstrated empathy for others who've had similar conditions, you can predict that they'll treat your situation with care and understanding as well.

For more about the pros and cons of self-disclosure, you can access a 50-page booklet on the topic titled *Self-Disclosure and Its Impact on Individuals Who Receive Mental Health Services* at `http://store.samhsa.gov/shin/content/SMA08-4337/SMA08-4337.pdf` (Hyman, I. Center for Mental Health Services, Substance Abuse and Mental Health Services Administration).

Talking to supervisors and coworkers

When you're the one who's ill, you shouldn't have to invest time and energy into educating others about your illness. As caring human beings, the people around you should already demonstrate some empathy, if not sympathy, and make it a point to understand your condition. The reality, however, is that if you don't educate and advocate for yourself, your situation at work (or home or school or wherever) isn't likely to improve. The more others know about bipolar, the less fearful and more accepting they tend to be.

So how do you go about educating your supervisor, colleagues, and others at your workplace? Here are some suggestions:

✔ Start by disclosing your condition to people whom you trust the most and who seem understanding and open minded. They can model acceptance to others.

✔ Play the role of teacher. Take a nonconfrontational approach to presenting the facts about bipolar. (Keep in mind that *you* control exactly how much you choose to disclose to each individual. You don't have to tell everyone everything.)

✔ If your employer has a human resources (HR) department, consider involving the HR staff in meetings with your supervisor. HR people should know employment law and be able to explain to your supervisors their responsibilities to you as an employee.

- Describe the way you feel when you're depressed or manic. Nobody can argue or become defensive when you simply describe how the disorder makes you feel.

- Describe your common symptoms. That is, tell your supervisor and coworkers how your behavior is likely to change when you're becoming manic or depressed. By describing symptoms, you accomplish two things. First, you let people know what to expect so they're better prepared to handle any behavioral changes. Second, you enlist them in helping you spot early warning signs, which you may not notice when you're feeling manic or depressed.

- Be sure to mention that not everything you say and do can be attributed to bipolar. You don't want a bunch of bipolar police sounding the alarm every time you raise your voice. Let them know that when you're healthy, you can be sad, angry, energetic, tired, frustrated, and so on — just like anybody else. Most people with bipolar want to be treated "just like everyone else."

- Point out that with treatment your symptoms usually remain in control.

- Keep in mind that it may take some time for people to absorb and accept the information and even longer to change their attitudes and behaviors.

If your company has in-services or guest speakers, consider inviting a psychiatrist, therapist, or qualified individual from a mental health group to speak or lead a discussion about mental illness — specifically bipolar.

Requesting Workplace Accommodations

When you receive a bipolar diagnosis (and disclose it to your employer), you gain protection under the law via the Americans with Disabilities Act (ADA). As long as you notified your employer of your condition and expressed some desire to get help, your employer is required to engage in a dialogue with you to determine whether reasonable accommodations can enable you to perform the essential functions of your job.

To qualify for protection under the ADA, your situation must meet the following conditions:

- You have a physical or mental impairment that substantially limits one or more of your major life activities.

✔ You have a record of such an impairment (your diagnosis, for example) or are regarded as having such an impairment.

✔ You are otherwise qualified to perform your job duties; that is, you must meet the skill, experience, education, and other job-related requirements of the position and, with reasonable accommodations, be able to perform the essential functions of the job.

So what exactly are *reasonable accommodations?* According to SAMHSA, the definition is this:

> *Accommodations are changes to the work environment or the way things are usually done that allow an individual with a disability to enjoy equal employment opportunities. An accommodation is not considered reasonable if it creates an "undue hardship" for the employer. Undue hardship refers not only to financial hardship, but also to accommodations that are overly extensive or disruptive, or that would change the nature or operation of a business.*

Reasonable workplace accommodations for employees with bipolar disorder may include the following:

✔ Flexible scheduling, along with leave-time allowances for doctor's visits and therapy sessions

✔ A work schedule that doesn't disrupt your sleep patterns

✔ Scheduling adjustments to reduce interruptions

✔ Longer or more frequent breaks

✔ Separate office or cubicle to reduce workplace distractions

✔ Clearly documented job requirements, responsibilities, and consequences for not meeting expectations

✔ Education for coworkers and supervisors about bipolar disorder

✔ Referrals to employee assistance programs and other supports

✔ Regular meetings with supervisors to assess needs and performance and to develop strategies for addressing any issues that arise

Establish a procedure to evaluate the effectiveness of each accommodation and make adjustments as needed to improve the overall work environment and respond to any changes that may arise.

For further assistance in adapting to your workplace or adapting your workplace to meet your needs, consult an occupational therapist who has training and experience in helping people with bipolar disorder. Occupational therapists aren't exclusively for people with physical disabilities.

Being self-employed with bipolar disorder

If you're self-employed, you may face unique challenges when managing your work life with bipolar disorder. Typically, you don't get sick leave or paid time off or even unemployment benefits in a self-employed position, so your income is immediately affected when you take a break. Yet, your expenses continue, including payroll and overhead. But self-employment also comes with greater flexibility in your schedule and, in most cases, freedom from reporting your whereabouts at any given time of day. In other words, you can give yourself reasonable accommodations and transition time. Not to mention, self-employment means you can manage the flow of information about your condition to your employees and coworkers.

Some advance planning can help with the potential downsides in this situation:

✔ Look into disability insurance, although this may be hard to obtain after you have your diagnosis.

✔ Develop an emergency plan for managing your business in case you're out of commission. Select a trusted person to step in and manage what he can for you while you're out. Try to work this out in some detail before a crisis arises.

✔ Try to stash away as much cash savings as you can to tide you over during times when you can't run your business.

✔ Try to ensure that your daily procedures and activities are well outlined somewhere, in writing, so that those covering for you can reference them in your absence.

Finding More Suitable Work

Some jobs just aren't conducive to mental health. Returning to such a job, even with reasonable workplace accommodations, could doom you to relapse. But just because you may not be able to return to the job you were doing doesn't relegate you to a life of unemployment. After all, you may be able to transition to a different position or profession, start your own business, or find a few enjoyable part-time gigs that pay the bills.

In the following sections, we provide guidance on how to choose work that's right for you and conducive to your mental wellbeing and then offer suggestions for how to pursue your work-related goals.

Recovery doesn't always mean returning to the life you had before your bipolar diagnosis. In fact, the disorder often provides an opportunity to move forward and make changes that lead to a more rewarding and fulfilling life.

Dreaming up your ideal work situation

Some people seem to know from the day they're born what they want to do when they grow up. Others keep asking themselves that question until the day they retire. When bipolar disorder prevents you from doing the work you've been doing, you have to ask the same question again in the context of your new reality. If you're unable or unwilling to return to the work you were doing before bipolar took a place in your life, ask yourself what you want to do for a living now. Try to formulate a vision of your ideal work situation:

✔ Do you prefer to work alone or with others?

✔ Do you prefer working at home or outside your home?

✔ How many hours per week can you work without jeopardizing your mental health? (Be sure to account for the time you need for doctor appointments, therapy sessions, and self-help activities.)

✔ Do you prefer fixed hours, or do you want to set your own schedule? (Even if you set your own schedule, regular hours may help stabilize your mood.)

✔ Are you self-directed or do you work better under close supervision with clearly defined goals, deadlines, and direction?

✔ Are you more of a leader/manager or a worker bee?

✔ Do you prefer working for someone or owning your own business?

✔ What do you do best? (See the next section for details.)

✔ What do you most enjoy doing? (See the next section for details.)

Taking a skills and interests inventory

When you're thinking of changing jobs, the goal is to find something that you're good at doing but that you'll also enjoy, so start your job search by making a tally of your skills, which may include any of the following examples or completely different activities:

✔ Working with children or teenagers

✔ Caring for the elderly

✔ Computer programming

✔ Writing

✔ Financial management/accounting

> ✔ Designing websites
>
> ✔ Repairing machines
>
> ✔ Gardening
>
> ✔ Teaching/training
>
> ✔ Organizing/scheduling

Then jot down a list of interests — what you like to do or feel drawn to do, regardless of whether you think you're qualified. What would you love to do even if you weren't getting paid to do it? What activities do you find most enjoyable and rewarding? Interests can include anything from interpretative dance to biochemistry.

Your lists of skills and interests point the way toward a variety of careers and can help you identify areas where you may need additional education and training. Consider consulting with an occupational therapist, psychiatric rehab professional, or career counselor to explore career options that match your skills, interests, and mental health needs.

Pursuing your dream job

Pursuing your dream job may be as easy as flipping through the Help Wanted ads or poking around on the Internet, but landing that job probably takes a bit more work. You may need to acquire additional education, training, or experience; establish contacts in a new field or industry; purchase special tools or equipment; or write a business plan (if you want to start your own business). To prepare yourself, consider exploring the following resources:

✔ **Family, friends, and colleagues:** Share your vision with supportive members of your inner circle. They may have information, advice, or professional contacts that can help you pursue your dreams. If your boss is supportive, you may even ask her for help in transitioning to a different position in the company or to a related business or industry.

✔ **Your doctor and therapist:** Keep your doctor and therapist in the loop about your plans for finding rewarding work. They may have information about local resources to help people with bipolar disorder return to work, and they may have professional contacts of their own who are willing and able to mentor you or perhaps even hire you.

✔ **Colleges or trade schools:** If you need additional education or training to enter a certain profession, contact local or online colleges or trade schools to find out what's available. Speak to someone in the financial aid office to see if you qualify for scholarships, grants, and loans. You can also find plenty of free courses and other educational opportunities online.

✔ **Businesses of interest:** If you want to work in a specific industry, contact businesses in that industry that you may like to work for. Try to arrange a meeting with the head of the department you're interested in to find out what you need to do to qualify for a position. Ask if the business has internship opportunities.

✔ **Volunteer organizations:** If you can't get on-the-job training and experience, look into volunteer organizations, where you can pick up all sorts of skills while donating your time and efforts to your community. Volunteerism also looks good on a resume.

✔ **Small Business Administration (SBA):** If you're thinking of starting your own business, head to www.sba.gov for information, guidance, and contacts for local counseling, mentoring, funding, and training. For example, during the writing of this book, Indiana's Division of Mental Health and Addiction was preparing to offer business grants to help people with mental illness start their own businesses.

✔ **Mental health support groups:** Don't forget to share your vision with the people in your support groups. Many people who attend support groups are professionals or small-business owners who may have job leads, connections, and information that can help you find the work you're looking for or start your own business.

The most successful job hunts start with personal conversations. Describe your dream job, and let people know what you're doing to prepare for it. Your network can offer help only if the people in it know what you need. For more job hunting advice, check out *Getting a Job after 50 For Dummies* by Kerry Hannon (John Wiley & Sons, Inc.). Even if you're not older than 50, this book is chock-full of valuable advice on finding a job or starting a business that's right for you.

Is Not Returning to Work Right for You?

An "occupational hazard" of bipolar disorder is that it can trigger snap decisions, especially in the midst of a manic or depressive episode. The illness can limit your foresight. For instance, if you're depressed and can't work or foresee a time in the near future when you'll be able to return to work, you may decide to quit, resign, or take early retirement. These options are certainly acceptable if you're in a position to take advantage of them and are making the decision in a state of sound mind and judgment. If you're not, however, making a snap decision to resign can seriously jeopardize your rights as an employee and your future prospects.

Before you submit that letter of resignation, consider what you have to gain and lose. Here are some suggestions for how to evaluate your situation:

- ✔ Take as much time as you need to feel better before making a final decision. Your employer probably isn't going to fire you when you're on medical leave and under a doctor's care; if he does, you have fertile grounds for a lawsuit.

- ✔ List the pros and cons of resigning. Spend some time reviewing your list so you clearly see what's at stake. Show the list to people you trust and ask them for any additional considerations.

- ✔ Discuss your options with your doctor and therapist as well as family members, friends, and associates you trust. Be honest with yourself and your support team as you sort through your thinking process; keeping your biggest worries hidden in the back of your mind doesn't help you find solutions.

- ✔ If you have a union at work, meet with your union representative to discuss your options and possible consequences of resigning. A union rep is likely to have experience with the situation and should be able to clearly explain what you stand to gain and lose if you resign. He may also have knowledge of lateral job positions that more effectively support mental health needs. Likewise, you may be able to access such information from HR or EAP (employee assistant program) professionals at your workplace.

- ✔ Before making a final decision, consider consulting your own attorney, preferably one who's well versed in employment law, to protect your rights as an employee. Even if your union rep and HR person are qualified to provide the guidance you need, they may feel more loyalty toward your employer than to you and offer you less-than-ideal advice.

We're not telling you to keep plugging away at a job that's making you miserable, but we hate to see people quit (especially when they're not feeling well) and then regret the decision later when it's possibly too late to do anything about it. But if you can't work or can't find employment to earn at least enough money to cover the bills, the last resort is to file for Social Security Disability benefits. See Chapter 18 for details.

Chapter 18

Overcoming Financial Setbacks

. . . .

In This Chapter

▶ Cracking the code to get public mental health services

▶ Navigating the process for disability coverage

▶ Finding affordable health insurance and low- or no-cost healthcare

▶ Leveraging other resources for financial survival

. . . .

*B*ipolar disorder often pushes families to the brink of financial collapse. Yet, people are often reluctant to ask for help because they take pride in working to earn enough money to pay their bills. Even when they clear that hurdle and decide to seek assistance, many people face the daunting double challenge of finding out where to get help and navigating a process that's more puzzling than a Rubik's Cube to receive it.

Unfortunately, no one-stop shop is available to access all available financial support for mental health situations, so you need to tap a variety of resources to stay afloat. We can't give you detailed step-by-step instructions on how to obtain financial assistance and affordable medical care, but in this chapter, we suggest starting points for finding the financial help you need and deserve.

The Public Mental Health System

In the United States, you may be able to find help by turning to the public mental health system — resources for people with severe mental illness and limited income — but these resources are highly variable in terms of availability, access, and funding by county or state. Your local system may seem like an obscure secret society that's nearly impossible to find and join. But cracking the code is well worth the effort because these public services are a crucial lifeline for people living with serious mental illness, including bipolar.

Some areas in the U.S. have a 211 or 311 phone number that connects callers to a sort of switchboard for obtaining local and national social services, including help with food, housing, employment, healthcare, counseling, and suicide prevention. Visit www.211.org to look up the number for your area.

Surveying available resources

Public mental health care isn't limited to community and low-cost clinics. In many states, the system includes a range of services — called *systems of care* in some places — that attempt to provide appropriate levels of proactive mental health care. Here are services that a public system may include:

- ✔ Outpatient therapy and medication services
- ✔ Day treatment
- ✔ Job training and coaching
- ✔ Housing and in-home services
- ✔ Assertive Community Treatment (ACT), or individualized, intensive 24/7 support for people with high levels of need
- ✔ Case management services to help coordinate needs and access services
- ✔ Outreach to homeless people with mental health care needs
- ✔ Coordination of general healthcare needs
- ✔ Substance abuse recovery programs
- ✔ Help to apply for Social Security Disability, Medicare, Medicaid, and other financial safety net programs
- ✔ Crisis intervention
- ✔ Inpatient hospital care

Unfortunately, many states offer only some of these services and on a very limited basis. Access is typically granted through a central agency that operates at the state or county level. Finding the front door can be tricky, and qualifying for services is even tougher.

Accessing local financial support

Public agencies can usually help you apply for disability benefits through the Social Security Administration, Medicaid, and other financial safety net programs. If you qualify for Medicaid or Medicare, your mental health care costs are offset by these programs as well (see the later section "Filing for Disability Benefits" for details).

Try these ideas for accessing your local public mental health services:

✔ Contact the mental health department for your state or county. Most of these departments have websites you can explore.

✔ Contact your local Mental Health Association (MHA) for assistance. Find the number for your state or county MHA in your telephone directory or by contacting the National Mental Health Association (NMHA) at 1-800-969-6642 or online at www.nmha.org. The NMHA has more than 340 affiliates.

✔ Visit the website for your local National Alliance on Mental Illness (NAMI) or Depression and Bipolar Support Alliance (DBSA).

✔ If you're in a hospital, the staff social worker likely has information about your local system and can help you mobilize these resources.

Public systems in Canada and the U.K.

The Canadian Mental Health Association (CMHA) has a central website at www.cmha.ca that guides you to the central mental health service agency in your province. The local agency helps you gather referrals, find treatment, and interface with other public health services. In general, the Canadian system seems to encourage people to first seek help through their primary-care doctor, who then makes a referral to mental health services.

Similarly, in the U.K., mental health services are part of the National Health Service (NHS), and people can access them through the primary-care system. Like the U.S., the U.K. is trying to develop more accessible and effective models of mental health care; but unlike the U.S., the U.K. system is centralized and available to all citizens. (For more about NHS and mental health services, visit www.nhs.uk.)

BIPOLAR BIO

Bruises heal, scars don't

After I was sacked due to my third breakdown and subsequent hospitalization, I soon realized I had two battles on my hands — a recovery and no income.

I'd just crossed a line where, at the age of 33, I'd committed to a number of large financial outlays when I became seriously ill, and was now in a precarious position where everything that I had worked for could be affected and taken away. It's a cruel side effect of my disorder that began even before the unknown side effects of my meds kicked in.

What I should've done was wait and adjust to my illness and my medication; instead, I fought the situation all the way, trying to get better faster. This only resulted in aggravating my depression. As time went on, I learned that going with my disorder was the best option, as it seemed to have its own agenda.

At the time, I was looking but not seeing and needed help with every piece of paperwork, an endless supply of forms to complete, from the repetitious benefits forms to notifying my mortgage lender of my current situation. Then I had to deal with my car payments and a costly pension plan. Fortunately, I was assigned to a social worker who removed most of the stress for me.

Time is what it takes to recover from a breakdown — lots of it. After all, I wasn't suffering from a simple flu virus. I'd spent years coping with high-stress problems, one after another, and I wasn't going to get well in a matter of days.

It's an arduous and grossly unfair disorder to deal with. I climbed the greasy pole every day for years only to slip back down again, but in time I learned to prioritize. I may have lost my job but soon realized my new one was recovery. It's a humbling experience, but I helped myself by rethinking my personal values. It was either that or face a bitter future and recurring ill health, because I would've kept revisiting the episodes I had no control over.

In the beginning I felt isolated, but it didn't take too long before I was surrounded with people who understood my disorder. One key point I did discover is, if you keep telling yourself you have emotional scars, they will never heal but, if you reinforce the thought that you have emotional bruising, the bruises will heal.

After everything I had survived and lost, I was grateful that I had clothes on my back, a meal on the table, and a roof over my head. And, no matter how clever I thought I was, I couldn't change the past, but the future on the other hand . . .

—Neil Walton, author, mentor,
mental health journalist, and
comedy writer. For more about Neil, visit
www.bipolar-expedition.co.uk.

Filing for Disability Benefits

If you're living in the U.S., you've been diagnosed with bipolar, and the disorder has reduced your income to the point that you need assistance, the first thing to do is file for the following two Social Security benefits:

✔ **Social Security Disability (SSD):** These benefits are based on the Social Security earnings record of the insured worker. If you qualify for SSD, you automatically get Medicare coverage after receiving SSD benefits for two years.

✔ **Supplemental Security Income (SSI):** These benefits are funded through general tax revenues, so benefits aren't based on prior work history. You qualify by having limited income and resources that meet the living arrangement criteria. In most states, if you qualify for SSI, you're automatically eligible for Medicaid coverage.

In some states, the only way to get public mental health services for children with severe mental illness that requires long-term or high-intensity care is to surrender your parental rights to the state. These states cover such care only if the child becomes a ward of the state's child protection agency. Advocacy groups are working with Congress to change this, but it's still the only option for parents in some parts of the country. Find out everything you can about the laws in your state from mental health advocacy organizations and get help from an attorney or legal-aid organization before signing any papers that take away your parental rights. (Chapter 21 offers information on children and teens with bipolar.)

Meeting the guidelines

When you file for disability because of a mood disorder, Social Security representatives evaluate whether or not you can perform "work-related tasks." Using a set of guidelines referred to as the Residual Function Capacity (RFC) evaluation, the SSA checks to make sure you meet the following conditions:

✔ **You meet clinical criteria for bipolar disorder.** Your doctor may be able to provide the necessary documentation to enable the SSA to make this determination. The SSA may also require that you see one of its recommended doctors for a second opinion.

✔ **Your disorder results in marked impairment in categories such as**

- Understanding and memory
- Significant social difficulty
- Concentration deficiencies that result in failure to complete tasks on time
- Impaired adaptability, which makes it difficult to respond to changes and demands without significant *decompensation* (deterioration of mental health and ability to function)

Disability doesn't have to be forever. Leaving your job and filing for disability may be painful, but remind yourself that you're doing what you must to regain your health and to prepare yourself to reenter the workforce in a healthier state than when you left it.

Improving your chances of approval

If bipolar disorder prevents you from holding down a job right now, consider applying for disability immediately — no matter how unsure you are about your chances of approval. Here are suggestions that may improve your chances of success:

- ✔ **Consult your doctor and therapist.** The approval, support, and assistance of your doctor or therapist are critical to helping you establish that bipolar disorder prevents you from working. If you're not currently seeing a doctor for treatment, the SSA is unlikely to approve your claim.

- ✔ **File immediately.** Disability claims can take several weeks or months to process, and you often need to file multiple appeals, so the sooner you file, the better. Most disability lawyers won't even talk to you until you've filed a claim and been denied, so don't waste your time consulting a lawyer at this point.

- ✔ **Appeal.** If the SSA denies your initial claim, which happens 60 to 70 percent of the time, consult a lawyer or other legal representative to file an appeal. A judge can override the SSA's original decision, but you may need to appear at a hearing, where a qualified legal representative is helpful. You may need to appeal several times.

- ✔ **Keep your doctor's appointments and maintain up-to-date health records.** Seeing your doctor regularly provides you with documented proof of your bipolar disorder and keeps your doctor in the loop. You can't expect your doctor to support your claim if she hasn't seen you in three months. Documented evidence can help your case.

- ✔ **Have your doctor complete an evaluation form for you.** Your doctor's evaluation of your ability to perform work-related tasks is a key component of your application. Usually, the SSA sends a form to your doctor as part of the process of applying for disability, so you may not have to request it from your doctor.

- ✔ **Be nice.** Treat the people involved in the application and approval process with courtesy and respect. Giving them grief can only hurt your case; it won't help. If you're upset, cool off before calling.

- ✔ **Keep copies.** Copy everything before submitting it and file your records in a safe place, keeping all your information together.

✔ **Document all communications.** Note the date and time of phone calls, appointments, and the names of people you interact with. Also jot down any details about the interactions that you may need to reference later.

✔ **Follow up.** Wait a few days after you mail your claim and any pertinent paperwork. Then call to make sure that the SSA received the documents. If you can establish a good relationship with an individual at your local SSA office, you have a better chance of keeping things straight.

Don't give up. The SSA may seem to do all it can to discourage you from filing for disability benefits, but persistence often pays off. To find out more about SSD and SSI and even apply online for benefits, visit www.ssa.gov, click the Benefits tab, and click the Disability or Supplemental Security Income link or call 800-772-1213. For specifics about benefits in your state, contact your local Social Security office.

Exploring Health Insurance Options

Living with bipolar disorder can be very expensive, especially if a severe mood episode lands you in a psychiatric facility, where the average cost per day is about $1,200. If you're lucky enough to live in a country that has universal healthcare or you have great, affordable health insurance through your employer, then you have little to worry about. If you're less fortunate, you face the prospect of paying out of pocket or finding an affordable health insurance plan that provides mental health coverage.

If you don't have health insurance, several options may be available, depending on your situation, income, and assets:

✔ **COBRA:** If you're about to lose your health insurance due to a job loss or change of jobs, under COBRA (Consolidated Omnibus Budget Reconciliation Act), your employer must offer to continue your group healthcare coverage for 18 to 36 months. Unfortunately, you have to pay your entire monthly premium; your employer doesn't have to pay a portion of it. Just keep in mind that keeping your old insurance through COBRA is usually less expensive than buying new insurance with comparable coverage on your own.

✔ **Medicare or Medicaid:** If you qualify for Social Security Disability or Supplemental Security Income, you may also qualify for Medicare or Medicaid:

   • **Medicare:** The federal health insurance program that focuses primarily on covering people over the age of 65 who paid into the program throughout their careers. It also covers younger people who qualify for Social Security Disability.

- **Medicaid:** The federal-state health insurance program that provides coverage for low-income people of every age. Federal, state, and local taxes help fund the program. If you qualify for Supplemental Security Income, you may also qualify for Medicaid. State and local governments run Medicaid under federal guidelines, so it varies from state to state.

- **Private insurance (federally subsidized):** With the passage of the Affordable Care Act, everyone in the United States is required by law to have health insurance. You can purchase private insurance through your state exchange (if your state has set it up) or the federal exchange. Depending on your income, you may qualify for a federal subsidy to reduce your premium. Visit www.healthcare.gov or call 800-318-2596 to register. After answering questions related to your financial situation, you're presented with options and rates for different policies.

- **Veterans Benefits Administration:** If you served in the military, you may be eligible for healthcare through the Veterans Benefits Administration. Visit http://benefits.va.gov or call 877-222-8387 to find out about healthcare benefits.

- **Children's Health Insurance Program (CHIP):** The federal government has mandated that all children be provided health insurance, and states have a variety of systems to provide this coverage. CHIP is meant to cover children who don't meet criteria for Medicaid but whose families can't afford private coverage. Eligibility criteria differ by state.

Parity for mental health coverage is now federal law. In other words, insurance companies aren't permitted to provide less or different coverage for psychiatric disorders, including bipolar disorder, than they do for any other medical condition. Parity isn't always being followed, however, so if you think your coverage is reduced or denied because you have a psychiatric diagnosis, contact your insurance company. If you don't get satisfaction, contact your state's insurance regulation agency to make a report.

Trying to obtain affordable healthcare for yourself or family members can be incredibly frustrating, even for someone with a clear mind. If you're ill, now is the time to enlist the aid of a friend or family member to help with what is often a very challenging process.

Low- or No-Cost Healthcare Resources

Having no health insurance doesn't mean that self-care or public mental health care are your only options. Services are still available, but you may need to cobble together your own treatment plan, using several resources. In the following sections, we highlight some of those resources.

Tracking down a university program

Universities are often on the cutting edge of research and may be able to provide the latest treatment options — possibly for free, especially if you're willing to take part in a study. If you do go through a university, try to talk directly to the bipolar expert in charge of the program. Most university psychiatrists have *residents* or *fellows* (doctors training after medical school graduation) studying under them, and if you get shuttled from one resident to another, you may find yourself constantly changing medications or treatments to your detriment. By recognizing this risk at the get-go, you can take steps to ensure continuity of care:

- ✔ **Keep in touch with the supervising physician or psychiatrist.** Notify him of any medication adjustments or other changes to your treatment plan. Get a phone number to his office and for emergency calls.

- ✔ **Request explanations for any changes to your medications or treatment.** Why is the resident requesting the change? What are the desired results? How long should it take before you see a positive change in your condition? What are the possible side effects? What should you do if your condition worsens?

- ✔ **Coordinate communication with all members of your treatment team.** If you have a therapist working with you outside of the university, be sure the university care providers keep him posted.

Although becoming involved in a controlled study is an excellent way to obtain access to the newest medications and to help the cause, ask yourself and your care providers some questions before you sign up. Discover the possible risks of the new medication and find out how likely it is that you'll receive a *placebo* (a "sugar pill" with no medication in it). Make sure your moods are stable enough to handle a change in medications, if that's what the study calls for. If you're doing well on your current medication and adjunctive treatments, we recommend that you stick with what's working.

Finding peer support

Everyone in your life has something valuable and unique to teach you — whether it involves a golf swing or a new therapy technique — and no one knows bipolar disorder better than someone who's living with it. You may feel reluctant to sit in a room full of strangers and talk about your life, but don't write off peer support until you've tried it. It can be a relief to be among people from whom you don't have to hide the fact that your brain short-circuits sometimes with unpredictable results. For details on tracking down peer support groups in your area, turn to Chapter 6.

Contacting religious organizations

Churches and other religious organizations often have qualified counselors on staff who provide therapy and other assistance. Many of these services are offered for free or at reduced cost to church members, but even if you're not a member, you may find that the organization has an open door.

Be at least as careful when shopping for free counseling as you are when exploring options for private therapy. The quality of training varies widely, and many religious organizations have their own agendas, which may not quite follow proven treatment protocols. Avoid any organization that's against the use of psychiatric medications or requires you to make drastic changes to your life that you aren't completely comfortable with.

Prescription assistance programs

Some pharmaceutical companies, healthcare groups, and local organizations offer assistance programs that provide medications at no cost or discount prices. You may need to provide the following information to qualify:

- ✔ Your doctor's written consent
- ✔ Proof that your insurance doesn't offer a prescription benefit or doesn't cover the medication you need
- ✔ Proof that you qualify financially to receive the assistance

Check out the following sources to find out about assistance programs:

- ✔ Find out whether you qualify for assistance at the Partnership for Prescription Assistance website at www.pparx.org or call 888-4PPA-NOW (888-477-2669).
- ✔ Mental health advocacy organizations can help you track down programs for which you qualify. See the section "The Public Mental Health System," earlier in this chapter.
- ✔ If you qualify for Medicare, you may be able to take advantage of its prescription drug programs. Go to www.medicare.gov to find out about these programs and to see whether you qualify for them.
- ✔ Some pharmaceutical companies offer their own prescription assistance programs for people with low household incomes. Your doctor or pharmacist, or sometimes your prescription label, can tell you the manufacturer of your medication, and you can find contact information online. In some cases, your doctor must contact the company on your behalf to get information on prescription assistance.

✔ An Internet search for *prescription assistance program* can help you find links to several other companies that provide information on prescription drug cards, generic medications, and other cost-saving plans.

Your doctor may be able to provide informal prescription assistance simply by supplying you with free samples.

Haggling with a psychiatrist or therapist

Some psychiatrists and therapists offer payment plans that allow their patients to pay off bills gradually. If you don't have insurance, your psychiatrist or therapist may offer you a discount. Many clinics and university settings and some private practitioners offer a *sliding scale,* where the fee is based on your ability to pay. You usually need to fill out some type of financial worksheet to determine whether you qualify for reduced fees. Most large insurance companies negotiate with providers in this way to save on costs, so doctors and therapists commonly offer similar discounts to uninsured patients. Always ask.

Other Ways to Survive the Hard Times

The old saying "Desperate times call for desperate measures" often applies to individuals and families dealing with bipolar disorder. When you can't pay the bills, you may find that the only options remaining are those you thought you would never have to consider. In the following sections, we describe a few other places to find financial support.

Asking family and friends for help

When you're strapped for cash, consider seeking help from your family and friends. If you're reluctant to ask people for money, consider this: If someone you care about needed money and you had the resources to help, wouldn't you want to know she needed help? Would you be willing to help her? You'd probably even feel hurt if you found out later that your loved one needed help and didn't come to you.

Self-reliance is one of the most overrated virtues in our society. People have an emotional and spiritual need to feel needed and to serve others. By asking for and accepting help from your loved ones, you're actually helping them fulfill a need.

Several online services enable you to set up a page for soliciting donations from friends, family members, and even complete strangers to help with paying medical bills and other expenses. Check out www.YouCaring.com, www.GiveForward.com, and http://fundly.com.

Finding temporary financial relief

When you're dealing with temporary cash-flow problems, you may be able to find some relief by taking the following actions:

✔ **Contact your creditors.** Call the banks, companies, or individuals to whom you owe money and let them know what's going on. They may be willing to work with you to accept lower payments or provide you with a grace period for paying bills. Utility companies may have assistance programs for helping to cover your monthly bills. Some lenders (for mortgages and student loans, for example) may allow you to temporarily stop making payments if you're experiencing a financial setback, especially if the setback is related to a medical condition.

✔ **Take out a home equity line of credit.** If you own a home and have equity built up in it, you may qualify for a home equity line of credit that lets you borrow against that equity. Contact local banks to see what they offer. If you qualify, the bank provides you with checks you can write and maybe even a debit card you can use to pay bills. You borrow only the amount you need only when you need it. Be careful, though: By putting your home up as equity for a loan, you may lose it if you can't make the payments on that loan or pay off the balance when it comes due. Use this tactic only to help with temporary cash flow problems and draw from the account only when you have a plan and timeline in place to pay back the money.

✔ **Borrow against your retirement savings.** If you have retirement accounts, you may be able to cash out some of that money or borrow against it without incurring a tax penalty, especially if you use the money specifically to pay for healthcare expenses. Consult your investment representative or an experienced accountant to find out more about your options. Again, use this tactic only for emergencies. You shouldn't have to put your future financial security at risk to deal with a current healthcare problem.

✔ **Transfer credit card balances to another credit card.** If you have two or more credit cards, you may be able to buy yourself some time by transferring the balance from one card to another. Just be sure to transfer high-interest balances to a lower-interest card and do your best to work toward paying down the debt and negotiating any breaks the credit card companies are willing to agree to.

Government safety net programs

Most people try hard to avoid asking for help, especially from the government. You value self-reliance and being able to pull yourself out of a hole. But sometimes, when bipolar disorder is a part of your life, you may need more help than you ever thought you would. Government resources are available specifically for situations like yours — when things become unmanageable and your basic health and safety are at stake. Here's a quick look at some of those resources:

- **Food assistance:** This program is now called Supplemental Nutrition Assistance Program (SNAP), and it's available for people whose income is low but not necessarily low enough to require other supports such as general assistance (welfare benefits). Don't be ashamed to seek out this benefit if you're struggling to keep food on the table. Benefits are usually managed at the county level.

- **Cash assistance/welfare:** These emergency cash-assistance benefits are managed through the state for families who are in severe financial situations. These benefits have many eligibility requirements and are available on a temporary basis, but they can be a lifesaver during critical periods. Applications are often filed at the county level.

- **Housing supports:** A variety of housing support programs are available at the federal and local levels. You typically need to speak to someone in a social services agency to access these kinds of benefits, but don't wait to do this if you're concerned about losing your current housing. These applications can take quite a while to complete, and you may have to add your name to waiting lists after you apply.

Part VI

Assisting a Friend or Relative with Bipolar Disorder

Seven ways to de-escalate a tense situation

- **Give your loved one plenty of space.** Back off and don't try to touch the person, unless he asks you to.

- **Move slowly.** Your loved one may interpret sudden, fast movements as threatening.

- **Engage your loved one in conversation.** Agitation often occurs as a result of someone's inability to communicate needs. Ask questions and listen actively. Conversing about light topics is also a good strategy, if the person is receptive.

- **Talk softly.** The louder your loved one speaks, the softer you should speak. Loud voices increase agitation.

- **Don't blame, criticize, judge, argue, order, or threaten.** All these actions escalate conflict.

- **Offer choices, not ultimatums.** Giving the person choices enables her to feel more in control instead of being controlled.

- **Offer something to eat or drink.** Or if the person smokes, suggest a cigarette break.

Check out www.dummies.com/extras/bipolardisorder for a bonus article on the principles that drive the strategies for helping a loved one with bipolar disorder.

In this part . . .

- ✔ Build empathy, lend a hand, and avoid becoming overbearing — all without letting the disorder drag you down.

- ✔ Find out what you can do to support your loved one, when you should step in, and when you should step back.

- ✔ Plan ahead for a crisis, so you know what to do when a mood episode spirals out of control, and develop a plan B for when bipolar throws you a curve.

- ✔ Understand the challenges of diagnosing, treating, and supporting a child or adolescent with bipolar disorder and find out about other conditions that may look a lot like bipolar but aren't.

Chapter 19

Supporting Your Loved One

In This Chapter

▶ Getting your head in the game

▶ Grasping what your loved one is going through

▶ Setting parameters for when to call for help

▶ Helping a person who refuses help and attending to your own needs and emotions

When bipolar disorder afflicts a friend or relative, it afflicts you, too. Symptoms can confuse and bewilder you, strain your relationship with your loved one, and leave you physically and mentally drained. You want to help, but how? What can you possibly do to remedy "wiring problems" in the brain? What can you say to your loved one when he loses all hope? What can you do when your friend seems determined to blow her retirement money and ruin her marriage? And how can you help when your loved one resists your attempt to intervene and answers your well-intentioned advice with arrogance and anger?

In this chapter, we confront the confusion and the sense of helplessness that friends and family members can face. We explain the cold, hard facts about bipolar disorder to prepare you for the struggles ahead; we provide exercises to steer you clear of any tendencies you may have to blame yourself or your loved one for what's happening; and we reveal what you can and can't do to help your loved one on the road to recovery. We also offer suggestions on how to care for yourself and find support so that you and your loved one can step out of the shadow of bipolar and into the light of a hopeful future.

Establishing the Right Mindset

Becoming an effective caregiver and support person has as much to do with what you think as it does with what you do. If you approach your role with false expectations and misunderstandings, you may be more apt to say and do all the wrong things, become easily frustrated, and blame yourself for situations and events outside your control. By establishing the right mindset, you can function more effectively as a support person while maintaining your own mental health. The following sections can help you begin.

Forming realistic expectations

Everyone needs hope, but false hope can lead to disappointment and frustration. It can also cause you to let down your guard. In the case of caring for a loved one with bipolar disorder, you may begin to think your problems are fixed, the illness is cured, and you've "put all this behind you." If you do, you're likely to drift back into old patterns. You forget about how important it is for your loved one to take his medications. You become less vigilant of the warning signs. You get careless. And bam! You're right back where you were, watching your loved one battle major depression or a manic episode.

To help your loved one win the battle against bipolar disorder, you must first establish the right mindset and confront the realities of the disorder:

- ✔ Your loved one is and will remain vulnerable to mood episodes.
- ✔ Your loved one can't will himself to overcome the illness.
- ✔ Preventive long-term medication is almost certainly required to prevent relapse and to control symptoms.
- ✔ Even with preventive medication, symptoms may recur.
- ✔ You and your loved one may need to adjust your future expectations and lifestyles to maintain wellness.
- ✔ Your loved one may not want your help at times, but he always needs your love and understanding.

You and your loved one have every reason to look forward to remission and a wonderful life. But your loved one must stick to the treatment plan, and you both need to remain vigilant when times are good so you can short-circuit any escalation in mood instability.

Disassociating the disorder from the one you love

Your loved one personifies bipolar disorder for you. The disorder expresses all its negative symptoms through your loved one's actions and words, which makes it tempting to associate the disorder with the person and blame your loved one for problems that result from the illness.

To successfully battle the illness, team up against it. Start by disassociating bipolar disorder from the person who has it. In the midst of a major mood episode, disassociation is easier said than done, but when you have time to think things through, try the following exercises:

- ✔ **Think back to a time before the first major mood episode disrupted your lives.** Did the person you love seem different? In what ways? Can you associate any behaviors with the disorder?

- ✔ **Look at photographs of pleasant times that you and your loved one experienced together.** Did you notice any symptoms back then? What has changed? Name some ways that the disorder affects your loved one's behavior during a mood episode.

- ✔ **List all the words and behaviors that seem out of character with the person you love.** Would your loved one say and do the same things if he were thinking clearly? What would be different?

Don't go too far when disassociating the disorder from your loved one. You may be tempted to attribute *every* negative behavior to the disorder, even behaviors that are consistent with your loved one's character. By attributing too much to the disorder, you diminish the importance and value of your loved one's personality and ability to think on his own, which can be just as damaging as attributing too little to the disorder.

Figuring out how not to take it personally

When you're on the receiving end of an angry tirade and when nothing you do seems to please your loved one, you may react by taking it personally and becoming defensive. This reaction is perfectly natural, especially when you're in a close relationship with someone you love. Your happiness and the happiness of your loved one may be intricately intertwined, and when one of you is unhappy, the other suffers as well. You begin to think that if you could just figure out the right way to act and the right words to say, the situation would improve. When it doesn't, frustration and bitterness often follow.

Try to *depersonalize* your loved one's hurtful words and deeds in order to overcome the common trap of taking them to heart. Depersonalizing consists of coming to terms with the fact that much of what your loved one says or does has very little to do with you. Your loved one's feelings, thoughts, reactions, words, and actions can arise from multiple sources, including depression, mania, distorted thinking, or paranoia. By knowing that the disorder and other factors often contribute significantly more to your loved one's behavior than anything you say or do, you may have an easier time shrugging off some of the reactions.

Nurturing a Sense of Empathy

You may not *know* what your loved one with bipolar is experiencing or feeling, but you can *empathize* — or imagine and share in what your loved one is going through to some degree. Unfortunately, your loved one is probably in no position to describe how she's feeling because she may not understand herself what's going on inside. This section is here to help you get a sense of what your loved one is going through.

Your loved one with bipolar disorder is wrestling with a severe mental illness that threatens her *self* — her self-esteem, self-control, self-confidence, self-determination, self-image, and so on. When she feels threatened, she instinctively resorts to fight or flight mode. In fight mode, your loved one may be angry, arrogant, or critical; refuse help; stop taking her medication; or blame others. In flight mode, she may turn to drugs or alcohol, break off a relationship, seem indifferent or self-absorbed, or deny she has a problem.

Everyone is guilty of maladaptive responses to perceived threats. People become defensive in the face of criticism, deny when blamed, lash out when others try to control them, refuse help even when they need it . . . and the list goes on. With mental illness, the negative spiral of events that drives maladaptive behaviors is compounded by at least two additional factors:

- ✔ **Major life changes:** In the midst of serious mental illness, a person may lose her job, friends, sense of financial security, and a host of other external supports that people tend to rely on to feel secure.

- ✔ **Diminished capacity to deal with situations:** A person who's unable to think clearly lacks a key tool for dealing with complex challenges in rational, constructive ways.

Although your loved one's words and actions may be counterproductive and seem irrational to you, they're actually normal and reasonable in the context of human psychology. In other words, under the same circumstances, most people, including you, would probably respond the same way. Empathy is all about accepting that fact and trying your best to see the situation through the eyes of your loved one.

Unfortunately, maladaptive behaviors tend to breed maladaptive behaviors, but you can begin to break the cycle by responding to maladaptive behaviors in more constructive ways and doing the following:

- ✔ Focusing less on criticizing negative behaviors and more on praising positive behaviors

- ✔ Becoming less demanding

- ✔ Avoiding confrontation and arguments

   ✔ Shifting from blaming to problem solving

   ✔ Focusing on the here and now instead of digging up the past

Recognizing Your Limitations

When a loved one has bipolar, you stand by and watch the drama unfold. On the main stage, the doctor diagnoses and prescribes, the therapist counsels and educates, and your loved one wrestles with mood episodes. You wander backstage like a lonely understudy, wondering whether you have a role to play and something to contribute.

Naturally, you want your loved one to get well, but the situation is totally new to you. Should you get out of the way so the doctor and therapist can do their jobs? Should you take control? What would be most helpful? And how can you avoid making matters worse? The first step toward becoming an effective support person is to determine what you can and can't do to help. Lucky for you, that's what this section is all about.

Doing what you can

Your presence, patience, understanding, and willingness to help are perhaps the most valuable contributions you can make. Beyond these, you can offer many types of help, but keep in mind that if your loved one is an adult, he has the option of accepting or rejecting your offers or limiting your level of involvement. Being too pushy or overbearing can cause feelings of resentment and additional resistance to treatment, and you definitely don't want that.

Here are some of the best and most effective ways you can help:

   ✔ Discover as much as you can about bipolar disorder and its symptoms and treatments, which you're already doing by reading this book.

   ✔ Keep in touch, especially during the tough times.

   ✔ Provide unconditional love and encouraging words while setting boundaries to keep your emotional reserves intact (such as "I need you to call me only three or four times in one day").

   ✔ Reassure your loved one that with the proper treatment, he will eventually manage the symptoms.

   ✔ Encourage your loved one to seek professional help when necessary (but don't nag).

   ✔ Help your loved one find a qualified doctor and therapist.

✔ Assist in following up on insurance coverage and claims.

✔ Help with tracking moods and medications and watching for signs of impending mood episodes.

✔ Ask for permission to attend appointments with your loved one's doctor and therapist.

✔ Talk to your loved one about when and how to call his doctor or therapist if you become concerned with his behavior.

✔ If your loved one can't make it to work, ask if he wants you to call his employer and what he wants you to say. If your loved one is self-employed, ask if you can do anything to help keep things running smoothly.

✔ Keep other people posted as directed by your loved one.

✔ Perform basic household tasks, such as grocery shopping, watching the kids, and paying bills.

Recognizing what you can't do

You can't control how your loved one chooses to deal with bipolar disorder. If your loved one is an adult, you can't force him to take medication, attend therapy, or even get sufficient sleep. If you attempt to take control, you risk taking ownership of a problem you can't fix.

You can and should step in at times when the illness makes your loved one incapable of making the right decisions, but the rest of the time, your job is to let go and allow your loved one to manage on his own. He needs to take responsibility for sticking with the treatment plan, making and keeping appointments, taking the prescribed medications, maintaining a healthy lifestyle, and asking for help.

You didn't cause your loved one to get bipolar disorder, nor can you cure it. Don't feel guilty for the onset of bipolar disorder and don't think you have the power or the resources to fix the problem on your own.

Remaining Vigilant for Warning Signs

One of the more sinister characteristics of bipolar disorder is that the person who has it may not be able to recognize the onset of symptoms until it's too late to interrupt the cycle. A valuable role you may be able to play as a support person is to keep in regular contact with your loved one and watch for early warning signs of a mood episode.

Not everyone has the knowledge, temperament, and sensitivity to differentiate between normal mood variations and symptoms and to intervene diplomatically. The ideal candidate for this job has the following qualifications:

✔ Knows and can recognize the signs of an oncoming mood episode

✔ Has close, regular contact with the person who has bipolar disorder

✔ Can openly communicate observations without instigating conflict

✔ Has permission to contact the person's therapist or doctor

During a period of relative calm, consult your loved one to determine if she's willing to allow one or two people to help monitor her moods. Avoid getting too many people involved. Too much vigilance and focus can make your loved one feel as though she lives in a fishbowl.

Knowing when to step in

If your loved one agrees to let you monitor her moods and watch for warning signs, ask for additional details to help you determine the severity of the symptoms and the actions you should take when you see them:

✔ Make a list of common warning signs. (See Chapter 15 for more about common early warning signs of mania and depression.)

✔ Find out at what point you should be concerned enough to act.

✔ Determine the actions you should take, including sharing your observations and concerns with your loved one, contacting the therapist or doctor, taking away credit cards or car keys, securing objects the person could use to harm herself, or contacting another support person for assistance.

Knowing when to step back

Everyone has good and bad days. Don't assume you need to contact your loved one's doctor or therapist just because she's irritable or seems a little down in the dumps. At these times, you can be a little more vigilant and convey your concerns, but try not to overreact.

In the midst of a major mood episode, don't step back simply because your loved one requests (or insists) you do so. Stick with her until she takes steps to obtain the treatment necessary to stabilize her moods. Encourage your loved one to contact her doctor or therapist immediately for evaluation and consultation. A short visit with a qualified therapist is often enough to get your loved one back on the right track, and if the therapist notices any disturbing behavior, she'll have a better idea of how to proceed.

When the crisis abates and your loved one regains control of her moods, be prepared to step back and let her manage her life once again. Let her know that you're there if she needs anything.

Making a deal: Drawing up a contract

The whole scenario surrounding mood instability and treatment is fraught with fear. Loved ones are afraid they'll be powerless in the midst of a major mood episode if the person with bipolar disorder refuses help. Nobody appreciates having hypervigilant friends and relatives micromanage their lives and force treatment when they believe they don't need it.

One solution is to draw up an agreement (a *treatment contract*) during a time of relative calm and stability that spells out who and under what circumstances that person can intervene and what that intervention may entail. An effective treatment contract contains the following information:

✔ List of people who are permitted to step in (and perhaps a list of people who aren't permitted to step in, if necessary)

✔ Descriptions of external signs and symptoms of depression and mania

✔ Descriptions of verifiable signs that your loved one can manage the disorder on her own

✔ Descriptions of observable signs that your loved one needs help

✔ Instructions on the types of help your loved one agrees to accept

✔ Instructions on the types of help your loved one absolutely refuses

✔ A clear statement that you may do whatever you think is best when you suspect that your loved one faces an imminent risk of harming herself or others

You can find a sample of a treatment contract at www.dummies.com/extras/bipolardisorder.

Helping Someone Who Refuses Help

One of the symptoms of bipolar disorder is a *lack of insight* — an inability (not unwillingness) to notice a significant shift in one's own mood or behavior. This symptom happens most often during an acute mood episode but can also be part of the bigger picture of living with the illness. Family members agonize over how to help someone who doesn't want help, and they some-times watch helplessly as the illness destroys their loved one's life. What to do to help someone who refuses help or treatment varies depending on the situation. The following sections offer some suggestions.

Solutions are very situation-specific. In some cases, if your loved one is man-aging on his own, just not in a way that meets your standards, backing off is the best approach. If the person is a danger to himself or others, you need to take more drastic measures, such as call for emergency services.

Taking action in an emergency

If your loved one is at risk of harming himself or someone else, get help immediately. If you believe he needs medical attention and you can safely transport him, take him to the nearest emergency medical center. If you're not completely confident that you can safely transport your loved one, call 911 or the emergency number for the area in which the emergency is occurring.

When you call an emergency number, tell the dispatcher that you believe the person you're concerned about is experiencing a "mental health crisis" and describe specifically the behaviors that are causing concern. When the police arrive, tell them that you want your loved one taken to a hospital or mental health facility and not to jail. You may not have a say in the final decision, but be sure to clearly express what you expect.

Some areas have *crisis intervention team (CIT)* officers trained to deal gently but firmly with situations that involve mental illness. If your area has CIT offi-cers, request that a CIT officer be sent.

Expressing your concerns

If you're trying to help someone who's refusing help, you've probably already tried to discuss your concerns and maybe even convince the person to get help. But trying to convince someone to get help doesn't always work. In a nonemergency situation, try listening more than talking and agreeing more than disagreeing or trying to convince the person to accept help.

Use the communication skills we describe in Chapter 13 to bring up your con-cerns and apply the problem-solving skills we describe in Chapter 14 to team up with your loved one to address your concerns.

Confrontation, criticism, and arguments are likely to be counterproductive and make your loved one even less likely to cooperate.

Calling the doctor or therapist

In a nonemergency situation, consider calling your loved one's doctor or therapist and expressing your concerns. The doctor or therapist can then provide guidance on how to proceed and may work with the family to get the person the care he needs.

Even if your loved one's healthcare provider says he can't speak with you, he *can* listen and take action on the information and insight you provide. Just remember that the provider may have an obligation to tell your loved one that he received information from you; your loved one may perceive this as a breach of trust.

Contacting a local support group

Contact a local chapter of the National Alliance on Mental Illness (NAMI) or the Depression and Bipolar Support Alliance (DBSA). Local support groups often maintain lists of local mental health clinics and other nearby resources that may be able to provide answers and assistance. Check out www.nami. org or www.dbsalliance.org for details.

Contacting a local mental health center

Depending on where your loved one lives, he may have access to a community or county mental health center or clinic. The Substance Abuse and Mental Health Services Administration (SAMHSA) has a searchable directory of mental health centers at http://store.samhsa.gov/mhlocator. Or you can search online for *mental health facility* followed by your loved one's location. Even if the mental health center can't directly intervene, it should be able to point you in the direction of useful local resources.

Seeking a court order

You can't detain or hospitalize a person against his will unless certain legal standards are met, and those standards vary among jurisdictions. In Indiana, for example, a person must have a mental illness and either be a danger to himself or others or be *gravely disabled* — basically unable to function independently and provide for his own food, clothing, and shelter. In some places, a doctor or police officer can order a brief involuntary hospitalization. In others, only a court-appointed mental health professional has that authority. Some places require a court order from a judge. Your local crisis line is probably the best source of information about the rules in your area.

The duration of a detention or forced hospitalization varies. In the U.S., initial involuntary hospitalization orders are usually for a short period of time — about 72 hours in many states — and require more extensive legal procedures to extend beyond that. A full court-ordered commitment may last for 90 days or be indefinite and subject to review after a predetermined time period.

If a court hearing is required, you may be asked to testify that your loved one needs longer hospitalization. Having to do so can be stressful, but it's sometimes necessary. If possible, don't file the petition yourself. Do your best to have a doctor or treatment facility file the petition on behalf of your loved one; a medical professional has more pull with the courts and helps shield you from any resentment your loved one may feel. The best way you can help is to provide detailed documentation of the current crisis and be available to present detailed information if requested by the court.

Taking Care of Yourself

As a caregiver, you may feel lonely. Friends and family may ask how your loved one is doing, showing little concern for how you're holding up. Even worse, your circle of friends may scatter, perhaps out of fear, ignorance, or the mistaken (or valid) belief that you don't want them "meddling" in your affairs. If you let this behavior continue, you and your loved one may become isolated.

Isolation isn't healthy for you or your loved one. If you mope around, consumed by thoughts of the life you lost and the added responsibilities you bear, your loved one will recognize the pain in your expressions and gestures and feel the pangs of guilt. Look for ways to blow off some steam, grieve for your losses, attend to your needs, get a life, and then return to the relationship refreshed and renewed.

BIPOLAR BIO

Getting better at supporting my daughter

People who love a person with a chronic illness like bipolar are part of their loved one's journey — whether they want to be or not. And while the symptoms of depression, anxiety, and mania are hardest for the person who has bipolar, mood episodes also have a profound effect on relationships. It can be difficult to stay steady and not react negatively when someone you care about struggles with severe depressions, anxieties, or manias. But there are many things you can do to provide understanding and support.

Throughout my journey with my daughter who has bipolar disorder, I've learned that taking care of myself and making sure I know as much as possible about bipolar are vital to my ability to offer real support. I cannot "fix" her symptoms, but I can change the way I react

to her illness. She needs me to be centered, solid, and knowledgeable. She also needs me to listen. I had to learn how to really listen to her — to hear what she's saying . . . and not saying — and to respond to her with openness and honesty. After all, I can't expect my daughter to be honest with me and trust me if I don't do the same. Learning these skills took more than a few sessions with my own therapist and support group.

Bipolar disorder is a lifelong illness; we will continue to talk, listen, and work toward a close and honest relationship with coping and communication skills we hone each day.

— Cinda Johnson, coauthor of *Perfect Chaos: A Daughter's Journey to Survive Bipolar, a Mother's Struggle to Save Her*

Although your loved one — whether a friend or relative — takes the direct hit from bipolar disorder, you deal with a lot of collateral damage. Suffering in silence forces you to hold back feelings that eventually find expression through blame and criticism. Try to find a healthy outlet for your emotions:

- ✔ **Attend a support group for friends and family members of people with mental illnesses.** A support group can provide a forum for sharing feelings and information. See Chapter 6 for a list of support groups.

- ✔ **Discuss problems with your family and friends.** Feeling angry over what you're dealing with is normal, and you have every right to talk openly about it, but do it in the right setting. Loading up your loved one who has bipolar disorder with your emotional responses, no matter how reasonable they are, only stirs up more negative feelings in someone who's poorly equipped to manage them.

- ✔ **See a therapist.** A therapist can help you through the grieving process and provide you with an outlet for your emotions.

Bipolar disorder may be a part of your life, but it shouldn't overshadow your life. While your time and energy may be severely curtailed, especially during crises, do everything you can to engage in some nourishing and refueling activities for yourself to avoid burnout. You want to maintain your own identity and your own life as much as possible. Start with some of the following possible activities:

- ✔ Connect with old friends.
- ✔ Pursue interests and hobbies that you enjoy outside of your relationship with your loved one.
- ✔ Get involved in community activities.
- ✔ Invite friends or family members to your home.
- ✔ Do something fun just for the heck of it once a week.

Chapter 20

Dealing with Crisis Situations

· ·

In This Chapter

▶ Communicating with your loved one's doctor and therapist

▶ Planning ahead so you know what to do when crisis strikes

▶ Managing different crisis scenarios

· ·

A family that lives with bipolar disorder tends to encounter more crisis situations than the average family. In the midst of these unsettling periods, friends and family members often experience a frustrating mix of chaos and isolation. If your loved one has bipolar disorder, you may not know what to do or even where to turn for help when a crisis hits. If you contact your loved one's doctor or therapist, you may be told that doctor-patient confidentiality rules prevent him from speaking to you. If you call the police, your loved one may resist and end up in jail instead of a hospital and, in either case, resent you for calling the authorities. So what should you do?

In this chapter, we try to help you answer that question, preferably *before* you need to ask it, so that you have a general idea of how to respond when a crisis occurs. But first, we look at something you'll probably need to do regardless of whether you have a more elaborate plan in place: Contact your loved one's doctor or therapist.

Consulting Your Loved One's Doctor or Therapist

In any mental health crisis, one of the first things you should do is call your loved one's doctor or therapist to let him know what's going on and to ask him what to do. We say "one of the first things you should do," because if you have reason to believe that your loved one may physically harm himself or someone else, you should first call 911 and describe the situation. Then you can call the doctor or therapist.

When calling 911, say specifically that your loved one is experiencing a "mental health crisis" and that he needs to be taken to the hospital. Use the phrase *mental health crisis* so the dispatcher can communicate this to law enforcement; some departments have crisis intervention team (CIT) officers who are specially trained to deal with cases that involve mental illness. Use the word *hospital* to send the message that you expect your loved one to be taken to a hospital, *not* to jail.

Calling your loved one's doctor or therapist certainly sounds easy enough, but in some cases, you may be unable to reach him, or he may tell you that the Health Insurance Portability and Accountability Act (HIPAA) Privacy Rule prohibits him from speaking with you about your loved one's medical condition without your loved one's consent. In fact, family members often report that this is one of the most frustrating aspects of dealing with mental illness.

Here are some insights that may help you overcome obstacles in obtaining information and getting the treatment your loved one needs:

✔ Although the doctor or therapist may not be able to tell you anything about your loved one's medical condition, no law prohibits him from

- Listening to you or reading a letter or email or text message from you

- Providing you with general information about a particular mental illness to help you develop a better understanding of what's going on and what to do in a certain situation

✔ If your loved one has signed and filed a release of information with the doctor or hospital authorizing you to receive information, the doctor or hospital can't withhold medical information from you. Chapter 15 contains a sample release of information form.

If your loved one is already hospitalized and hasn't filed a release of information form, insist that the hospital ask your loved one if he's willing to sign an authorization.

✔ Your loved one's healthcare provider can share information with you if your loved one is present and has an opportunity to object to disclosures.

✔ A doctor or therapist isn't prohibited from sharing information with you if, in his professional judgment, it's in the patient's "best interest" — for example, if you need to know that your loved one is feeling suicidal so you can be more vigilant. When requesting information, explain that you need information to act in your loved one's *best interest.* Of course, the doctor must agree with your assessment of the patient's best interest

> before he'll release information to you without the patient's consent. In addition, doctors can share only information that's necessary for the patient's care.
>
> ✔ A doctor or therapist is likely to have more power than you in getting your loved one the help he needs if he's resisting that help.
>
> ✔ If your loved one is not yet receiving psychiatric care or if his doctor or therapist isn't being helpful, try contacting your county or community mental health center (CMHC) for guidance.

If you talk to your loved one's doctor or therapist, keep in mind that he may feel obligated to let your loved one, his patient, know that you have spoken to each other and some or all of what you spoke about.

Discussing the Emergency Plan

The worst time to decide what to do when your loved one is in a crisis is during the crisis. With a little planning, you'll know what to do (and not to do) when a crisis hits, including when to take action, whom to contact and how, and where to take your loved one if hospitalization becomes necessary. During a time of relative calm, arrange a meeting with all family members who may be called into action to manage a crisis, including the person with bipolar. (If possible, keep your loved one's doctor and therapist in the loop, too.) In the following sections, we provide details on topics to cover during this meeting.

To make your meeting most productive, follow the communications guidelines we present in Chapter 13, focusing especially on setting the stage for effective communication.

Figuring out how involved to be

The first topic of a crisis-intervention meeting needs to be what role each person should play in the event of a crisis. When determining what your specific role in managing your loved one's crisis will be, consider the various levels of support. For instance, will you play cheerleader, stepping in only when a crisis looms? Will you act as a referral service, calling others when you sense trouble? Or will you land a starting position on the mood-management team — going to the doctor, managing medications, and assisting your loved one directly? And when you do step in, how much power should you have?

Consider, too, some important questions that affect your ability to follow through on your commitment:

- **How available are you?** Geography and time may limit your availability. Are you close enough to your loved one to show up within moments of a problem, or do you need to hop on a plane? Can you take time off work or away from household responsibilities to devote to crisis prevention and management? Do you have ready access to childcare? Is your boss understanding about the situation?

- **How do you typically respond when tensions rise?** If you're the type who faints when someone at the office gets a paper cut or if you wig out when the basement floods, perhaps you're not the best person for a leading role during a crisis. To help your loved one, you need to keep a cool head, identify the signs of an impending mood episode, and act rationally in the midst of chaos.

- **How involved were you before the crisis?** The more involved you've been in everyday management, the more helpful you'll be when responding to crises. Do you have a sense of the patterns that lead up to a crisis? Do you know what's been happening with your loved one's medications? Do you regularly talk with your loved one about the stresses in her life or are you more on the sidelines?

- **To what degree are you willing and able to intervene?** Do you want to have power of attorney so that you can freeze credit cards and bank accounts and make other financial decisions? Is your loved one with bipolar willing to share information and control of her finances? Will you be in her home, taking away car keys and alcohol? Answer such questions prior to a crisis to eliminate hesitation and guesswork during a crisis.

- **How much intervention can your loved one endure from you?** If the person you're helping has patterns of becoming explosive or dangerous during a crisis, you can do only so much before involving other levels of intervention, such as a crisis team or hospital emergency room. Your role in crisis management may have an early stopping point if your attempts to intervene trigger outbursts or destructive reactions.

The limits you set for your involvement depend a great deal on temperaments, trust, and willingness to work as a team. You must identify what your loved one's personal preferences are and what she feels are reasonable levels of involvement. Just as importantly, communicate your comfort level for dealing with deeply personal issues such as money and healthcare. Your level of involvement isn't a given; it's a matter of negotiation. However, your loved one should have someone on the support team who's willing and able to step in during a crisis.

Determining when to intervene

Identifying the proper intervention point can be quite a challenge. You don't want to hit the panic button whenever your loved one looks a little glum or gets excited, but you also don't want to wait until your loved one becomes completely unreceptive or threatens harm.

Ideally, you can communicate your observations and concerns to your loved one well before a crisis occurs, assuming that you can identify the warning signs early enough and that your loved one is open to feedback. In such cases, you may say something like, "I hear more talking from you than usual" or "I think you seem less energetic than you were a couple weeks ago." Stick to describing what you see and hear and avoid making diagnoses, such as "You seem to be getting manic" or "You seem depressed today." Let your loved one draw her own conclusions based on your observations. If she accepts the situation, she can see her doctor or therapist for evaluation and any necessary treatment. If you feel doubt about when to speak up, these guidelines may help:

- ✔ **Act early and often.** Work on establishing open communication with your loved one about the disorder and how it affects her, as we explain in Chapter 19. Such discourse gives you greater knowledge of the warning signs and improves your ability to identify them early. It also makes your loved one more comfortable when talking about the illness with you and others and more receptive to your observations and concerns.

  The sooner you can identify a mood cycle and take action, the more likely you are to be successful. As a mood cycle gains momentum, your loved one's resistance to your intervention is likely to increase, and your efforts can backfire.

- ✔ **Keep an eye on the mood chart.** If you live with your loved one, you may not notice the subtle escalation of mood from one day to the next, but a quick glance at a one- or two-week period on a mood chart can alert you to a growing problem. To be proactive, you and your loved one may agree to look at the mood chart together at regular times. If your loved one agrees, you may chart your observations as well. Sometimes comparing notes from her chart and yours can help you both see patterns in your observations. (Chapter 11 has a sample mood chart that you can use; a number of mood-monitoring smartphone apps are also available.)

- ✔ **Identify "red flag" behaviors.** Is your loved one sleeping dramatically less or more? Is she beginning to lose whole evenings to shopping or planning numerous big projects? Is she eating much more or less? Has your musician friend stopped listening to music or playing instruments? Behavioral changes that indicate trouble are often very unique to the individual.

✔ **Err on the side of caution.** Balance your fear of hurting your loved one's feelings and making her angry at your desire to keep her safe. You can't manage everything in her life, but if you're worried and things don't feel right, taking action is the way to go. Your loved one may be angry with you for it, but if your actions make a difference in her safety and survival, your efforts are well worth it.

If your friend or relative is talking about suicide or behaving recklessly, you must act immediately. If she can't or won't listen to you, call for help, as we instruct later in the section "Suicidal threats or attempts."

Knowing whom to call for help

While you work on a crisis-intervention plan with your loved one, be sure to address the issue of who may become involved and at what point. Make a list of the people your loved one wants you to contact and the people you consider helpful and then edit as necessary. Cross off people who may cause more problems than they solve; you both know who they are. Record your final list of names and numbers on the Crisis Information Sheet we provide in Chapter 15. Regularly update contact information and keep a digital copy.

Keep in mind that you may need to call more than one person on your list. If you're trying to act early and dangerous symptoms aren't present, you're more likely to deal with the doctor and therapist. If you're acting during a dangerous episode, you're likely to call the hospital or 911 first, but you need to call the psychiatrist and therapist as well.

Bring your list of contact information to the emergency room or hospital. Doing so saves a lot of time for the admitting team. Also keep an updated list of medications with your contact list so you can tell the healthcare professionals exactly which medications and doses your loved one is supposed to be taking.

Deciding where to go

You need to know where to take your loved one in the event that she needs hospital care. Have a list of at least three options, such as these:

✔ **First choice:** Ask your loved one where she prefers to go. In Chapter 15, we offer guidance on choosing a psychiatric facility before a crisis hits.

✔ **Second choice:** In the event that the first choice is unavailable (the facility has no available beds, for instance), you need a backup.

✔ **Emergency room:** The hospital emergency room is the choice of last resort. From here, doctors can determine the next steps.

In addition to this list, obtain directions on how to get to each hospital or treatment facility as well as a phone number, just in case. You don't want to be looking up this information in the middle of a volatile situation. If you're taking your loved one to the emergency room, you can just show up. If you're taking her to a psychiatric facility, you need to call ahead to see if a bed is available and if your loved one's insurance covers that facility.

The hospital or psychiatric facility will get approval from the insurance company before admitting your loved one. However, having information about which hospitals and facilities are covered by insurance before a crisis hits is of the utmost importance. Encourage your loved one to contact her insurance company to find out which emergency and inpatient facilities are covered. (The insurer is unlikely to speak with loved ones due to confidentiality concerns.)

In a medical crisis, most insurers cover care received in any emergency room, but if that hospital's psychiatric units aren't covered, the ER staff will work with the insurer to find a bed in a covered facility.

Responding in a Crisis

People think nothing of buckling up for safety or wearing a bicycle helmet, but they often hesitate to take car keys away from someone who's driving recklessly or to snatch credit cards from someone whose spending is out of control. When you and your loved one discuss crisis prevention and management, be sure to cover risky behaviors and agree on a plan for dealing with them. Your loved one's prior approval to intervene can strengthen your resolve to act forcefully during a crisis and perhaps make your loved one more receptive to your efforts.

In this section, we list risky behaviors that are common to bipolar disorder and offer suggestions for dealing with them in a crisis. How you choose to handle the behaviors is up to you and your loved one, but the best way often requires creative thinking and serious planning.

The clever plans you develop during your rational meeting of minds may seem completely unacceptable to your loved one during a crisis, particularly a manic episode. Having a solid plan and taking early action can increase your chances of success, but be prepared to encounter unexpected resistance.

Suicidal threats or attempts

A person with severe depression is at high risk for suicide. The risk may be elevated if the person has recently started treatment for depression because he may still be depressed but now have enough energy to actually go through with it. If you suspect that your loved one may be considering suicide, take the following steps:

1. **Keep watch; don't leave your loved one alone.**

   If you can't stay around, call someone to come over and then stay until your replacement arrives.

2. **Listen, remain supportive by telling your loved one how much he means to you, and encourage him to talk about how he's feeling.**

   Keep your own distress in check — staying calm is critical. At this point, don't try to argue about why life is worth living and don't dismiss his feelings.

3. **Remove any weapons or medications that your loved one could use in a suicide attempt.**

   Don't leave anything around that could make suicide an easy option.

4. **Call your loved one's doctor or therapist or call 911.**

   If you can't connect with the doctor or therapist, don't hesitate to drive your loved one to the emergency room (if you can do so safely) or dial 911.

5. **Get help from other friends or family members.**

   They can help support your loved one, as well as you, through the crisis.

Don't be afraid to ask about suicidal thoughts. Your loved one won't become suicidal just because you ask questions; the risk comes when you don't ask. Also, trust your perceptions and instincts. When dealing with a loved one who's becoming increasingly violent or suicidal, you may try to talk yourself out of believing that something bad can actually happen. If the situation is escalating, get help before it's too late.

Agitated behavior

If agitated behavior accompanies a mood episode, don't try to fight fire with fire. Try to defuse the situation and deescalate the conflict.

Safety is first. Position yourself so that you have access to an exit. Don't let the agitated person get between you and the only way out. Avoid talking in the bathroom or kitchen, where the risks of getting hurt are greater. Don't be alone with someone who is becoming increasingly agitated; call friends or family members to help or call 911.

Deescalating potentially volatile situations is all about effective communication, which we cover in Chapter 13. Following are some additional do's and don'ts for tense situations:

- ✔ **Give your loved one plenty of space.** A person who's experiencing a severe mood episode may have an altered sense of personal space, so back off and don't try to touch the person.

- ✔ **Move slowly.** Your loved one may interpret sudden, fast movements as threatening.

- ✔ **Remain calm.** Doing so is essential.

- ✔ **Don't blame, criticize, judge, order, or threaten.** All these actions escalate conflict.

- ✔ **Speak softly.** Try using a soothing tone of voice.

- ✔ **Engage your loved one in conversation.** Aggression often occurs as a result of someone's inability to communicate needs. Ask questions and use active listening skills, as we explain in Chapter 13, to get your loved one talking. Distracting conversation about light topics is also a good strategy if the person is receptive.

- ✔ **Offer something to eat or drink.** Or if the person smokes, suggest a cigarette break. These distractions can also help defuse a situation.

If someone if aggressive, call 911; don't try to handle the situation yourself. The preceding recommendations help defuse situations before aggression occurs or while you're waiting for emergency services.

Reckless driving

Mania and depression can impair your loved one's ability to drive safely. Mania lifts inhibitions, essentially disabling the speed regulator inside the brain and pressing your friend or relative to disregard speed limits and defensive-driving techniques. Depression, on the other hand, can impair concentration and reflexes, slowing response times and resulting in erratic driving. A driver who feels hopeless and despondent and who doesn't care whether he lives or dies may be unable to make safe driving decisions.

The obvious intervention in this case is to take away the car keys — obvious, that is, until you consider some of the ramifications. Driving is central to many people's lives and represents adulthood and independence. By grabbing the car keys, you remove your loved one's sense of independence and freedom and his ability to get to work, do his shopping, get to doctor's appointments, and perform other tasks that help him stay on track and avoid a major mood episode. So before you snatch the car keys, plan for these contingencies:

✓ Can someone take your loved one to work?

✓ How will your friend or relative get to the doctor and therapist?

✓ Who can pick up your loved one's kids, take them to soccer, and buy groceries?

Taking away the keys is the easy part. Keeping your loved one's life going afterward requires serious planning and attention to detail. Ideally you and your loved one mutually agree that he'll stop driving for some time. However, if someone is ramping up into mania, the situation may escalate quickly, and you may have to take away the keys without the opportunity for discussion. Ideally in your crisis planning, you can address the possibility that during a rising manic episode your loved one may not be able to think clearly and he'll give you permission to take this action unilaterally when necessary.

Overspending

Unrestrained spending is almost a cliché in stories about manic episodes. The logical intervention is deceptively simple: Hide the cash and checkbook, snatch the credit and debit cards, and transfer the cash from the savings account to an account that your loved one can't touch. Just be aware that your loved one can find ways to work around these minor inconveniences and get to the cash. For example, he could

✓ Memorize the credit card numbers.

✓ Use stored account information on Internet shopping sites to place orders.

✓ Shop by phone.

✓ Apply for new credit cards over the phone or on the Internet.

To stay one step ahead of the mania, you need to think creatively and invent ways to counter the preceding tactics:

✔ **Contact the credit card companies to place a hold on the accounts or change account numbers.** Procedures may vary, depending on the companies and the state in which you reside, so research the policies and credit card company phone numbers ahead of time. Remember that you may also need to change the card number at any places that use the card for regular or automatic payments.

✔ **Report the credit cards stolen.** Technically speaking, the bipolar disorder has stolen them, so you're not really lying. (Do this only in a pinch.)

✔ **Inspect the mail for any new credit card applications.** Most mailboxes receive a steady stream of tempting offers; shred them or simply write "Return to Sender" on the envelopes and drop them in the mail.

✔ **Monitor your loved one's Internet use and email for any activity regarding credit card applications or transactions.** This particular step is possible only if you have login information for your loved one's accounts. It can also backfire if it causes a breach of trust. This is one of those interventions that's best done by planning ahead and getting permission from your loved one when he's feeling well.

✔ **Try to avoid saving credit card numbers on favorite shopping sites or remove them if a crisis is brewing.** That way, your loved one can't just log in to his favorite site and make extravagant purchases when he's in the middle of a manic or depressive episode.

Of course, potential drawbacks accompany these clever plans. For example, if your loved one shares accounts with a spouse or significant other, how can that person access money to buy groceries and pay bills? One solution is to keep at least one separate account that the person with bipolar disorder can't access — money available during a crisis. You may also want to consider keeping most accounts only in the spouse's name to reduce the potential sources of money and credit during a crisis, but make sure everyone is on board with this plan.

Hypersexual behavior

Hypersexuality — a supercharged state of sexual confidence and desire — is a diagnostic feature of mania that often results in risky sexual behavior. It stirs up boatloads of trouble for the person with bipolar disorder and his family. Trying to reduce this risky behavior presents unique challenges. Sexual behavior is private stuff. Without trailing the manic person 24/7, how can you prevent dangerous sexual behavior? For starters, try the following:

✔ **Take the car keys and credit cards.** No car, no money, no sex. Well, it may not be that easy, but taking driving and spending off the table blocks the main access routes to unsafe sexual connections. Of course, taking away the car keys and credit cards presents other drawbacks, which we describe in the previous two sections.

✔ **Restrict or monitor Internet access.** The Internet is everywhere — phone, computers, tablets, TVs — providing constant access to a menu of sexual opportunities, including pornography, which may be the least of your worries. Hookup apps, social media platforms, online dating sites, and other virtual pickup joints are packed with people looking for sexual connections. Pornography doesn't carry the risk of sexually transmitted diseases or pregnancy, but hookup apps and dating sites can lead to physical encounters.

Restricting Internet access has some potential drawbacks to discuss with your loved one during your planning meeting. Can you restrict Internet access without eliminating communications (phone/texting, email, and work communications)? Should you limit texting or phone access? Will your loved one allow you to monitor or restrict his Internet activities and communications? Tailor your plan so that both of you feel comfortable with it and confident that it will produce the desired results. Talk, talk, and more talk is the only way to cover all your bases.

Substance abuse

Bipolar disorder doesn't mix well with drugs or alcohol. In a person whose inhibitions are already compromised, these substances melt away any vestiges of good judgment. With depression, alcohol can result in a much higher risk of completed suicide. Helping your loved one stay away from these dangerous substances can be lifesaving, but your options are limited:

✔ **Cut off access to money and transportation.** If your loved one can't afford drugs and alcohol and can't get to them, he can't use them. However, even if funds are restricted, he can still steal what he needs or trade stuff for them.

✔ **Restrict phone and Internet access.** If a friend or acquaintance delivers drugs or alcohol to your loved one, you can cut off communications to the outside world, if possible, to help block the courier route.

✔ **Monitor your loved one's activity.** Keeping watch is incredibly intrusive and restrictive for both you and your loved one, but standing guard is the most effective option in controlling almost every risky behavior we cover in this section. Obtain assistance from others, if possible, to reduce burnout.

Runaways and disappearances

If your loved one disappears — you can't find him or track him down within a reasonable time frame — you must notify the police. If the police department has a unit trained to deal with people with mental illness, ask to speak to someone in that department. In any case, be sure to tell the person taking the report that your loved one has a mental illness and is at risk of unpredictable behavior. Although you may not have reached the required time frame for reporting a person missing, by identifying the mental illness, you may help law enforcement officials respond more quickly than standard operating procedure calls for.

Making this report in person rather than over the phone may be more effective because doing so allows you to assess how the police officer is reacting to the information you're giving him. If you feel that you're not being heard or not being taken seriously, with respect and courtesy, ask to speak to a supervisor.

If your loved one is missing, contact his doctor and therapist, who may have some idea of where to look. They may have more sway with law enforcement as well. Make sure to contact friends and relatives (as many as you can think of) to broaden the network of people looking for your loved one.

Arrests

If your loved one with bipolar disorder is arrested, your goal is to transition the person as quickly as possible from the legal system to the healthcare system. Here are several guidelines you can follow to help achieve that goal:

- ✔ **Be supportive.** Remain calm and remind your loved one of his right to legal representation. If charges are filed and you have the resources, consider hiring an attorney to represent him — preferably an attorney experienced with cases that involve mental illness.

  NAMI offers a lawyer referral service to its members and the general public. To contact the NAMI Legal Center and request a referral, email legal@nami.org or call 1-800-950-6264. Provide your full name, address with ZIP code, and telephone number.

- ✔ **Don't sign a police report unless you want your loved one arrested.** Feel free to give a statement to police, but hold off on signing the report until you've discussed the options with the police and are comfortable with the decision of where your loved one will be taken. To make an arrest, the officers will probably need a sworn (signed) statement.

- ✔ **Be proactive.** Have consent and be proactive in your communications with your loved one's attorney, especially if the attorney is a public defender who's been assigned to the case. Ask questions whenever you encounter something you don't understand or if you don't know the potential consequences of something you or your loved one is asked to do or sign.

✔ **Report the arrest to your loved one's psychiatrist, treating physician, and therapist.** If your loved one has been in treatment, keep the doctor and therapist in the loop.

✔ **Document everything.** Keep a journal of everything that happens and everything you and your loved one do to seek help. Keep copies of any letters, emails, text messages, and faxes you send and receive. Document phone conversations and messages you leave, including the date, time, and name of the person you speak with.

✔ **Don't discuss any criminal charges with authorities.** You don't want to inadvertently say something that hurts your loved one's case.

✔ **When speaking with the jail supervisor or watch commander, ask the following questions:**

- When can I expect my loved one to be released?

- Where will he be released?

- Does he need to post bail? If so, find out how much and in what form; for example, cash, credit card, or certified check. If you can't afford to post bail, request information about bail bonds services. (Make sure your loved one has legal representation at the bail hearing.)

Avoid the temptation to merely bail out your loved one. Always consider the endgame — if you bail him out, then what? You're usually better off working through the justice system to try to transition your loved one to a mental health facility for treatment. The justice system may have more power than you do to help someone who doesn't think he needs help or who refuses treatment.

- If charges are filed, when and where will the hearing take place?

- When and where can I visit my loved one?

- Does the jail have a medical or mental health services department? If it does, get the name, phone, and fax number of the person in charge.

✔ **Consult your loved one's attorney and obtain permission before discussing your loved one's diagnosis with authorities.** The people you're dealing with may not fully understand or accept mental illness. Mention of the mental illness can positively or negatively affect your loved one's situation, and a local attorney usually has a better sense than you do of how sensitive and knowledgeable a particular individual is.

✔ **Remember that medication may be withheld until your loved one's competency for trial is assessed.** Withholding medication is cruel, but defense attorneys sometimes fight to have medication withheld so their clients are more likely to be found *not competent to stand trial,* in which case the clients are more likely to be committed to a mental health facility and the charges are likely to be dropped.

Not competent to stand trial isn't an insanity defense. It means the person can't, at this time, understand the nature of the proceedings against him or help his lawyer prepare his defense.

✔ **Keep in mind that the insanity defense may be an option, especially if charges revolve around violent behaviors.** If you think your loved one lacked the ability to recognize the wrongfulness of his actions at the time he committed those actions, the insanity defense may be helpful in transitioning him from the criminal justice system to a psychiatric facility.

✔ **Speak with your loved one's attorney about providing sentencing input if a conviction results.** Several sentencing scenarios may unfold that vary according to jurisdiction and the nature of the crime:

- In some jurisdictions, sentences are mandated for specific types of crimes, and the judge has little or no leeway in sentencing, in which case your input really doesn't matter.

- In the case of a felony, a parole officer usually writes a pre-sentence report that the judge refers to in determining the sentence. You may be able to provide the parole officer with details about your loved one's mental illness to sway the sentencing toward treatment rather than incarceration.

- In the case of a misdemeanor, the judge may proceed to sentencing immediately after ruling on the case, so the defense attorney needs to inform the judge at the appropriate time of your desire to provide input regarding sentencing.

✔ **Advocate for a *jail diversion program,* if one is available.** Some jurisdictions have jail diversion programs. For cases that involve mental illness, jail diversion is likely to require the person charged with the crime to receive treatment and stay out of trouble for a certain period of time to have charges dropped. This can help your loved one avoid a criminal record.

✔ **Write letters.** If the system is being irresponsive and you sense that your loved one is about to experience an unjust conviction, research the chain of command and work your way up until you find someone who listens and is sympathetic to what you're going through. You may end up having to write a letter to your state governor.

✔ **Contact the press.** If you're not getting satisfactory results through the system, contact the local press and tell them your story. Public exposure can often correct an injustice and help to fix a broken system.

If your loved one is ultimately convicted and jailed, then you can advocate for treatment for your loved one without having to consult with your loved one's attorney. If the jail has a medical or mental health services department, fax the following information to both the jail supervisor or watch commander and the medical or mental health services department:

- ✔ Your loved one's full legal name, date of birth, booking number, and current residential address

- ✔ Your loved one's diagnosis or the reasons why you believe his behavior is the result of a mental illness

- ✔ The name, phone number, and address of your loved one's psychiatrist or treating physician

- ✔ A list of all current medications, dosages, time(s) of day to be administered, and the name and number of the pharmacy

- ✔ Information about medications that have proven to be effective versus ineffective or that have caused serious negative side effects

- ✔ Any history of suicide attempts or threats

- ✔ Information about other medical conditions that may require attention

- ✔ A written release of information consent form if your loved one has given you one; if he hasn't, a request that he be asked to sign one while in jail

Chapter 21

Backing Your Bipolar Child or Teen

In This Chapter

▶ Accepting the challenges of diagnosing children and adolescents

▶ Seeking out a professional evaluation

▶ Developing a treatment plan for your child and family

▶ Figuring out how to parent your child after bipolar enters the picture

*Y*ou may notice that something's not quite right with your child. It may be that she's always been more sensitive and irritable than other kids, but now she isn't herself at all. She's exhausted; even the tiniest task overwhelms her. She doesn't seem to enjoy much of anything, and she's hardly talking to friends anymore. You're worried about depression.

But after a few weeks, she seems better. Then, gradually or suddenly, she's over the top, again not herself. She never seems to sleep, she talks a mile a minute, and it's hard to follow her thinking. She's started several ambitious projects but can't seem to focus on any of them. She's texting everyone in her class — even kids she really doesn't know — and talking about strange discoveries she's made about the universe. Or maybe she's angrier than ever and convinced that kids are following her home and erasing stuff on her computer. Up all day and all night, she damages the computer and confronts her peers, scaring everyone.

Need some advice? When it comes to raising children, everyone's an expert. But trying to tough out the situation with advice from daytime television and the neighborhood peanut gallery isn't going to help you or your child. You're likely dealing with a complicated medical problem that needs the same care and attention you'd give to diabetes, severe asthma, or other chronic illness.

In this chapter, we describe how bipolar disorder typically affects children and teenagers and why the diagnosis can be tricky. We also point out what a professional evaluation should involve and how to obtain one for your child. Finally, we lay out treatment options for a child with bipolar disorder and offer a brief introduction to what you can do as a parent (at home and at school) for your child with this condition.

Recognizing the Diagnostic Difficulties

The idea of childhood bipolar disorder was dismissed as a rare event until about 20 years ago when some researchers began to explore the idea that pediatric bipolar disorder was more common than previously thought. The researchers noted that many adults with bipolar disorder reported that their symptoms started before age 18. Some case reports over the years also suggested that mania could occur in younger adolescents and pre-pubertal children.

Over the next few years a theory evolved that childhood mania may look different than adult mania; specifically, childhood mania looks more irritable than euphoric and more chronic than episodic when compared to adults. Chronic emotional *dysregulation* — a range of difficulties with modulating emotional responses — was identified as a core component of pediatric bipolar disorder. This was quite different from the defining feature of bipolar disorder being discrete mood episodes, which had defined the bipolar I diagnosis in adults for many years.

This theory took hold and became accepted practice quickly, in part because chronic irritability and emotional dysregulation are primary symptoms in many of the most challenging children seen by child psychiatrists. Bipolar diagnoses in children skyrocketed, as did the use of powerful antipsychotics and mood stabilizers to treat the children with these diagnoses. Since then, experts in the field have diverged into two general schools of thought:

- ✓ The *narrow,* more conservative approach to diagnosing bipolar disorder in children relies on the presence of well-defined episodes of mood and energy changes. This approach is similar to the approach used to diagnose bipolar in adults. It's helpful in avoiding overdiagnosis and unnecessarily exposing children and teens to powerful antipsychotics and mood medications.

- ✓ The *broad* approach looks at chronic mood dysregulation as part of a spectrum of mania and bipolar disorders. Proponents of this approach are more concerned about the potential harm of missing a diagnosis of bipolar disorder in children and teens.

Research continues to try to sort out the differences between bipolar disorder in children and adults, but because of different underlying diagnostic approaches, the studies often measure different things and can be quite conflicting.

Currently, the most rigorous research indicates that although some children who are irritable and dysregulated ultimately develop bipolar disorder, most don't. The ultimate goal is to be able to diagnose bipolar disorder accurately in children and teens so as not to miss a diagnosis of bipolar disorder when one is warranted and not to apply the diagnosis when something else is the root cause.

A brief interview isn't adequate for a diagnosis of bipolar disorder in a child or teen. Get a careful evaluation, preferably with a board-certified child and adolescent psychiatrist, before you accept a bipolar diagnosis for your child. (See the later section "Requesting a Professional Evaluation" in this chapter for details.)

Diagnosing Bipolar Disorder in Children

Arriving at a diagnosis of bipolar disorder in children and adolescents is problematic because manic episodes typically first appear in late adolescence or early adulthood. A diagnosis of bipolar I disorder requires the presence of at least one manic episode. (See Chapter 2 for the criteria used to determine when a certain mood episode qualifies as a manic episode.) Using these criteria, mania (and therefore bipolar I) is much less common in younger adolescents and children, but it does occur.

A key feature in the criteria used to diagnosis mania is that the episode represents a *change from baseline.* A child may be chronically hyperactive, inattentive, or irritable, but the behavior isn't considered a manic episode unless the symptoms are substantially worse than usual for a period of time. The diagnosis can be tricky because many other childhood disorders have the same symptoms as bipolar disorder in children and teens, including the following:

- *Irritability* and *agitation* can be due to many conditions including, but not limited to, autism spectrum disorder, language disorders, unipolar depression, anxiety, trauma, substance abuse, and attention deficit hyperactivity disorder (ADHD).

- Chronic *hyperactivity/high energy, talkativeness,* and *distractibility* are core symptoms of ADHD and may be associated with substance abuse, trauma, and developmental disorders.

- *Sleep disturbances* are common in childhood for a variety of reasons. Daytime fatigue from staying up too late, for example, isn't the same as the decreased need for sleep seen in mania. Trouble falling asleep has many causes, including typical adolescence, depression, and anxiety.

- The subjective sensation of *racing thoughts* can be associated with anxiety as well as mania.

- *Impulsivity* (poor judgment and high levels of risk taking) is often found in ADHD; it can also be related to typical adolescence, substance abuse, depression in which someone has given up and shows no regard for his own safety, and other developmental disorders.

The growing consensus is that some form of episode — a change from baseline — needs to happen to identify bipolar disorder in children and distinguish it from other childhood psychiatric or developmental disorders. The following sections briefly describe some of the most common conditions that complicate the diagnosis of bipolar disorder in kids — conditions that should be considered before arriving at a diagnosis of bipolar disorder.

Attention deficit hyperactivity disorder (ADHD)

The diagnostic criteria for mania clearly overlap with those for ADHD. Distinguishing between the two conditions is critical because treatment for ADHD is different from treatment for bipolar. For instance, the stimulants used to treat ADHD, such as Adderall (a combination of dextroamphetamine and amphetamine) and Ritalin (methylphenidate), can wreak havoc in a manic child, and antimanics, which can help with mania, don't help kids with ADHD. Here we explore the similarities and differences between ADHD and bipolar disorder and the possibility of the two conditions existing together.

Identifying shared symptoms of mania and ADHD

Mania and ADHD share a number of core symptoms that center on energy, impulse control, and mood reactions. Some important overlapping symptoms include

- High energy levels
- Excessive talking
- Poor impulse control
- Inattention/distractibility
- High risk taking/stimulus seeking

✔ Impatience/trouble delaying gratification

✔ Moodiness/short fuse (although this isn't a diagnostic criterion for ADHD, it's a commonly occurring associated symptom)

Distinguishing bipolar from ADHD

What are the differences between symptoms of mania and those of ADHD? How do you sort them out? The following considerations are important to evaluate when making a diagnosis:

✔ **Cycling/change from baseline:** In bipolar disorder, the manic and hypomanic symptoms typically come in episodes. In ADHD, the symptoms are *chronic* (present all the time).

✔ **Grandiosity:** Mania causes a person to be full of irrational confidence and certain that she can do anything and achieve everything that she imagines. Markedly distorted feelings of power and ability aren't part of ADHD. In fact, kids with ADHD typically struggle with low self-confidence and a sense that they're doomed to failure. Grandiosity is a red flag for mania.

✔ **Sleep disturbance:** Kids with ADHD often have trouble quieting their minds to sleep; these kids are usually fatigued the next day and have a difficult time waking up. In mania, kids need little sleep; they stay up late, get up early, and keep on going. They eventually crash, exhausted, but they have sustained periods of high energy with less need for sleep.

✔ **Euphoria:** Mania can be diagnosed in someone who has only angry, irritable moods — a symptom that's also associated with ADHD. However, the presence of *euphoria* — an expansive, overly happy mood with a persistent sense that everything is beyond wonderful, that everything is easy, even when life throws its usual curve balls — is part of mania, but not part of ADHD.

Considering comorbidity: ADHD and bipolar

How common is it for kids with bipolar disorder to also have ADHD? Can a child have both conditions? Research shows that bipolar disorder causes problems with attention and concentration, even between mood episodes. If a child is diagnosed with bipolar disorder, she'll likely have problems listening, focusing, and following directions. Teasing out the two diagnoses is a challenge for treating doctors and researchers. If your child has been diagnosed with both disorders, she'll require especially careful treatment planning.

Oppositional defiant disorder (ODD)

All children are oppositional at times; it's part of growing up and developing independence and personality. For most kids, rebellious behaviors respond fairly well to the usual carrot-and-stick parenting techniques, but oppositional kids exhibit a much more tenacious defiance. Parents describe the child as being stubborn, strong-willed, or simply a pain in the neck. When this pattern creates significant problems in function — at school, at home, with friends, or during activities — a doctor or therapist may suggest a diagnosis of oppositional defiant disorder (ODD), which is described in the *DSM-5* as:

> A pattern of angry/irritable mood, argumentative/defiant behavior, or vindictiveness lasting at least 6 months . . . and is not exclusively directed at siblings.

ODD's irritable mood and behavioral difficulties — not doing as one's told — can overlap with mania. Although this is often a confusing area, the child with ODD demonstrates these symptoms chronically and not episodically. Furthermore, ODD doesn't include other manic symptoms such as energy changes and grandiosity as we describe in the previous section on ADHD.

ODD is a problematic diagnosis in many regards, because its core symptoms are nonspecific. Irritable mood and defiant behavior can be associated with a wide range of developmental and psychiatric conditions. Your child needs a careful medical and psychiatric evaluation to help understand the mechanisms underlying these difficult symptoms. Bipolar disorder/mania is one possible explanation, but others can include unipolar depression, ADHD, language disorders, autism spectrum disorder, and trauma, among others.

Unipolar depression

Even though a manic episode is needed to make the diagnosis of bipolar disorder, most people with bipolar also experience periods of depression. In fact, bipolar depressive episodes typically occur more frequently and last longer than mania.

Depressive episodes often present long before manic ones do. Before treating depression, the doctor tries to assess the risk that someone will eventually develop mania, which is important because antidepressants alone can sometimes trigger manic symptoms if someone's brain is wired for bipolar disorder. Additionally, the treatment for bipolar depression differs from that for unipolar depression, and research suggests that they're different in their underlying brain changes (refer to Chapter 2). Without clear-cut mania, however, differentiating bipolar depression from unipolar depression is difficult even for the most experienced psychiatrists. In the following sections, we highlight differences in depressive symptoms that may help to predict the likelihood of bipolar depression now or in the future.

Sorting out depression in children and teens

Depression in children and teens can be especially difficult to sort out. People who develop depression early in life have a higher risk of developing bipolar disorder than people who experience depression at a later age; still, most kids who suffer from depression don't develop bipolar disorder. To sort out the risks of your child having bipolar disorder, her doctor may explore some of the following warning signs:

- ✔ **Repeat depressive episodes:** A kid who experiences numerous episodes of depression is a more likely candidate for an eventual bipolar diagnosis. If the episodes are brief (three months or less), the risk increases.

- ✔ **Family history:** Having a first-degree relative, such as a parent or sibling, with bipolar disorder increases the risk of developing bipolar disorder by 5 to 10 percent. Check out Chapter 2 for details regarding family history and genetics.

- ✔ **Response to antidepressants:** How someone responds to antidepressants is suggestive of, but not part of, the diagnostic criteria for bipolar disorder. Any of the following responses to antidepressants may lead a doctor to suspect the possibility of bipolar disorder:

  - Mania or hypomania occurs. (Note that people can become manic or agitated on antidepressants without having bipolar disorder, but if the mania persists after the antidepressants are removed, then this is part of the diagnostic criteria for mania/bipolar disorder.)

  - Antidepressants don't work.

  - Antidepressants work initially but then stop working, even after dose increases and trials of different antidepressants.

- ✔ **A larger-than-life temperament:** People with baseline hyperthymic personalities are considered a high bipolar risk. *Hyperthymic* is a medical term for high energy — meaning extremely outgoing and active — often highly confident, and sometimes seen as arrogant or narcissistic.

Repeat depressions, a family history of bipolar disorder, certain responses to antidepressants, and a hyperthymic personality aren't diagnostic for bipolar disorder; rather, you should consider them red flags. If your child's doctor spots several of these warning signs, she may develop a different treatment plan than she would for a kid without the possible bipolar indicators.

Whether it's unipolar or bipolar, child and adolescent depression is a condition that tragically results in one of the leading causes of death in teenagers: suicide. Depression is a serious medical condition that requires appropriate evaluation and care.

Recognizing depression in your child

Depression can be tricky to spot, particularly in teens who already seem moody and impulsive. Depressed kids and teens can appear angry, bored, or withdrawn rather than sad and dejected. In children and adolescents, irritability, instead of sadness, can be the major mood state in depression. Because irritability is also often prominent in manic episodes, sorting out mood symptoms in kids can be slippery.

In order to determine whether your child is being dramatic or is sinking into a serious depression, look for the following signs:

- **Persistent changes in function:** Everybody has good and bad days — sometimes even a few in a row, but when your child or adolescent begins to experience extended periods of time when she's not herself, you need to pay attention. Explore further any significant changes in grades, friends, activities, energy, and enthusiasm that go on for more than a couple of weeks.

- **Any self-harm or references to suicide:** These are critical red flags that you must respond to immediately. Even if you think your child just wants attention or is trying to manipulate you, the fact that she's using suicide or self-injury as her tool is a real problem.

   Always take threats of suicide seriously. Don't try on your own to determine whether your child really means it. Involve a professional immediately.

- **Withdrawal:** Kids like their personal space, and adolescents, in particular, spend plenty of time in their rooms. But kids who hardly leave their rooms, lose interest in spending time with friends, or drop out of activities are showing signs of depression. This behavior can happen gradually and be easily overlooked.

- **Sleep/energy shifts:** Kids change their sleep patterns throughout development. Teenagers typically develop a need to stay up late and sleep later into the day. However, a kid who changes her patterns and starts sleeping a lot more or a lot less than usual may be depressed. If your child's energy levels seem to drop and not rebound after a couple of weeks, schedule a medical exam. If the doctor finds no other medical cause, depression may be a possibility.

- **Substance use:** Drinking and marijuana use seem to be ubiquitous in high schools nowadays. Keeping kids away from these experiences is a

difficult challenge, but a kid who uses drugs and alcohol regularly or significantly increases her use may be self-medicating. Don't convince yourself that all kids do it. If your child gets high or drunk most weekends,
you need to look into it. Even if depression isn't present, substance
abuse in a teenager is a big problem and needs to be addressed as early
as possible.

Disruptive mood dysregulation disorder

DSM-5 introduced a new diagnosis that grew out of research on children
with chronic mood dysregulation — irritability and emotional/behavioral
outbursts. As we previously discuss in this chapter, the concept of chronic
mood dysregulation has overlapped with the diagnosis of bipolar disorder,
but they're not the same. This diagnosis helps to capture children with
baseline irritability and outbursts who don't exhibit the cycles or episodes
needed to diagnose mania and therefore bipolar disorder.

Disruptive mood dysregulation disorder (DMDD) is listed under Depressive
Disorders in the *DSM-5,* and its diagnostic criteria are as follows:

A. Severe recurrent temper outbursts manifested verbally (for example,
   verbal rages) and/or behaviorally (for example, physical aggression
   toward people or property) that are grossly out of proportion in intensity or duration to the situation or provocation.

B. The temper outbursts are inconsistent with developmental level (they
   look like more typical reactions in a younger child, for example).

C. The temper outbursts occur, on average, three or more times per week.

D. The mood between temper outbursts is persistently irritable or angry
   most of the day, nearly every day, and is observable by others (for
   example, parents, teachers, and peers).

E. Criteria A–D have been present for 12 or more months. Throughout that
   time, the individual has not had a period lasting three or more consecutive months without all the symptoms in Criteria A–D.

F. Criteria A and D are present in at least two of three settings (at home, at
   school, with peers) and are severe in at least one of these.

G. The diagnosis should not be made for the first time before age 6 years or
   after age 18 years.

H. By history or observation, the age at onset of Criteria A–E is before
   age 10 years.

I. There has never been a distinct period lasting more than one day during which the full symptom criteria, except duration, for a manic or hypomanic episode have been met.

J. The behaviors do not occur exclusively during an episode of major depression and are not better explained by another mental disorder (for example, autism spectrum disorder, post-traumatic stress disorder, separation anxiety disorder, persistent depressive disorder).

K. The symptoms are not attributable to the physiological effects of a substance or to another medical or neurological condition.

Importantly, this diagnosis can't coexist with bipolar disorder or oppositional defiant disorder. If mania or hypomania is present, bipolar is the diagnosis. If symptoms of ODD present, then the DMDD diagnosis is used instead. DMDD can coexist with depression, ADHD, substance use, and other disorders.

Currently no specific treatment recommendations are available for DMDD. Because it's considered a subset of depression, treatment for depression is often the first place to start. If coexisting conditions, such as ADHD or anxiety, are present, those are targeted. Multiple resources are typically needed for effective treatment in these children, including psychotherapy, parenting support, educational accommodations, as well as possible medications. The diagnosis of DMDD can be helpful to families who are trying to understand these difficult behaviors in their children. Realize that these responses aren't just children being difficult or willful, but rather are due to problems in their nervous system circuits that help to regulate mood and behavior. Understanding this difference in cause changes the treatment and parenting approaches considerably.

An important consideration with this diagnosis is that if your child is diagnosed with bipolar disorder, certain medications, such as antidepressants and stimulants, may be avoided. The DMDD diagnosis doesn't carry these restrictions beyond baseline caution in using these medications in children. This is extremely helpful, because the overuse of the bipolar disorder diagnosis can lead to restricting the use of medications that may be helpful for diagnoses such as depression, ADHD, and anxiety disorders.

Anxiety disorders

Anxiety disorders are common in children, and they trigger changes in mood and behavior that can look like manic or depressive symptoms. Anxiety disorders cause fear and distress that are out of proportion to any actual threat. The fear and distress then trigger behavioral responses to try to reduce the threat, typically in one of two forms — fight or flight. Fight looks angry and out of control — the brain trying to save itself from a perceived danger. Flight can include running away from something, but can also present as avoidance and refusals and shutting down. Anxiety can mimic symptoms of bipolar disorder in some of the following ways:

- ✔ **Irritability:** Fear triggers a need to control the environment, to reduce threats, and to keep things safe. When the world doesn't cooperate (if children must do things that trigger fear or must stop doing something that is helping them stay calm), they can become angry and sometimes explosive. This behavior looks like the mood dysregulation found in mania and depression.

- ✔ **Racing thoughts:** Anxious people's brains are always scanning the environment for threats and are very busy worrying about potential dangers. This often presents as a subjective sensation of racing thoughts, also a symptom of mania.

- ✔ **Demanding and controlling behaviors:** People with anxiety work hard to control their environments. Parents are tasked with getting children to do things they don't want to do, which can be particularly difficult with anxious children, leading to hours of struggle with escalating tempers and mood changes.

- ✔ **Oppositional/defiant behaviors:** The flight response of anxiety can present as refusals and shutting down when given demands that trigger anxiety or distress. When the adult escalates the demands and becomes firmer (or even angry), the child's anxiety escalates, creating further paralysis and even less likelihood of meeting the adult's demand. This can easily turn into angry or sobbing outbursts that look like a mood disorder.

Obsessive compulsive disorder (OCD) isn't technically an anxiety disorder, but is related. Children with OCD have repeated and out-of-the-ordinary fears (for example, that the doors are unlocked and a stranger will come in and hurt them) that they control with a variety of mental or physical rituals and behaviors (for example, checking door locks over and over before being able to sleep). If people with OCD aren't allowed to perform their behaviors, their level of distress can escalate dramatically and quickly. It can present as irritability with explosive mood and behaviors that are puzzling to parents and teachers and that look like mania or depression. Kids often can't or won't communicate their fears, which can make OCD difficult to diagnose. Your child's doctor should consider OCD, if your child has explosive outbursts.

Trauma

Children and adolescents who have been exposed to trauma, including neglect, abuse, domestic violence, death or loss of parents, bullying, or other extremely distressing/fear-inducing events and situations, are at risk of a variety of psychiatric disorders. Trauma and severe life events are contributing factors to the development of bipolar disorder in someone with underlying genetic risks (as we discuss in Chapter 2). However, trauma can present with a variety of emotional and behavioral symptoms, including sadness, anxiety, irritability, distractibility, impulsivity, and sleep disturbances that may look like mania but are instead directly related to the trauma.

Trauma must be considered and *ruled out* (determined to not be present) whenever children present with marked changes in their function. The term *trauma-informed care* has evolved to help healthcare professionals keep trauma at the front of their thinking at all times, because if trauma is present, the single most important step is removing the traumatic triggers and addressing them.

Autism spectrum disorders

Autism spectrum disorders (ASD) are developmental disorders that present with impaired social interactions/communications and repetitive patterns of language and behavior. The severity can range from very impaired (with severe intellectual disability and little or no language) to average or superior intellectual function and typical verbal language skills.

Irritability and temper outbursts aren't uncommon symptoms in children with ASD, related to many factors, including the following:

- Rigid/inflexible thinking and behaviors
- Difficulties with self-expression
- Impaired social interactions and relationships

Additionally, anxiety is a common co-occurrence in ASD, which can cause moodiness and temper outbursts sometimes seen in bipolar disorder. ADHD may also be present in kids with ASD, and depression can occur more frequently than in children without ASD.

More severe presentations of ASD are usually diagnosed early in life, but children with less severe symptoms can be harder to accurately diagnose. If mood symptoms are especially pronounced, especially in young children, these symptoms may become a target of evaluation and treatment, and the ASD diagnosis may be missed or less clear-cut. Identifying these conditions is important, because the care and support include many features that aren't necessarily needed in bipolar disorder, such as speech/language therapy and other interventions to address the core symptoms of ASD.

Toxic exposures

The term *toxic exposures* refers to substances that are known to damage the body. Regarding the presentation of bipolar disorder in children and teens, toxic exposure specifically regards substances that harm the central nervous system. These types of effects may be part of the development of bipolar disorder in some people (research is still trying to uncover what may trigger the development of bipolar in people who are vulnerable), but the outcomes of these exposures can also be confused with bipolar disorder. Some examples include the following:

- ✔ **Prenatal alcohol exposure:** Alcohol exposure in the developing fetus can cause a wide range of developmental problems. Many children with *fetal alcohol effects* can exhibit growth and learning problems, and many also have severe problems with mood and behavioral regulation as well as social interactions.

- ✔ **Lead toxicity:** Lead exposure damages developing brains. Even though children are monitored for lead, and lead paints are no longer allowed, many children, especially those living in poverty, have elevated lead levels. Emotional and behavioral dysregulation can be a prominent symptom in these children.

- ✔ **Alcohol and drug use:** In teens, substance use and misuse becomes a crucial part of the diagnostic workup of bipolar disorder. Intoxication, withdrawal, and dependence/addiction can all create severe changes in mood, thought, and behavior. Marijuana use is particularly noted to increase the risk of developing psychosis in young people who are vulnerable.

Requesting a Professional Evaluation

If you've read the first half of this chapter, you may still have no clear idea of what's going on with your child. All you know is that your child has *some* characteristics that *may* be caused by any one or more of a dozen different things, such as normal adolescent angst, ADHD, depression, anxiety, lack of sleep, or a host of other conditions and contributing factors. You can now get your child to a professional who can help sort out the possible issues and pinpoint one or two factors that can steer you toward proper treatment. The following sections help you locate the right doctor and determine what you need to do as a parent.

Finding the right doctor

A good starting point in identifying the right professional to conduct a psychiatric evaluation for your child is your family doctor or pediatrician. Pediatricians are becoming increasingly familiar with psychiatric diagnoses in kids; yours can likely guide your family to the appropriate psychiatric help. Involving the pediatrician early is also beneficial, because he can conduct a full medical examination to rule out the presence of any illnesses that may be contributing to your child's symptoms. In addition, the doctor can address general health issues, such as sleep and growth, which may be important factors in a mood disorder.

If you still have serious concerns about a mood disorder after a physician has ruled out other conditions, the next step is to consult a board-certified child and adolescent psychiatrist. Some adult psychiatrists work with adolescents and may be comfortable diagnosing and treating kids older than 16. Younger teens and children, however, should see a psychiatrist who's trained and experienced in working with kids.

Beware of doctors who proceed with a *diagnosis by prescription.* In this approach, the doctor spends 15 minutes with you and your child, hands you a prescription for methylphenidate (Ritalin) or an antidepressant, and then when your kid ends up in the hospital, tries a different medication to see if it works. A thorough evaluation takes time, input from various sources, and detective work. Continue your search if the psychiatrist you see doesn't seem genuinely invested in discovering the most accurate diagnosis for your child.

Finding a child and adolescent psychiatrist may take some work, depending on where you live. This field has a shortage of qualified professionals, particularly in some areas of the country. And even if you can locate a number of these doctors in your area, finding one covered by your insurance plan can be a nightmare. Look to the following sources for leads:

- ✔ Your child's pediatrician or family physician (in the U.K., this is necessary before accessing a mental health evaluation)

- ✔ The school counselor or special education department

- ✔ Friends or relatives

- ✔ A counselor or therapist who works with your child

- ✔ The American Academy of Child and Adolescent Psychiatry (www.aacap.org)

- ✔ Your local medical society

- ✔ A local support group, such as the National Alliance on Mental Illness (NAMI) or Depression and Bipolar Support Alliance (DBSA), where members often exchange information, recommendations, and concerns about specific doctors and therapists

✔ The Balanced Mind Parent Network, whose website (`www.`
`thebalancedmind.org`) offers access to a professional directory,
which includes names of doctors with expertise in working with kids
with bipolar disorder

✔ A local children's hospital or a medical school or university hospital that
may have a department of psychiatry

Flip to Chapter 5 for tips on finding and choosing a psychiatrist, and check
out Chapter 6 for guidance on assembling a mood-management team and
support network. This information can help you put together and work with a
team that's focused on your child's care.

If your child expresses suicidal thoughts or behaviors, *run,* don't walk, to the
nearest mental health professional or emergency room. Get immediate help
and sort through your long-term options later.

Knowing what to do when seeking help

As a parent or guardian, your role at this early stage of investigating the possibility that your child has a mood disorder is to find a doctor who's qualified
to evaluate and treat your son or daughter and then to provide that doctor
with the most accurate and complete history possible. Your child may be
unable or unwilling to describe symptoms or to relate the details of various incidents that can help the doctor accurately assess the situation, so
you need to supply that information in a way that protects your child's self-
esteem as much as possible.

The following suggestions come from others who've been in the trenches:

✔ **Be open and honest.** If you and your spouse are having marital problems or if one of you has a drinking or substance abuse problem, don't
keep it a secret. Family problems are important to consider when formulating a diagnosis. Don't let your child be misdiagnosed because you
want to protect a family secret. Family therapy may be a necessary first
step in treating your child.

✔ **Mention any family history of mental illness.** Genetics plays a strong
role in bipolar disorder. If your family has a history of bipolar disorder,
schizophrenia, depression, or other mental illness, tell the psychiatrist.

✔ **Share the history.** When did you and others first become concerned
about your child's moods? Record details of any incidents involving
your child that have raised concern. Also be sure to record periods of
relative calm, when you observed few problems. Along with your child,
try keeping a mood chart and sleep log or using a mood monitoring app
for one or two weeks before your appointment.

You can find a sample mood chart and instructions about how to use it at www.dummies.com/extras/bipolardisorder. Keep in mind, however, that symptoms may differ significantly in children.

✔ **Gather input from others.** Ask caregivers, teachers, youth ministers, coaches, and others who interact with your child for their observations and input. Some therapists and psychiatrists have standard forms for collecting this data as part of their evaluation process.

✔ **Meet with the doctor personally.** Everyone who's closely involved with your child's situation should get a chance to meet with the doctor privately. Parents need to honestly report their concerns without shaming the child, and the child needs to be free to speak openly about his symptoms. Exactly how this plays out depends on the child's age and temperament, but the doctor needs information from both sources. Confidentiality weighs heavily in this situation, especially with teenagers. The usual arrangement is that a doctor won't tell parents what the patient says unless a safety risk is involved. Clarify the boundaries of confidentiality with your child's doctor from the start.

✔ **Obtain a copy of the evaluation.** In this day and age, people change doctors more often than they change clothes. Having a copy of your child's psychiatric evaluation(s) and any diagnoses can smooth the transition from one doctor or therapist to another.

If you don't feel confident about the diagnosis or treatment plan that a doctor provides or if you're uncomfortable with the answers to your questions, obtain a second opinion. Given the complexity of a mental health situation, a second viewpoint can help you make the best decisions and treatment choices for your child.

Breaking Out the Treatment Toolbox

With a diagnosis in hand and the assistance of your child's doctor and support network, your family can prepare to embark on a course of treatment. Your journey will meander along a path strewn with starts and stops, successes and failures, excitement and fatigue, and financial drain, but it will eventually lead to the land of stabilization for your child and family. Fortunately, you have several support vehicles to help you reach your destination:

✔ **Medications:** Balancing and calming an overcooked (overstimulated) nervous system usually requires at least some period of medication. Although you and your doctor may have concerns about using medications in children and teenagers, the right medication combination can ultimately be a lifesaver.

✔ **Therapy:** Individual therapy, family and parenting supports, and group and social skills therapy are the building blocks of treating children with bipolar disorder.

✔ **School support and intervention:** Kids spend much of their daily lives in school, and mood disorders disrupt school life in many ways. Building the right educational setting and support system, which we address in the later section "Tending to school matters," is critical to a child's wellbeing.

✔ **Lifestyle/expectations management:** Throughout this book, we point out the beneficial effects that lifestyle changes can have on the treatment outcome. These lifestyle changes apply to children, too; but for children, parents must accept, implement, and encourage the lifestyle changes so the kids don't feel pressured to fulfill unrealistic expectations.

✔ **Hospitalization:** Hospitalization is a last resort, but it may be the only option if your child is likely to harm herself or others. Managing bipolar without hospitalization is possible, but children with the disorder are commonly hospitalized at least once for the illness.

The idea of treating a child with psychiatric medications may send shivers down your spine. If so, you're not alone. People often find it difficult to accept that a child's brain can misfire and experience mood instability beyond that of a normal child. The fact that bipolar disorder is a physical illness is tough enough to grasp when adults are struggling with it; in kids, for some reason, people seem to be even more resistant to accept this scientifically clear reality.

Considering medication issues

When a child's mood problems threaten to destroy her chances of safely making the transition to adulthood or symptoms disrupt her development, medications are often the only viable solution. That is, despite all the diagnostic challenges, when a child's depression or mania hijacks her life, biological treatment is often necessary. Yet, the process of medicating a child is complicated.

The study of psychiatric medication in children is still in its infancy. Pediatric treatment for some disorders, such as ADHD and anxiety, has been studied for decades, but scientists are just beginning to look closely at biological treatments for bipolar disorder in kids — including medication for depression, mania, and mood cycling.

We detail many of the medications used to treat bipolar disorder in adults in Chapter 7. Doctors prescribe most of these medications for children as well, using the adult-based research along with the scant information available about kids with the disorder. However, for many reasons, doctors must be especially careful when treating children and teenagers. Here are just some of the difficulties:

- ✔ **Different brains, different reactions:** Child and adolescent brains differ from adult brains, so medications may work differently in children. The potential benefits and side effects of different meds aren't as predictable in children as they are in adults because current research comes from studying adult brains.

- ✔ **Changing brains, changing reactions:** Not only do young brains differ from those of adults, but they're also developing more rapidly. You may get things stabilized, but when puberty strikes or some physiological event occurs, brain circuits evolve and change, requiring adjustments to medication combinations.

- ✔ **Murky diagnostic process:** The diagnosis of bipolar disorder in children can be challenging. (See the section "Recognizing the Diagnostic Difficulties" earlier in this chapter for details.) When a child rages, for example, you need to figure out whether it's a symptom of an oncoming or worsening mood episode or a result of sleep deprivation or social problems. Teasing out the answers needed to choose the best response or treatment can be difficult.

- ✔ **Lack of understanding/noncompliance:** A child's understanding of her illness and her ability to manage it varies with age and developmental stage. Including her in conversations and decisions as much as possible in age-appropriate ways is important. But given that many symptoms of bipolar disorder include opposition and emotional outbursts, convincing a kid to cooperate with treatment isn't easy. Like adults, kids can feel flattened by the medicine or dislike side effects enough to stop taking it.

- ✔ **Parental conflict:** Parents often disagree on the diagnosis of bipolar disorder and the necessity of medication for the child. Media images of psychiatric medication and the stigma associated with mental illness can weigh heavily on parents' minds. If a parent has bipolar, her personal experiences may influence decisions about treating her child. And if parents don't see eye to eye, the child often gets caught in the middle.

So what do you do? How can you decide what the best course of action is for your child's wellbeing? Your best bet is to gather as much information as you can before making a decision.

Understanding the diagnosis and treatment plan

Before you make decisions about medication and treatment for your child, be sure you understand the situation as it stands. Ask your child's doctor some of the following questions to draw out diagnosis and treatment details and to gain a clear picture of what you're facing:

✔ **How did you make this diagnosis?** You want to know the doctor's thought process, not just a pronouncement. Given the complexity of a bipolar diagnosis in kids, don't accept it without a careful review of how the doctor arrived at her conclusion.

✔ **How did you choose this particular medication?** Just like making a diagnosis, picking a medication is a layered process with many pieces. You want to know your doctor's thought process so you can understand and then evaluate her recommendations. If the doctor hands you a prescription with no explanation, find another doctor.

✔ **Have studies in children been done with this medication?** Find out if the medication has been studied in kids and how often it has been used for children. Ask if the medication has an *FDA indication* for treating bipolar in children, which means that the US Food and Drug Administration (FDA) approves the medication for this particular use. Many psychiatric medications don't have FDA indications in children; they're used *off-label.* The off-label practice is completely legal, common, and often the right choice, but you want to know what information is available.

✔ **What are the target symptoms?** The answer to this question tells you what the goals of a particular medication are and how you can determine whether it's working. Keeping mood charts, rage counts, and sleep journals are ways for you and the doctor to follow your child's progress (see Chapter 11). Without these records, sorting out the response to medication can be quite difficult.

✔ **What are the possible side effects?** Find out what side effects to look for, whether any of them are dangerous, and how to measure them. Be sure you know what to do if you become concerned about a side effect. Also find out how to get in touch with the doctor — get her office and emergency number and an estimate of how long it typically takes her to return phone calls.

✔ **How often will you see my child?** You want to know how closely the doctor needs to monitor your child on this medication and how often and how long the doctor will talk to you, the caregiver. Check to see whether you need to follow up with laboratory tests or medical exams.

✔ **How long will my child be on this medication?** This question addresses how long your child needs to stay on the medication if she does well on it. If she doesn't do well, ask how long your child must continue taking it before trying something else. You also want to know what the criteria are for stopping or changing a medicine and how the doctor makes that decision.

Getting the right medication combination can take months. Avoid the temptation to throw in the towel and give it all up when nothing seems to work. Persistence pays off.

✔ **Will you collaborate with other caregivers?** You want to know if the doctor will communicate with your child's therapist, pediatrician, neurologist, and/or teacher. Ask whether the doctor can give you a written report and whether this kind of documentation costs more.

Bring a written list of questions with you to your child's appointment and write down the answers. Keeping this information in your computer, smartphone, or other organizer can help you keep it accessible and updated. During appointments, you and the doctor exchange a lot of information in a short period of time; you won't remember it all if you don't write it down. Don't be embarrassed to take notes during the appointment. Doctors are usually supportive and know that detailed notes can help you follow through on the treatment plan.

Finding my way

If you're a child with bipolar disorder, you know you're different, and it's scary. I know because I was a child with bipolar, but I had no idea what was wrong and why I was different from all my friends. I was angry and would rage whenever my parents left the house. I got into a lot of trouble at school, and I seemed to be getting worse over time, not better. When I wasn't angry and breaking things, I was depressed, hopeless. At one point, when I was 12, I even threatened to kill myself.

My parents and teachers asked me what was wrong, but how could I explain to the adults in my life what was wrong with me when I had no idea what was going on in my brain?

Fortunately, my parents didn't give up. They took me to a therapist who was able to figure out what was wrong and sent me to Dr. Fink to confirm my diagnosis. But of course that's not the end of the story. Finding the right medications seemed to take forever, and the

side effects were terrible. Antidepressants and antianxiety medications helped, but they also made me goofy. Lithium worked, but it made me gain a bunch of weight. On some of the meds, I couldn't concentrate at school. In junior high, I was so fed up with the side effects that I stopped taking my meds and ended up in the hospital.

My mom took some time off work to focus on helping me get better and return to school. She never gave up on me. My doctor encouraged me to be more open about my concerns regarding the medication side effects, and we were able to make some trade-offs.

After a hard teenage life and several tries at school, I moved to California and am now attending College of the Redwoods for cars and manufacturing technology. My life is going very well.

— Matthew Durand

Parenting a Child with Bipolar Disorder

Parenting is a formidable challenge even when kids have the standard amount of control over their thoughts and emotions, but parenting children with bipolar disorder is even more demanding. Sure, medication can help stabilize the neurons and chemistry in your child's brain, but the chaos of everyday life outside the brain — bedtime, the morning rush, sibling rivalries, family discord, and other commotion — requires intensive care. Many of the therapeutic approaches we describe in Chapter 11 work well for both adults and children, but child therapy usually requires a higher dose of family training and coaching. Here, we bring you up to speed on what you can do as a parent to help your child more effectively navigate childhood with bipolar disorder.

Fine-tuning your parenting skills

Some standard parenting approaches not only are ineffective, but they also aggravate a child's condition, negatively affect his self-esteem, and make parents feel powerless, guilty, and resentful toward their child. To survive as a parent and avoid the "everybody loses" confrontations, try the following suggestions:

- ✔ **Don't take your child's behavior personally.** You're not a bad parent just because you can't control your child's mood and behavior.

- ✔ **Don't blame your child for negative behaviors that are symptoms of the illness.** Remember that bipolar disorder significantly impairs a person's self-control, especially during an active depressive or manic episode but often between these periods as well. Many negative behaviors grow out of your child's distress, not from a desire to break the rules or anger you. Staying calm and avoiding power struggles can buy you some peace of mind.

- ✔ **Avoid shaming your child or using highly punitive discipline.** These tactics only make matters worse. If your child can't meet the demands you place on him because of his mood symptoms, anxiety, or low energy, for example, then consequences won't change his inability to meet your expectations. You both just end up feeling more hopeless and angry.

- ✔ **Do what you can to help your child accept himself as he is and to integrate the disorder into his life.** Acceptance and integration are the primary goals of therapy, and as a parent, you can help tremendously. Like adults with this disorder, children must work toward understanding that they *aren't* bipolar; they *have* bipolar disorder. It's a big, frustrating part of their lives, but it doesn't define them.

✔ **Let your child and yourself grieve.** Your child grieves over the differences between himself and his peers. As a parent, you grieve the loss of the child you expected and some of the dreams you may have had for him. A skilled therapist can guide you and your child through what's often a long and arduous grieving process to help everyone move forward.

Parenting a child with special emotional and behavioral needs requires specialized skills. A child therapist or psychiatrist can provide you with strategies and techniques for managing everything from the biggest crisis to mundane matters, such as getting your child out of bed in the morning.

Judgment, criticism, and demands may seem to have a place in parenting, but other, more positive ways to communicate with your child are far more successful, particularly when your child is dealing with bipolar disorder.

Tending to school matters

Kids with bipolar disorder are often sensitive and reactive, especially during mood episodes but often in between as well. They have a lower tolerance than most kids and can be extremely reactive to teacher temperament, schedules, task demands, peer conflict, and unanticipated change. Oppositional behavior, meltdowns, and social drama dot the school landscape for a child with bipolar disorder. Teachers and administrators can develop negative attitudes and expectations for your child, which only make success more difficult.

In the following sections, we provide suggestions to help you minimize the damaging impact of bipolar disorder on your child's school experience and include school-based resources as part of the process of reducing the negative effects of the illness and recovering into wellness.

Taking advantage of available services

Kids with special needs, such as physical challenges and language differences, are entitled to appropriate modifications in the educational setting. Similarly, children with bipolar disorder deserve appropriate services that enable them to participate in the educational process. If your child is struggling in school, look into the following options, both of which are mandated by law:

✔ **Special education services:** The Individuals with Disabilities in Education Act (IDEA) is a federal law that ensures students with a disability are provided with a free appropriate public education (FAPE) that is tailored to their individual needs. To take advantage of special education services, follow this process:

- **To obtain services, you, the parent, must request, in writing, that your child be evaluated for special education services.** Usually, this request goes to the director of special education in your school district.

- **The school district has a designated timeframe to respond to your request.** Schools typically have 30 days to respond — 30 school days, not 30 calendar days.

- **The evaluation includes a minimum of three types of assessments: psychological, educational, and social.** School or district psychologists and social workers usually conduct these evaluations.

- **An individualized educational plan (IEP) team considers your child's case.** After the evaluations are complete, an IEP team holds a meeting to determine whether your child meets the criteria for services. The team must include you, your child's teacher, a district special education representative, and a special education teacher. States often require that a *parent advocate* (often another parent from the district) be on the team as well. You may also bring your own advocate.

- **The team develops an IEP.** If your child is eligible to receive services, the team develops an IEP to outline where and how the school will educate your child, based on his needs.

- **You must agree with and sign off on the IEP for it to proceed.** This step ensures that you have the final say in the IEP.

✔ **Section 504 and ADA services:** Section 504 of the Rehabilitation Act of 1973 and the Americans with Disabilities Act are laws to provide for reasonable accommodations to the educational program that allow your child to participate without being discriminated against for a disability. Here are a few key points about these services:

- **Services typically accommodate less severe needs than do special education services.** You may have more success convincing your child's school to provide special services under Section 504 than under the IDEA. School districts have tight budgets, and this option involves more modifications than actual supports, so it's less expensive. If your child's needs are clear but not extreme enough to meet criteria for an IEP, this may be the way to go.

- **Section 504 services are defined locally.** Procedures for obtaining these services vary from district to district.

- **The evaluation process varies.** In some cases, the school may need to evaluate your child; in other cases, you simply need to produce a letter or report from your child's doctor that indicates a need for services.

- **Accommodations are based on your child's unique needs.** Accommodations can include providing extended time on testing, separate testing locations, oral rather than written tests, and computer use in class, to name a few.

Educating the educators about bipolar disorder

The process of obtaining an appropriate education for your child is often daunting. Schools are inundated with demands for services, and budgets are stretched thin. The education community has a track record of inconsistent understanding and awareness of mental health needs in kids. Stigma and a lack of understanding about bipolar disorder are rampant everywhere, including in schools.

During the process of securing services and modifications for your child, you'll probably need to educate the educators. Advocacy is your mission. Consider the following suggestions as you get started:

- **Remember that communication is key.** Begin by talking with and staying in touch with your child's teachers to get their perspectives on your child's needs. Get to know the guidance counselor or social worker who's involved. Ongoing communication provides you with information and demonstrates your concern and involvement — important tools in your ongoing negotiations with the school and district.

- **Gather supporting data.** Get reports from your child's psychiatrist and therapist. Bring them to meetings. Encourage phone or email communication between the school and your child's medical team.

- **Know your rights.** Federal education law mandates that every state maintain parent resource and training centers that provide guidance and information for parents as they navigate the special education system. The centers are sometimes referred to as *advocacy centers.* Your state department of education or your district's special education department should be able to give you a list of these centers.

- **Network with other parents.** Special education PTAs or informal gatherings of parents in your child's school system can provide a wealth of information, as well as camaraderie and support.

Practicing lifestyle management

Lifestyle changes can enhance the management of bipolar disorder and often alleviate symptoms. Many of the suggestions we offer here and in Chapters 11 and 12 apply to children with bipolar disorder as well as adults:

- Ensure proper health and nutrition (see Chapter 12).

- Adjust expectations and develop structured but flexible schedules and routines (see Chapter 12).

✔ Pace your family life and your child's activities (see Chapter 12).

✔ Map and track moods (see Chapter 11).

These techniques can contribute to your child's treatment success, but battling with your child over things like food and exercise may not always be advisable — if, by doing so, you create rages or meltdowns, for example. Over time, though, working in small increments when possible to establish some healthy lifestyle habits eventually pays dividends.

Self-check your expectations and demands for your child, and try to let go of some unspoken expectations that may be driving your responses. Embrace the child you have, not the child you expected, in order to empower and liberate you both.

Recognizing suicidal red flags

Bipolar disorder is a potentially lethal disease. An agonizing fact is that some people with this disorder do kill themselves. Suicide is a leading cause of death in adolescents, and bipolar disorder increases this risk significantly. To prevent suicide, follow these guidelines:

✔ **Never ignore threats of suicide or self-harm.** Don't try to determine if your child really means it. Let an expert evaluate your child to assess the risk.

✔ **Pay attention to substance abuse.** Alcohol intoxication dramatically increases the risk of completed suicide.

✔ **Watch for covert signs.** Seek professional help if you notice your child organizing and giving away belongings (preparing for when he's gone), experiencing sudden and extreme changes in activity levels or socialization, or talking of despair and hopelessness or death, even if you don't hear him speak of suicide in particular.

✔ **When possible, keep an eye on social media, such as Facebook, especially with younger children.** Kids may be more open about their thoughts and feelings in these contexts, even though doing so may not be advisable for many reasons. The older a child is, the more privacy is appropriate; monitoring his Facebook or Instagram page or Twitter feed without consent only causes more conflict. But some kids are comfortable with their parents or another trusted relative (maybe a younger aunt or uncle or family friend) accessing their social media, so don't be afraid to bring it up as a possible way to help stay in their loop.

✔ **If you have concerns about your child, don't be afraid to talk about them.** Bringing up suicide won't give your child the idea; you don't create suicidal thoughts by talking about them. Not talking about your worries is much more dangerous.

If your child appears suicidal or out of control, your doctor may recommend hospitalization. Don't panic if that happens. Psychiatric hospitalization is only for brief periods of time (often fewer than ten days) and is only for safety and crisis management.

Here are some things to do when considering hospitalization for your child:

- Talk to your doctor about where he admits people or whether he uses a hospital where another doctor does the inpatient treatment. (Such policies vary regionally.)

- Review hospital choices with your insurance company because it may contract with only certain hospitals.

- Expect a long day during admission and plan to spend as much time at the hospital as you can during your child's stay. Being present, even when your child says he doesn't want to see you, is critical for getting good care and for improving your child's wellbeing.

- Ask the hospital staff about the policies regarding seclusion and restraint and *prn meds* — meds administered to a child who's out of control. Find out what the protocol/staff training model is to deescalate crises and avoid seclusion, restraint, and involuntary medication. You may be able to get information on frequency of restraints on the unit, but that data is often kept out of public hands. Ensure that the staff understands that you expect to be informed if any of these measures are necessary. Create a big stink if you're not contacted. Make sure they know you're watching.

In some cases, children can't stabilize at home and may require long-term care at a residential facility. This process is beyond the scope of this chapter, but you can obtain additional information from your doctor, your child's school system, the American Academy of Child and Adolescent Psychiatry (www.aacap.org), or the Balanced Mind Parent Network (www.thebalancedmind.org).

Part VII
The Part of Tens

Visit www.dummies.com/extras/bipolardisorder for a list of ten questions to ask your psychiatrist.

In this part . . .

✔ Focus on practical steps you can take to help yourself or a loved one with bipolar disorder.

✔ Discover ten ways to manage bipolar mania and depression and fend off future episodes, nine of which have nothing to do with taking medication.

✔ Find ten ways to help your loved one with bipolar disorder. Consider them the do's and don'ts of helping your loved one.

Chapter 22

Ten Tips for Managing Bipolar

In This Chapter

▶ Seeing your doctor and therapist and sticking with the agreed-upon treatment plan

▶ Regulating your sleep and monitoring your moods

▶ Developing daily routines and practicing mindfulness

▶ Remaining alert for early warning signs and being prepared to act

*E*very illness has a better prognosis when the people who have it are informed, invested, and involved in their treatment plans. This is especially true for serious mood disorders, including bipolar. In general, the more involved you are in your recovery and mood maintenance, the better the outcome. This entire book is packed with strategies and skills for managing bipolar, but this chapter boils them down to the top ten.

Team Up with Your Doctor and Therapist

Managing bipolar disorder effectively is a team sport. To win, all team members must respect each other and communicate openly so that everyone remains well informed and can work together to achieve common goals. To team up with your doctor and therapist, put these suggestions into practice:

✔ **Make and keep regular appointments.** *Regular* may mean every six months when everything is going fine or once a week when warning signs appear.

✔ **Be open and honest.** Doctors and therapists are only as effective as the accuracy of the information you provide them. Be honest about how you feel, whether or not you've been following their advice and taking your medications, how much and what quality of sleep you've been getting, what your drug and alcohol use has been, and so on. Don't assume your doctor or therapist can read your mind.

✔ **Consult your doctor before making any medication or treatment changes.** If you feel the urge to reduce or stop taking a medication, contact your doctor before doing so. Your doctor may be able to suggest solutions for any concerns you have about your medications.

✔ **Ask questions.** When you know why your doctor or therapist recommends a certain medication, treatment, or therapy, you're more likely to stick with the treatment plan. Your doctor and therapist are usually the best sources of information, because they know your specific situation. If you obtain additional information on the Internet or through friends and acquaintances, ask your doctor or therapist for confirmation of its validity.

Visit www.dummies.com/extras/bipolardisorder for a list of ten questions you definitely want to ask your doctor or therapist.

✔ **Don't hesitate to speak up.** You're a consumer of the medical services and products you're using, so you have a right to tell your doctor and therapist what's working and what's not, what you like and dislike, what makes you feel better or worse, and which side effects are unacceptable. Be patient and remember that some medications may require some time before they take effect and certain side effects diminish. But at the same time, realize that sometimes you need to speak up to get the results you expect and deserve.

Take Medications as Prescribed

The single most important step for stopping and preventing a major mood episode is to take your medications as prescribed. Keep in mind that some medications require several weeks to establish a therapeutic level in the bloodstream and alleviate symptoms. If you're concerned about a medication's effectiveness or undesirable side effects, consult the prescribing doctor. When you start or change a medication, be sure to ask when (hours, days, weeks) you may notice any positive effects or side effects.

Don't stop taking your medication when you start feeling better. The meds are likely what's making you feel better. Plus, abruptly stopping an antimanic medication or antidepressant can trigger mania, depression, or seizures.

Regulate Your Sleep

Too much, not enough, or poor-quality sleep is both a symptom and a contributing factor to bipolar mania and depression. You should be getting eight to ten hours of quality sleep per day/night. Whether you sleep eight hours solid or divide it into smaller chunks is up to you, but try to establish a regular routine so you're sleeping at the same time(s) every day.

Sleep deprivation can really throw your moods out of whack. For tips on getting some restful sleep, visit www.sleepfoundation.org. If you're having trouble getting to sleep or staying asleep, consult your doctor. Don't try to tough it out, thinking you'll eventually get tired enough to fall asleep.

Develop Daily Routines

Daily routines relieve stress, level moods, and help regulate sleep. Start with the basics, such as a specific bedtime and wake time and then add in your mealtimes. Track your schedule over the course of a week to spot any severe variations and try to bring them more in sync with your scheduled times. Some variation, especially on weekends and over the holidays, is probably not a big deal, but work toward reducing any major deviations in your daily routine. See Chapter 12 for tips on establishing healthy daily routines.

Build Mindfulness and Other Self-Centering Skills

Mindfulness is a mental state of active attention to your present experience, which is conducive to deliberate thought and action. In mindfulness, you focus on your thoughts, feelings, and sensations in the here and now, trying not to attend to past regrets, future worries, and negative self-talk. In addition, studies show that mindfulness has positive effects on how the brain processes sensory information. Try these basic mindfulness exercises to help you center on the present:

- **Breathe.** Close your eyes and focus on your breathing. Don't try to change it; just notice the rising and falling of your breath.

- **Focus on sensations.** Pay attention to what you see, hear, smell, taste, and feel at this given moment in time.

- **Shift from *doing* mode to *being* mode.** Most of the time, people are in *doing* mode — setting goals and trying to achieve them. In *being* mode, you accept your current situation and the way you're feeling instead of fighting or analyzing it.

- **Observe thoughts without judging them.** As you have thoughts, avoid the temptation to view them as good or bad or to become emotionally involved in them. By observing your thoughts objectively, you reduce their ability to trigger emotional reactions.

✔ **Accept yourself.** Comparing yourself to someone else or measuring your situation based on someone else's often leads to feelings of inadequacy and resentment. Focusing on gratitude can be a useful mental exercise in building self-acceptance.

✔ **Spend time in nature.** Leave your cellphone and any other gadgets at home and enjoy a walk in the woods or at the local park. In the midst of nature, people tend to become more aware of what's around them at the given moment and less absorbed in inner thoughts about past and future events in their personal lives.

You can practice mindfulness regardless of what you're doing by taking a sensory inventory. What are you seeing, hearing, smelling, tasting, and touching right now? This sensory inventory allows you to focus on the here and now instead of getting lost in the usual mental chatter about past and future events and concerns.

Clearly Communicate Your Needs

Even if you have the most supportive network of family and friends on the planet, get into the habit of advocating for yourself. Tell people what you need from them, express your preferences, and if they don't seem to understand, say so. You can say something like, "I think maybe I wasn't clear. What I really need/want is . . . ."

Asking for what you want and need isn't selfish. Thinking that others should know what you want and need is ineffective. It places unrealistic expectations on others — namely, the expectation that they can read your mind. When you tell others clearly what you need, you're doing them a tremendous service.

Avoid Alcohol and Stimulants

When you and your doctor are working hard to stabilize your moods with medication and therapy, avoid consuming any substances that may throw off that delicate balance. These include the following:

✔ **Alcohol:** Moderate alcohol consumption when you are stable (one or two occasional drinks) is okay, but you're asking for trouble if you have more than that. Drinking alcohol can neutralize the beneficial effects of medications, trigger a wide range of damaging mood and behavior changes, and interact with some medications to cause liver damage, seizures, unpredictable shifts in mood, and other health problems. If you can't drink in moderation, don't drink.

> ✔ **Stimulants:** Caffeine, nicotine, energy drinks, and other stimulants can tip your mood balance, especially if they cause you to lose sleep.
>
> ✔ **Drugs and other substances:** Marijuana, cocaine, meth, ecstasy, and other drugs and medications that your doctor hasn't prescribed for you may also contribute to severe mood instability.

Talk with your doctor about any supplements or over-the-counter medications you use or are thinking of using. Some of these products can have powerful effects on sleep, mood, and energy.

Monitor Your Moods

Early intervention is essential in preventing major mood episodes, and mood monitoring is the best way to tell when intervention is necessary. Hang a calendar on your wall, keep one in your purse or on your computer, or download a mood-monitoring app on your phone. Rank your mood and other symptoms such as sleep and energy on a daily basis. If your mood drifts from the middle ranges to higher or lower levels for more than a few days, contact your doctor.

You may not always be in the best position to assess your own mood. Consider enlisting a trusted friend or family member whom you see regularly to help you keep track of your moods.

Identify Your Early Warning Signs

Bipolar disorder has telltale signs, but they differ depending on whether you're experiencing mania or depression, and they vary among individuals. By learning what your early warning signs are and becoming more sensitive to these signs, you're in a better position to seek help before the mania or depression spirals out of control.

Common external signs of escalating mania include the following:

> ✔ Missing an entire night's sleep and not feeling tired
>
> ✔ Rapid speech or racing thoughts; people tell you to slow down
>
> ✔ Being less sexually inhibited than usual
>
> ✔ Spending significantly more money than usual
>
> ✔ Engaging in reckless behaviors, including driving too fast
>
> ✔ Dressing flamboyantly or wearing makeup that's out of the ordinary

Common external signs of escalating depression include the following:

- Hearing more and more people ask you, "What's wrong?"
- Getting plenty of sleep and still feeling tired
- Eating a lot less or a lot more than normal
- Being more socially withdrawn
- Crying or being upset for no specific reason

Get Help at the First Sign of Trouble

No matter how carefully you care for yourself, monitor your moods, and remain alert for early warning signs, you can't always prevent symptoms. Through early intervention, however, you may be able to reduce the severity and duration of a mood episode by following these suggestions:

- Ask your doctor and therapist what to do if you begin to notice signs of depression or mania. Your doctor may be able to prescribe something for short-term relief.
- Contact your doctor or therapist as soon as you notice your early warning signs or a shift in mood that causes concern.
- Be prepared to call 911 or head to the emergency room if you feel that your moods are escalating out of control. (Don't drive yourself unless you're confident that doing so is safe.)

Chapter 23

Ten Ways to Help a Loved One with Bipolar Disorder

In This Chapter

▶ Educating yourself about bipolar disorder and medication options

▶ Sharpening your communication and problem-solving skills

▶ Teaming up with and encouraging your loved one and disengaging when necessary

▶ Keeping impeccable records and remaining vigilant for shifts in mood

▶ Avoiding bipolar disorder from taking over your life

When a loved one experiences a major mood episode, you may be at a loss for what to do. In this chapter, we suggest ten practical ways to help your loved one.

Ultimately, the task of managing bipolar disorder is the responsibility of the person who has it, except for periods during which the person is incapacitated by a severe mood episode. Don't let help turn into enabling. Your job is to assist most of the time and to take charge only when necessary.

Find Out More about Bipolar Disorder

By reading this book, you're already doing the single most important and valuable thing to help your loved one with bipolar disorder — you're taking time to figure it out. Knowledge is power and provides the basis for developing the empathy necessary to grasp the challenges that your loved one faces.

Without making bipolar disorder the sole focus of your life, continue to pursue additional information and insight about bipolar disorder. Consider the following resources:

- ✔ Websites and blogs, including `www.nami.org`, `www.dbsalliance.org`, and `http://psychcentral.com` (and our own blog at `blogs.psychcentral.com/bipolar`).

- ✔ Books, including bipolar memoirs, several of which have been written by those who contributed bipolar bios for this book. (We also host `bipolar-story.com`, where you can read stories that people have shared, comment on stories, and post your own story of living with bipolar disorder.)

- ✔ Movies, documentaries, and theater productions about bipolar disorder, including *Next to Normal* and *Silver Linings Playbook*.

- ✔ *BP* magazine (`www.bphope.com`).

Search Google News (`news.google.com`) for "bipolar disorder," scroll to the bottom of the search results, click Create alert, and follow the onscreen instructions to create a news alert. Google emails you a notification whenever news about bipolar disorder is published on the web.

Treat Your Loved One with Respect

Whenever your loved one becomes ill, you launch into caregiver mode, but when you're caring for an adult, treat the person as an adult. As caregivers, people often slide into parent-child mode, treating the ill relative as a dependent. The caregiver may talk down to the ill relative, establish rules and punishments for noncompliance, or talk about the person in her presence as though she's not even in the room.

Be careful not to *infantilize* your loved one, treating the person as a child. Treat your loved one as an equal, deserving of your respect.

Hone Your Communication Skills

Effective communication not only enables you to express yourself clearly, but also makes others more receptive to what you have to say. Here are a few communication techniques, strategies, and tactics that may help:

- ✔ **Listen.** Really listen to what your loved one tells you. If you can demonstrate that you heard and understood your loved one, she'll be more inclined to listen to you. Ask questions if you're unclear about what your loved one has said.

- ✔ **Verify that you understand.** Repeat back in your own words what you heard to demonstrate that your understanding is correct.

- ✔ **Show *empathy*.** Genuinely try to put yourself in your loved one's shoes and validate his feelings. For example, you may say something like, "I understand that you're feeling so sad (or whatever emotion he's expressing) right now, and I want to understand more." This gives you a good place to start.

- ✔ **Speak softly.** Loud talking intensifies the emotion. Set the tone of the conversation by example.

- ✔ **Speak in "I" statements.** Use "I" statements to express how you feel and what you think, so your loved one will be less defensive and less able to argue against whatever you have to say.

- ✔ **Be specific and focused.** Stick to one issue or problem to keep the conversation on track. Stay in the present; don't dredge up past issues.

- ✔ **Avoid blame, criticism, and demands.** Blame, criticism, and demands undermine the spirit of cooperation required to make progress.

Become a Problem Solver

Whenever disagreements arise, approach the issue as a problem to be solved instead of an argument to be won. Think less in terms of *issues* and more in terms of *interests* or *needs*. Both you and your loved one have needs that you're seeking to meet. The right solution ensures that everyone's needs are met and all concerns are addressed.

Problem-solving rarely, if ever, needs to be a zero-sum endeavor in which one side has to lose something in order for the other side to gain something. Effective problem-solving involves teamwork and results in a win-win outcome, often *creating* value, so neither side must compromise.

Disengage When Tensions Rise

When attacked, most people tend to respond in kind, but keep in mind that an emotional reaction is often what bipolar disorder craves. It thrives on emotional energy. Disengage when tensions rise to prevent a situation from boiling over.

Disengagement isn't a solution. Take a timeout with the understanding that you'll address the cause of the conflict when you've both had time to cool down and approach the issue or situation more rationally.

Keep Detailed Records

To manage bipolar disorder effectively, you need to be able to make well-informed decisions about medications and therapies. Although doctors and therapists keep detailed records, you may not have access to those records, and information can get lost whenever you change doctors or therapists. Hence, someone on the treatment team should keep a log of all medications and therapies that have been tried, side effects, and so on, to avoid repeated trials of treatments that didn't work or caused more problems.

Establish a system for collecting and storing records. If you're tech savvy, you may keep a record on your smartphone and back it up regularly to a computer. If you're old school, you can keep a notebook, folder, or binder and log noteworthy information about each visit to a doctor or therapist, medication changes, therapy trials, and so forth.

Partner with Your Loved One

Partnering with your loved one means working together to manage bipolar. It requires effective communication and problem solving along with cooperation as your loved one works toward making lifestyle changes that promote mood stability. It means not blaming your loved one for the challenges brought on by the illness, but working together to target the actual culprit — bipolar disorder.

Depending on your relationship with your loved one, an effective partnership may call on you to make some lifestyle changes, as well, such as establishing predictable routines, going to bed earlier, joining your loved one on walks, planning healthier meals together, and (when appropriate) accompanying your loved one to doctor visits and therapy sessions.

Brush Up on Medications

After the bipolar diagnosis is made, finding and managing effective medical treatment becomes a primary goal. You and your loved one will learn an entirely new vocabulary and digest all kinds of new information and instructions. It can feel overwhelming. Many sources outside of your loved one's treatment team will also provide information and opinions about medications (with or without being invited to do so). Some ways you can be helpful regarding medications include

- **Seek out reliable and accurate information about medications.** Some of the websites presented in the earlier section "Find Out More about Bipolar Disorder" may help. You can also find information at sites such as www.mayoclinic.org/drugs-supplements. Avoid sites or pages that are dominated by advertisements for medications. Share what you discover with your loved one and encourage her to do her own research.

- **Take opinions and information from family and friends with a grain of salt.** Family members or friends will offer their experiences with and feelings about medications. These stories can be helpful, terrifying, or somewhere in between. Every person responds differently to medications. Although an immediate family member's response to a certain medicine may be important information for your loved one's doctor, anyone else's experience with a particular medication doesn't predict anything about how your loved one will feel on it.

- **Play a role in doctor visits, if allowed.** If your loved one allows you to come to the doctor's appointment with her, listen carefully (take notes even) and ask questions if you need more information. If you're unable to come, help your loved one prepare for the appointment and encourage her to report side effects and to ask the doctor any questions she has.

- **Keep tabs on medication effectiveness and side effects.** Using empathy and other communication skills described earlier in this chapter, ask your loved one about her experiences on the medications and help her keep track of the positive and negative effects she's noticing. Encourage her to contact her prescriber if she's not feeling well.

- **Team up with your loved one for medication reminders, if allowed.** If your loved one is agreeable, help her set up ways to remember to take her medicine — and encourage her to let you know if she's having trouble with it. Don't offer judgments or criticism. If your loved asks you to remind her, create a system that doesn't feel like nagging. You can find apps to set alarms for medicine times, and, if she wants, your loved one can set you up as a medication buddy or friend who will also be reminded if she hasn't taken her medication.

Flex Your Expectations

Bipolar disorder often wreaks havoc on the lives of those it touches, but it's not a death sentence. You may find yourself grieving over the losses or being angry over the injustices suffered at the hands of the illness. If you expect your life to return to what it was before bipolar disorder entered the scene, you're likely to be disappointed. The truth is that your reality has changed.

Grieving the loss is normal, but the sooner you can begin to accept the new normal, the sooner you can begin to adjust your course and explore new paths and opportunities. Be open to new ways of thinking and living, so you can adjust your ideals, goals, and lifestyle to match your new reality.

Enjoy Your Life

People who have bipolar disorder tend to lug around a lot of guilt for becoming a burden to their loved ones. If you mope around feeling sorry for yourself, you reinforce your loved one's guilt and shame, which isn't helpful. Grieving is natural and acceptable. Throwing yourself a pity party every now and again is okay; preferably don't do it around your loved one. Enjoy your life, both for your own sake and for the sake of your loved one. Strive to build healthy, pleasant activities into your life and get enough sleep and eat healthfully. You can't help anyone else if you're burnt out. As they say at the start of a flight, you have to put on your own oxygen mask before taking care of anyone else.

Index

Numerics

5-HTP, 163
911 call, 305, 312, 319, 360

• *A* •

AACAP (American Academy of Child and Adolescent Psychiatry), 77, 340, 352
Abilify, 115, 135, 152
ABPN (American Board of Psychiatry and Neurology), 80
acceptance of the diagnosis, 143
accompanying features, 19–20
acquired immune deficiency syndrome (AIDS), 65, 184
acting "as if," 193
acutane, 67
acute bipolar depression, 52
acute mania, 52
acute symptoms, 51
ADA (Americans with Disabilities Act), 270, 271, 272, 349
Adderall, 330
ADHD. *See* attention deficit hyperactivity disorder (ADHD)
advanced directive, 251–252
advanced statement, 251–252
aftershock, 262–263
agitated behavior, 318–319, 329
agranulocytosis, 117
AIDS, 65, 184
akathisia, 114–116, 119, 152
alcohol
  avoidance with bipolar disorder, 358
  bipolar disorder accompanied by abuse, 7, 23–24, 34
  effect on mood, 66
  interactions with medication, 148, 218
  teen use, 334–335, 339

Alidina, Shamash (author), 199
all-natural remedies, 219
allopurinol, 139
alothisia, 114
alprazolam (Xanax), 124, 148
Alzheimer's, 65, 161, 181
Ambien, 53, 126
American Academy of Child and Adolescent Psychiatry (AACAP), 77, 340, 352
American Board of Psychiatry and Neurology (ABPN), 80
American Psychiatric Association (APA), 8, 77, 259
Americans with Disabilities Act (ADA), 270, 271, 272, 349
amitriptyline (Elavil), 125, 177
amphetamines, 67, 218, 330
amygdala, 40, 42
androgen, 73
angiotensin-converting enzyme inhibitors, 181
anitdepressant monotherapy, 52
anterior cingulate cortex, 38, 40
anticonvulsants, 112–114, 134, 182
antidepressants
  ADHD and anxiety disorder treatment, 133
  avoiding with DMDD, 324
  bipolar treatment, 51, 52, 74, 84, 118, 135, 137, 172
  depression treatment, 182, 185
  dosage and benefits, 119, 120, 122–123
  mechanism of action, 45
  side effects/risks, 8, 21–22, 37, 52, 84, 119, 120, 122–123, 128, 145, 149, 153, 332, 346, 356
  sleep aid, 125
  unipolar depression treatment, 134
  use during pregnancy, 177

antidepressants *(continued)*
  use for disruptive mood
    dysregulation, 336
  use for menopause, 180
  use for PMS, 168
  use in diagnosis, 333, 340
antihistamines, 67
antimanic agents, 52, 330
antioxidants, 164, 213
antipsychotics
  bipolar treatment, 52, 134
  dosage and benefits, 182
  drug interactions, 131
  side effects/risks, 145, 153–155,
    172, 176, 177
  types, dosage, benefits, 114–117, 151–152
antiseizure medications, 50
antisocial disorder, 24
anxiety, 19, 21, 83, 338
anxiety disorders
  in children, 336–337
  comorbidity with bipolar disorder, 21,
    30, 133, 166
  medication, 119, 120, 123, 125
  ruling out, 87
  substance abuse associated with, 85
  symptoms, 22, 26, 31, 337
  treatment, 23, 343
  types of, 23
anxiolytics, 123
APA (American Psychiatric Association),
  8, 77, 259
apologizing, 225, 268
aripiprazole (Abilify), 115, 135, 152
arrests, 323–326
ASD (autism spectrum disorder),
  22, 30, 338
asenapine (Saphris), 52, 115
assumptions, 2
Ativan, 53, 124
attention deficit hyperactivity
    disorder (ADHD)
  bipolar disorder compared to,
    329, 330–331
  comorbidity with bipolar disorder,
    24, 30

comorbidity with disruptive mood
    dysregulation, 336
  ruling out, 87
  symptoms, 21
  treatment, 121, 133, 198, 343
atypical antipsychotics, 114–117,
    154, 177, 182
atypical features, 20
atypical neuroleptics, 114
autism spectrum disorder (ASD),
    22, 30, 338
autoimmune diseases, 65
axon, 40, 41

• *B* •

Balanced Mind Parent Network, 341, 352
*Balancing the Beast: A Bright View of
    Schizoaffective Disorder–Bipolar or
    Manic-Depressive Type*, 199
bariatric surgery, 154
B-complex vitamins, 161–162
Beat, Bipolar, 101
Beck Depression Inventory, 81
Behrman, Andy (bipolar patient), 27
Belsomra, 126
Benadryl, 125
benzodiazepines, 123–124, 125, 126, 176
benzos. *See* benzodiazepines
Bipolar Bio icon, 3
bipolar depression, 134–135
bipolar disorder
  brain and body science of, 29–45
  cause, 29–45
  in children and teens, 7, 25–26, 328–344
  comorbidity, 22–25
  crises. *see* crisis situation
  definition of, 7
  diagnosis. *see* diagnosis
  distinguishing from similar
    conditions, 20–22
  lifestyle adjustments, 54–55, 152, 154, 211,
    343, 350–351
  medication. *see* medication
  in older adults, 180–183
  poles of, 9–13

prognosis, 47–48

psychiatric evaluation and treatment plan. *see* psychiatric evaluation and treatment plan

reactive and proactive response, 48–50

ruling out other health issues, 63–74

specifiers, 17–20

support. *see* family support; friends; support group

treatment. *see* treatment

types of, 13–16

in women, 172–179

bipolar I, 7, 14, 135, 329

bipolar II, 7, 14, 30, 135, 172

bipolar mood app, 188, 265, 359

Bipolar Scotland, 105

Bipolar UK, 105

birth control, 175

blame, 227–228, 363

blogs, 101

blood tests, 72

body language, 224

borderline personality disorder (BPD), 21–22, 24, 88, 133

boundaries, 58

BP magazine, 362

BPD (borderline personality disorder), 21–22, 24, 88, 133

brain

in bipolar disorder, 41–44

care of, 211

structures and function, 37–41

brain injury, 22

brain stem, 37, 38, 39

brain tumors, 22

Branch, Rhena

Cognitive Behavior Therapy For Dummies, 194

breakthrough episodes, 245

breathing exercise, 199

Brintellix, 122

Bristol Mind, 252

bupropion (Wellbutrin, Zyban), 121, 123, 177

Buspar, 124–125

buspirone (Buspar), 124–125

Bussell, Gaynor

PCOS For Dummies, 176

● **C** ●

caffeine, 67, 208, 218

CAM (complementary and alternative medicine), 159

Canadian Mental Health Association (CMHA), 283

carbamazepine (Tegretol, Carbatrol, Epitol, Equetro)

bipolar treatment, 112

dosage and benefits, 113

side effects/risks, 175, 176, 177, 182

carbohydrates, 211–212

career counseling, 57, 278

caregiver. *See also* family support

dealing with crisis situations, 307–309, 311–326

helping bipolar patients, 361–366

CAT scan, 72

catatonia, 20

CBT (cognitive behavioral therapy), 56, 192–193, 198

CDC (Centers for Disease Control and Prevention), 172

celecoxib (Celebrex), 144

Celexa, 119

cell body, 40, 41

cellular signaling, 110

Centers for Disease Control and Prevention (CDC), 172

cerebellum, 37, 38, 39, 42

cerebral hemisphere, 37, 38, 39

cerebrospinal fluid, 40

challenging, 193

Champagne, Natalie Jeanne (bipolar patient), 131

change from baseline, 329, 331

Cheat Sheet, 3

chemical restraint, 257

chief complaint, 81, 82

child and adolescent psychiatrist, 340–341

children
  diagnosing bipolar in, 7, 25–26, 329–339
  diagnostic difficulties, 328–329
  education and protection of, 206–207
  professional evaluation of, 339–342
  treatment for bipolar disorder, 342–344
Children's Health Insurance Program
    (CHIP), 288
chlorpromazine (Thorazine), 114
chocolate, 213
cholesterol, 214–215
cholinergic system, 140
chronic emotional dysregulation, 328–329
chronic traumatic
    encephalopathy (CTE), 66
church, 105
Churchill, Winston (English prime
    minister), 13
Cibalith-S, 111, 112
circadian rhythm, 35, 39, 44
circuitry of brain, 42
circuits, 193
circuits, stress, 43–44
CIT (crisis intervention team), 305
citalopram (Celexa), 119
clean bill of health, 73–74
clonazepam (Klonopin), 124
clozaoine (Clozaril), 117
club drug, 67
clueless helper, 102
CMHA (Canadian Mental Health
    Association), 283
CMHC (community mental health
    center), 313
COBRA, 287
cocaine, 66, 359
coenzyme Q10, 163
Cognitive Behavior Therapy For Dummies
    (Willson and Branch), 194
cognitive behavioral therapy (CBT), 56,
    192–193, 198
cognitive skill problem, 25
college, 278
communication
  adding mood symptoms, 225–226
  apologizing, 225

body language, posture, and position,
    224
  clear, honest, and accurate
    conversations, 223
  disengaging from unproductive
    conflicts, 230–231
  within the family, 305–306, 315
  ground rules for, 222–223
  "I" statements, 228–229
  place and time, 221–222
  positive tone, 224
  self-advocation, 358
  within support group, 102–103
  with teachers, 350
  tiff-makers, 226–228
  validating others feelings, 229–230
communication skills, 58, 362–363
community mental health center
    (CMHC), 313
comorbidity, 22–25, 133, 172, 331
complementary and alternative medicine
    (CAM), 159
compliance, 142, 344, 356
compulsive behaviors, 83
conflict reduction, 203, 363–364
conflict resolution. *See* problem-
    solving skills
continuity of care, 59
contraindications, 182
controlling behavior, 337
cortex, 40
cortico-limbic theory, 42–43
corticosteroids, 67
cortisol, 43–44, 73
cough suppressants, 219
course of illness, 19
court order, 306–307
court-ordered commitment, 307
Crisis Information Sheet, 247–248
crisis intervention team (CIT), 305
crisis situation
  preparation, 243–251, 313
  response, 305, 311–313, 317–326
criticism, 203, 204, 226, 300, 348, 363
CTE (chronic traumatic
    encephalopathy), 66

cultural differences, 183–184
current or most recent episode, 17
Cushing's syndrome, 65, 73
cyclothymic disorder, 14, 30
Cymbalta, 120

• *D* •

daily routines, 357
Dalmane, 126
DBS (deep brain stimulation), 53, 167, 170
DBSA. *See* Depression and Bipolar Support Alliance (DBSA)
decongestant, 67, 219
deep brain stimulation (DBS), 53, 167, 170
degenerative brain diseases, 65
delusional disorder, 13
demanding behavior, 337
demands, 227, 363
dementia, 181
dendrite, 40, 41
denial, 142–143
Depakote/Depakene. *See* valproate (Depakote, Depakene)
depersonalization of hurtful deeds, 299
depression, 12, 172, 244. *See also* mood episodes; unipolar depression
Depression and Bipolar Support Alliance (DBSA)
  information resource, 98, 252
  pediatric psychiatrists resource, 340
  support group, 100, 105
  treatment facility and professionals list, 78, 306
  wellness tracker, 188
depression-related questions, 82
depressive episode, 118, 134–135. *See also* mood episodes
desensitization, 193
desipramine (Norpramin), 177
desvenlafaxine (Pristiq), 120
desyrel (Trazodone), 122, 125, 177
dextroamphetamine, 330
dextromethorphan, 219
DHA (docosahexaenoic acid), 161

diagnosis
  of children and teens, 7, 25–26, 329–339
  definition, 8
  disclosure of, 272–274
  parental understanding, 344–346
  psychiatric evaluation and treatment plan, 29, 75–92, 94–95
  ruling out other health issues, 20–22, 63–74
diagnosis by prescription, 340
Diagnostic and Statistical Manual of Mental Disorders (DSM)
  bipolar criteria, 17–18
  disruptive mood dysregulation disorder criteria, 335
  oppositional defiance disorder criteria, 332
  use in diagnosis of bipolar disorder, 7, 8, 15
dialectical behavioral therapy (DBT), 57, 194, 198
diazepam (Valium), 124, 148
diet, 54, 154, 210–215, 350
diet pills, 218, 219
differential diagnosis, 87–88
diphenhydramine (Benadryl), 125
disability benefits, filing for, 284–287
disappearances, 322–323
disassociation of person from disorder, 298–299
disruptive mood dysregulation disorder (DMDD), 335–336
distinct period, 9
distractability, 329
divalproex sodium (Depakote, Depakene), 113
DMDD (disruptive mood dysregulation disorder), 335–336
docosahexaenoic acid (DHA), 161
doctor. *See also* psychiatrist; therapist and doctor
  caregiver's role at visits, 365
  changing, 104
  communication with, 67–71, 306, 311–313, 355–356
  finding one for children, 340–341

doctor *(continued)*
  preparation for mood episodes,
      243–244, 360
  times to contact, 360
documentation of essential
      information, 247–248
dopamine, 43
doxepin (Silenor), 125
drowsiness, 152–153
drug-induced mania, 10
drugs, legal and illegal, 85, 218, 339, 359
  alcohol. *see* alcohol
  medication. *see* medication
  substance use/abuse. *see* substance use
      disorder; substance use/abuse
*DSM-5. See Diagnostic and Statistical
      Manual of Mental Disorders* (DSM)
duloxetine (Cymbalta), 120
Dummies website
  mood chart, 188, 265, 342
  questions to ask psychiatrist, 79, 356
  treatment contract, 304
durable power of attorney, 251
Durand, Matthew (bipolar patient), 346

• *E* •

ecstasy (NMDA), 67, 359
ECT. *See* electroconvulsive therapy (ECT)
EE (expressed emotion), 203
EEG (electroencephalogram), 72
Effexor, 120
eicosapentaenoic acid (EPA), 161
Elavil, 177
electroconvulsive therapy (ECT)
  alternative to medications, 53, 137, 152
  effectiveness, 167–169
  for older adults, 182, 183
  during pregnancy, 179
Elliott, Charles H.
  *Seasonal Affective Disorder For
      Dummies,* 166
emergency cash-assistance benefit, 293
emergency plan, 305, 313
emotional reactions to
      medications, 142–149

empathy toward patient, 300–301, 363
encephalitis, 22
endocrinologist, 73
energy shifts, 334
environmental effect, 29
enzyme, 138–139
EPA (eicosapentaenoic acid), 161
ephedra, 67, 219
ephedrine, 67
epigenetics, 33–34
Epitol, 112, 113, 175, 176, 177, 182
Equetro, 112, 113, 175, 176, 177, 182
escitalopram (Lexapro), 119
Eskalith, 111, 112
estrogen, 73, 173
eszopiclone (Lunesta), 126
euphoria, 331
exercise, 54, 209, 211, 217–218, 264
expectations
  for children and teens, 351
  establishing to eliminate conflict, 204–206
  for life with bipolar loved one,
      298, 365–366
  for medications, 129–130, 143–144
expressed emotion (EE), 203

• *F* •

family history, 84–85, 333, 341
family support
  bipolar patient's responsibilities, 98–100
  communication skills, 58, 102–103,
      362–363
  consulting patient's doctor, 311–313
  dealing with crisis situations, 59, 305
  deciding where to go, 316–317
  determining involvement, 101–102,
      267–268, 313–316
  determining when to intervene,
      303–304, 315–316
  disengaging from unproductive
      conflicts, 363–364
  emergency plan, 313
  empathy toward patient, 300–301
  establishing boundaries, 58
  expressing concerns, 305–306

in financial crisis, 291–292
for healthy routines, 209
helping someone refusing help, 304–307
mindset for, 297–298
partnering with loved ones, 364
problem-solving skills, 58, 363
psychoeducation, 58, 100–101,
    268, 361–362
recognizing limitations, 301–302
record keeping, 364
responding in crisis, 317–326
self-care, 58, 307–309
teamwork, 104
treating patients with respect, 362
treatment contract, 304
understanding and monitoring
    medication, 364–365
watching for warning signs, 244, 302–304
who to call in crisis, 316
family therapy, 200, 265
Family-to-Family, 101
FAPE (free appropriate public
    education), 348
fatigue, 152–153
fats, 214–215
FDA (Food and Drug Administration),
    109, 161, 214
fibromyalgia, 65
fight-or-flight response, 336–337
financial setbacks, 281–293
financial-resource guidance, 57
first-degree family members, 30
first-generation antipsychotics, 152
first-generation neuroleptics, 114
fish oil, 53, 160
fluoxetine (Prozac), 52, 119, 145
flurazepam (Dalmane), 126
fluvoxamine (Luvox), 119, 177
fMRI (functional resonnance
    imaging), 82
folic acid, 53, 162
Food and Drug Administration (FDA),
    109, 161, 214
forced hospitalization, 307
free appropriate public education
    (FAPE), 348

friends, 98–104, 267–268, 291–292, 309
fruits, 212–213
full remission, 19
functional impairment, 10
functional magnetic resonance imaging
    (fMRI), 82

• *G* •

GABA (gamma-aminobutyric acid),
    43, 123, 163
gabapentin (Neurontin), 112, 124, 125
Gabitril, 114
gamma-aminobutyric acid (GABA),
    43, 123, 163
general questions on thought processes
    and processes, 83
generalized anxiety disorder, 23, 133
genetic factors, 29, 30–34, 36, 45, 136,
    338
genetic research, 82
genome, 33
Geodon, 116
Getting a Job After 50 For Dummies
    (Hannon), 279
glial cell, 40
Glucophage, 154
glutamate, 43, 137, 163
glutathione, 163
Google News, 362
gout, 139
government safety net programs, 293
grandiosity, 331
gravely disabled, 307
gray matter, 40
grieving, 348, 366
grieving process, 12, 147, 305, 307–308

• *H* •

Haldol, 114, 117
hallucinogen, 67
haloperidol (Haldol), 114, 117
Hannon, Kerry
    Getting a Job After 50 For Dummies, 279

Haynes, Janine Crowley
  electroconvulsive therapy, 168
  lifestyle adjustments, 211
  My Kind of Crazy, 168, 211
health insurance options, 287–288
Health Insurance Portability and
    Accountability Act (HIPAA), 248, 312
healthy routines, 56, 207–210, 211,
    264, 356–357
heavy, the, 102
hemoglobin A1C, 153
hepatitis, 65
herbs, 66–67, 164, 219
heritability, 30
Hines, Kevin (mental health advocate), 36
HIPAA (Health Insurance Portability
    and Accountability Act) Security
    Rule, 248, 312
hippocampus, 38, 39, 42
history, 67, 71, 82, 83–85
histrionic disorder, 24
HIV (human immunodeficiency
    virus), 65, 184
home environment, 201–207
honesty, 103
hormonal changes, 64, 172–174
hormone imbalance, 22, 35, 64
hormone replacement therapy (HRT), 180
hormone tests, 72–73
hospitalization
  of children and teens, 343, 352
  coping, 255–261
  crisis management, 49, 134, 307, 343, 352
  as criteria for bipolar diagnosis, 9, 10
  doctors' communication, 104
  facility selection, 245–246
  prevention, 56, 59
  release from, 104, 262–268
housing support program, 293
HRT (hormone replacement therapy), 180
human immunodeficiency virus
    (HIV), 65, 184
Hyman, I. (author)
  *Self-Disclosure and Its Impact on
    Individuals Who Receive Mental Health
    Services*, 273

hyperactivity/high energy, 329, 331
hypercortisolism, 65
hypericum, 164
hypersexual behavior, 321–322
hyperthymic personality, 333
hyperthyroidism, 64, 72
hypomania, 87, 244
hypomania episode without major
    depression or manic episodes, 16
hypomanic episode, 10–11, 12
hypothalamus, 38, 39
hypothyroidism, 64, 72

• I •

"I" statements, 228–229, 363
ibuprofen, 219
ICD (*International Classification of
    Diseases*), 8
icons, 3
IDEA (Individuals with Disabilities in
    Education Act), 348, 349
IEP (individual education plan), 349
iloperidone (Fanapt), 114
I'm Not Crazy Just Bipolar (Williamson), 149
imipramine (Tofranil), 177
impaired social interaction, 338
impulsivity, 330, 331
indication, 117
individual education plan (IEP), 349
Individuals with Disabilities in Education
    Act (IDEA), 348, 349
infection, 35, 65
inflammation, 44
information authorization release,
    249–250, 312
inositol, 164
insanity defense, 325
insight, 142
insomnia, 208
instructive directive, 251–252
insulin, 73
intensive outpatient therapy (IOT), 49, 245
intercellular communication, 45
*International Classification of
    Diseases* (ICD), 8

internist, 76

interpersonal and social rhythm therapy (IPSRT), 57, 195–198

intracellular signaling, 40–41, 43, 45

intravenous injections, 140

Invega, 114

IOT (intensive outpatient therapy), 49, 245

IPSRT (interpersonal and social rhythm therapy), 57, 195–198

iron deficiency, 66

irritability, 329, 337

• J •

jail diversion program, 325

Johnson, Linea (author)
  family support, 103
  Perfect Chaos, 103, 308
  supporting loved one, 308

journaling, 193

judgment, 227, 348

• K •

Kabat-Zinn, Jon (researcher), 198

kava, 164, 219

Keppra, 114

ketamine (Special K), 67, 137–138

kindling hypothesis, 52

Klonopin, 124

Kraynak, Cecie (teacher and author)
  recovery from mood episode, 267, 271
  Spanish Grammar For Dummies, 271

Krystal, Phyllis (meditation director), 199

• L •

label, 16

lack of insight, 304–305

lamotrigine (Lamictal)
  bipolar treatment, 52, 112, 182
  dosage and benefits, 113
  drug interactions, 131, 175
  side effects/risks, 113, 135, 177, 182

larger-than-life temperament, 333

Latuda, 52, 115

lead toxicity, 339

lesbian, gay, bisexual, or transgender (LGBT) patients, 184

levetiracetam (Keppra), 114

Lexapro, 119

LGBT (lesbian, gay, bisexual, or transgender) patients, 184

lifestyle adjustments
  avoiding bad stuff, 218–219
  diet, 54, 152, 154, 210–215, 343, 350
  exercise, 54, 152, 154, 209, 211, 217–228, 264
  healthy home environment, 201–207, 343, 350
  healthy relationships, 55, 215–217
  healthy routines, 56, 207–210, 211, 264, 356–357

life-threatening emergencies, 176

light therapy, 53, 166–167

limbic system, 40

limitations, 301–302

Lincoln, Abraham (president), 13

Linehan, Marsha (therapy developer), 194

Lithane, 111

lithium
  acute mania treatment, 52
  alcohol use with, 133, 218
  bipolar treatment, 25, 52, 89, 110–112, 128, 129, 134, 135
  cost effectiveness, 165
  dosage and benefits, 111
  drug interactions, 131, 219
  effect on thyroid tests, 72
  effective time period, 143
  exercise risks, 218
  mechanism of action, 45, 139, 162, 164
  side effects/risks, 111, 145, 153, 176, 181, 182, 346
  unconventional treatment interactions, 165
  use during pregnancy, 177–179

lithium carbonate (Eskalith, Cibalith-S), 111, 112

lithium citrate (Lithane, Lithonate, Lithotabs, Lithobid), 111

lithium orotate, 112
Lithobid, 111
Lithonate, 111
Lithotabs, 111
local financial support, 283
local mental health center, 306
local support groups, 104–106, 306
lorazepam (Ativan), 53, 124
low- of no-cost healthcare
    resources, 288–291
LSD, 67
Lunesta, 126
lupus, 65
lurasidone (Latuda), 52, 115
Luvox, 119, 177
Lyrica, 124, 125

• *M* •

magnesium, 162
maintenance treatment, 52, 135, 141, 144
major depression, 87
major depression with hypomania failing
    criteria for hypomanic episode, 15–16
major depression with short-duration
    hyponmanic episodes, 15
major depressive episode, 11–12
management, 355–360
mania, 87
mania-related questions, 83
manic episode, 9, 12, 134, 244. *See also*
    mood episodes
MAOIs (monoamine oxidase
    inhibitors), 121, 177
marijuana, 66, 218, 359
MBSR (mindfulness-based stress
    reduction), 198–199
mechanism of action of medications, 45
mediation, 199
medical conditions, 10, 15, 88
medical history, 83–84
medical power of attorney, 250–252
medical treatment, 10. *See also*
    medication; therapy
Medicare/Medicaid, 287–288
medication

anticonvulsants, 112–114, 134
antidepressants, 134, 135
antipsychotics, 114–117, 134
anxiolytic sand sleep agents, 123–127
for children and teens, 342, 343–344
for comorbid conditions, 133
compliance, 356
contribution to symptoms, 245
cost of, 148
cost-benefit analysis, 149–150
ethnicity and metabolism of, 184
expectations, 129–130, 143–144
future of, 137–140
goal of, 53
information concerning, 365
interactions, 128
for life-threatening emergencies, 176–177
list for doctor, 71
lithium. *see* lithium
mechanism of action in bipolar
    disorder, 45
mixing, 130–133
mood-boosting antidepressants,
    66–67, 118–123
objections to taking, 142–148
off label, 109
for older adults, 181–183
over-the-counter medications, 219, 359
practicing safety, 131
pregnancy and, 176–177
prophylactics, 51–53
psychotropics, 127–133
selection, 128–129, 131
side effects, 130–155. *see also specific
    medication*
switching, reducing, and stopping,
    151–152, 154, 156–157, 245, 256–257
taking, 55, 145–146
treating and preventing episodes,
    49, 134–137
medication-induced bipolar
    disorder, 15, 172
melancholic features, 19–20
melatonin, 67, 127, 164
memantine (Namenda), 138
memingitis, 22

memory problem, 25, 133, 155
menarche, 173
menopause, 174, 180
menses/menstruation, 173
Mental Health America, 105
mental health centers, 105
mental health facility, 306
mental health history, 83
Mental Health Humor blog, 240
metformin (Glucophage), 154
methylphenidate (Ritalin), 330, 340
mild depression, 12
MIND, 105
mindfulness, 57, 198, 357–358
Mindfulness For Dummies (Alidina), 199
mindfulness-based stress reduction
    (MBSR), 198–199
minerals, 162–163, 213
Mini Mental Status Examination
    (MMSE), 181
mirtazapine (Remeron), 122, 125, 177
missing persons report, 322–323
mixed episodes, 172
mixed features, 19
MMSE (Mini Mental Status
    Examination), 181
Moban, 117
molindone (Moban), 117
monitoring moods, 56, 187–188, 244, 245
monoamine oxidase inhibitors. *See* MAOIs
    (monoamine oxidase inhibitors)
monotherapy, 52, 135
mood chart, 188, 265, 315, 341–342, 359
mood episodes
  family's role in dealing with,
      303–307, 311–313
  getting help early, 360
  preparation for, 243–251, 313
  prevention, 245
  warning signs, 244, 302–303, 315, 359–360
mood-congruent psychotic features, 20
mood-incongruent psychotic features, 20
moodiness, 12
mood-management team, 93–106, 261,
    265, 355–356
mood-monitoring app, 188, 265, 359

MRI, 72, 82
muscarinic receptor, 140
mushroom, 67
My Kind of Crazy: Living in a Bipolar World
    (Haynes), 168, 211
myelin sheath, 40

• *N* •

NAC (n-acetyl cysteine), 53, 138, 164
n-acetyl cysteine (NAC), 53, 138, 164
nagger, 102, 204
Namenda, 138
NAMI. *See* National Alliance on Mental
    Illness (NAMI)
naproxen, 219
narcissistic personality disorder, 24, 133
Narcotics Anonymous, 218
Nardil, 177
National Alliance on Mental Illness (NAMI)
  contact information, 105
  Family-to-Family course, 101
  information resources, 98
  Legal Center, 323
  resource for pediatric psychiatrists, 340
  service provider lists, 306
  support groups, 105, 340
  website, 252, 362
National Health Service (NHS), 283
National Institute of Mental Health
    (NIMH), 98
Nature Genetics journal, 33
Navane, 117
n-desmethyl aspartate (NDMA), 137
nefazodone (Serzone), 122, 177
neurologist, 79
neurons, 40–41, 118
Neurontin, 112, 124, 125
neuropeptides, 41
neuroplasticity, 44
neuroprotective factors, 45, 110
neuropsychological tests, 42, 82
neurostimulation, 169–170
neurotransmitter, 41, 43, 45
Next to Normal These are two different films.
    (film), 362

NHS (National Health Service), 283
nicotine, 218
NIMH. *See* National Institute of Mental Health (NIMH)
NMDA (ecstasy), 67, 359
NoDoz, 67
nondurable power of attorney, 251
nongenetic factors, 29, 34–36
nonsteroidal anti-inflammatory medications (NSAIDs), 111, 181
norepinephrine, 43
normalcy, 146–147
Norpramin, 120, 177
nortriptyline (Pamelor), 177
not competent to stand trial, 324–325
NSAIDs (nonsteroidal anitinflammatory medications), 111, 181
nucleus, 41
nutrition, 35, 54

• O •

objective information, 81
obsessive compulsive disorder (OCD), 23, 133, 337
obstetrician/gynecologist, 79, 178
occupational therapist, 275, 278
OCD (obsessive compulsive disorder), 23, 133, 337
ODD (oppositional defiance disorder), 332, 336
olanzapine (Zyprexa, Relprevv, Zydis, Symbyax), 52, 115, 135, 151–152
olanzapine fluoxetine combination (Symbyax), 52, 118, 119, 123
older adults, 180–183
omega-3 fatty acids, 53, 160, 214
oppositional defiance disorder (ODD), 332, 336
oppositional/defiant behaviors, 337
orexin, 126
overspending, 320–321
over-the-counter medications, 219, 359
oxcarbemazapine (Trileptal), 112, 175
oxidative stress, 163

• P •

paliperidone (Invega), 114
Pamelor, 177
panic disorder, 23, 133
parental conflict, 344
parenting a bipolar child, 347–352
parity, 288
Parkinson's, 65
Parnate, 177
paroxetine (Paxil), 52, 119, 145, 177
partial remission, 19
party animal, 102
past life questions, 83
patient rights, 259–260
Paxil, 52, 119, 145, 177
PCOS For Dummies (Bussell and Perkins), 176
PCP (primary-care physician), 78–79
PDD (pervasive developmental disorder), 22
p-doc. *See* psychiatrist
pediatrician, 340
peer support, 289
Perfect Chaos: A Daughter's Journey to Survive Bipolar, a Mother's Struggle to Save Her (Johnson), 103, 308
perfection, 208
perimenopause, 174, 180
peripartum onset, 20
Perkins, Sharon
  PCOS For Dummies, 176
perphenazine (Trilafon), 117
personal suppot staff, 98–104
personality disorders, 24–25, 30, 133
pervasive developmental disorder (PDD), 22
phenelzine (Nardil), 177
phototherapy, 53, 166–167
PHQ-9 depression scale, 81
physical exam, 71
physical restraint, 257
PKC (protein kinase), 138
plasticity, 44

PMDD (premenstrual mood dysphoric disorder), 173
PME (premenstrual exacerbation), 173
PMS (premenstrual syndrome), 173
POA (power of attorney), 250–251
pole of episode, 127
poles of bipolar disorder, 9
postmenopause, 180
postmortem examination, 42
postpartum, 174, 178
post-traumatic stress disorder (PTSD), 23
power of attorney (POA), 250–251
pramiprexole, 139
preferred provider, 76–77
prefrontal cortex, 38, 39
pregabalin (Lyrica), 124, 125
pregnancy, 174–179
premenstrual exacerbation (PME), 173
premenstrual mood dysphoric disorder (PMDD), 64, 173
premenstrual syndrome (PMS), 173
prenatal alcohol exposure, 339
prescription assistance programs, 290–291
prevention of flare-ups, 50, 52, 134, 144, 245
primary-care physician (PCP), 78–79
Pristiq, 120
private insurance, 288
proactive response, 48–49
problem-solving skills
  avoiding unproductive approaches, 240–241
  brainstorming solutions, 238
  identifying the problem, 235–237
  letting go of unsolvable problems, 241–242
  planning and implementing agreed-upon solutions, 239
  redefining the problem/conflict to unmet needs, 237–238
  in relationships, 58, 363–364
  setting the stage, 234–235
  through self-education, 240
problem-solving therapy (PST), 233–234
professional counseling, 56–58
progesterone, 73, 173
prognosis, 47–48

progressive muscle relaxation, 199
prophylaxis, 51, 144
protein, 213–214
protein kinase C inhibitors, 138–139
protein kinase (PKC), 138
proxy directive, 252
Prozac, 52, 119, 145
pseudoephedrine, 67, 219
PST (problem-solving therapy), 233–234
psychiatric evaluation and treatment plan, 75–92, 339–342
psychiatric facility, 245–247
psychiatric rehab professional, 278
psychiatrist, 74, 76–81, 94, 291
psychoeducation
  for family and supporters, 58, 100, 201–202
  for patient, 56, 191–192
  for supporters, 361–362
  for teachers, 350
psychopharmacology, 127–133
psychosis, 87
psychosis, presence of absence of, 88
psychotherapy, 56–58, 183
psychotic disorder, 13
psychotropic medications, 127–133
PTSD (post-traumatic stress disorder), 23
public mental health system, 281
pulmonary hypertension, 177

• Q •

questions psychiatrists ask, 82–83
quetiapine (Seroquel), 52, 116, 122, 129, 135, 176

• R •

racing thoughts, 330, 337
ramelteon (Rozerem), 127
rapid-cycling bipolar disorder, 7, 19, 172
reactive response, 48–49
reasonable accommodations, 275
receptor sites, 41
reckless driving, 319–320

reclaiming your life, 266–268
record transfer, 104
recovery, 262–266
referral service, 97
relationships, 55, 58–59, 215–217, 264, 267–268
release from hospital, 104, 259, 262–268
release signing, 249–250
religious organizations, 290
Relprevv, 52, 115, 135, 151–152
Remember icon, 3
Remeron, 177
remission, 19
remitting symptoms, 136–137
repetitive transcranial magnetic stimulation (rTMS), 53, 167, 169
respect, 362
response to diagnosis, 90
Restoril, 126
restraint policies, 257
reuptake, 41
reuptake transporter, 41
review of systems, 67, 82
rigid thinking/behaviors, 338
riluzole (Rilutek), 138
risky behaviors, 317–326, 331
risperidone (Risperdal), 52, 116, 152
Ritalin, 24, 330, 340
role-playing, 193
Rozerem, 127
rTMS (repetitive transcranial magnetic stimulation), 53, 167, 169
rule out, 87, 338
runaway, 322–323

• *S* •

S-adenosylmethionine (SAMe), 164
safety, 131, 165–166
SAMe (S-adenosylmethionine), 164
SAMHSA (Substance Abuse and Mental Health Services Administration), 273, 306
Saphris, 52, 115
scheduling
  of discussions, 222

homelife, 202, 209–210
problem solving and conflict resolution, 234
schizoaffective disorder, 13, 21, 87, 114
schizophrenia
  bipolar disorder compared to, 13
  comorbidity with bipolar disorder, 30
  family history, 22, 31, 84, 88, 341
  genetic factors, 33
  ruling out, 87
  symptoms, 21
  treatment, 114, 117
schizophreniform disorder, 13
school, 343, 348–350
scopolamine, 140
Seasonal Affective Disorder For Dummies (Smith and Elliott), 166
seasonal patterns, 20
seclusion policies, 257
second opinion, 74
second-generation antipsychotics, 114, 152
Section 504 of Rehabilitation Act (1973), 349
sedative hypnotic, 125
sedatives, 53
seizure disorder, 22, 50
Selective Serotonin and Norepinephrine Reuptake inhibitors (SSNRIs)
  anxiety treatment, 123
  dosage and benefits, 120
  mechanism of action, 118
  side effects, 120, 121
  timing of therapeutic effect, 124
  use in pregnancy, 177
Selective Serotonin Reuptake inhibitors (SSRIs)
  anxiety treatment, 123, 125, 133
  dosage and benefits, 119
  drug interactions, 121, 131, 163, 211, 219
  mechanism of action, 118
  PMS treatment, 174
  side effects, 119, 121, 145, 155, 177
  timing of therapeutic effect, 124, 125, 143
  unipolar depression treatment, 134
  use during pregnancy, 177

self-acceptance, 358

self-advocation, 358

self-centering skills, 357

self-diagnosis, 67

Self-Disclosure and Its Impact on Individuals Who Receive Mental Health Services (Hyman), 273

self-eduction, 240

self-employment, 276

self-expression difficulties, 338

self-harm, 334

self-help, 55–56, 58, 187–191, 199

selfishness, 263–264

self-medicating with drugs or alcohol, 31, 34, 50, 334–335

sentencing input, 325

Seroquel, 52, 116, 135

serotonin, 43, 118, 163

serotonin syndrome, 163

serotonin-related antidepressants, 121, 122

sertraline (Zoloft), 119, 145

severe depression, 12

severity of illness, 17–18

sexual dysfunction, 155

short-duration cyclothymia, 16

side effects, 150–155. *See also specific medication*

Silenor, 125

Silver Linings Playbook (film), 362

skills and interest inventory, 277–278

sleep, 35, 54, 207–209, 211, 356–357

sleep disorders, 183

sleep disturbances, 330, 331

sleep log, 86, 188–189

sleep medication, 53, 67, 123, 125–127, 219

sleep shifts, 334

sliding scale, 291

Smith, Laura L.
 Seasonal Affective Disorder for Dummies, 166

Smole, Helena (author)
 Balancing the Beast: A Bright View of Schizoaffective Disorder–Bipolar or Manic-Depressive Type, 199

SNAP (Supplemental Nutrition Assistance Program), 293

SNRIs. *See* Selective Serotonin and Norepinephrine Reuptake inhibitors (SSNRIs)

social activities, 209–210

social anxiety, 23, 133

social media, 351

Social Security Disability (SSD), 285

Sonata, 126

Spanish Grammar For Dummies (Kraynak), 271

special education services, 348–350

Special K, 67, 137–138

specifiers of bipolar disorder, 17–20

spinal tap, 72

springing power of attorney, 251

SSD (Social Security Disability), 285

SSI (Supplemental Security Income), 285

SSRIs. *See* Selective Serotonin Reuptake inhibitors (SSRIs)

St. John's wort, 164, 219

standard neuroleptics, 114

standards of practice, 109

Stewart, Chato (mental health advocate), 240

stigma, 27

stimulants, 67, 208, 218, 336, 359

stress
 effect on bipolar condition, 34, 35, 36, 50, 55
 identifying stressors, 189–191
 relief, 217–218

subjective information, 81

Substance Abuse and Mental Health Services Administration (SAMHSA), 273, 306

substance use disorder, 7, 31, 88, 133, 136

substance use/abuse. *See also* drugs, legal and illegal
 bipolar disorder accompanied by, 7, 23–24, 27, 30, 50, 70
 comorbidity with psychiatric problems, 30, 128, 172, 336
 dealing with loved ones, 322
 drug interactions, 148
 effect on mood, 35, 66, 85, 88, 218–219, 358–359

substance use/abuse *(continued)*
  genetic factors, 34
  red flag for suicide, 351
  symptoms, 317, 330
  teens' use, 334–335, 339
  treatment, 57, 67
substance-induced bipolar disorder, 15
suicidal threats or attempts, 316, 318, 334, 351–352
Supplemental Nutrition Assistance Program (SNAP), 293
Supplemental Security Income (SSI), 285
supplements, 132, 159–166, 359
support group, 78, 200, 264–265, 308, 340
survival tips, 260–261
suvorexant (Belsomra), 126
syanptic cleft, 41
Symbyax, 52, 115, 118, 119, 123, 135, 151–152
symptoms
  evaluation, 86–87
  information the doctor needs to know, 69–70
  of major depressive episode, 11–12
  of manic episode, 9–10
synaptic bulb, 41
synaptic vesicle, 41
systems of care, 282

• T •

Tai Chi, 199
talkativeness, 329, 331
tamoxifen, 139
tardive dyskinesia, 114, 152
taurine, 165
teens. *See* children
Tegretol, 112, 113, 175, 176, 177, 182
temazepam (Restoril), 126
temper outbursts, 335
temporary financial relief, 292
testosterone, 73, 173
tests, 71–73, 82, 130
thalamus, 38, 39
therapist and doctor
  advice on medication, 150

advice on work, 270, 275, 278, 280
advocation for services, 59
for caregivers, 308
caregiver's contact, 311–313, 316, 318, 323, 324
for children and teens, 340, 348
communication with, 251, 267, 306, 311–313, 355–356
doctor's communication with, 77, 91, 104, 346
documenting contact information, 247, 260
evaluation form, 342
finding, 58, 301, 340
frequency of visits, 179, 272
goals, 143
help for caregiver, 301, 302
help with benefits and services, 59, 286
help with grieving process, 308
help with relationship and parenting issues, 190
information sharing, 90, 91, 104, 311
locating, 58, 301, 340
mediation, 223, 235, 242
mood team member, 93, 95–98
payment options, 291
psychoeducation, 192, 274
records and reports, 350, 352, 364
referrals, 77, 97, 105, 246
relationship with, 355–356
review of mood charts, 188
switching, 59, 104, 342, 364
teaching thought control, 193
time to contact, 50, 236, 243–244, 251, 302, 303–304, 306, 360
treatment plan, 94–95
therapy
  for children and teens, 343
  in hospital, 257
  problem-solving therapy, 233
  seeking, 191
  types of, 191–200
thiazide diuretic, 182
thinking problem, 25, 133, 155
thiothixene (Navane), 117
Thorazine, 114

thyroid dysfunction, 64, 72
thyroid scan, 73
thyroid tests, 72–73
tiagabine (Gabitril), 114
tiff-makers, 226–228
Tip icon, 3
Tofranil, 177
topiramate (Topamax), 112, 152, 154, 175
toxic exposure, 339
trade school, 278
tranquility, 264–265
tranquilizers, 123, 124–125
tranylcypromine (Parnate), 177
trauma, 337–338
trauma-informed care, 338
trazodone (Desyrel), 122, 125, 177
TRD (treatment-resistant depression), 169
treatment. *See also* medication
  brain stimulation therapies, 53, 137
  for children and teens, 342–346
  components of effective plan, 51–59
  electroconvulsive therapy (ECT), 53, 137, 152, 167–169, 182
  lifestyle adjustments, 54–55
  light therapy, 53, 166–167
  neurostimulation, 169–170
  for older adults, 181–183
  parental understanding, 344–346
  for personality disorders, 24
  psychotherapy and other professional counseling, 56–58
  repetitive transcranial magnetic stimulation (rTMS), 53, 167, 169
  self-help treatments, 55–56
  therapies, 56–57, 191–200
  vitamins and supplements, 53, 159–166
  for women, 171–180
treatment contract, 304
treatment plan, 91–92, 94
treatment-resistant bipolar disorder, 136–137
treatment-resistant depression (TRD), 169
tricyclics, 121, 177

trigger identification, 56, 189–191
Trilafon, 117
Trileptal, 112, 175
trust, 98–99
Two Bipolar Chicks Guide to Survival: Tips for Living with Bipolar Disorder (Williamson), 149
type 2 diabetes, 153, 176
types of bipolar disorder, 13–16
typical, first-generation antipsychotic, 117, 182

• U •

unipolar depression
  bipolar disorder compared to, 134, 332–333
  in children and teens, 332–335
  comorbidity with bipolar disorder, 30
  definition, 21
  genetic factors, 30, 33
  ruling out, 87
  symptoms, 329
  treatment, 52, 116, 119, 120, 122, 123, 134, 137, 160, 164
United Kingdom, 283
unspecified bipolar disorder, 16
uric acid, 139

• V •

vagus nerve stimulation (VNS), 167, 170
valerian, 67, 165, 219
Valium, 124, 148
valproate (Depakote, Depakene)
  acute mood episode treatment, 52, 112, 134, 135
  dosage and benefits, 113
  drug interactions, 182
  mechanism of action, 45, 112, 139, 164
  side effects/risks, 88, 113, 145, 176, 177
  treatment of acute mania, 52
  use during pregnancy, 176, 178
valproic acid. *See* valproate (Depakote, Depakene)

van Gogh, Vincent (artist), 13
vegetables, 212–213
venlafaxine (Effexor), 120
ventricles, 40, 42
verapamil, 139
Veterans Benefits Administration, 288
vilazodone (Viibryd), 122, 177
visiting hours, 258
visualization technique, 193, 199
vitamin D, 162
vitamin deficiency, 66
vitamins, 53, 161, 213
Vivarin, 67
VNS (vagus nerve stimulations), 170
vocational therapy, 57
volume reduction, 202–203
vortioxetin (Brintellix), 122

• W •

Walton, Neil (author), 284
Warning! icon, 3
warning signs, 244, 302, 315, 351–352,
    359–360
Web extras icon, 3
WebMD, 77
websites, 101
weight gain, 153–155
Wellbutrin, 121, 123, 177
white matter, 40
WHO (World Health Organization), 8
Williamson, Wendy K. (author)
    I'm Not Crazy Just Bipolar, 149
    Two Bipolar Chicks Guide to Survival,
        148
willingness to communicate, 80
Willson, Rob (author)
    *Cognitive Behavior Therapy For
        Dummies*, 194

withdrawal, 334
women
    hormonal changes, 172–174
    menopause, 180
    nature of illness, 172
    pregnancy and bipolar disorder, 174–179
Woolf, Virginia (author), 13
work, returning to
    changing jobs, 271, 272, 276–279
    disclosing your diagnosis, 272–274
    getting back in the swing, 271–272
    readiness, 269–270
    rightness for you, 279–280
working diagnosis, 81
workplace accommodations, 270,
    272, 274–275
World Health Organization (WHO), 8

• X •

Xanax, 124, 148

• Y •

yoga, 199
Young Mania Rating Scale, 81

• Z •

zaleplon (Sonata), 126
zinc, 163
ziprasidone (Geodon), 116
Zoloft, 119, 145
zolpidem (Ambien), 53, 126
zonisamide (Zonegran), 114
Zyban, 121, 123, 177
Zydis, 52, 115, 135, 151–152
Zyprexa, 52, 115, 135, 151–152

About the Authors

Candida Fink, MD, is a board-certified adult, child, and adolescent psychiatrist in private practice in the New York area. Dr. Fink graduated from Boston University School of Medicine and did her postgraduate training through Harvard Medical School. She has worked extensively with children and adults with complicated psychiatric illnesses. Mood disorders, including the diagnostic and treatment questions surrounding bipolar disorder in children, comprise much of her current practice. She also consults frequently with schools and other institutions regarding developmental and psychiatric issues. Dr. Fink grew up with mood disorders in her family, so she has seen them from every angle and knows the importance of mobilizing the family as a part of any successful treatment. She previously coauthored the first and second editions of *Bipolar Disorder For Dummies* and, with Judith Lederman, *The Ups and Downs of Raising a Bipolar Child: A Survival Guide for Parents* (Fireside). She frequently writes and speaks on bipolar disorder in children. For more about Dr. Fink, visit www.finkshrink.com.

Joe Kraynak, MA, is a freelance writer who has written and coauthored dozens of books on topics ranging from slam poetry to personal computers. Joe received his degree in bipolar disorder from the College of Hard Knocks. On December 10, 1999, Joe's wife, Cecie, a Spanish teacher, was diagnosed with bipolar disorder. Since that day, they have bounced around to a half dozen doctors and even more therapists, broken in a few young marriage counselors, survived several changes in health insurance coverage, attended dozens of support group meetings, helped launch a NAMI support group, and endured the career changes and financial hardships that often accompany bipolar disorder. In this book, Joe offers his experience and insight from a family member's perspective. For more about Joe, visit www.joekraynak.com.

The authors also host Psych Central's *Bipolar Beat* at blogs.psychcentral.com/bipolar and a site called *Bipolar Story* (bipolar-story.com), where you can post your story of living with bipolar disorder and read and comment on stories posted by others.

Dedications

To my daughters, Julia and Jessica, who never cease to amaze me with their boundless love, generosity of spirit, and insights. They lift me to new places every day. — Candida

To my wife, Cecie, whose zest for life and genuine interest in the lives of others engage and inspire everyone she touches. — Joe

Authors' Acknowledgments

Although we wrote this book, dozens of other talented individuals contributed to its conception, development, and shine. Special thanks to Tracy Boggier, who chose us to author this book. Chad Sievers, project editor, deserves a round of applause for acting as the choreographer — developing chapters, shepherding the text and illustrations through production, making sure any technical issues were properly addressed, and serving as unofficial quality control manager.

We owe special thanks to our technical editor, Matthew Lowe, MS, DO, for ferreting out technical errors in the manuscript and helping guide its content.

And we thank our agent, Faith Hamlin, of Sanford J. Greenburger Associates, Inc., for managing the contract negotiations so we could focus on writing this book instead of on all the legal stuff.

We would also like to thank all the people with bipolar disorder and their family members and friends whom we've met along the way, especially those who contributed their Bipolar Bios:

Andy Behrman (www.electroboy.com), author of *Electroboy: A Memoir of Mania*

Natalie Jeanne Champagne, author of *The Third Sunrise: A Memoir of Madness*

Matthew Durand, a young man living with bipolar since childhood who wanted to share his experience to bring hope to others

Janine Crowley Haynes (janinecrowleyhaynes@gmail.com), author of *My Kind of Crazy: Living in a Bipolar World*

Kevin Hines (www.kevinhinesstory.com), mental health advocate, speaker, and author of *Cracked, Not Broken: Surviving and Thriving After a Suicide Attempt*

Cinda Johnson (www.lineacinda.com), coauthor of *Perfect Chaos: A Daughter's Journey to Survive Bipolar, a Mother's Struggle to Save Her*

Linea Johnson (www.lineacinda.com), coauthor of *Perfect Chaos: A Daughter's Journey to Survive Bipolar, a Mother's Struggle to Save Her*

Cecie Kraynak (www.ceciekraynak.com), Spanish teacher and author of *Spanish Grammar For Dummies,* among other *Spanish For Dummies* titles

Stacy Pershall, author of *Loud in the House of Myself: Memoir of a Strange Girl*

Helena Smole (www.helenasmole.com), author of *Balancing the Beast: A Bright View of Schizoaffective Disorder — Bipolar or Manic-Depressive Type*

Chato Stewart, husband, father, and mental health advocate and cartoonist for MentalHealthHumor.com

Neil Walton (www.bipolar-expedition.co.uk), author, mentor, mental health journalist, and comedy writer

Wendy K. Williamson (www.wendykwilliamson.com), author of *I'm Not Crazy Just Bipolar* and *Two Bipolar Chicks Guide to Survival: Tips for Living with Bipolar Disorder*

Without these brave souls, along with their stories, their struggles, and their achievements, this book wouldn't be possible. Finally, we acknowledge nonprofit organizations, including the Depression and Bipolar Support Alliance (DBSA) and the National Alliance on Mental Illness (NAMI), for their valuable contributions and continued dedication to educating, supporting, and advocating for all those in the bipolar community.

Publisher's Acknowledgments

Senior Acquisitions Editor: Tracy Boggier

Project Manager: Chad R. Sievers

Development/Copy Editor: Chad R. Sievers

Technical Editor: Matthew Lowe, MS, DO

Art Coordinator: Alicia B. South

Project Coordinator: Antony Sami

Cover Photos: A I R/Shutterstock

ple & Mac

d For Dummies,
Edition
-1-118-72306-7

ne For Dummies,
Edition
-1-118-69083-3

s All-in-One
Dummies, 4th Edition
-1-118-82210-4

K Mavericks
Dummies
-1-118-69188-5

gging & Social Media

ebook For Dummies,
Edition
-1-118-63312-0

ial Media Engagement
Dummies
-1-118-53019-1

dPress For Dummies,
Edition
-1-118-79161-5

iness

k Investing
Dummies, 4th Edition
-1-118-37678-2

sting For Dummies,
Edition
-0-470-90545-6

Personal Finance
For Dummies, 7th Edition
978-1-118-11785-9

QuickBooks 2014
For Dummies
978-1-118-72005-9

Small Business Marketing
Kit For Dummies,
3rd Edition
978-1-118-31183-7

Careers

Job Interviews
For Dummies, 4th Edition
978-1-118-11290-8

Job Searching with Social
Media For Dummies,
2nd Edition
978-1-118-67856-5

Personal Branding
For Dummies
978-1-118-11792-7

Resumes For Dummies,
6th Edition
978-0-470-87361-8

Starting an Etsy Business
For Dummies, 2nd Edition
978-1-118-59024-9

Diet & Nutrition

Belly Fat Diet For Dummies
978-1-118-34585-6

Mediterranean Diet
For Dummies
978-1-118-71525-3

Nutrition For Dummies,
5th Edition
978-0-470-93231-5

Digital Photography

Digital SLR Photography
All-in-One For Dummies,
2nd Edition
978-1-118-59082-9

Digital SLR Video &
Filmmaking For Dummies
978-1-118-36598-4

Photoshop Elements 12
For Dummies
978-1-118-72714-0

Gardening

Herb Gardening
For Dummies, 2nd Edition
978-0-470-61778-6

Gardening with Free-Range
Chickens For Dummies
978-1-118-54754-0

Health

Boosting Your Immunity
For Dummies
978-1-118-40200-9

Diabetes For Dummies,
4th Edition
978-1-118-29447-5

Living Paleo For Dummies
978-1-118-29405-5

Big Data

Big Data For Dummies
978-1-118-50422-2

Data Visualization
For Dummies
978-1-118-50289-1

Hadoop For Dummies
978-1-118-60755-8

Language &
Foreign Language

500 Spanish Verbs
For Dummies
978-1-118-02382-2

English Grammar
For Dummies, 2nd Edition
978-0-470-54664-2

French All-in-One
For Dummies
978-1-118-22815-9

German Essentials
For Dummies
978-1-118-18422-6

Italian For Dummies,
2nd Edition
978-1-118-00465-4

e **Available in print and e-book formats.**

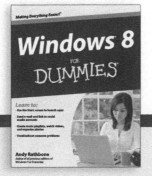

Available wherever books are sold. **For more information or to order direct visit www.dummies.com**

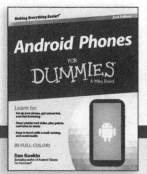

Take Dummies with you everywhere you go!

Whether you are excited about e-books, want more from the web, must have your mobile apps, or are swept up in social media, Dummies makes everything easier.

Leverage the Power

For Dummies is the global leader in the reference category and one of the most trusted and highly regarded brands in the world. No longer just focused on books, customers now have access to the For Dummies content they need in the format they want. Let us help you develop a solution that will fit your brand and help you connect with your customers.

Advertising & Sponsorships

Connect with an engaged audience on a powerful multimedia site, and position your message alongside expert how-to content.

Targeted ads • Video • Email marketing • Microsites • Sweepstakes sponsorship

21 Million Monthly Page Views & 13 Million Unique Visitors